**"Inspiration frees the mind
and allows the soul to stroll
through imagination's playground
and create beautiful paintings."**

~ Candice James

Poetry books by Candice James

Blue Silence *(Silver Bow Publishing)* 2024
Short Shots 2 *(Silver Bow Publishing)* 2023
Spiritual Whispers *(Silver Bow Publishing)* 2023
Imagination's Reverie *(Silver Bow Publishing)* 2023
Atmospheres *(Silver Bow Publishing)* 2023
The Depth of the Dance *(Silver Bow Publishing)* 2023
Behind the One-Way Mirror *(Silver Bow Publishing)* 2022
The Call of the Crow *(Silver Bow Publishing)* 2021
The Path of Loneliness *(Inanna Publications)* 2020
Rithimus Aeternam *(Silver Bow Publishing)* 2019
Haiku Paintings *(Silver Bow Publishing)* 2019
The 13th Cusp *(Silver Bow Publishing)* 2018
Fhaze-ing *(Silver Bow Publishing)* 2018
The Water Poems *(Ekstasis Editions)* 2017
Short Shots *(Silver Bow Publishing)* 2016
City of Dreams *(Silver Bow Publishing)* 2016
Merging Dimensions *(Ekstasis Editions)* 2015
Colors of India *(Xpress Publications India)* 2015
Purple Haze *(Libros Libertad)* 2014
A Silence of Echoes *(Silver Bow Publishing)* 2014
Shorelines *(Silver Bow Publishing)* 2013
Ekphrasticism *(Silver Bow Publishing)* 2013
Midnight Embers *(Libros Libertad)* 2012
Bridges and Clouds *(Silver Bow Publishing)* 2011
Inner Heart, a Journey *(Silver Bow Publishing)* 2010
A Split in the Water *(Fiddlehead Poetry Books)* 1979

A Potpourri of Paintings

by
Candice James

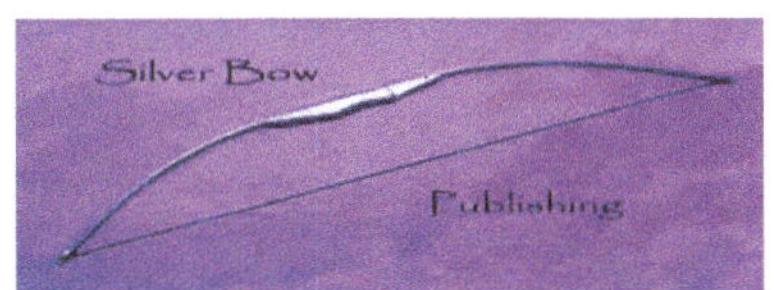

720 –Sixth Street, Box # 5
New Westminster, BC V3C 3C5
CANADA

Title: A Potpourri of Paintings
Author: Candice James
Cover Painting: "Pale Desert Moon" painting by Candice James
Cover Layout Design: Candice James
Editor: Candice James
All artwork/paintings in the book are by Candice James

© Silver Bow Publishing
9781774033272 prints
9781774033289 ebook

Library and Archives Canada Cataloguing in Publication

Title: A potpourri of paintings / by Candice James.
Names: James, Candice, 1948- artist
Identifiers: Canadiana (print) 2024048780X | Canadiana (ebook) 20240487818 | ISBN 9781774033272
   (softcover) | ISBN 9781774033289 (Kindle)
Subjects: LCSH: James, Candice, 1948-
Classification: LCC ND249.J34497 A4 2024 | DDC 759.11—dc23

Author's Note

Colors ... vibrant colors, are what I mostly paint, but sometimes the mood for a muted soft toned painting edges its way into my being and suddenly I have a painting I didn't expect to arrive. I can't copy and I can't draw, so I'm an off the cuff, spontaneous painter. Everything I paint comes from my mind.

My method of painting is: I choose the colors that appeal to me at the time and then just start putting them onto the canvas and then I look at the colors and shapes to see what I can see and once I see something, I build on it to create a painting. I paint mostly with palette knives, but I do also use brushes. The majority of my paintings and all the paintings in this book are acrylic but I also dabble in watercolor occasionally and I've done one oil painting.

The paintings are a variety of sizes but have been sized to fit on each page to their best viewing advantage.

All my paintings are on my website: www.candicejames.com

~ Candice James

PAINTINGS

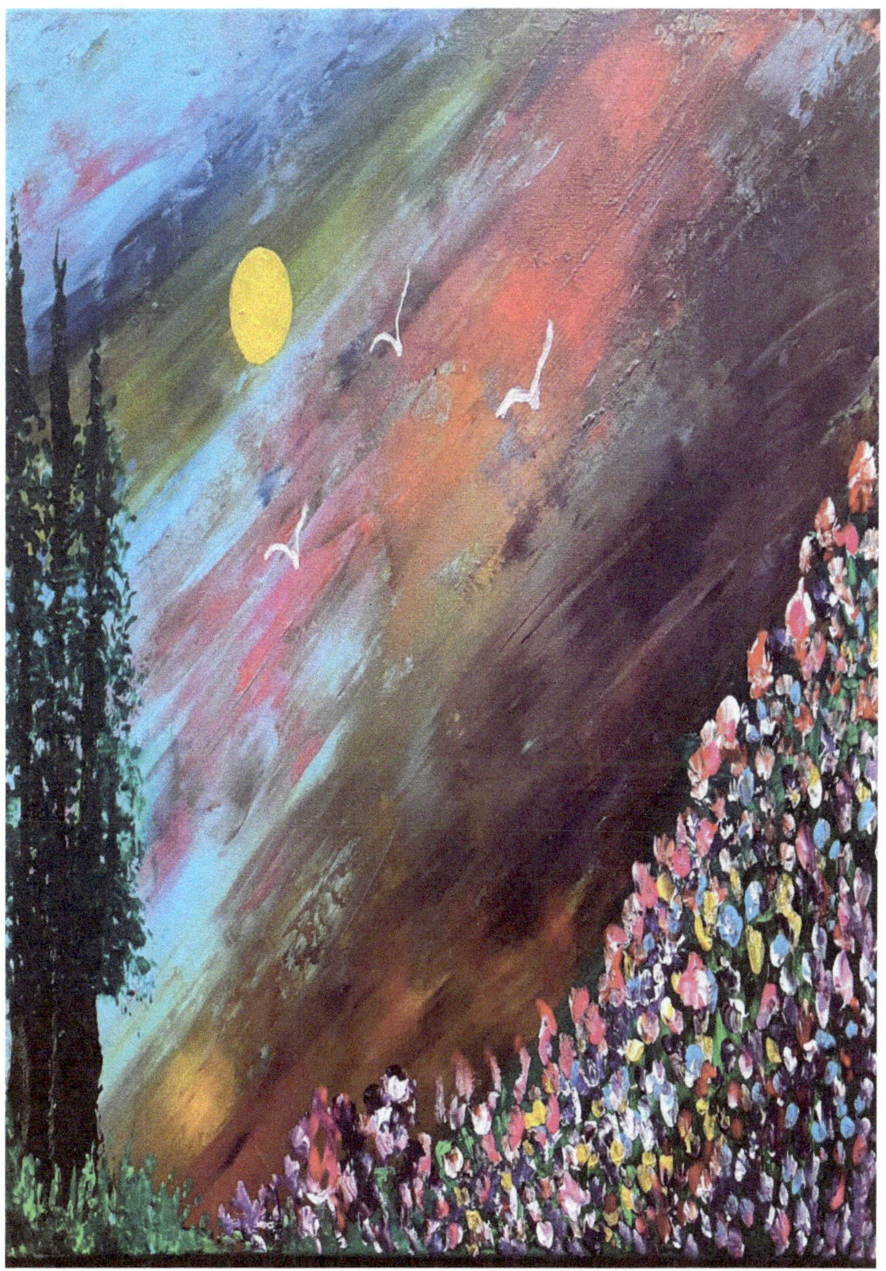

Sunny Day, Birds And Hillside Flowers

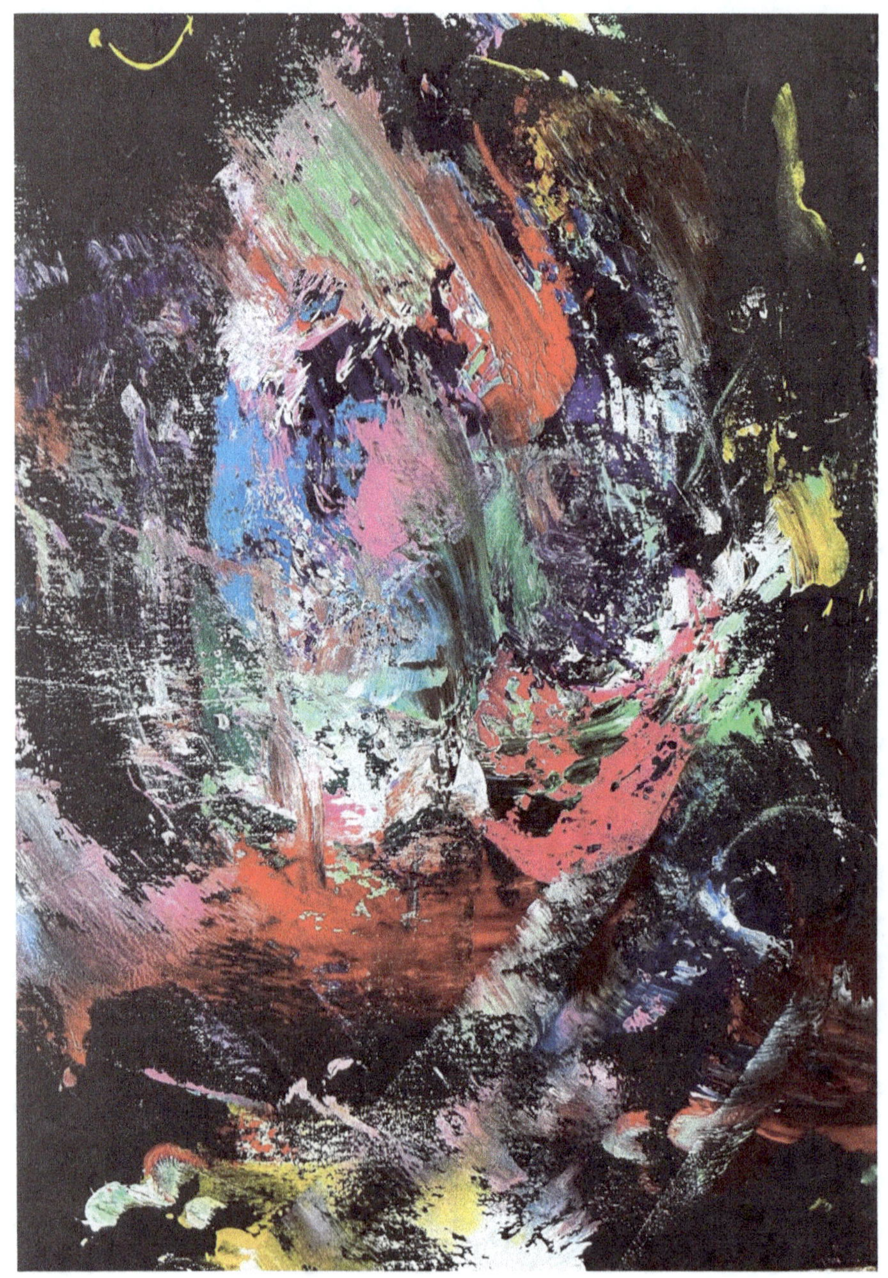

Interrogatory Man

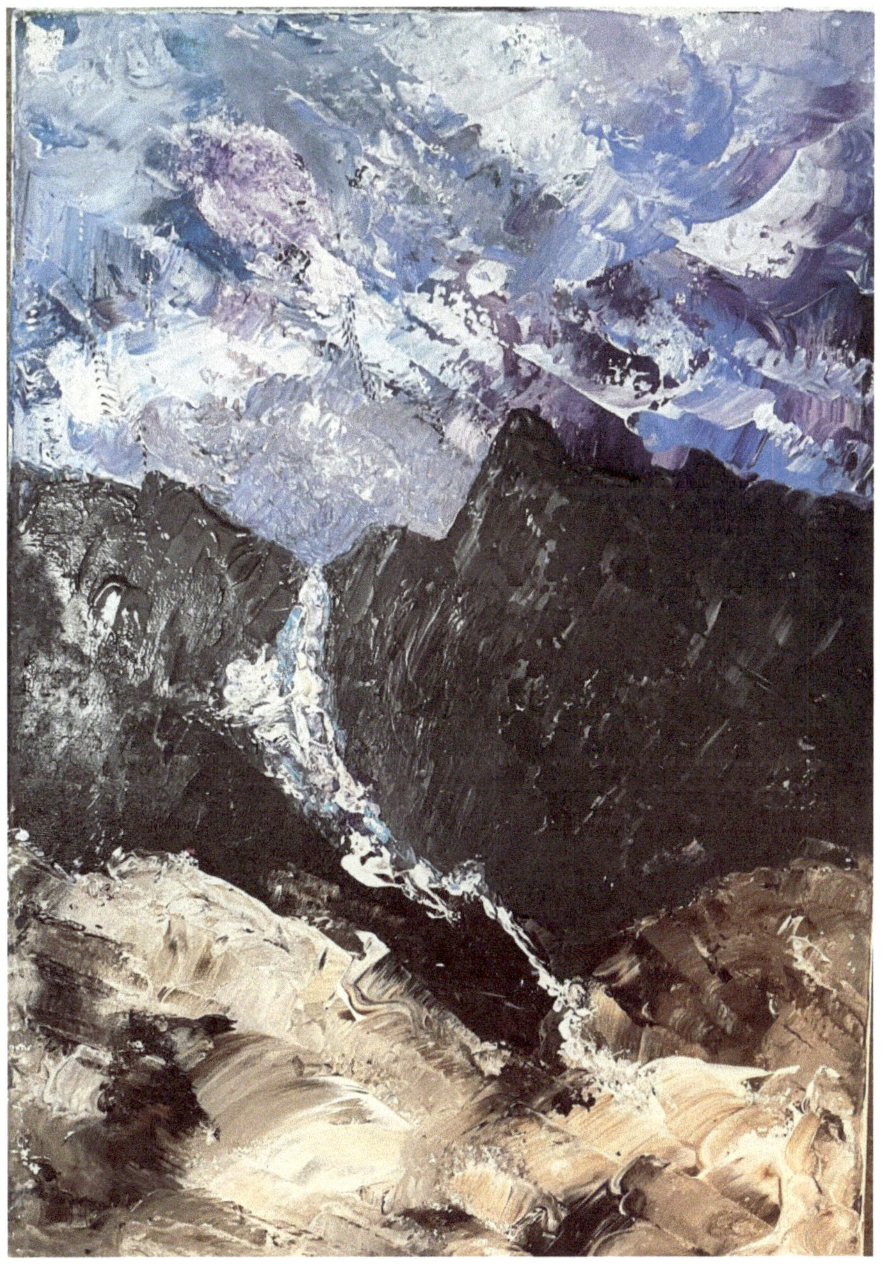

Haifoss Falls (Iceland)

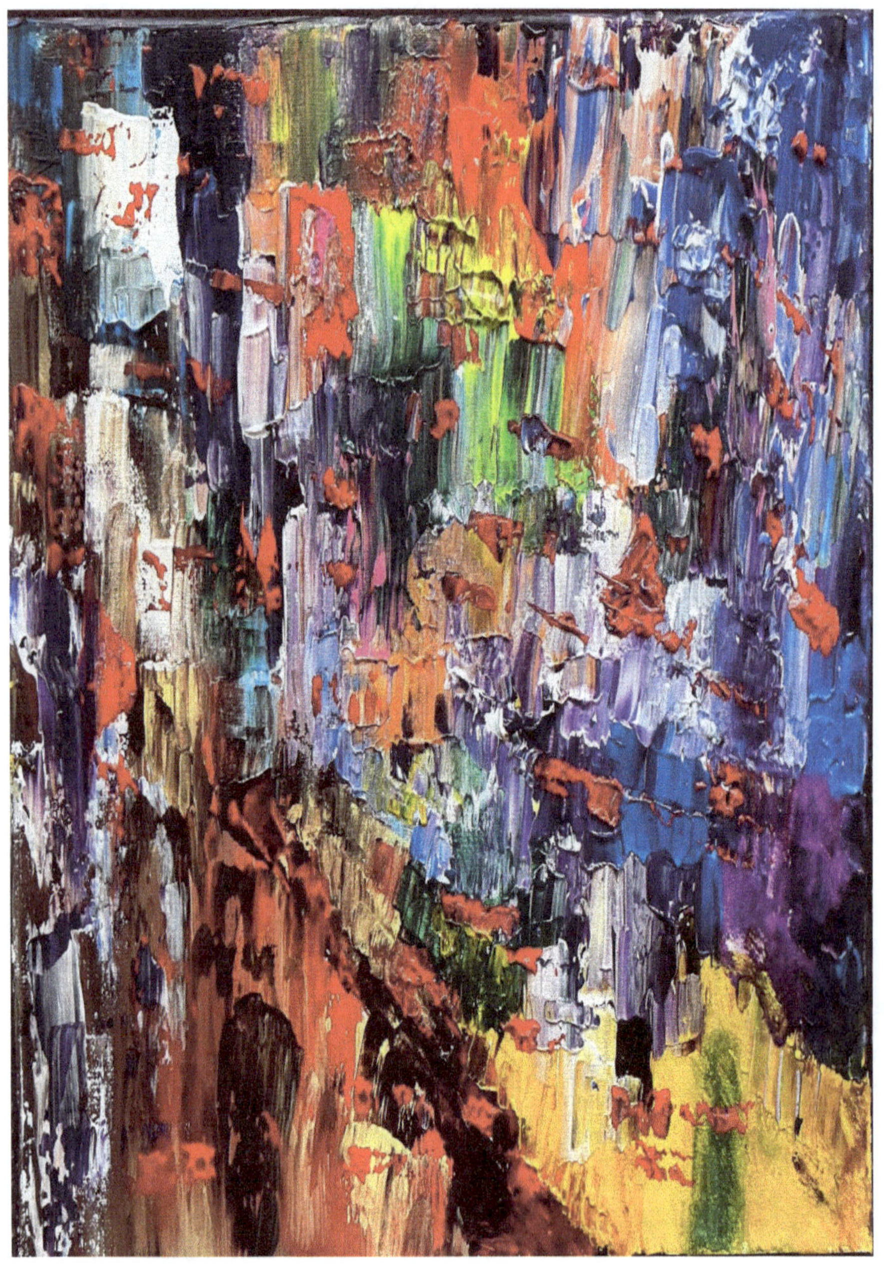

Aerial View, Madison Ave, New York

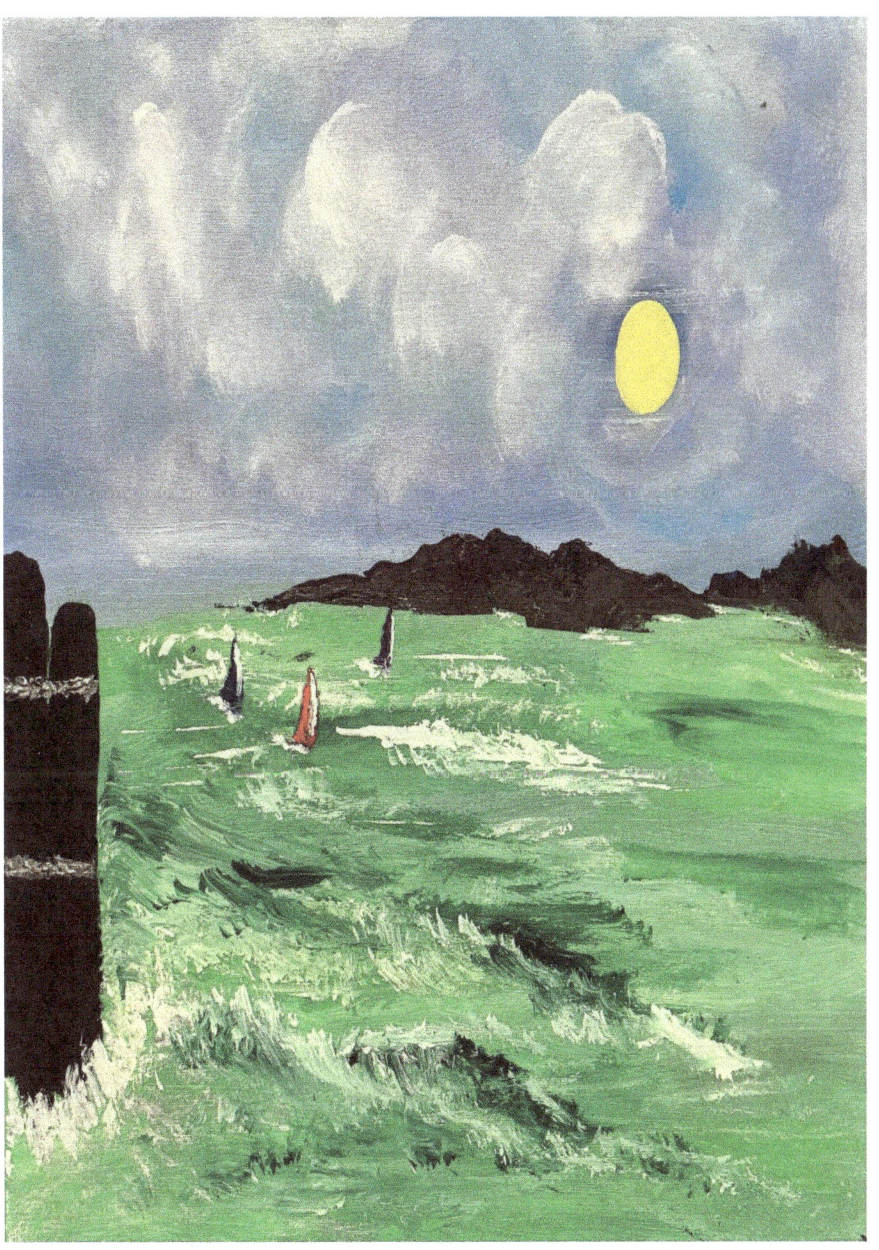

Crescent Beach Afternoon

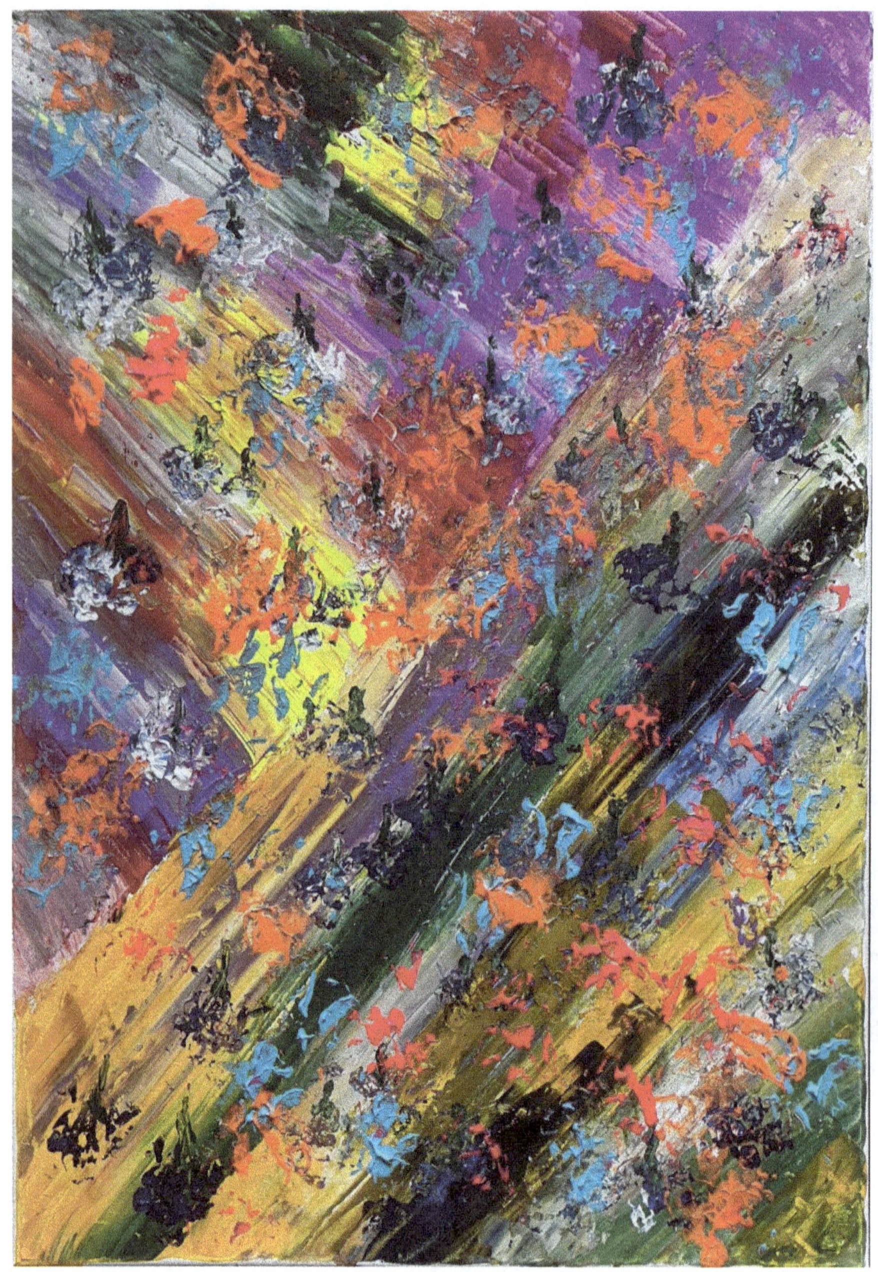

Unfinished Symphony

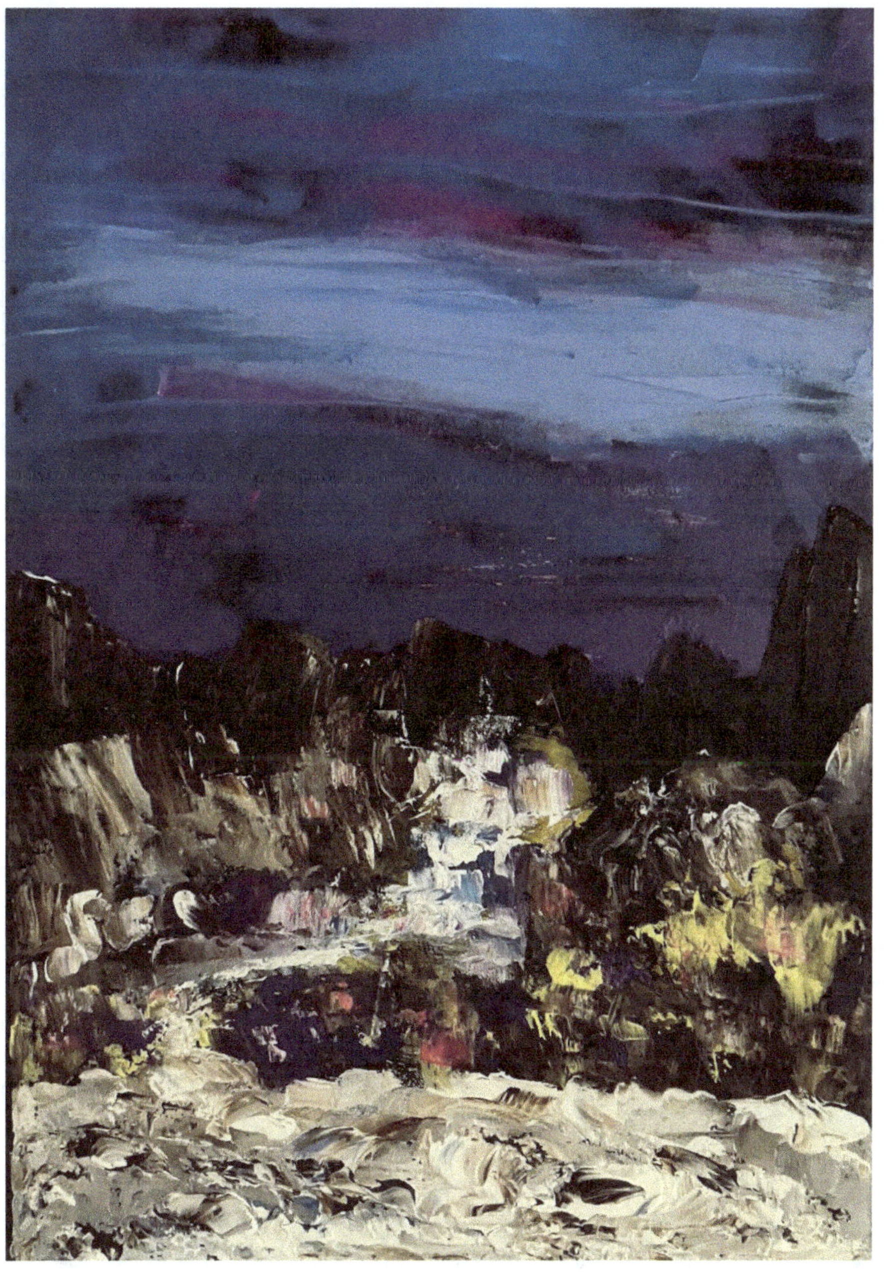

Rocky Point

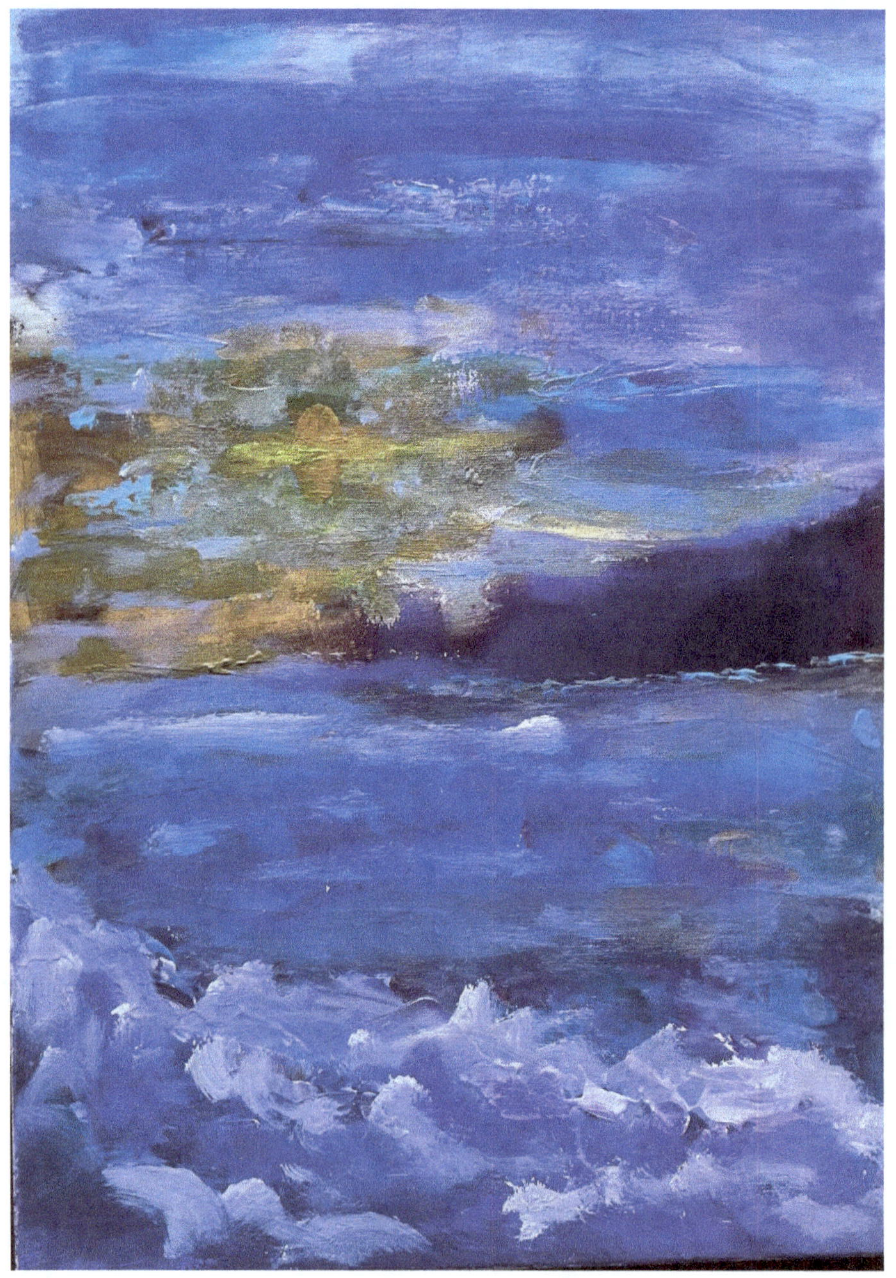

Bay Of Fundy Sundown, New Brunswick Canada

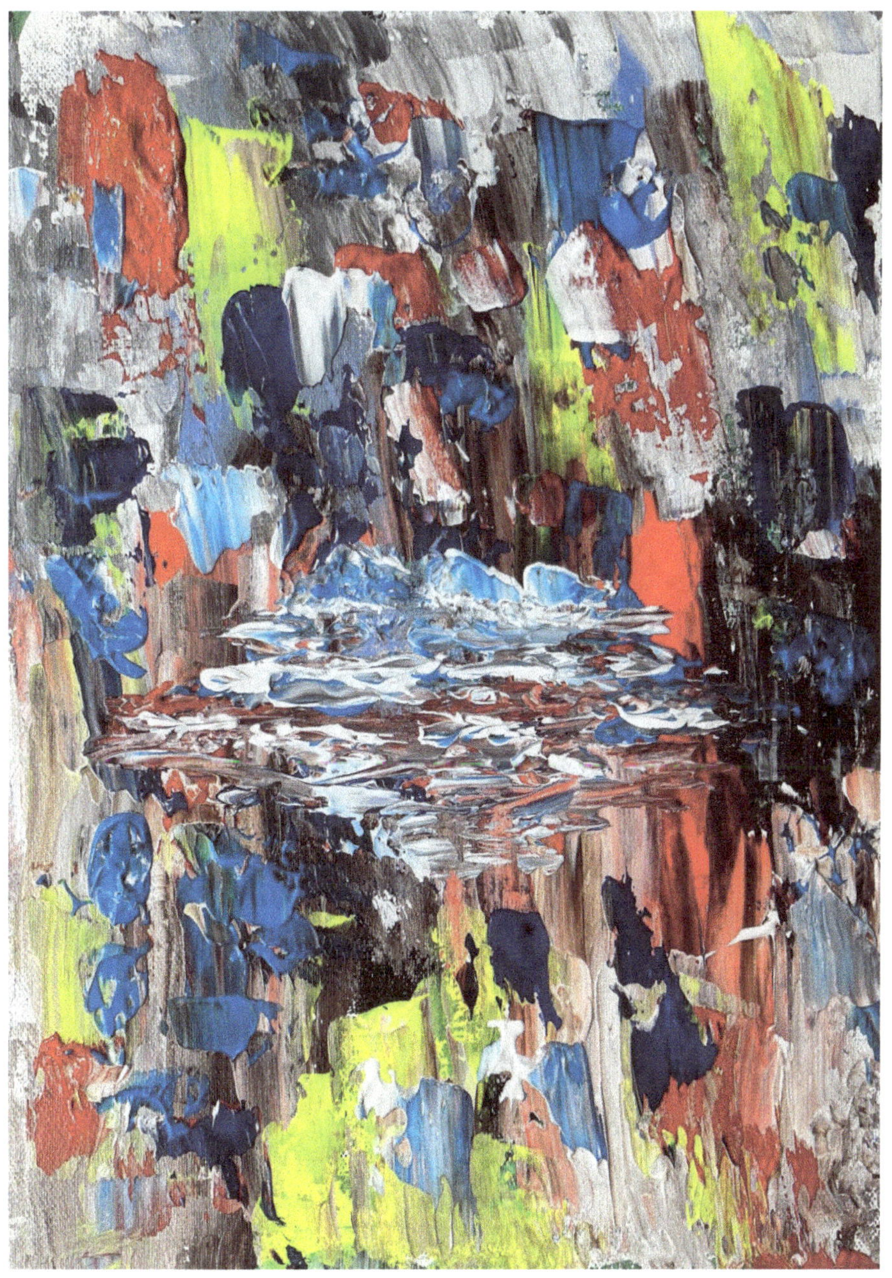

Whale Wonderland

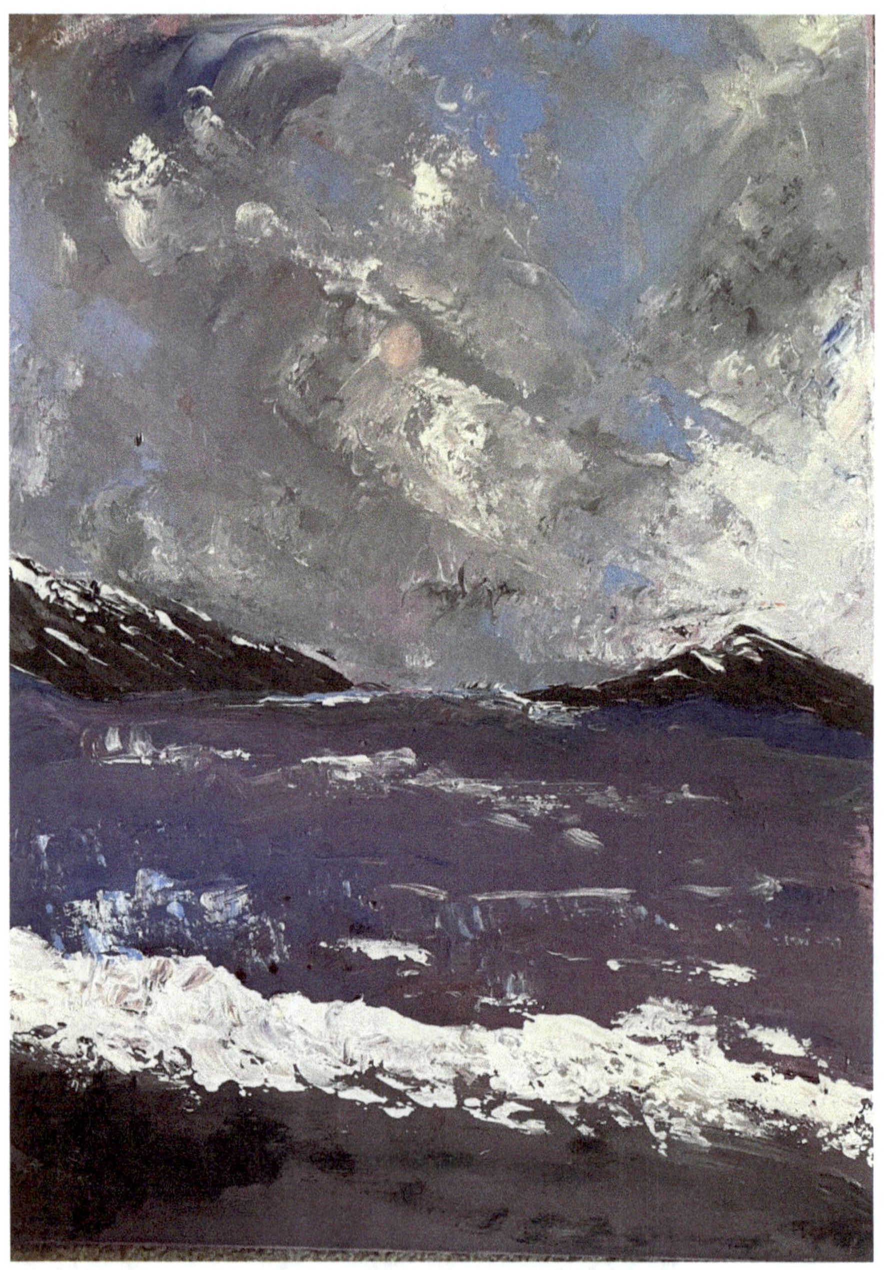

Moody West Coast Sky

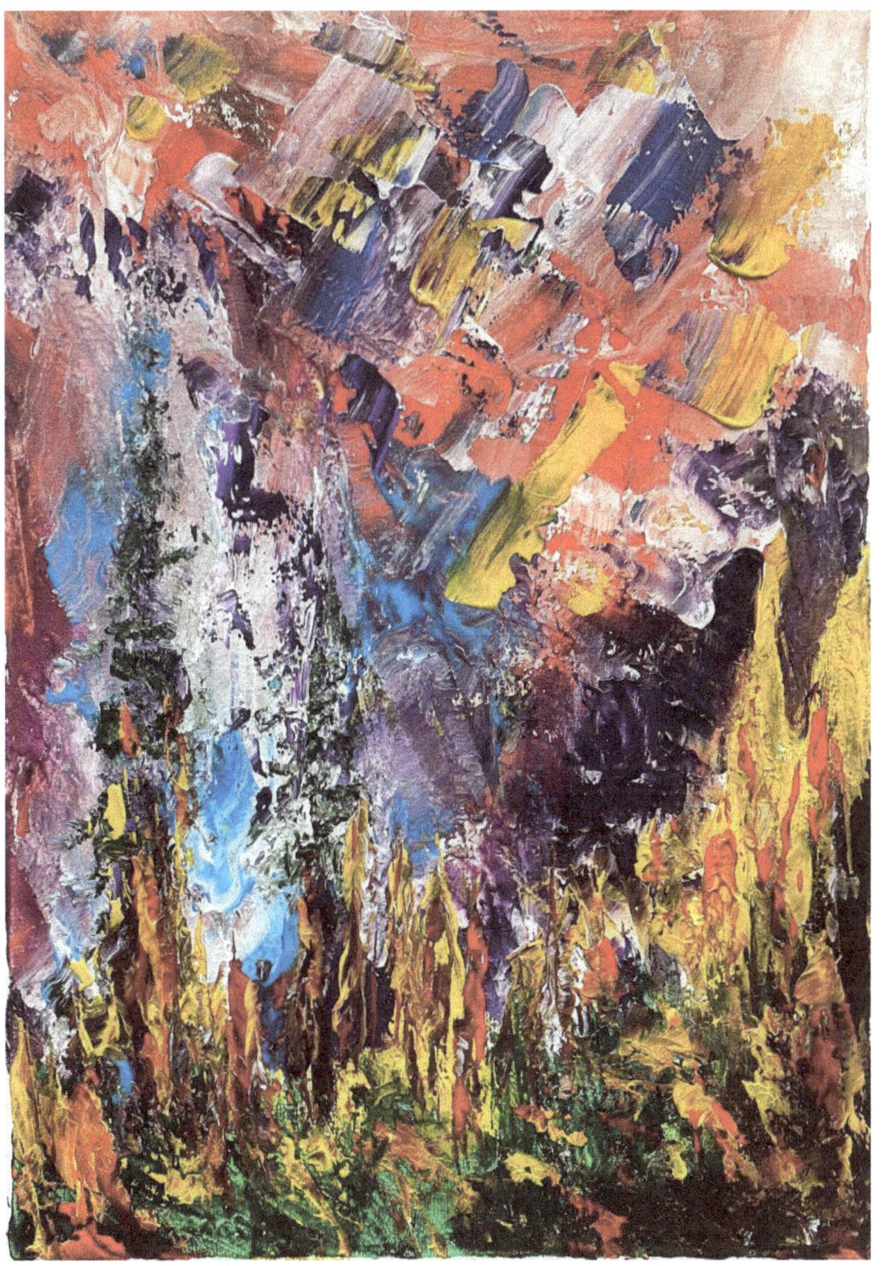

Wildfire

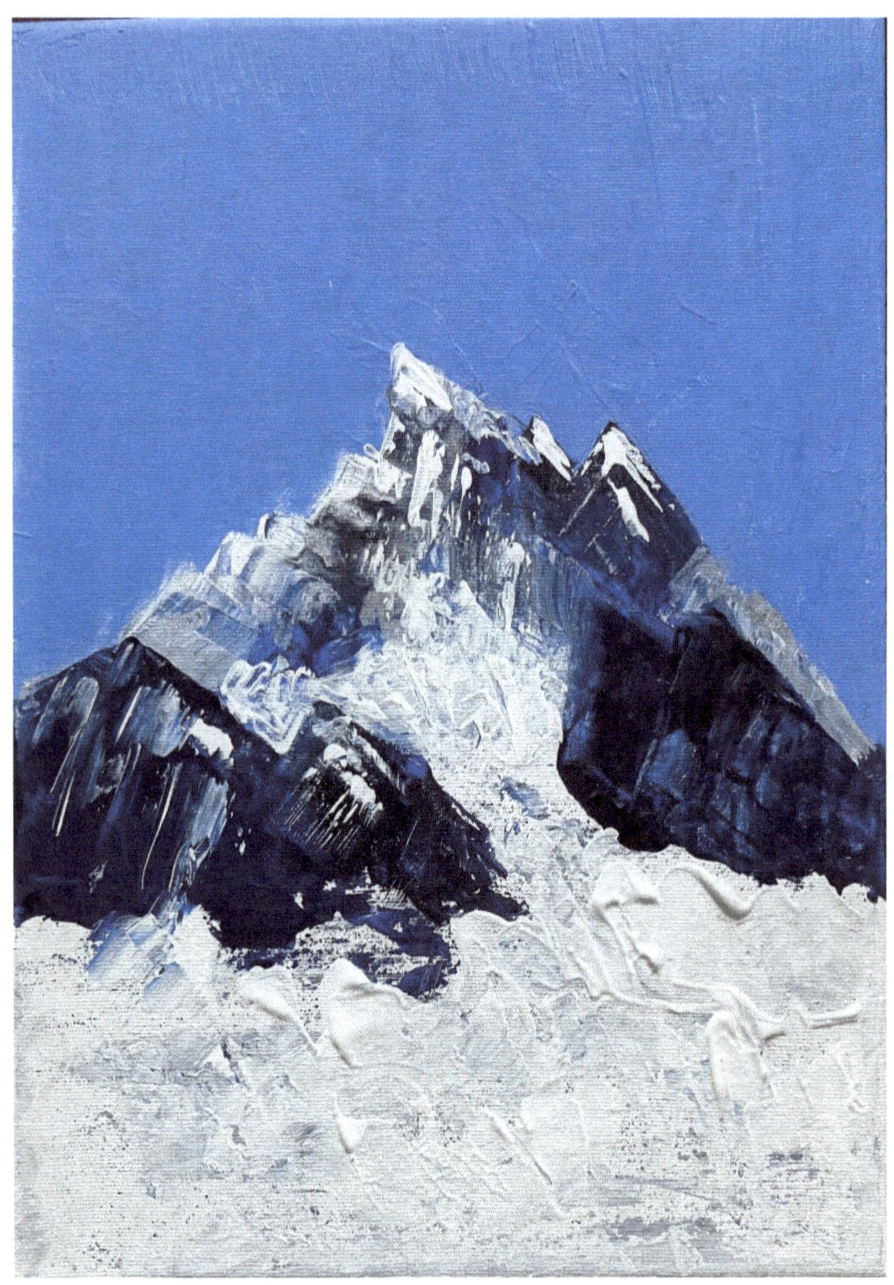

Everest

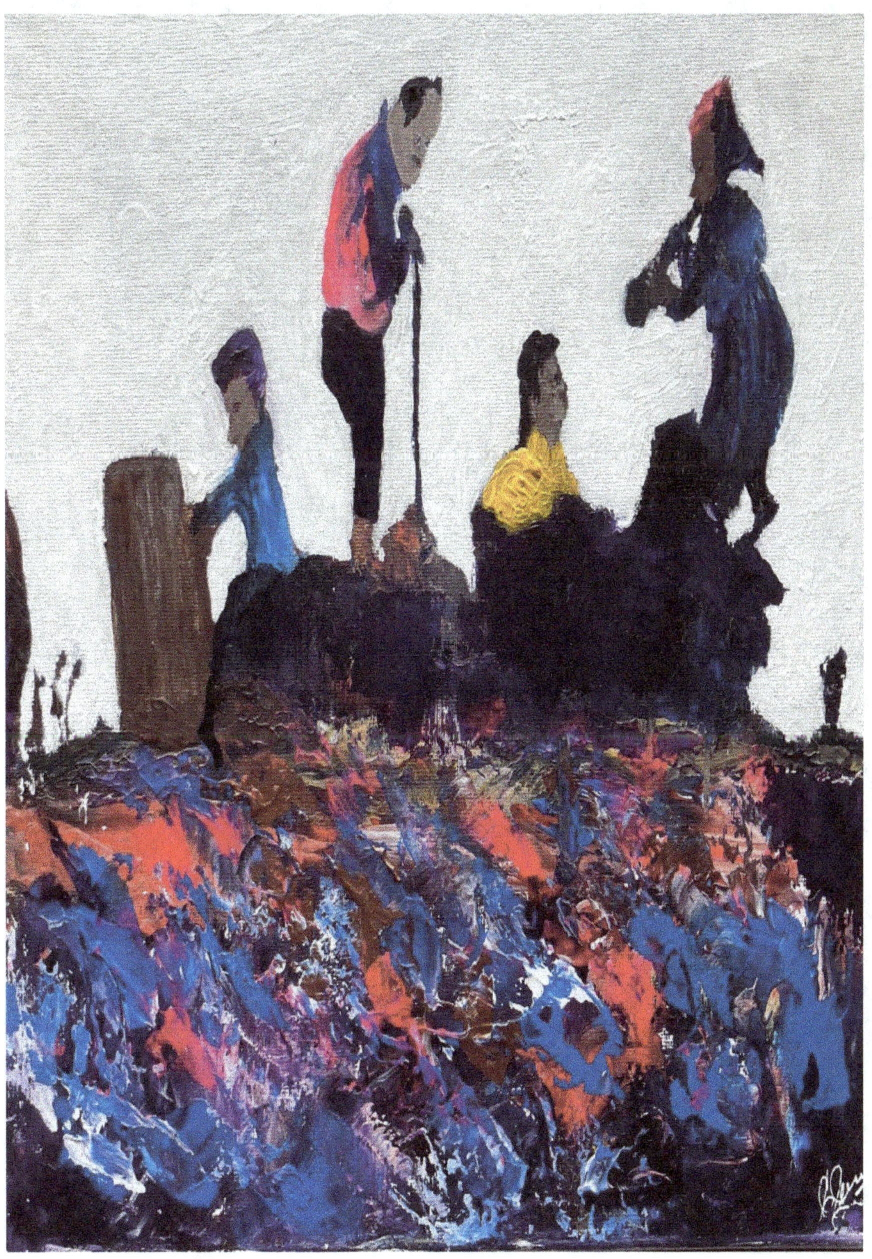

Groove-Yard Jam Session

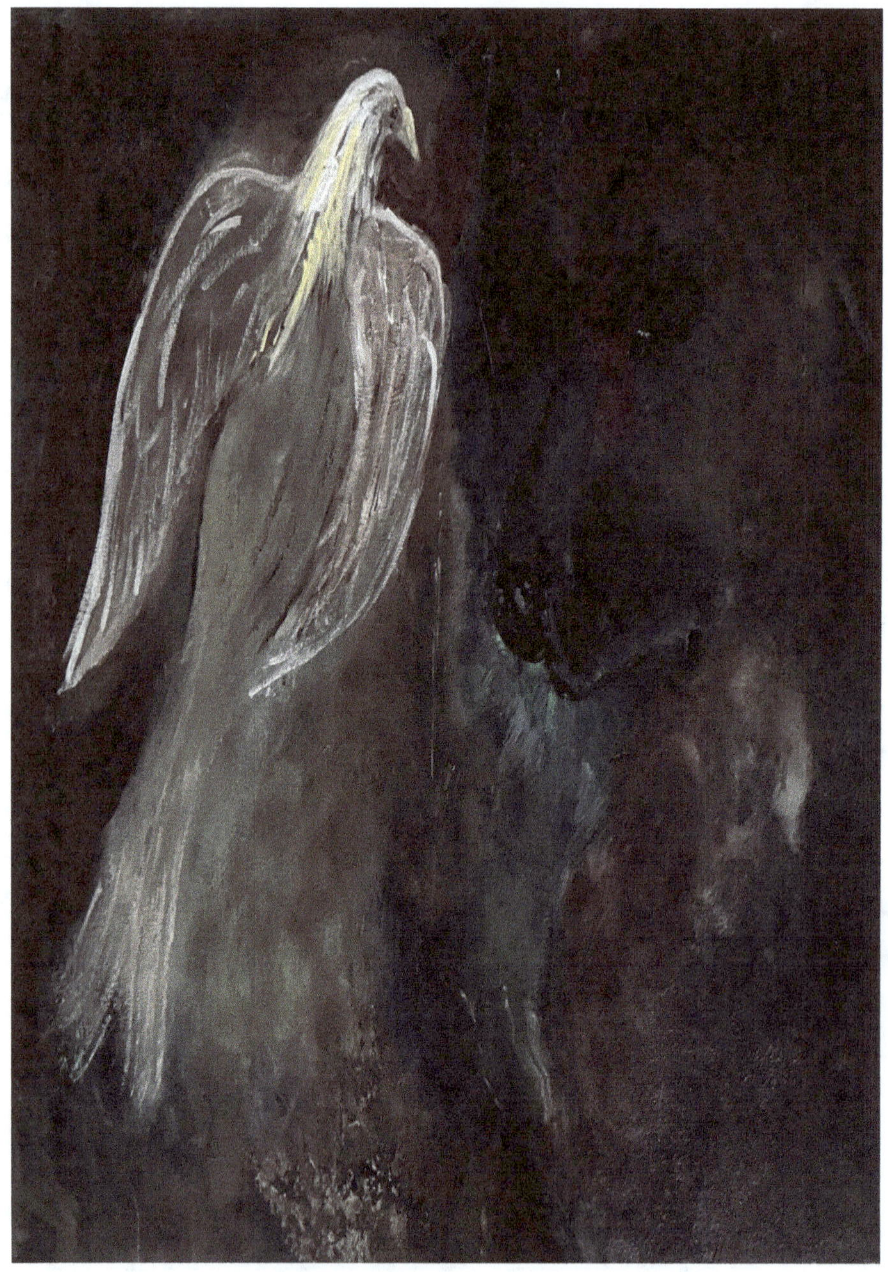

The Eagle And The Wolf

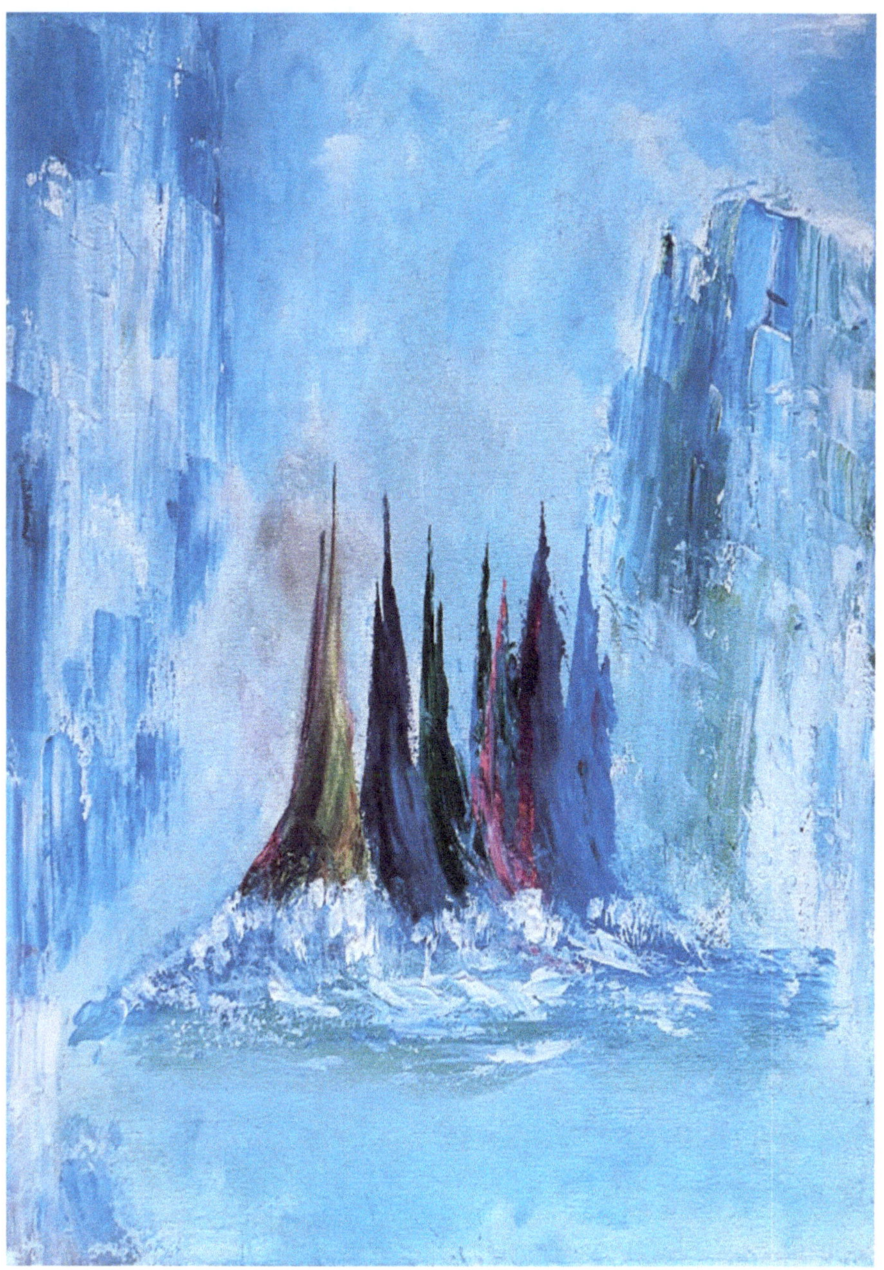

Sailboats Of Narnia

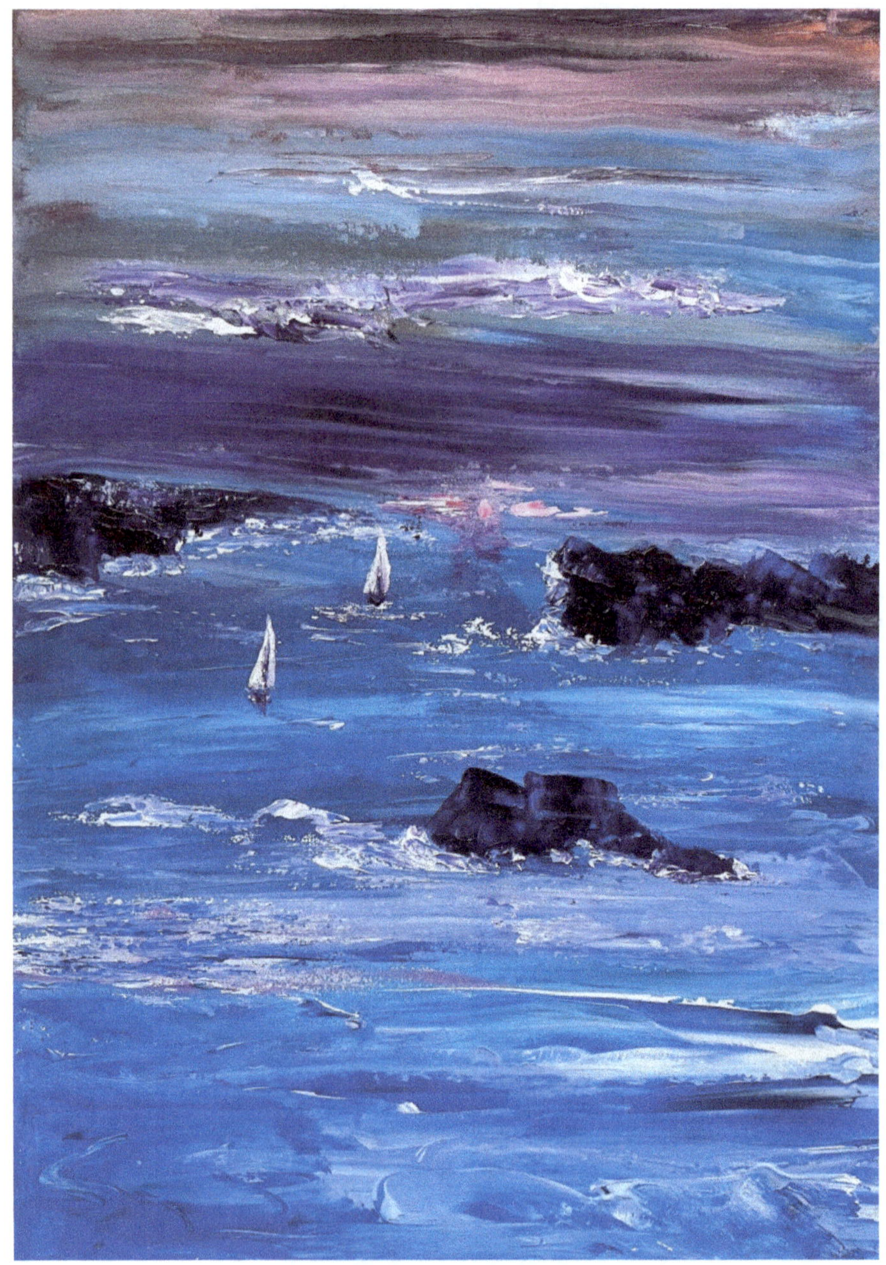

Dusk In The Pass

Northern Tangerine Moon

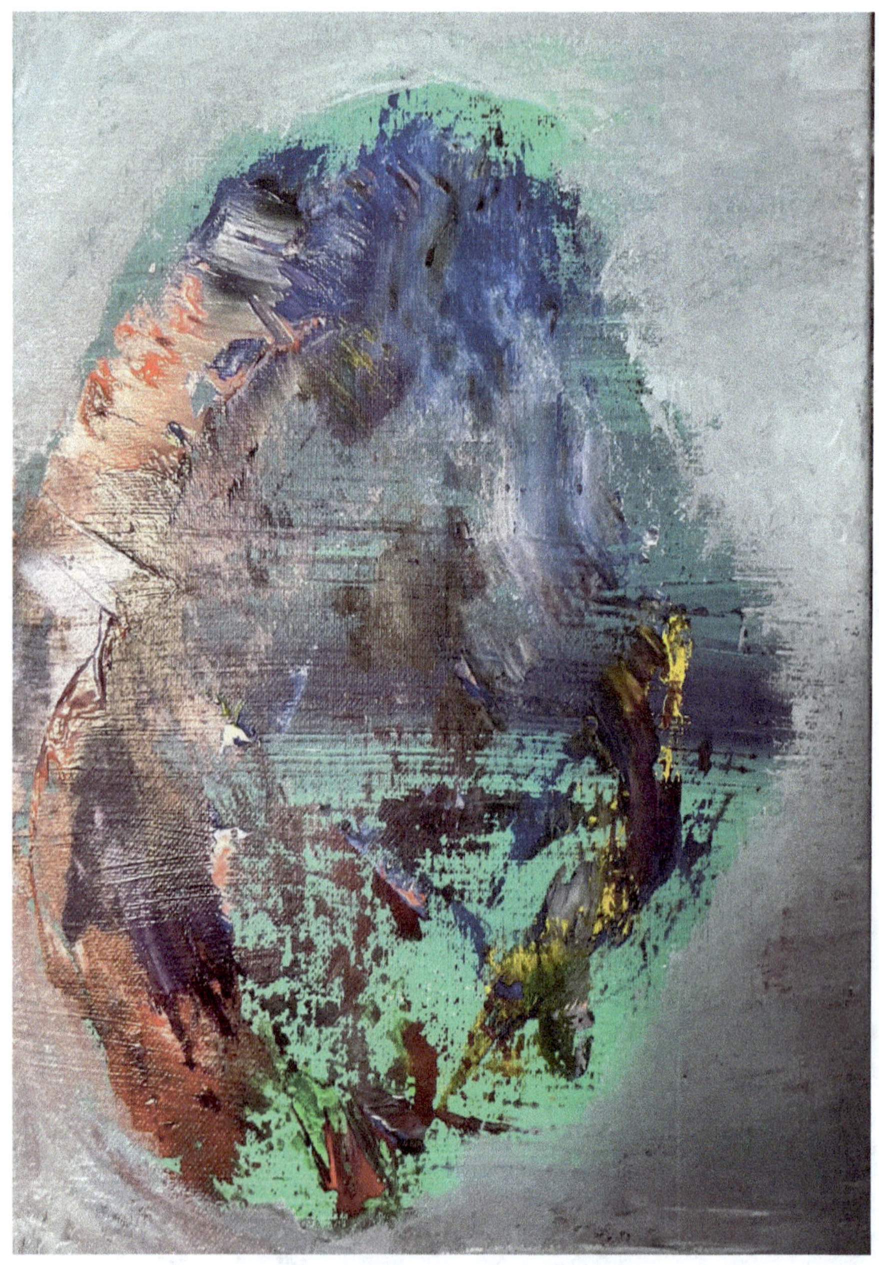

Bird And The Speaker

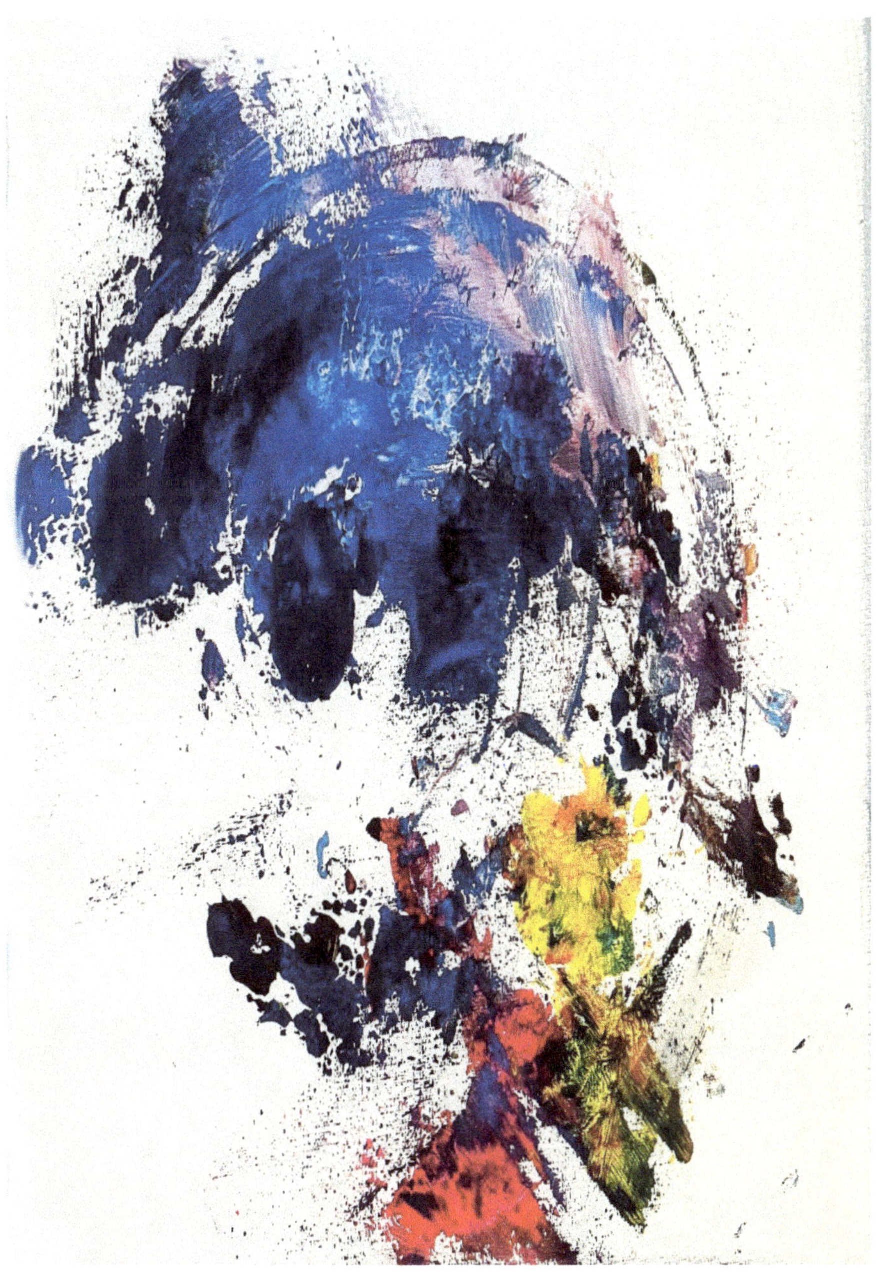

Concussion (Inner Workings Of The Mind)

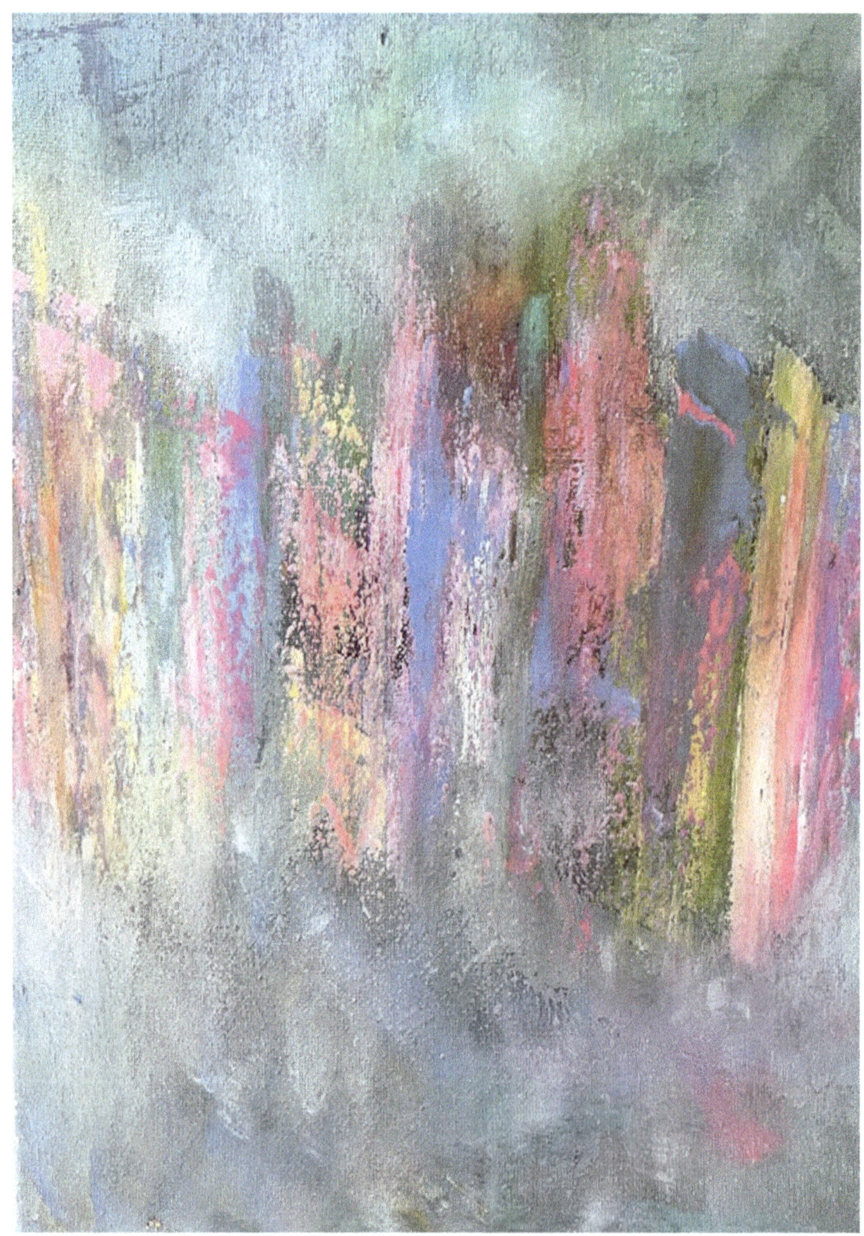

People Of The Foggy Surreal Cityscape

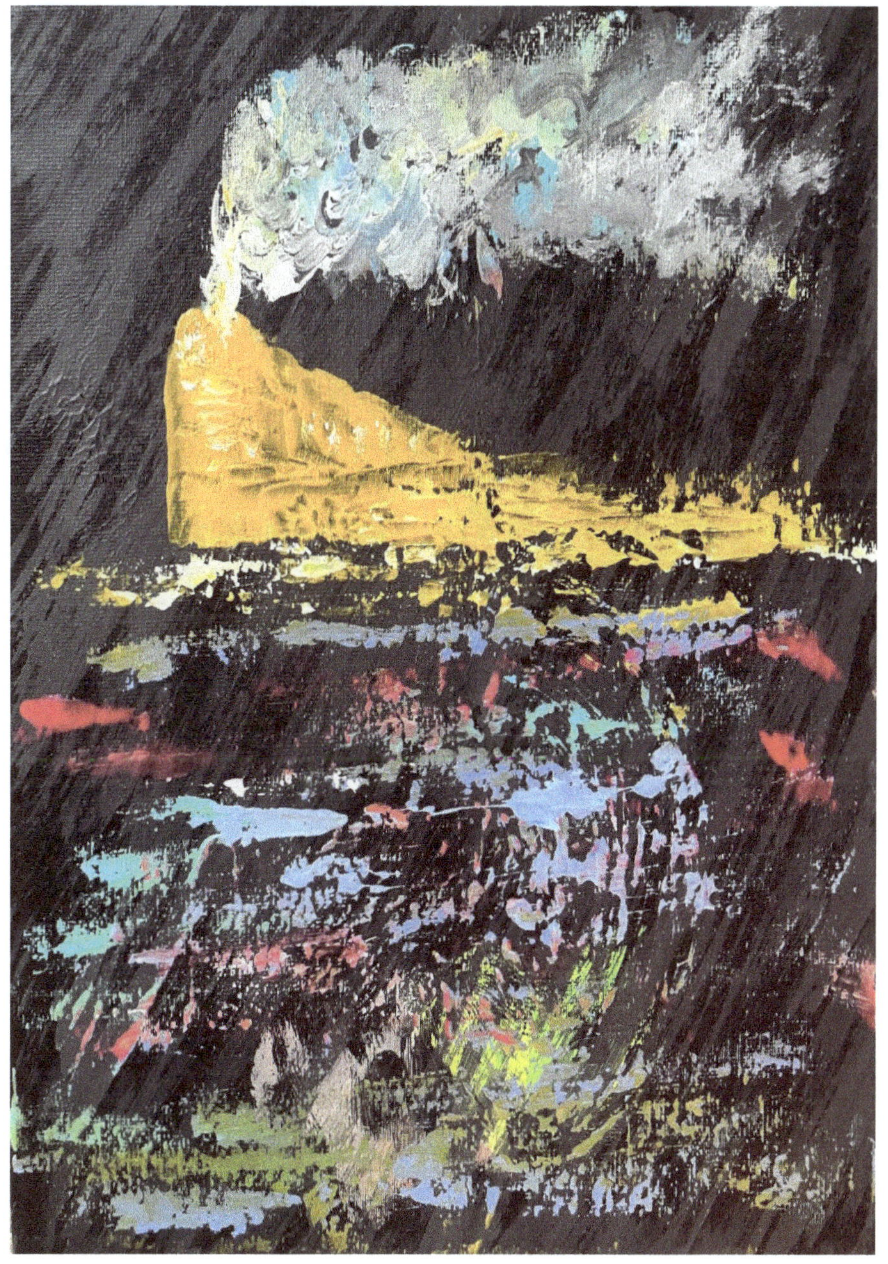

Last Train To Avignon

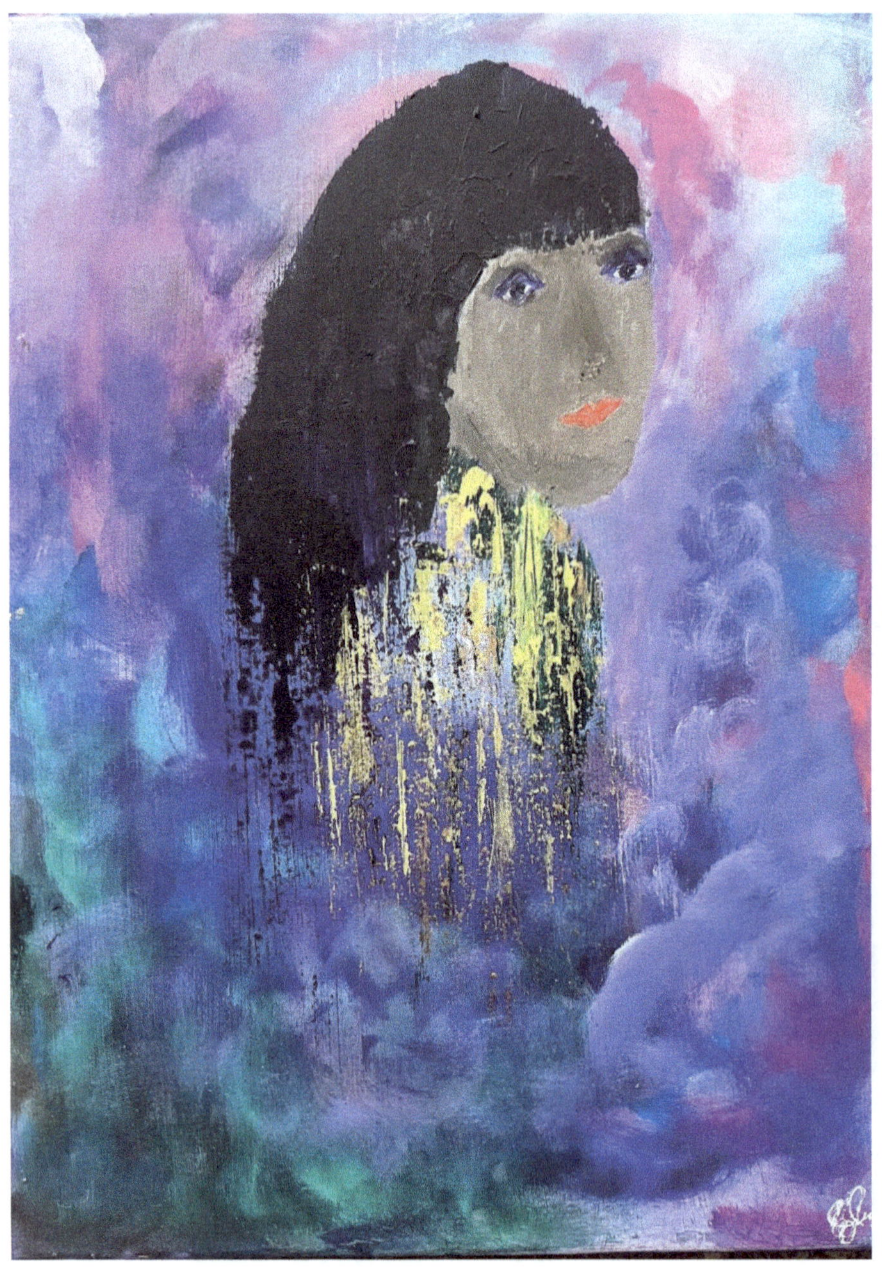

Cleohontas

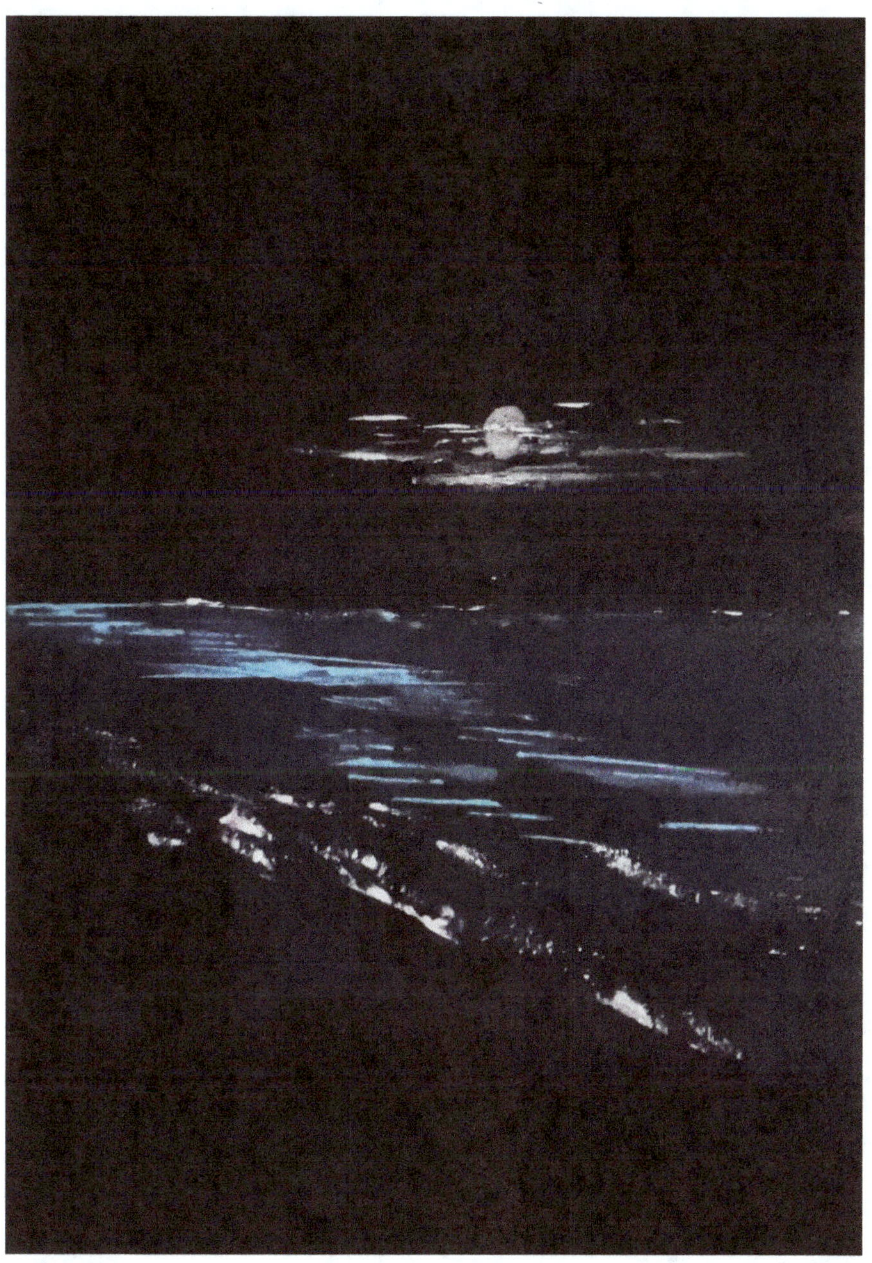

Moonlight Bay

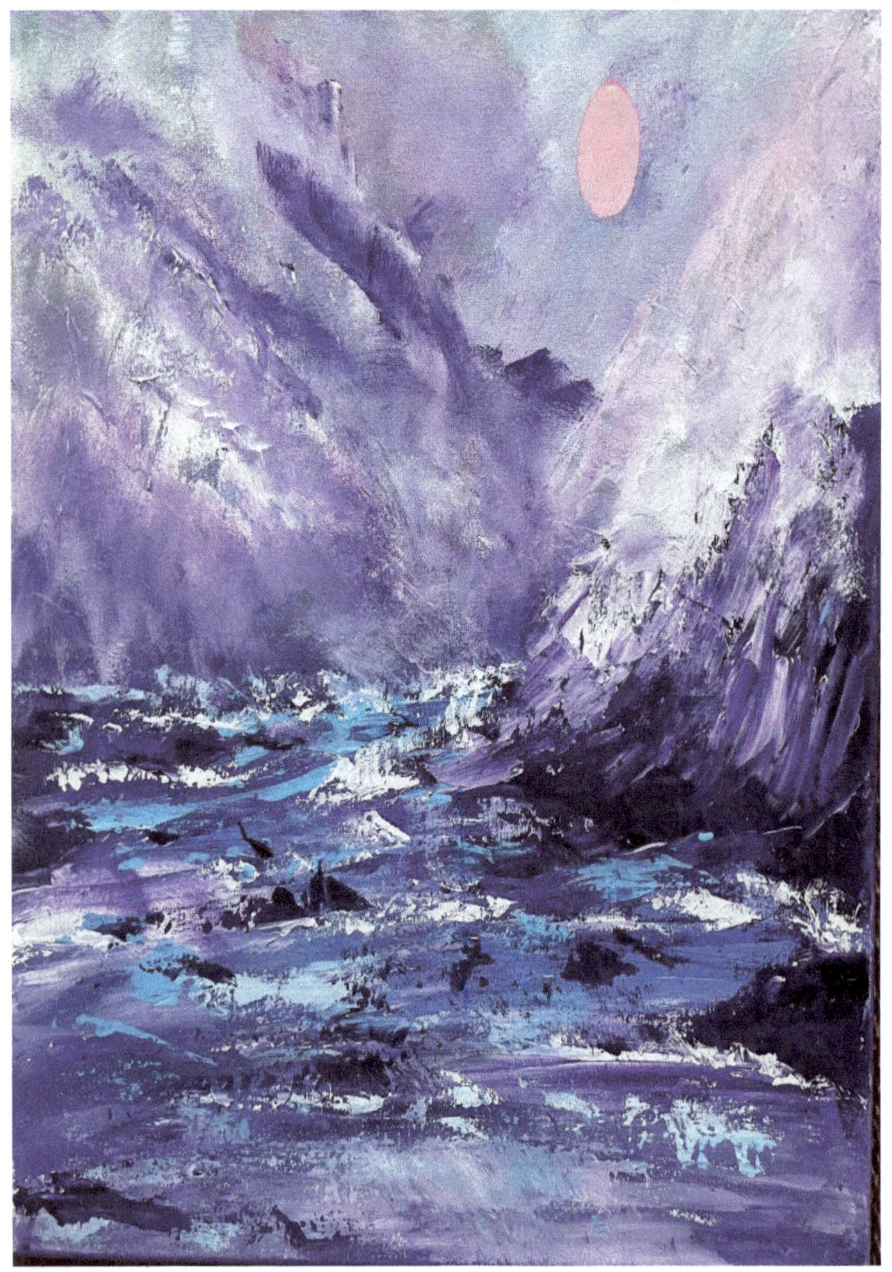

Arctic Twilight Moon

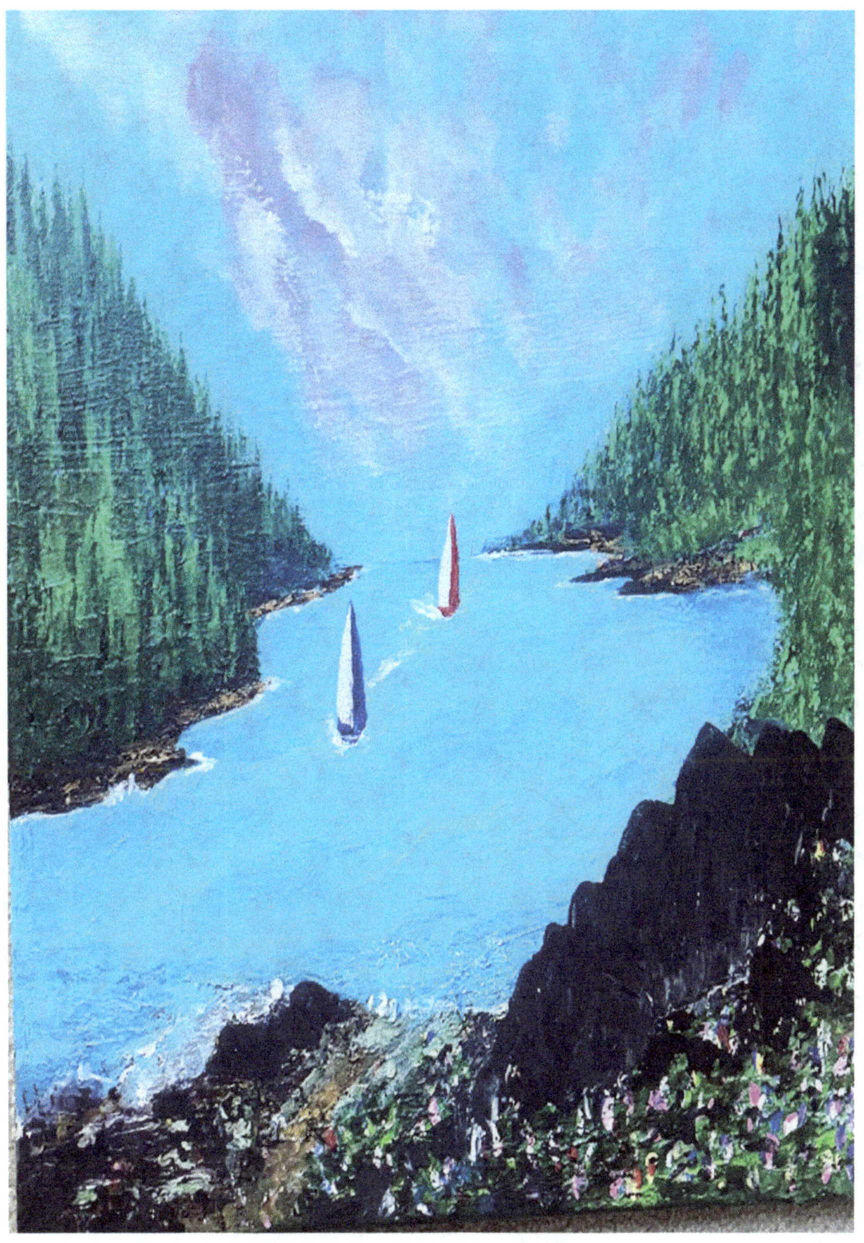

Entering The Harbour

Pale Desert Moon

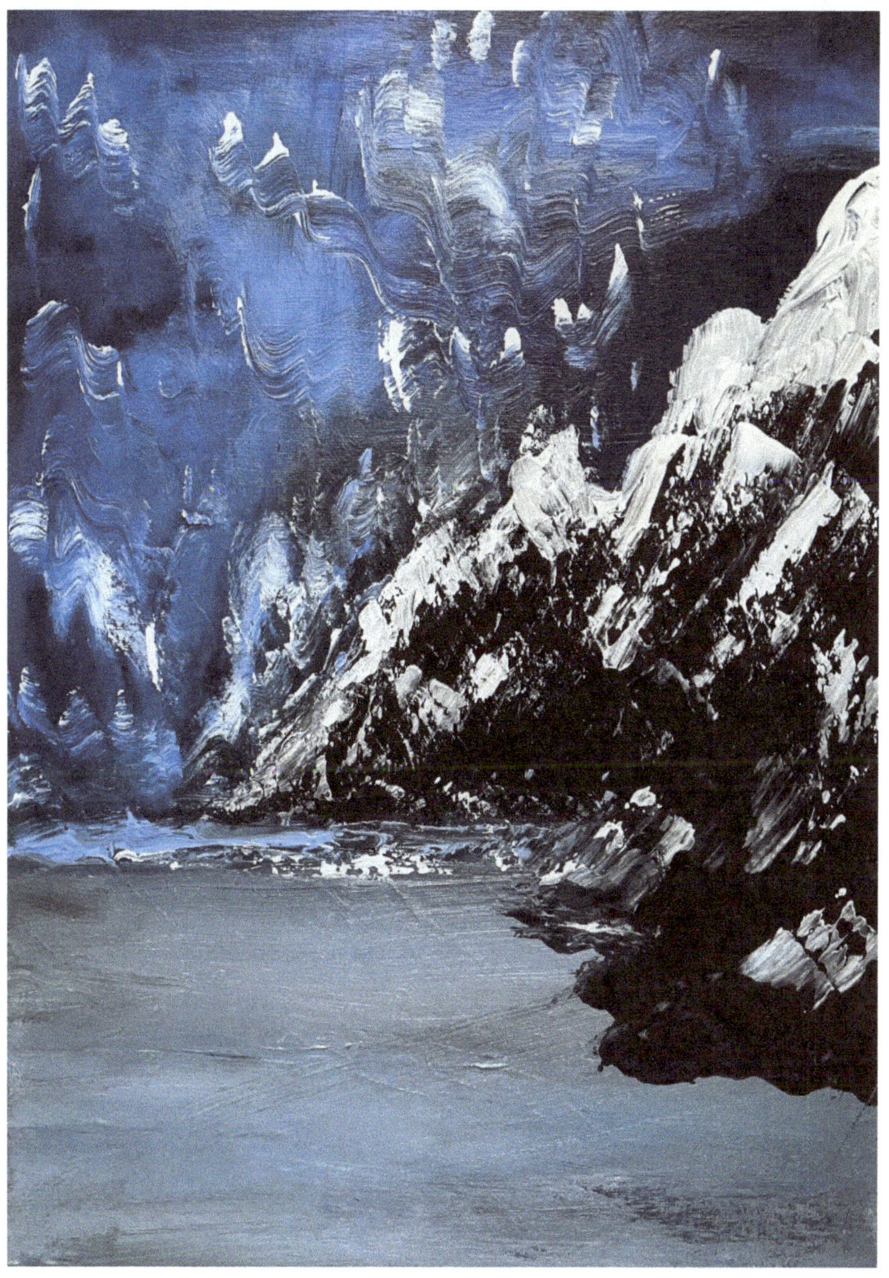

Northern Nights

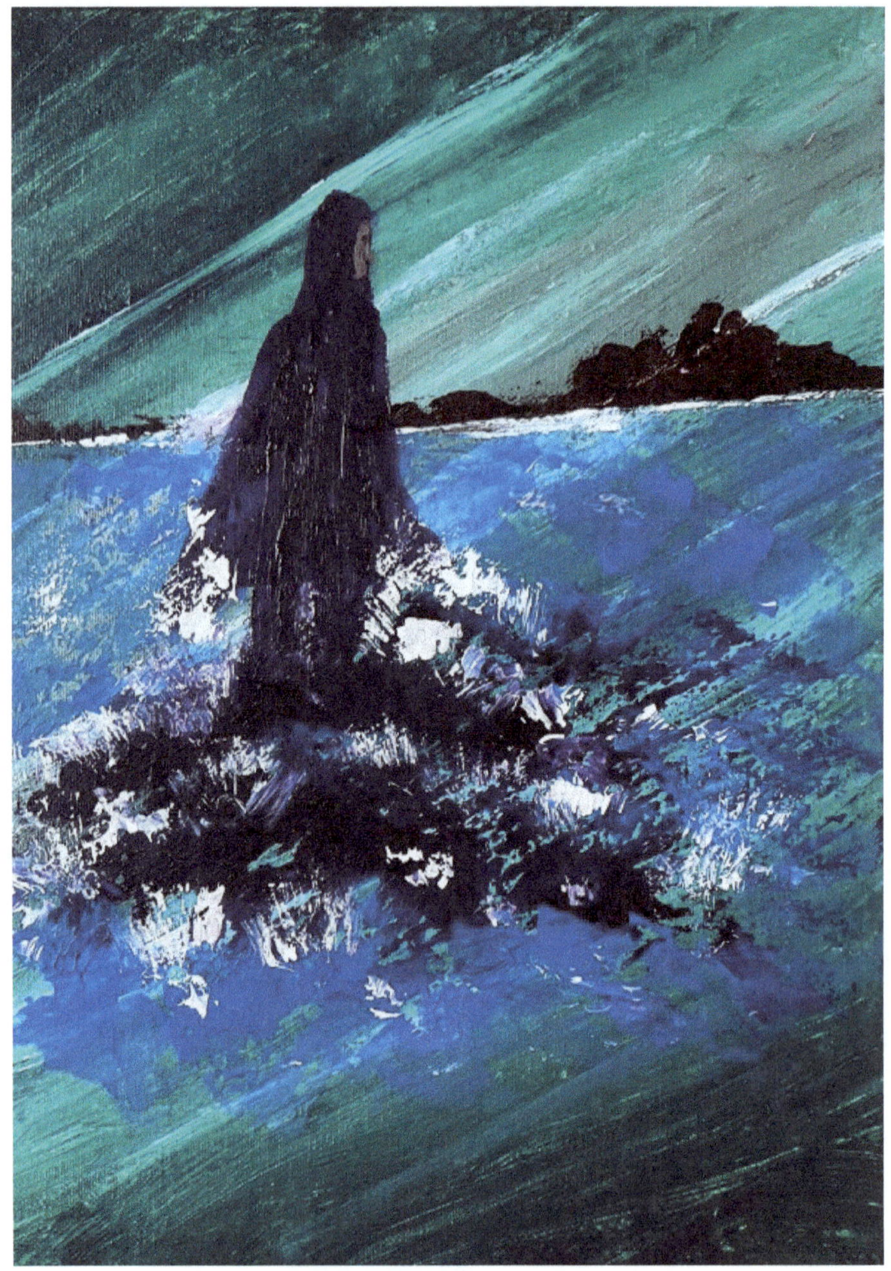

Self-Imposed Exile

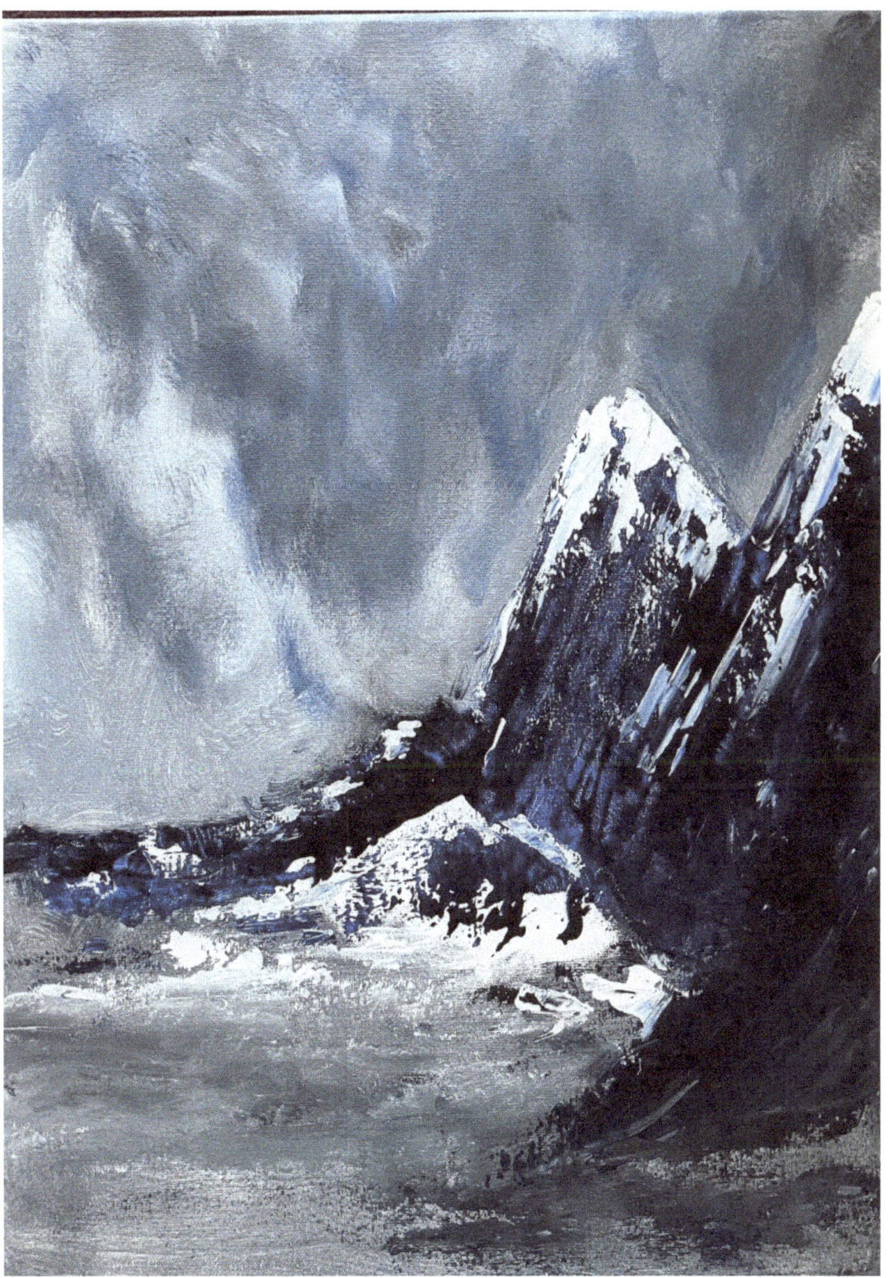

Snows Of Kilimanjaro

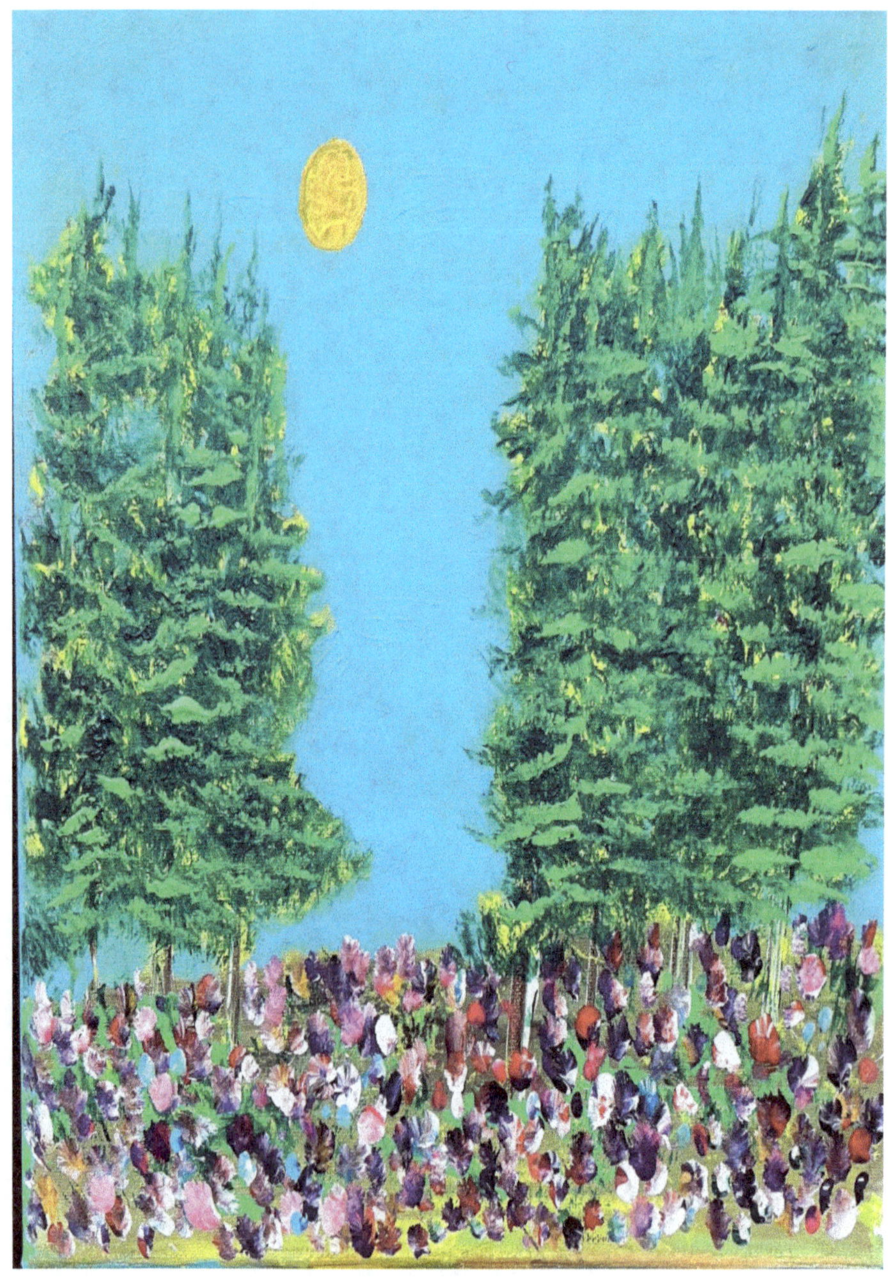

Sun Worshippers

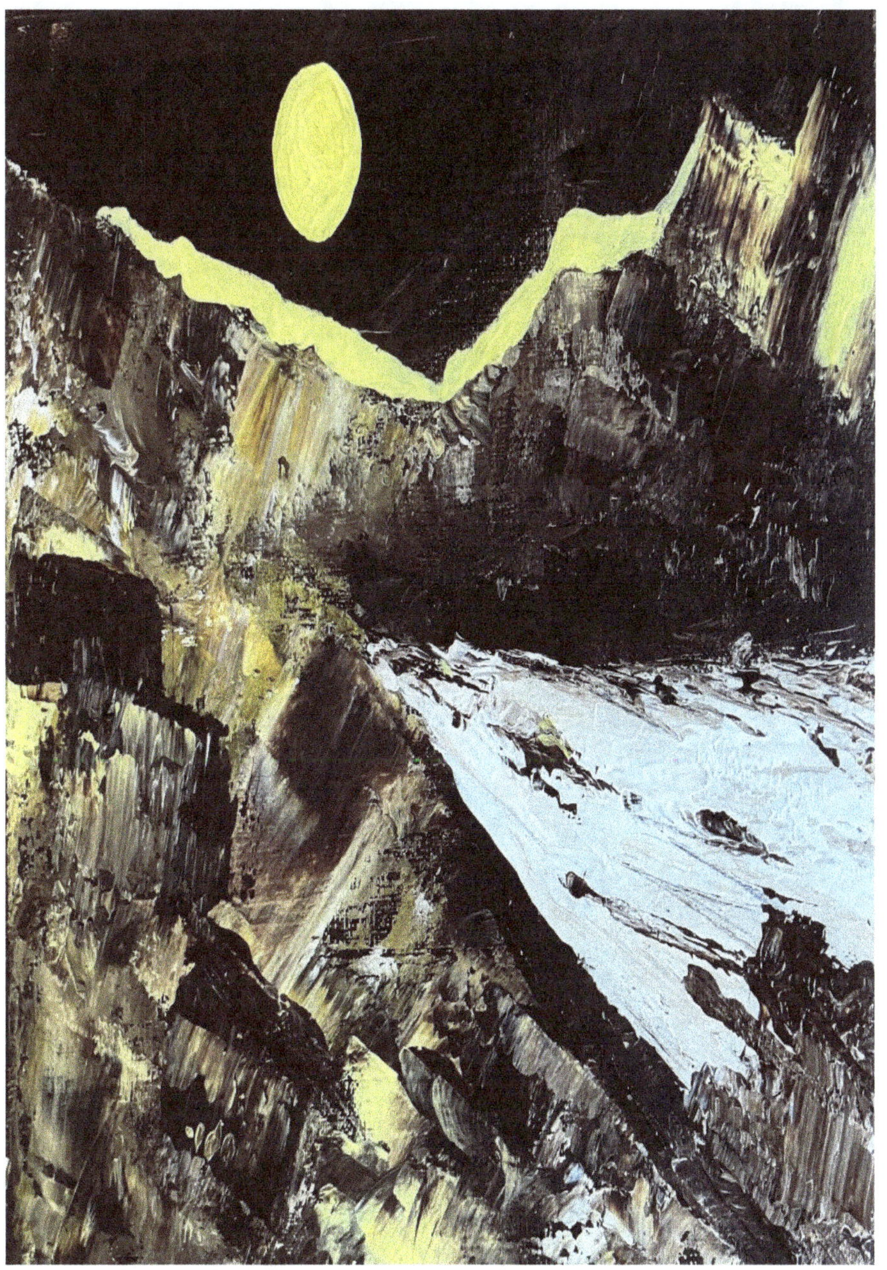

Tartan Mountain Glacial Lake

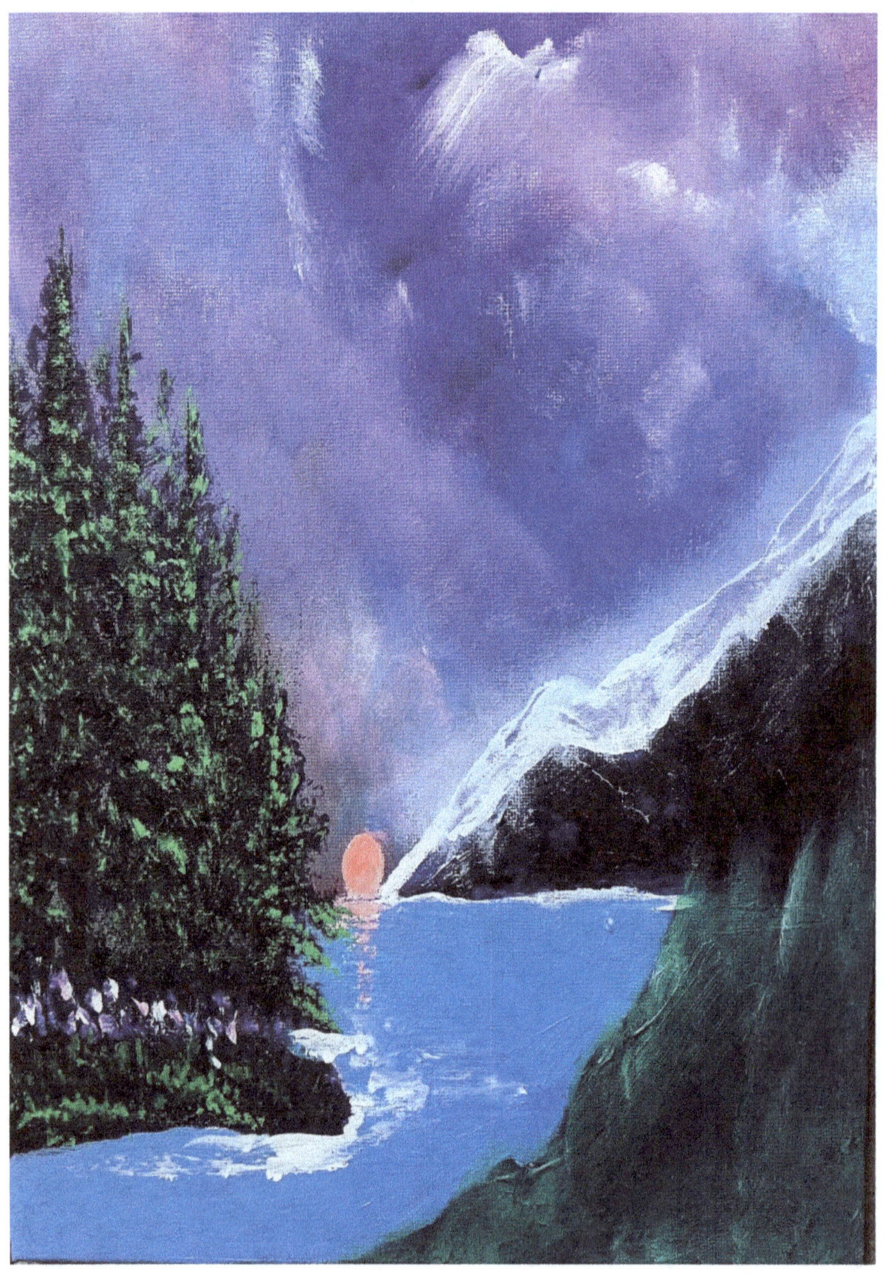

Sun Falling Into Water

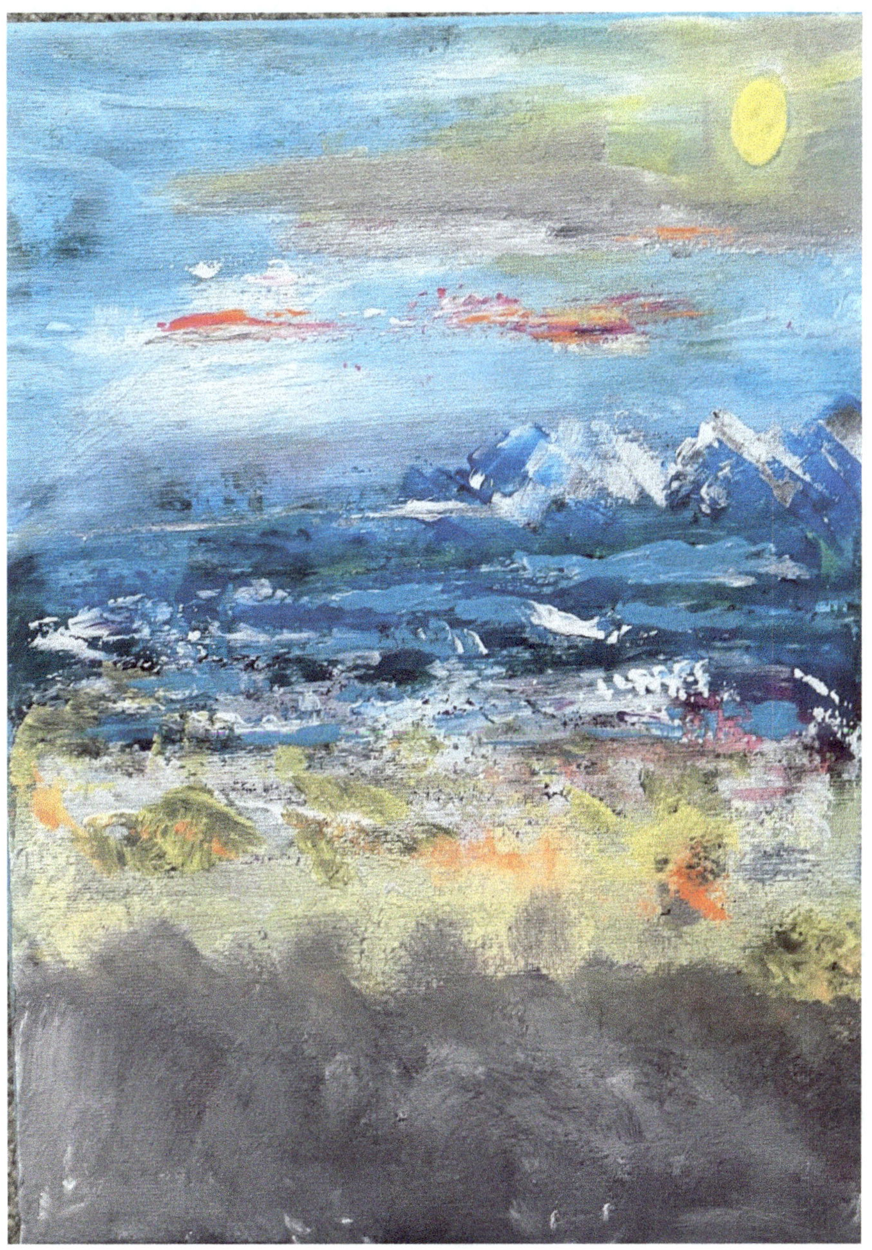

Choppy Waters

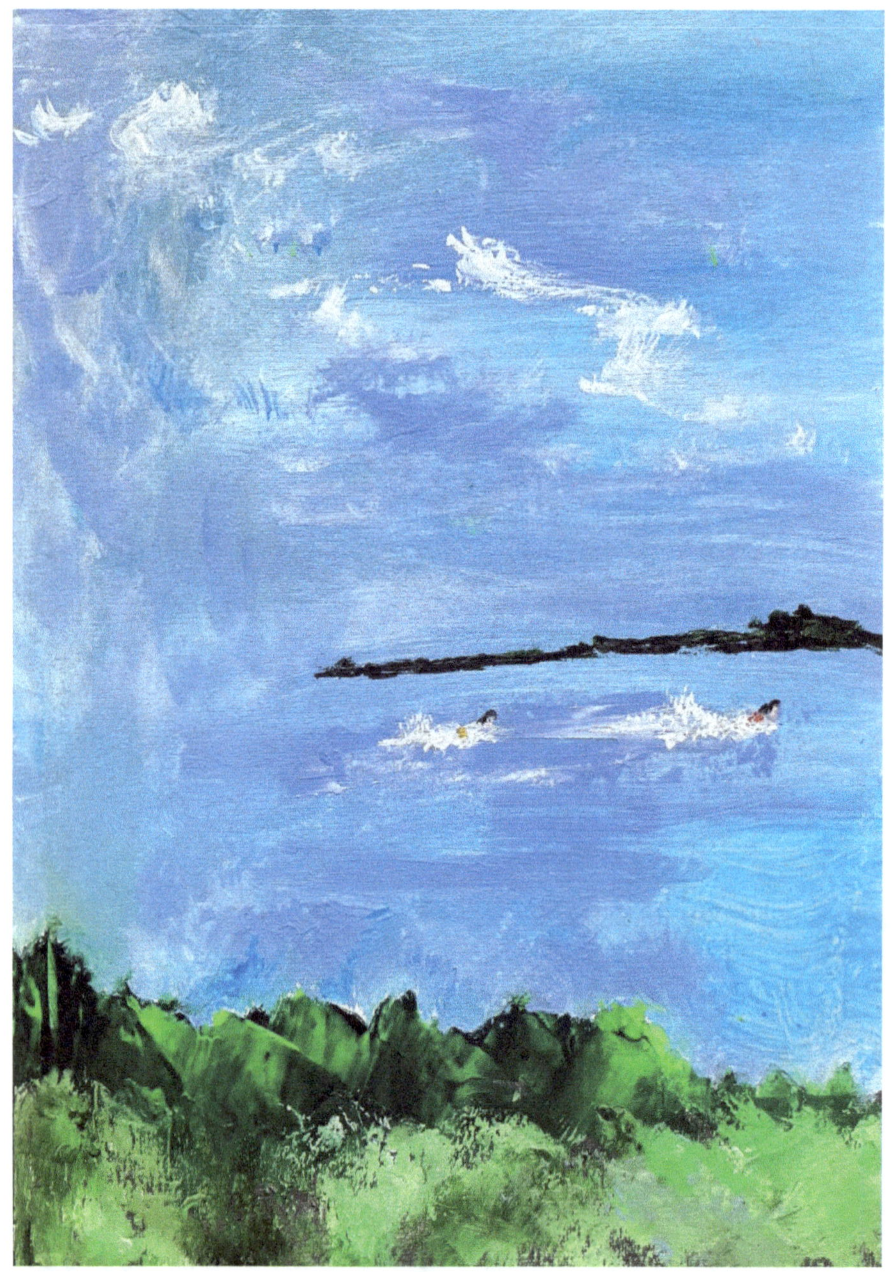

The Swimmers

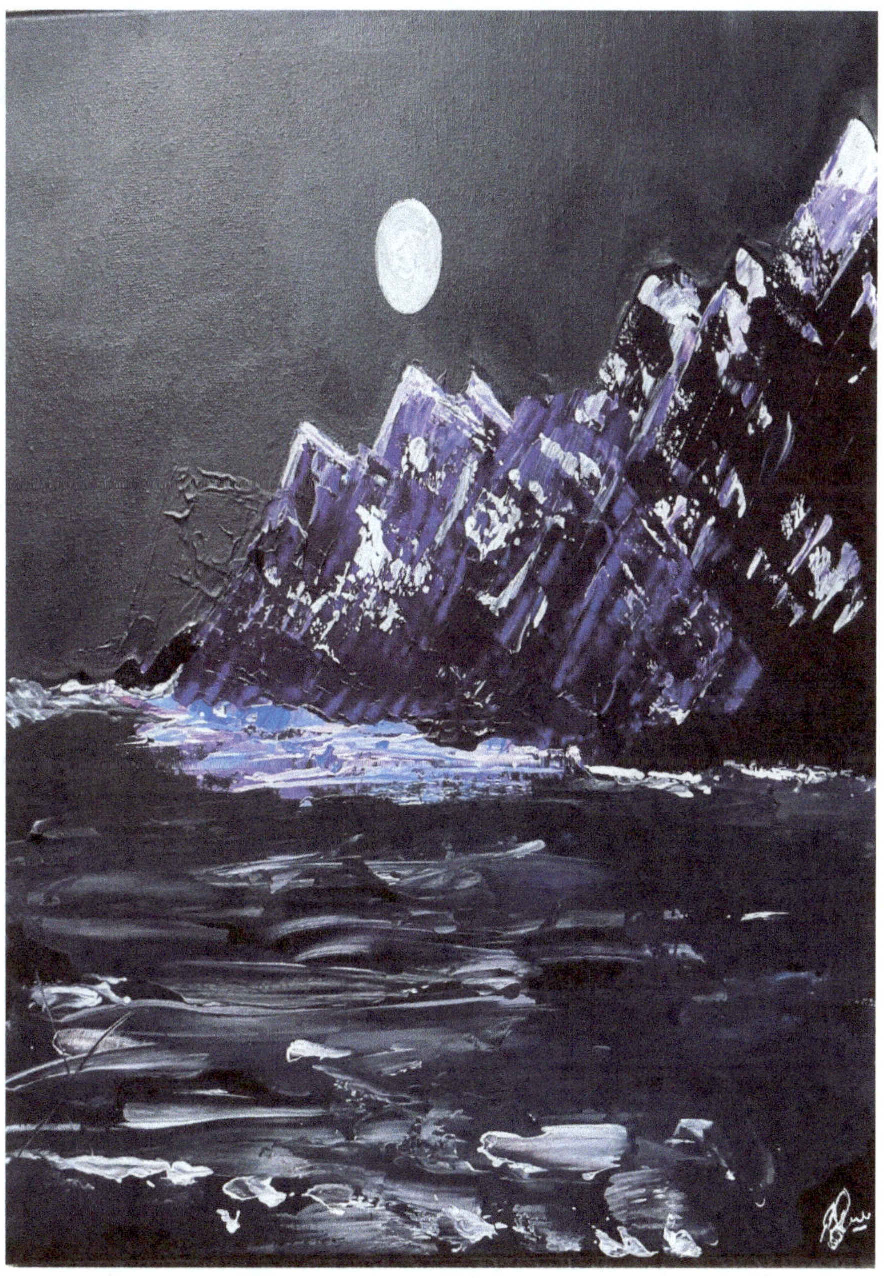

Arctic Melt

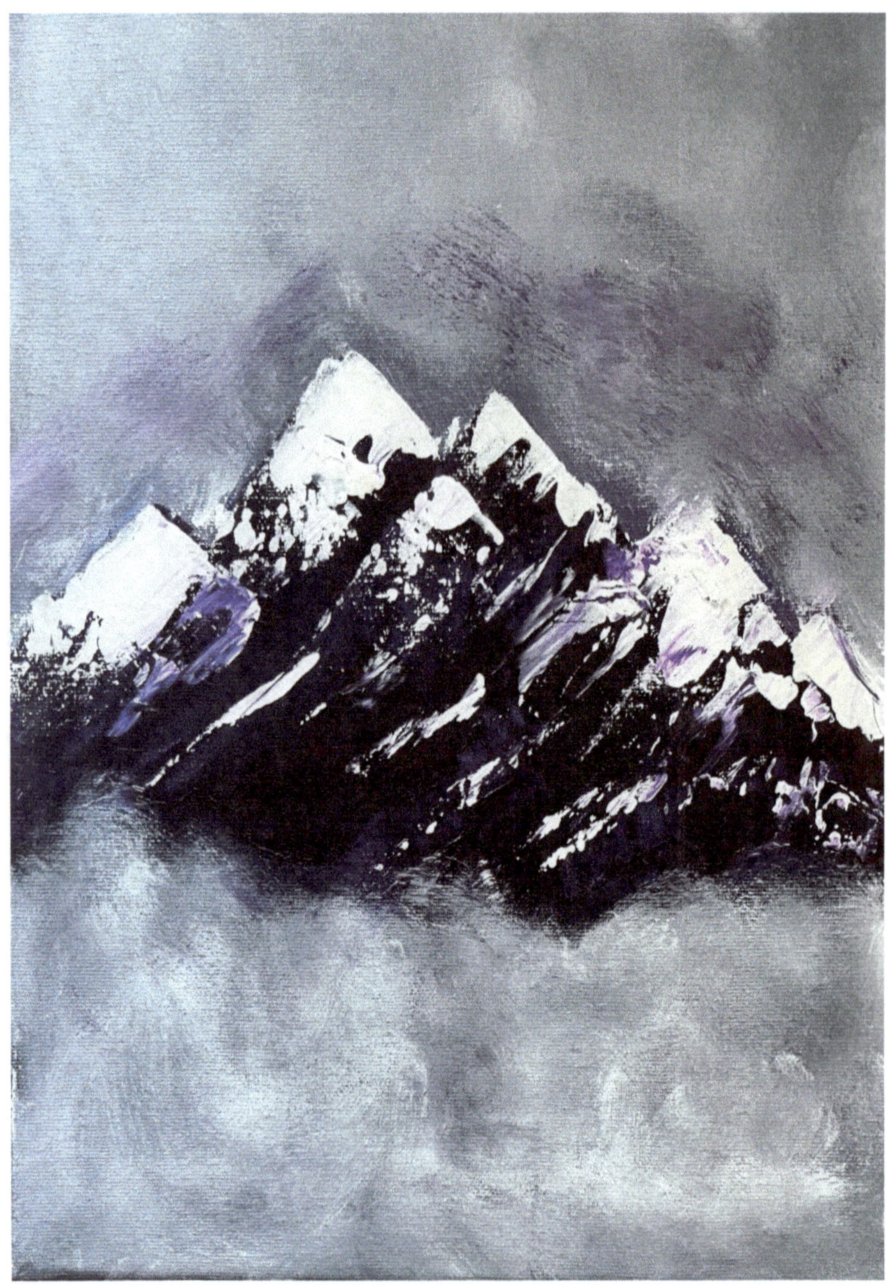

Impending Fog

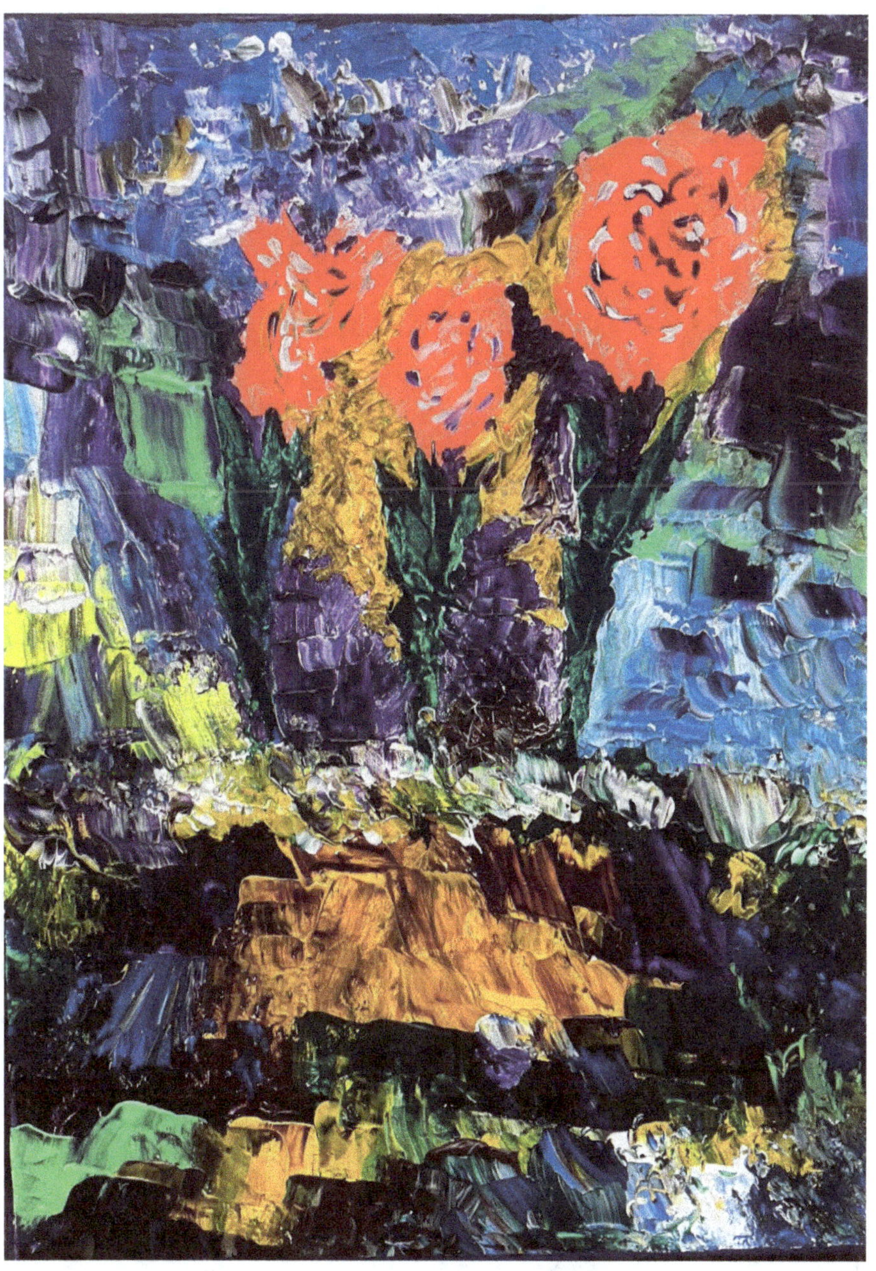

Inner Sanctum Playground

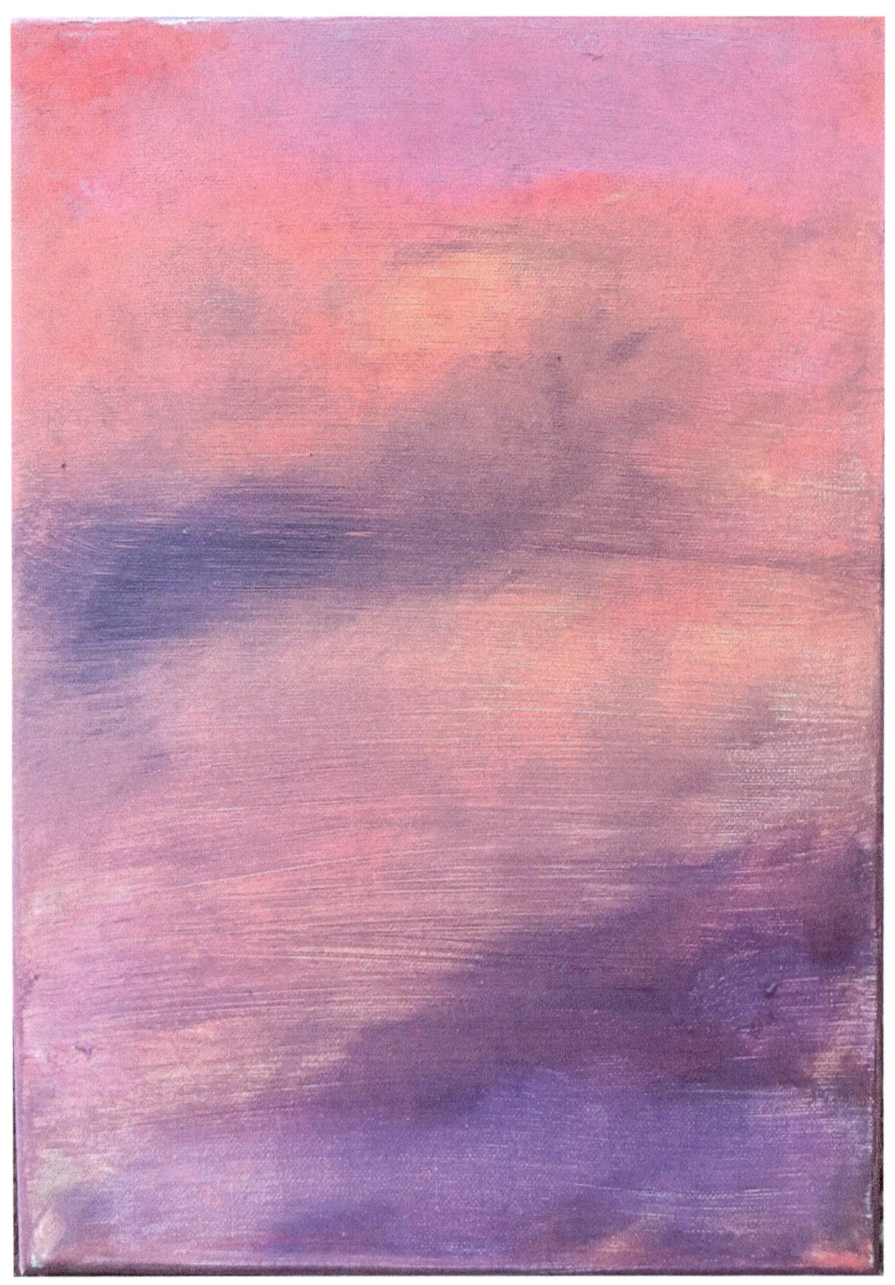

Muted Mojave Desert

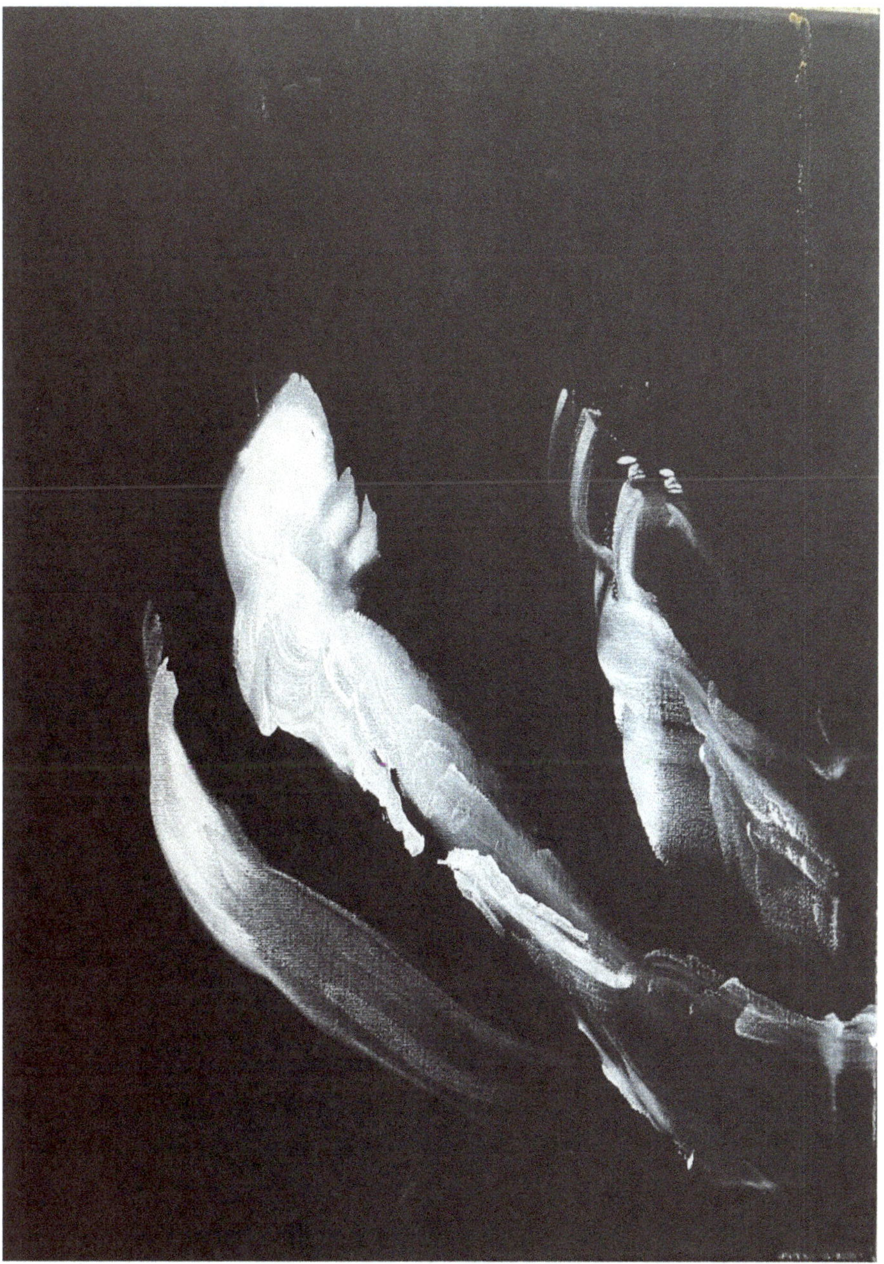

Dance of the Ghosts

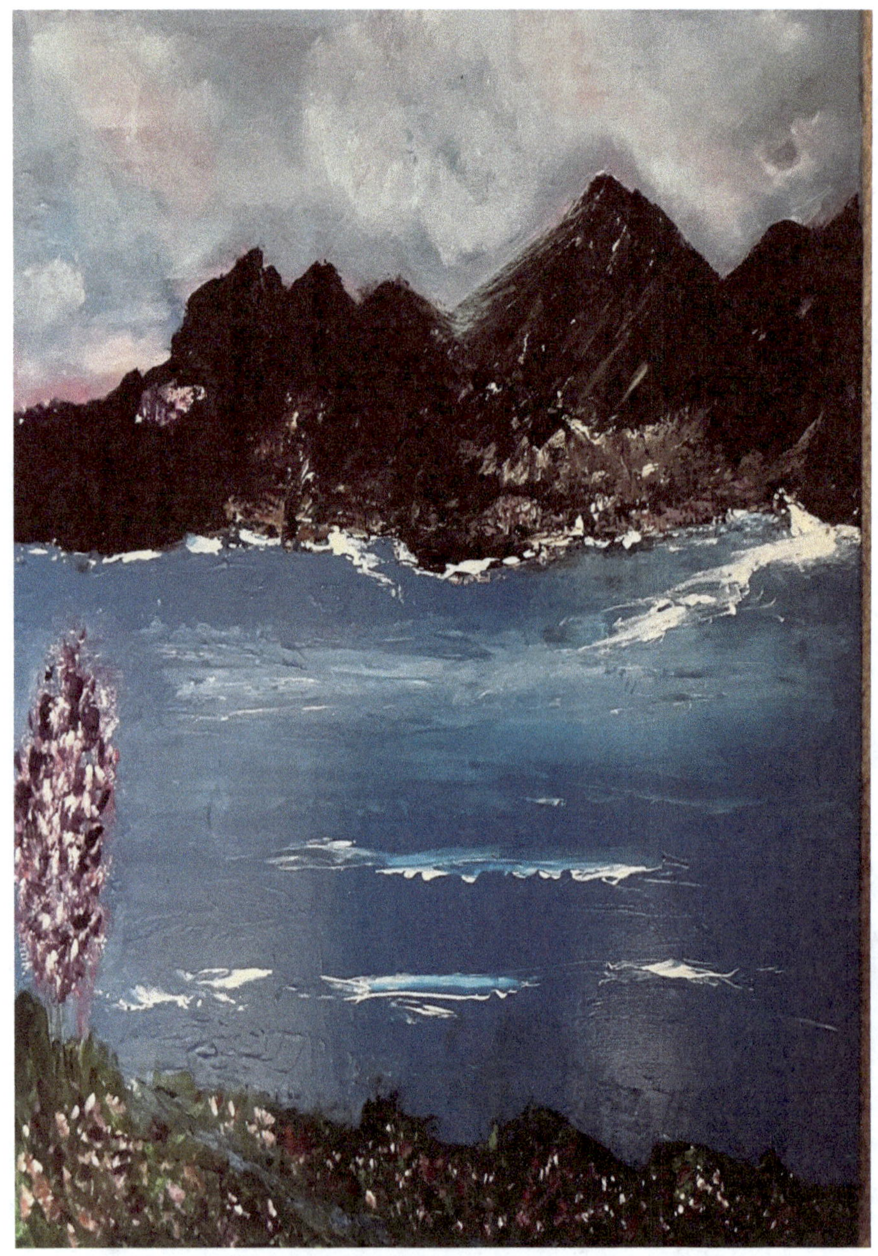

Distant Settlements

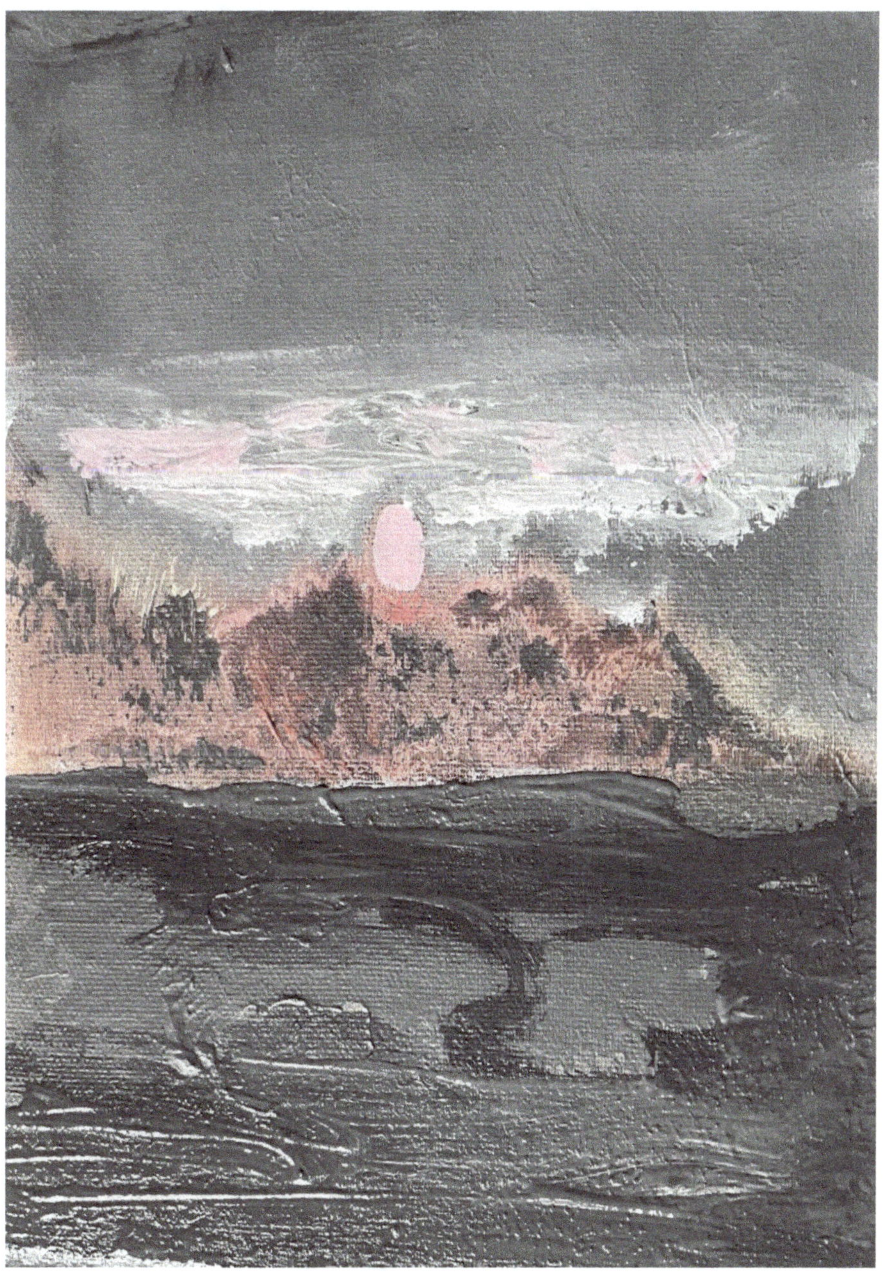

Mendoza Moon

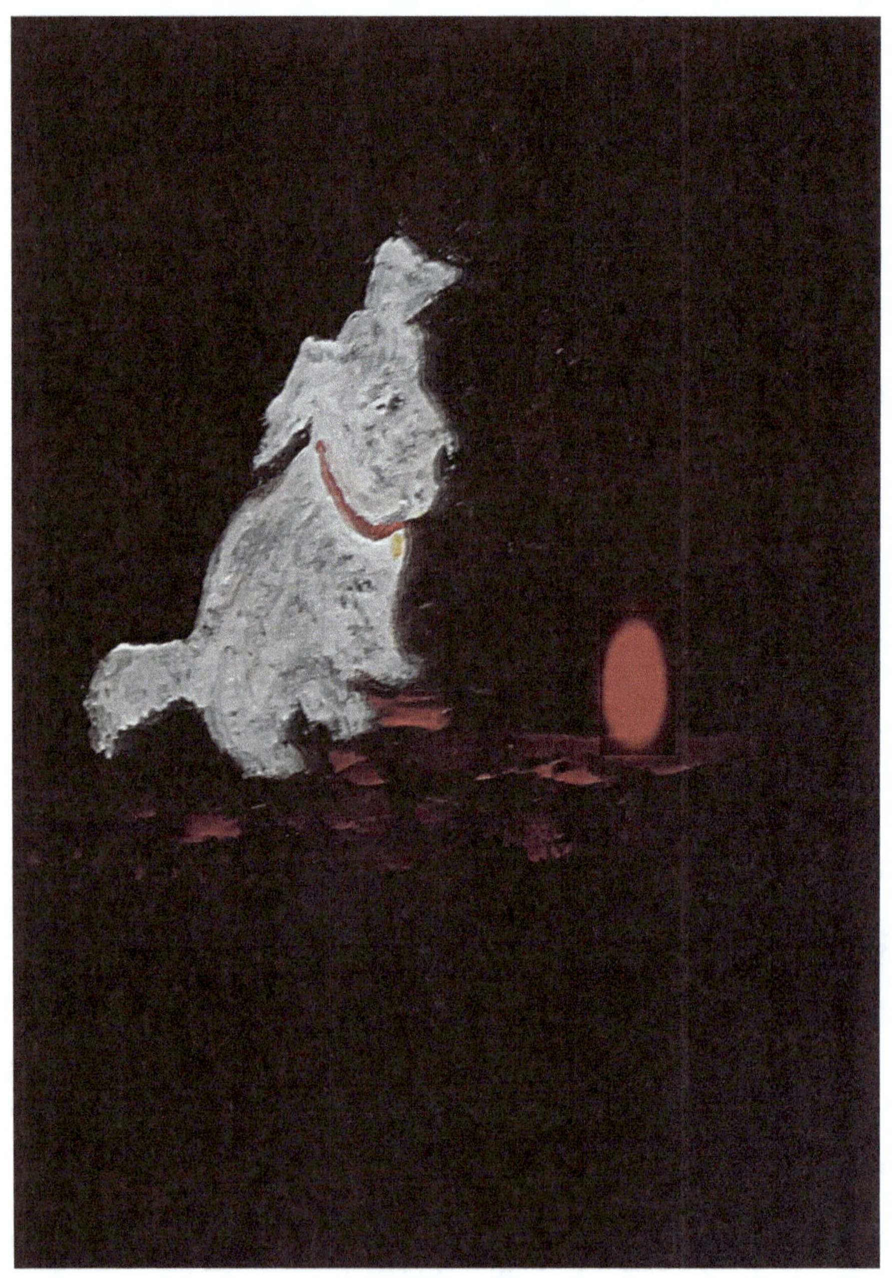

Stay

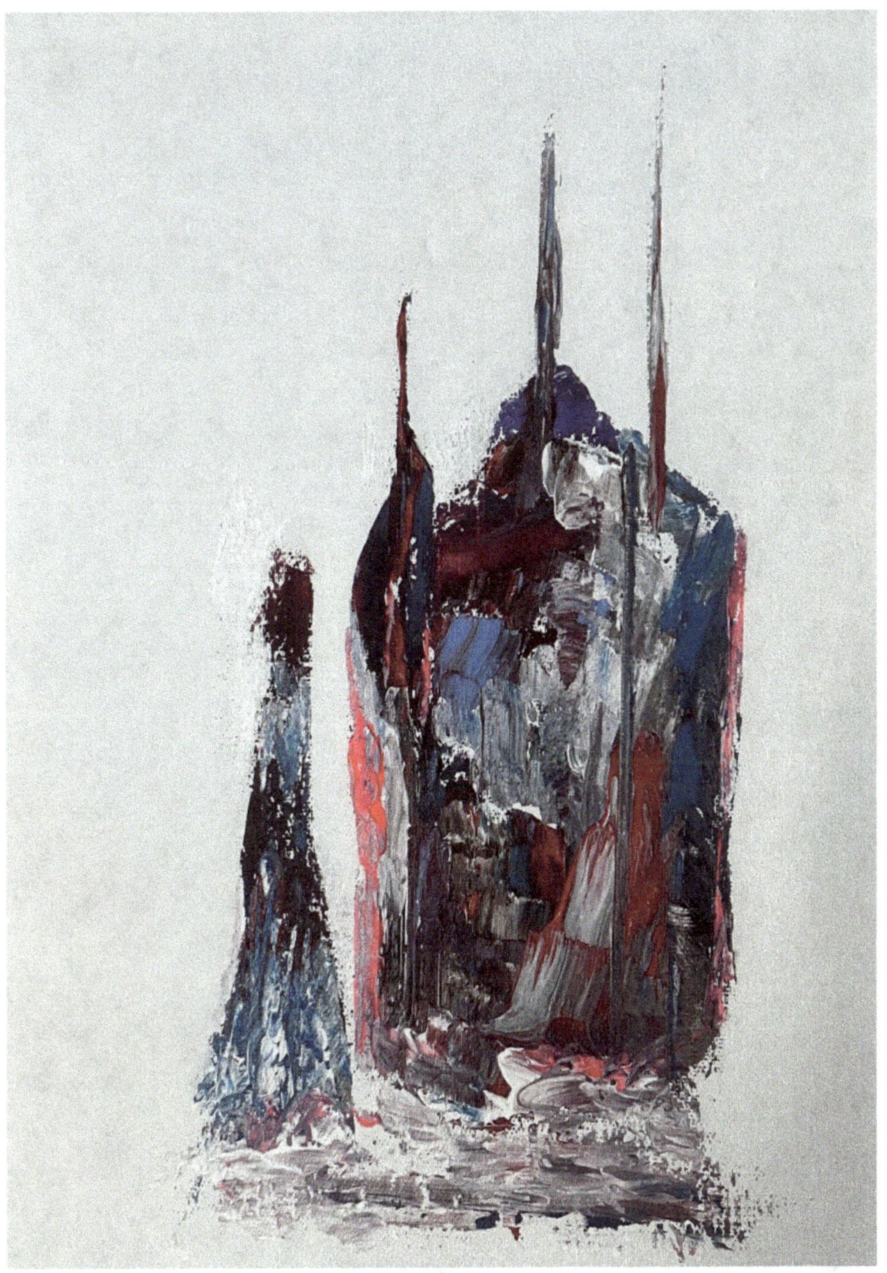

Arabesque

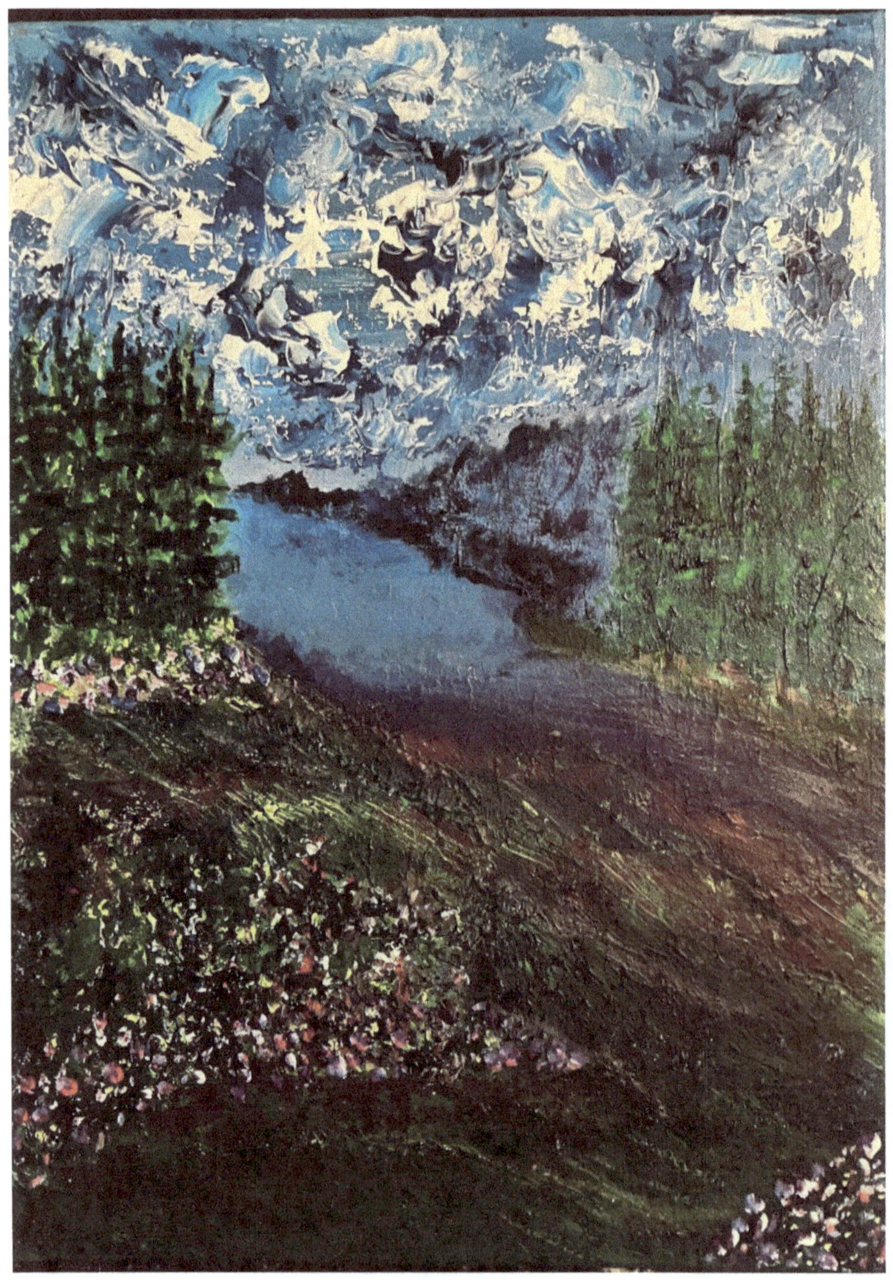

Blue Dahlia Skyfall

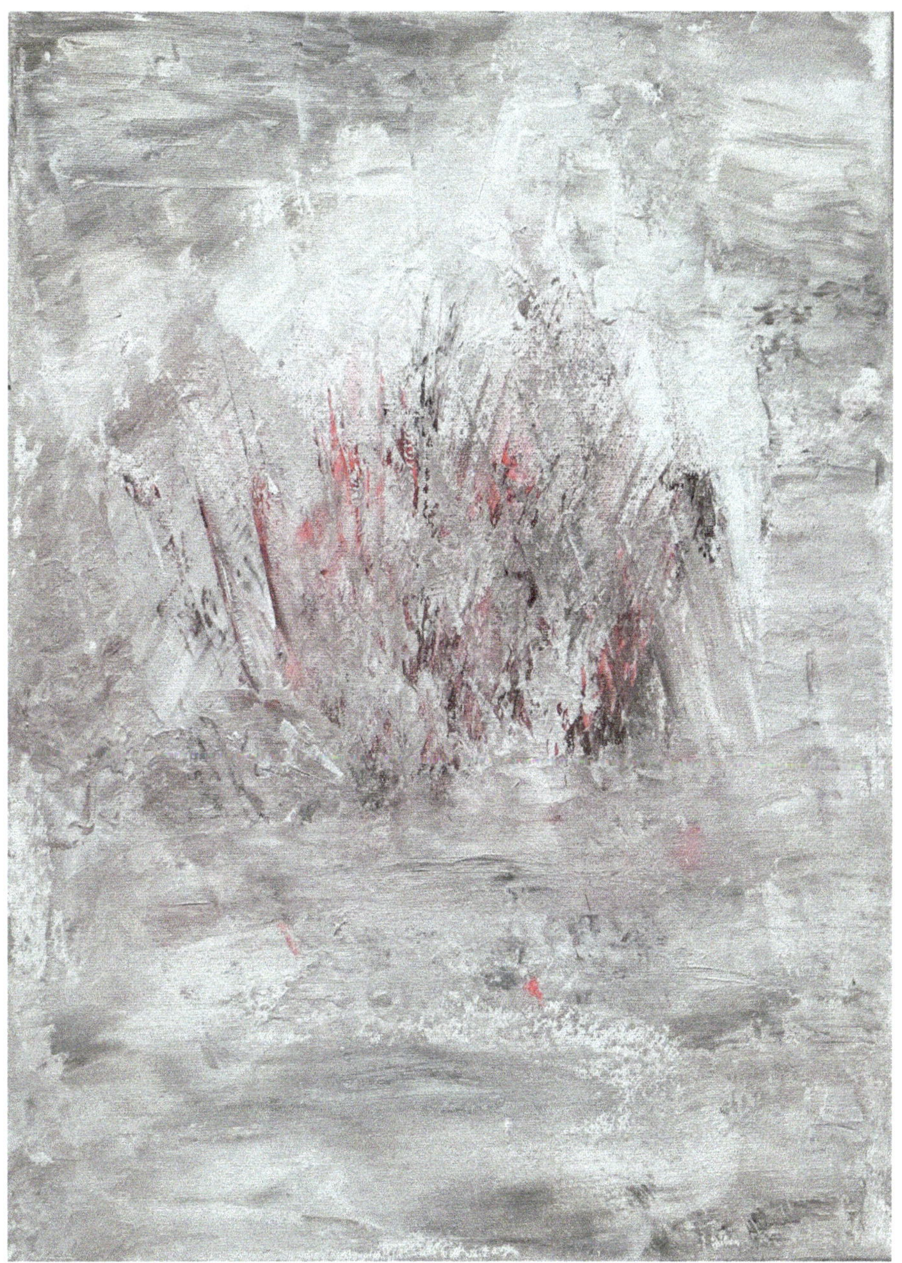

Misty Morning Floral

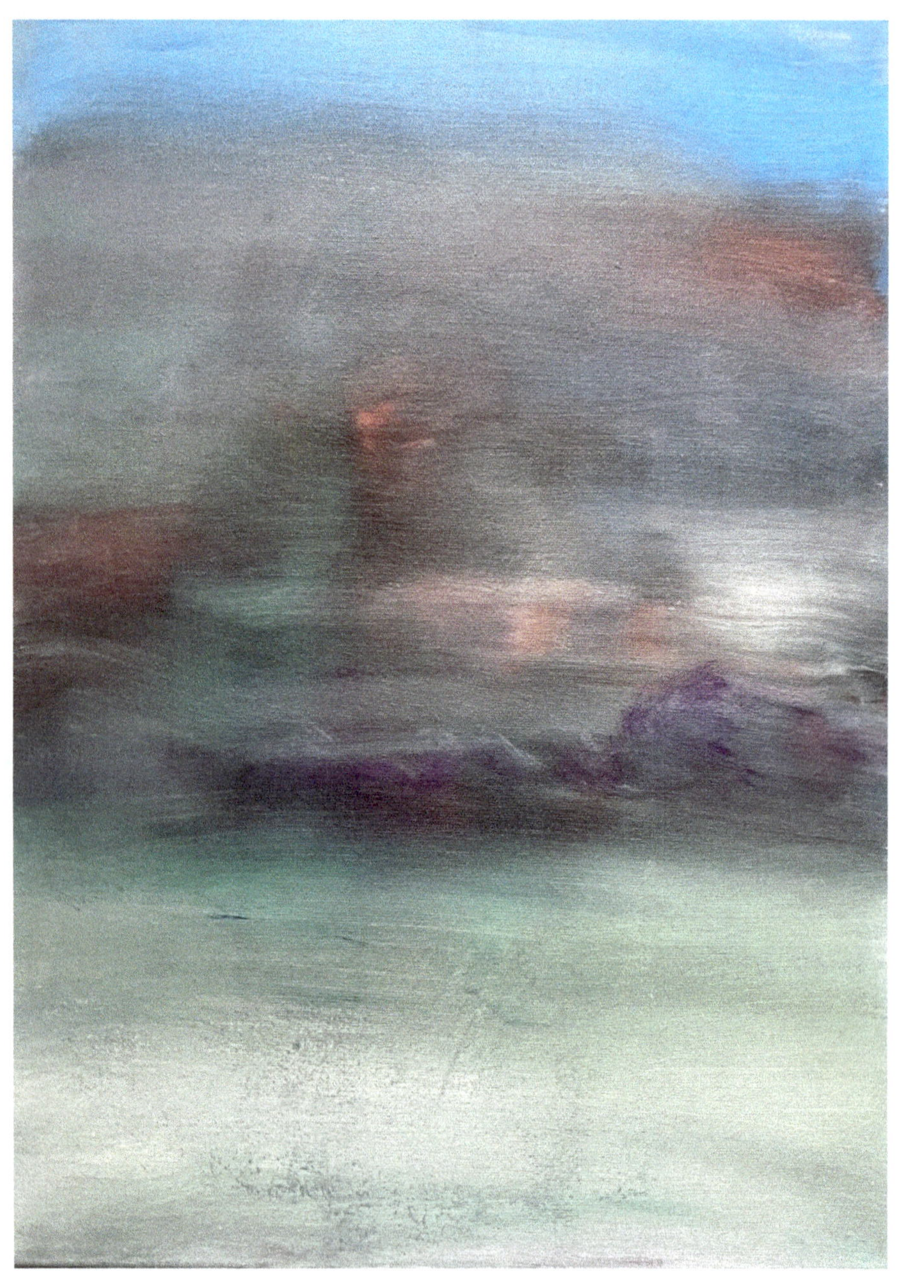

Misty Morning Lights

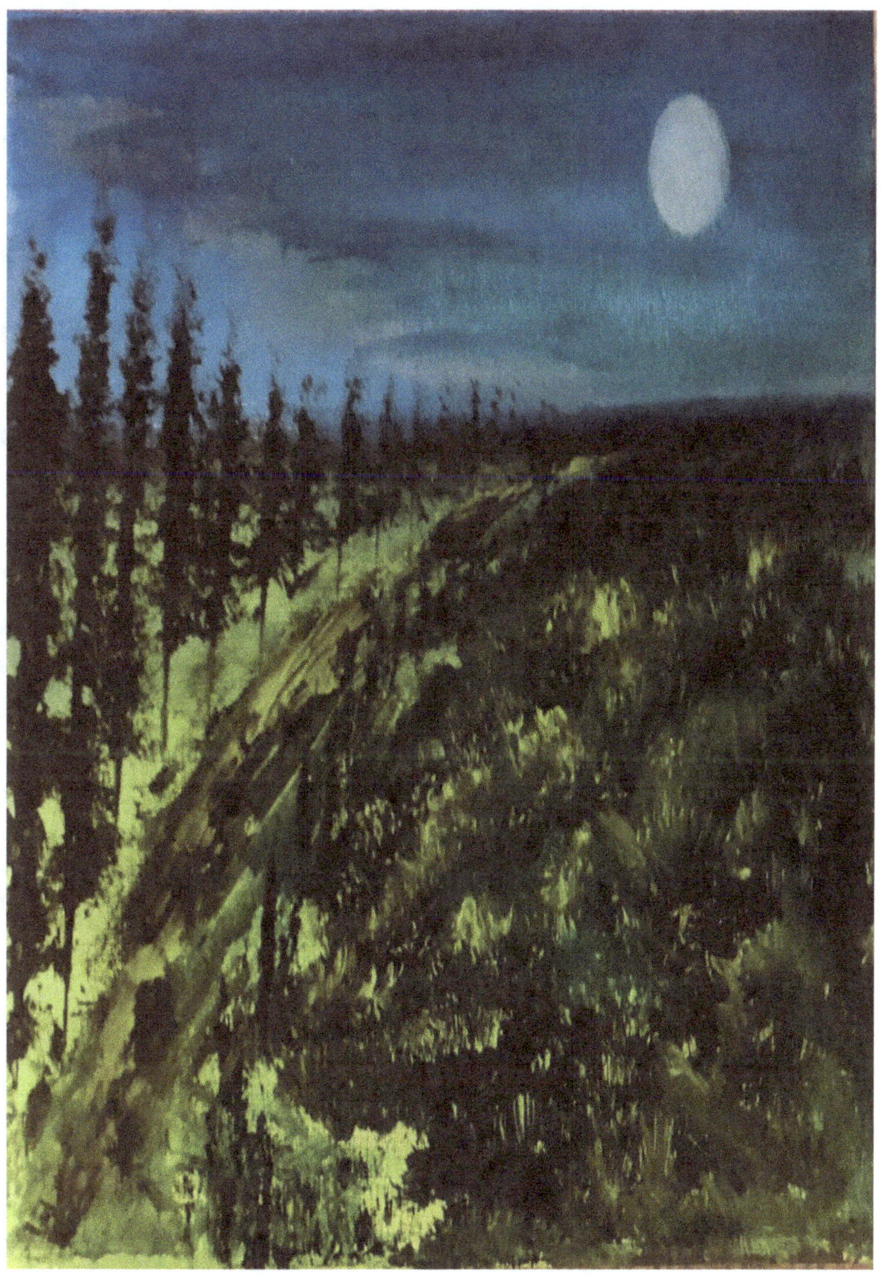

Clashindougal, Scotland

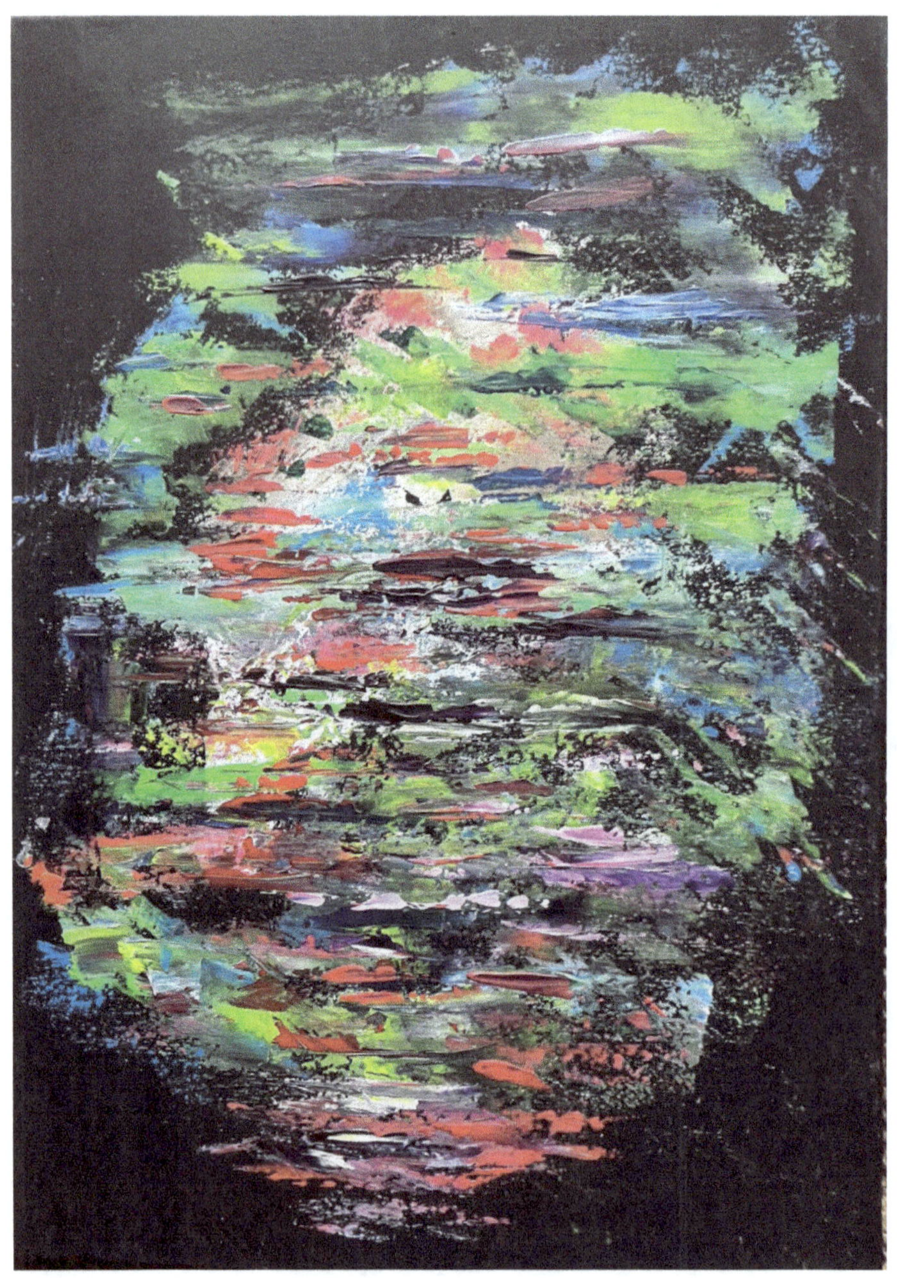

Peeking Through

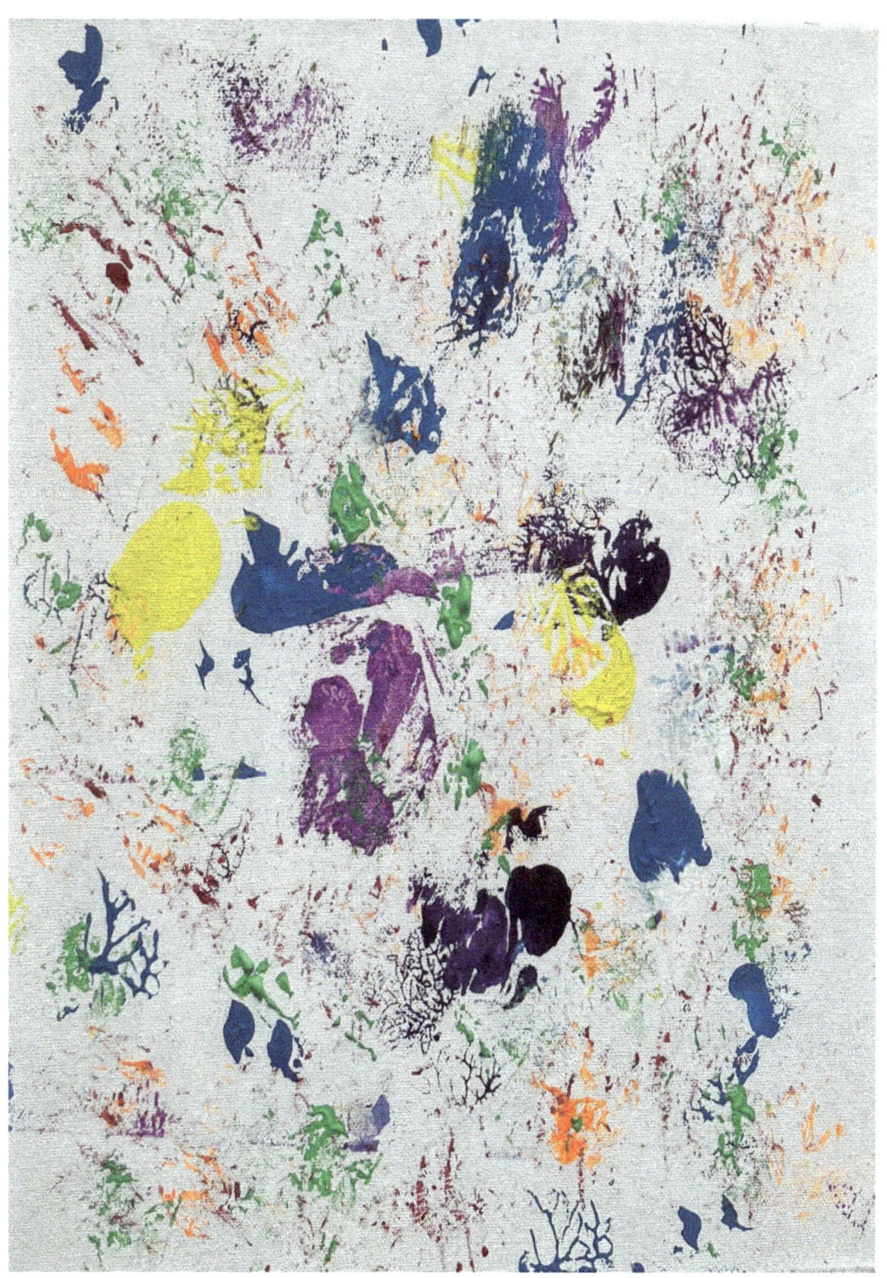

Conversational Jazz

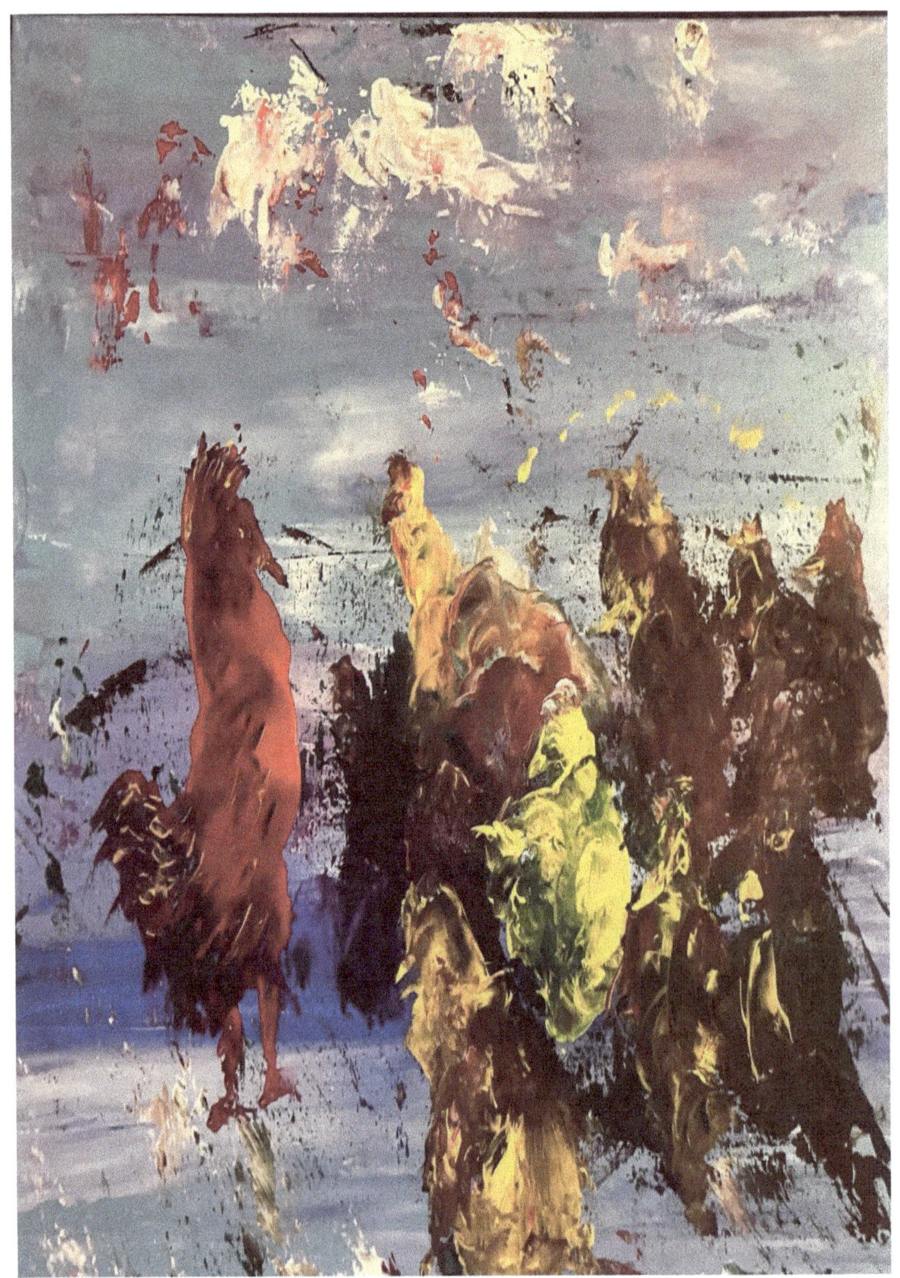

Rooster In The Hen House

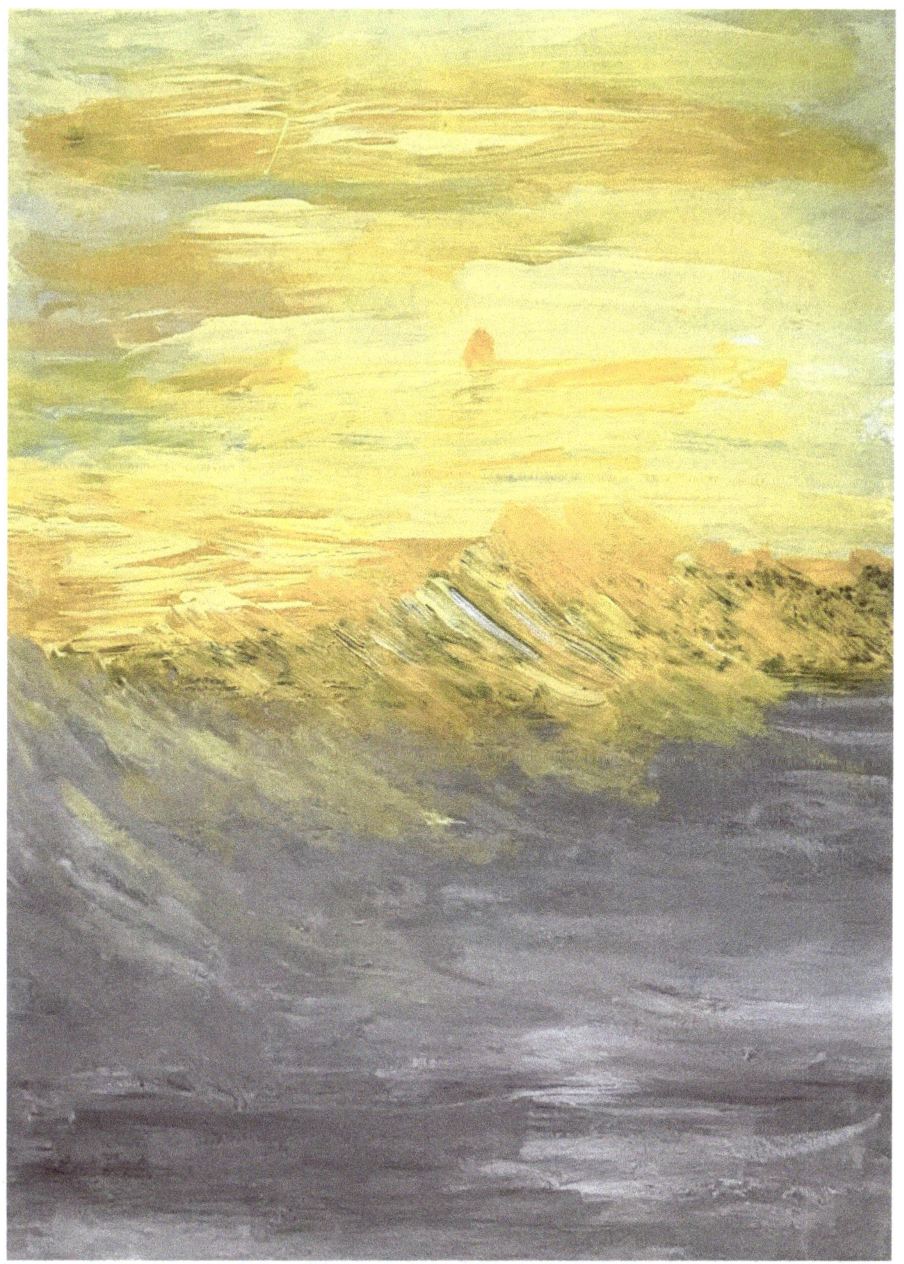

Sahara Sundown

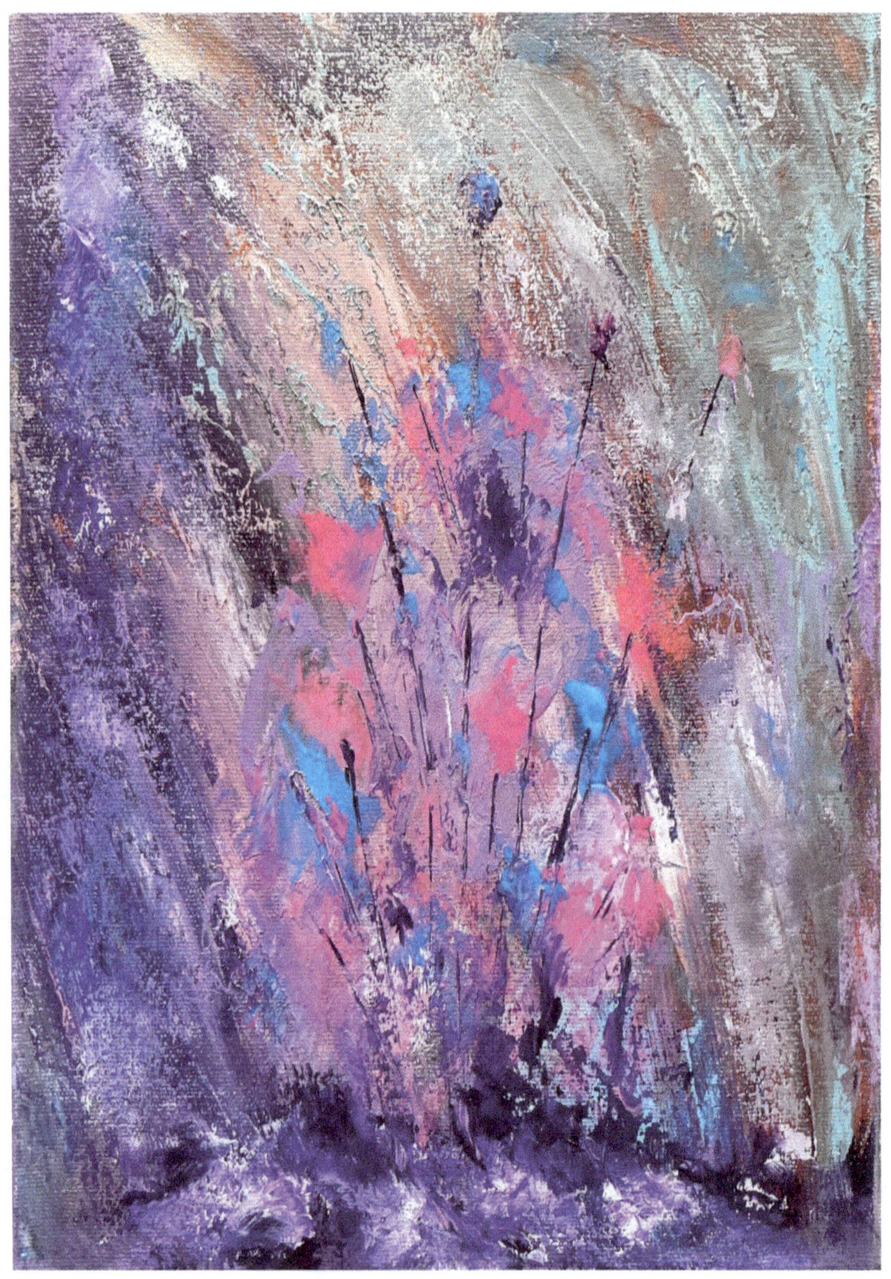

Snow White's Garden

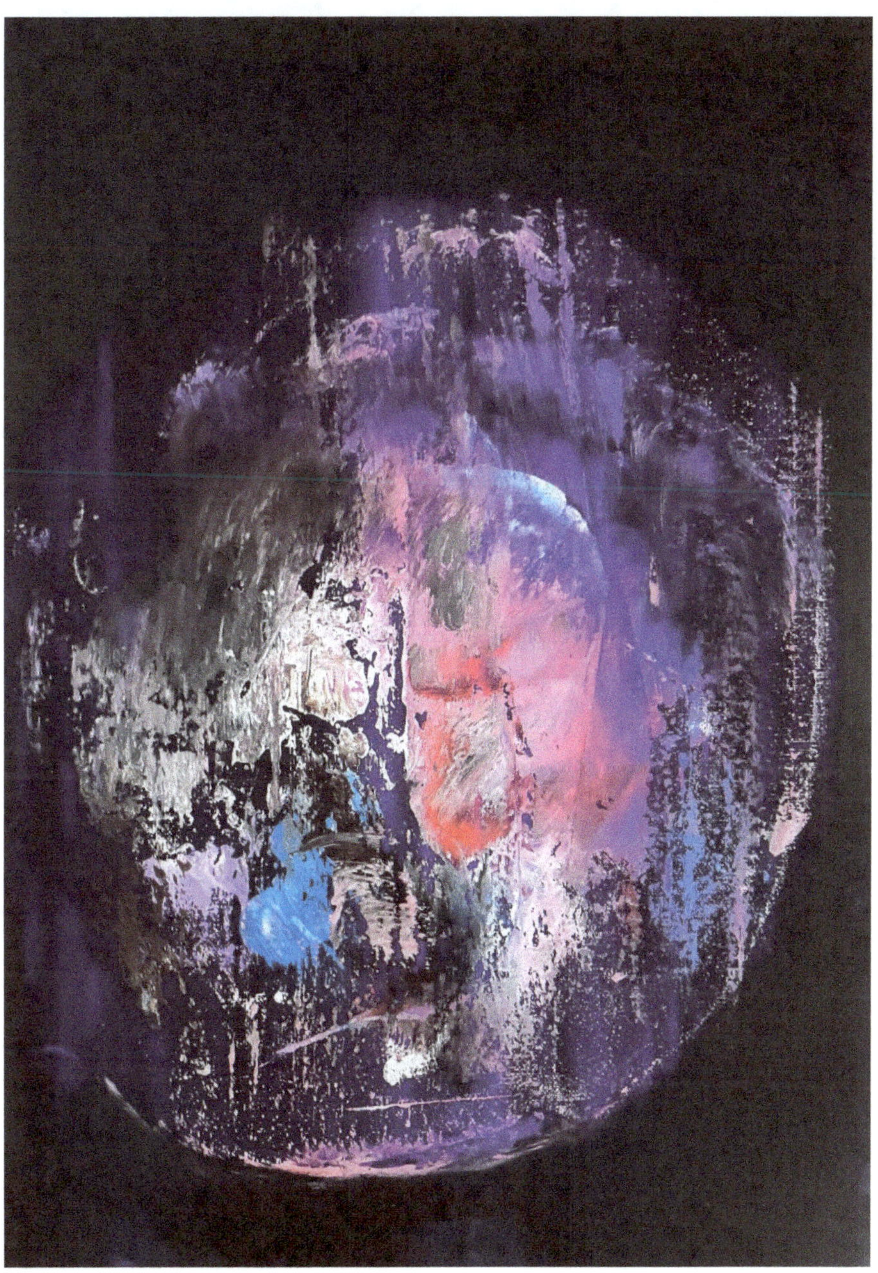

Space Shaman

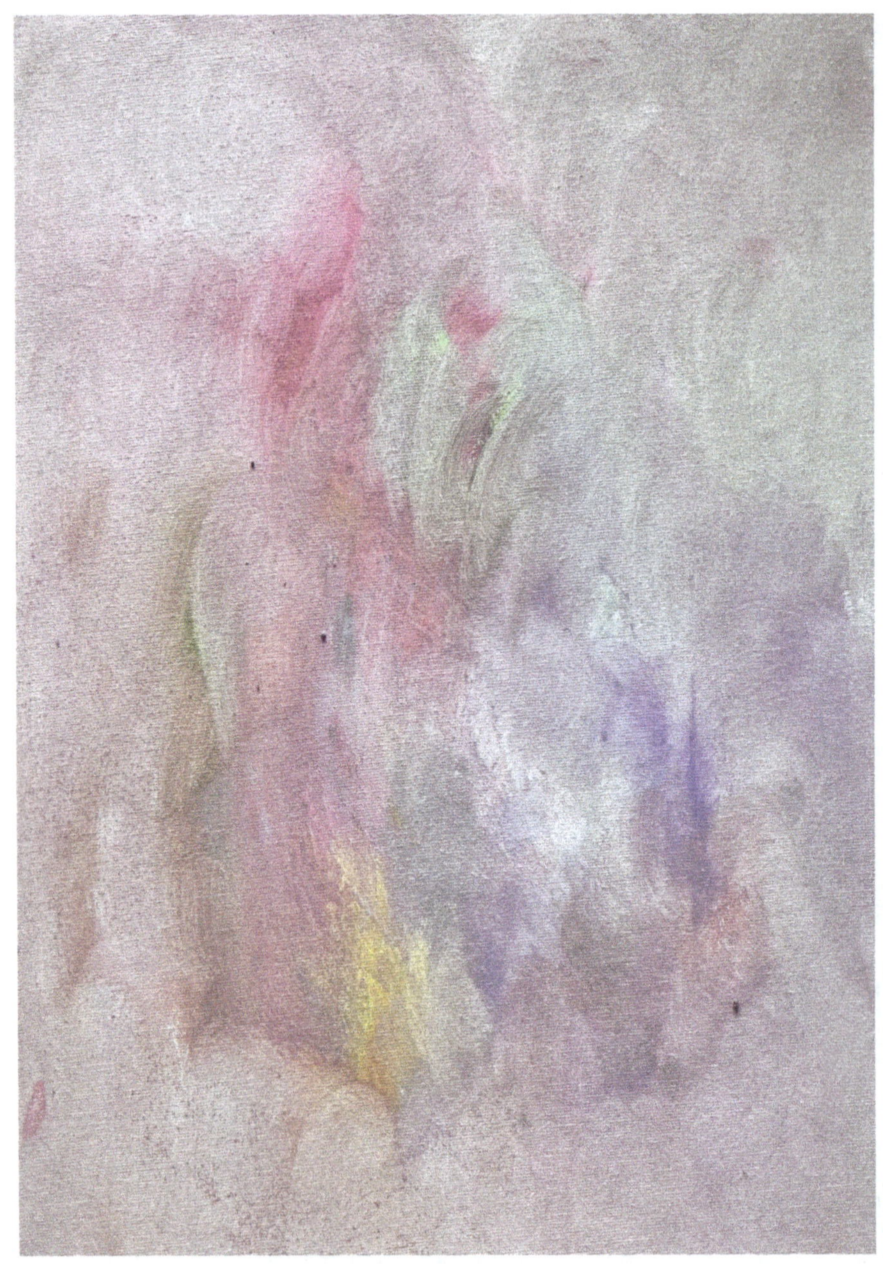

Surreal Pastel Tulips

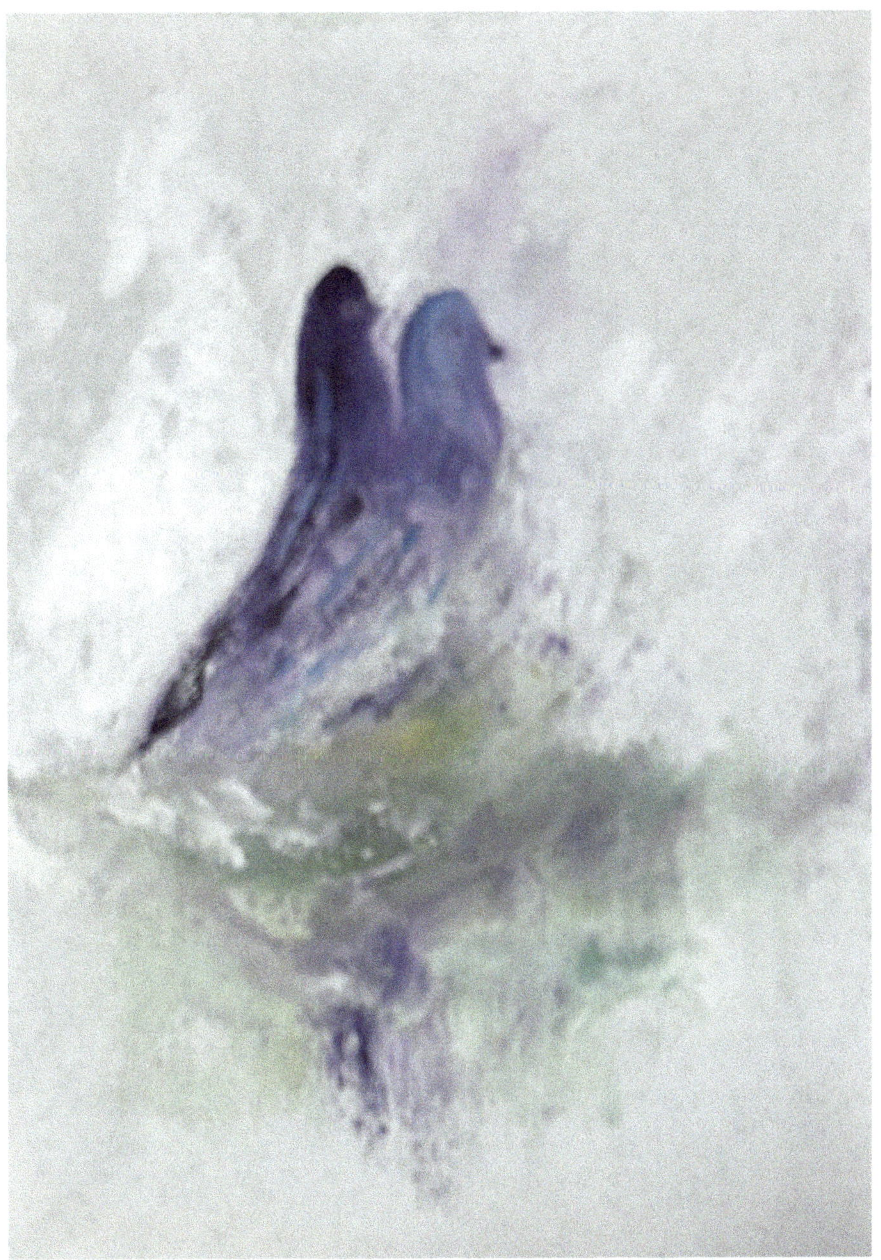

The Love Birds

Violet Moon Reflections

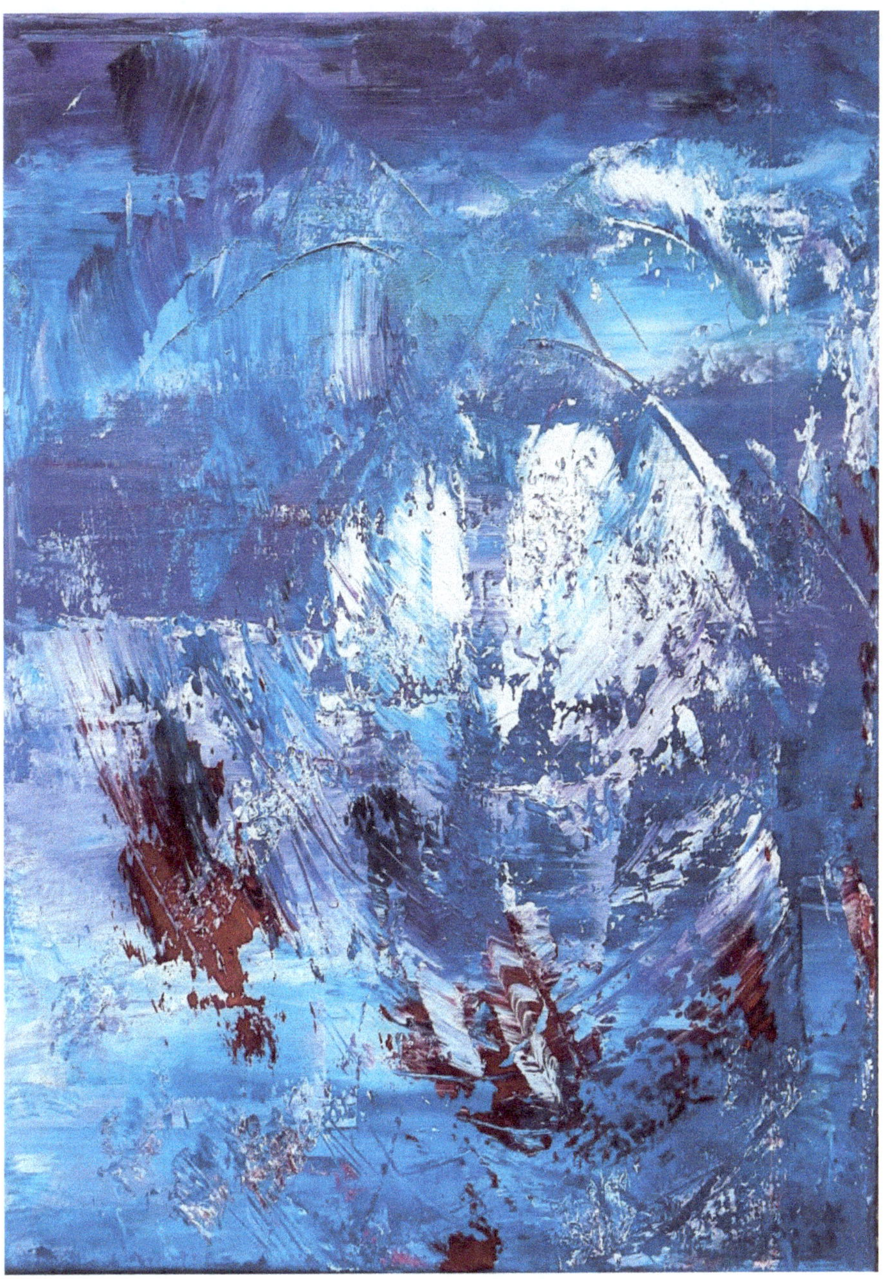

Viking Ghost Ships

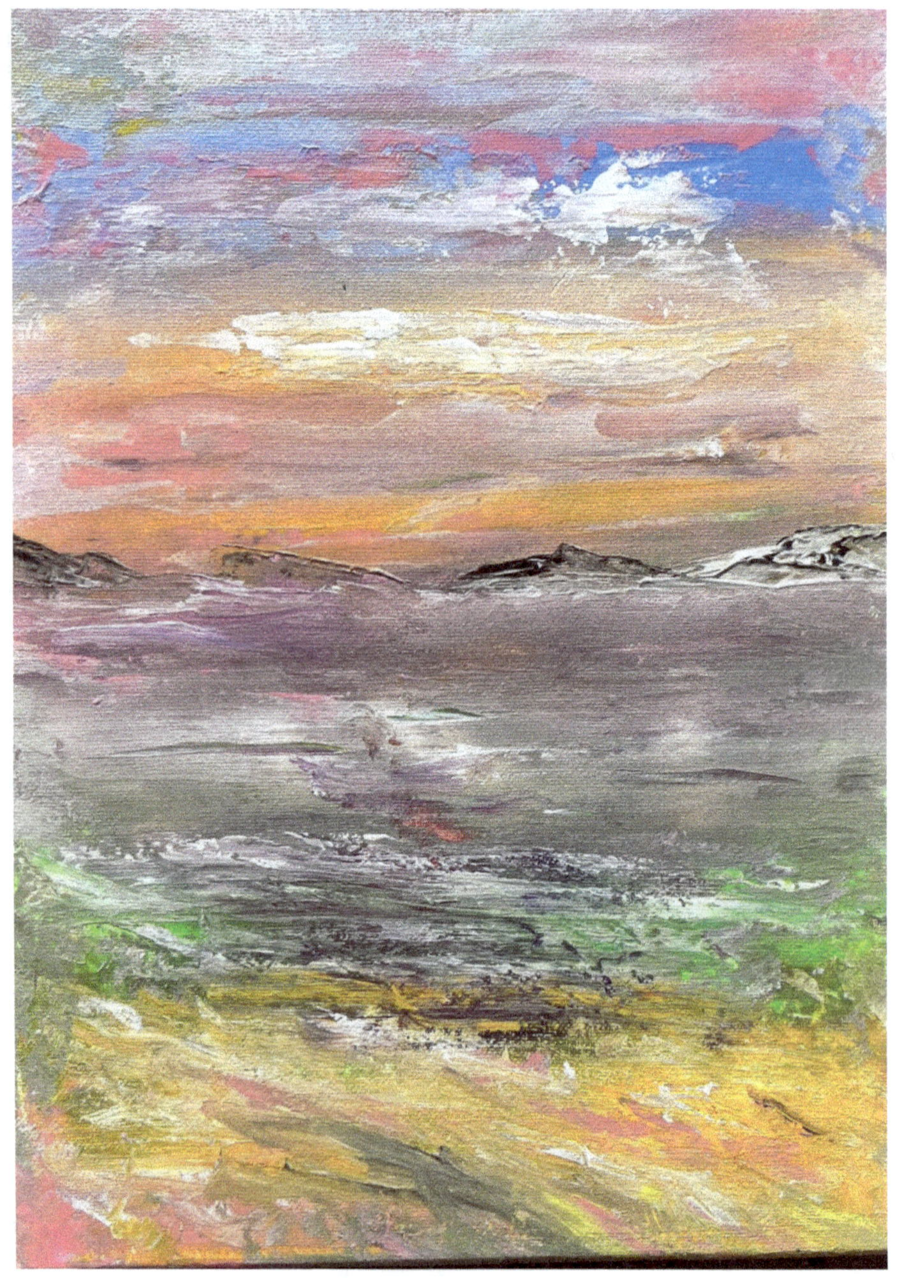

Windy West Coast Afternoon

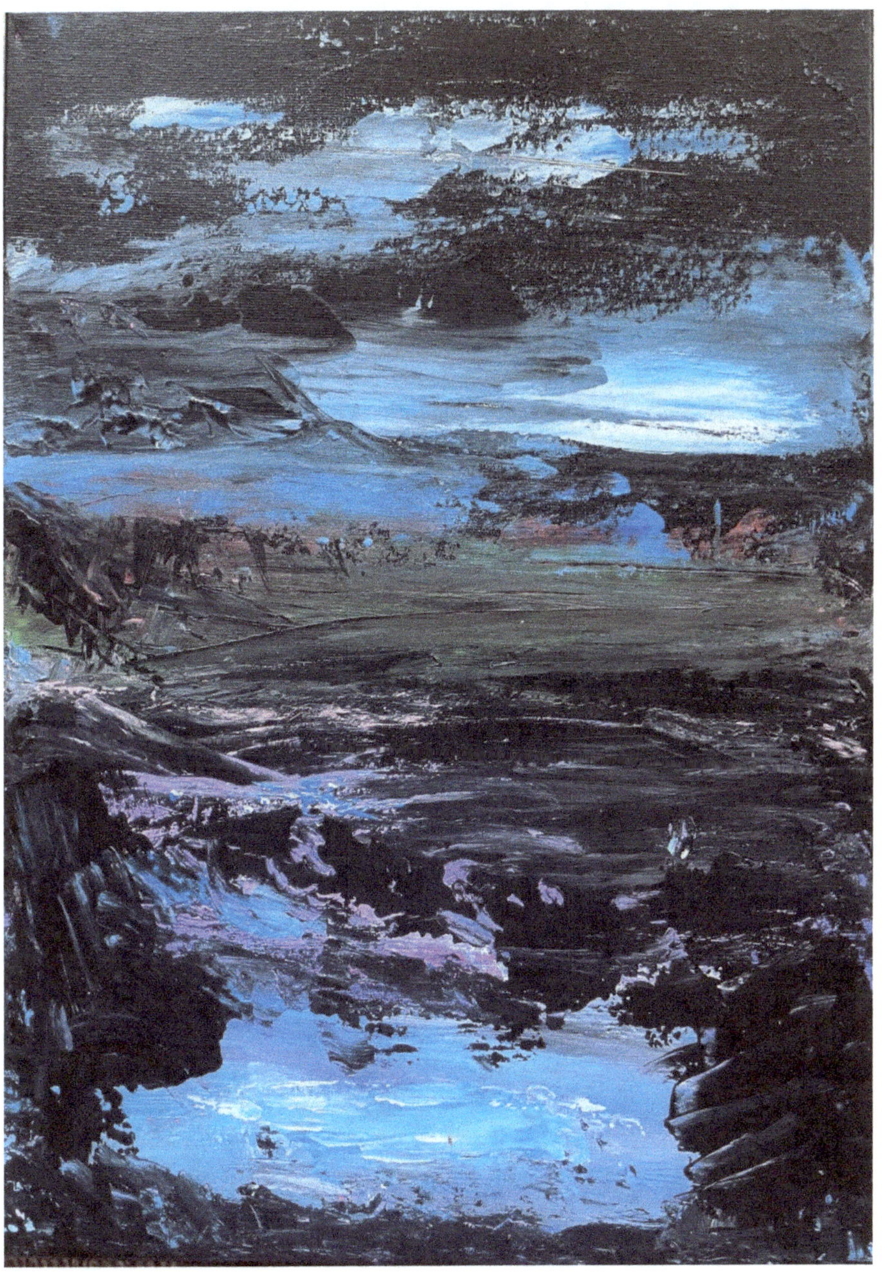

And The Lord Said, "Let there be light."

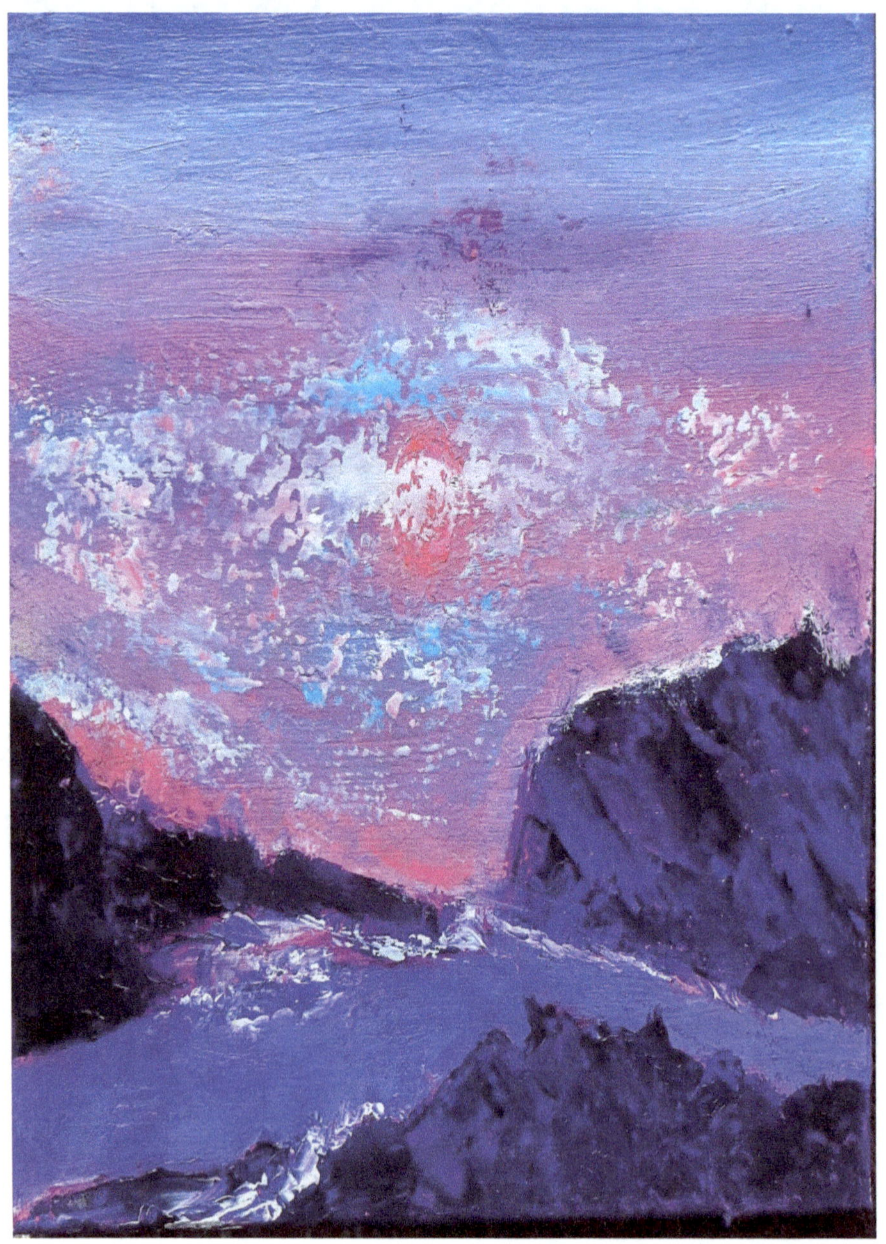

And There Shall Be Signs

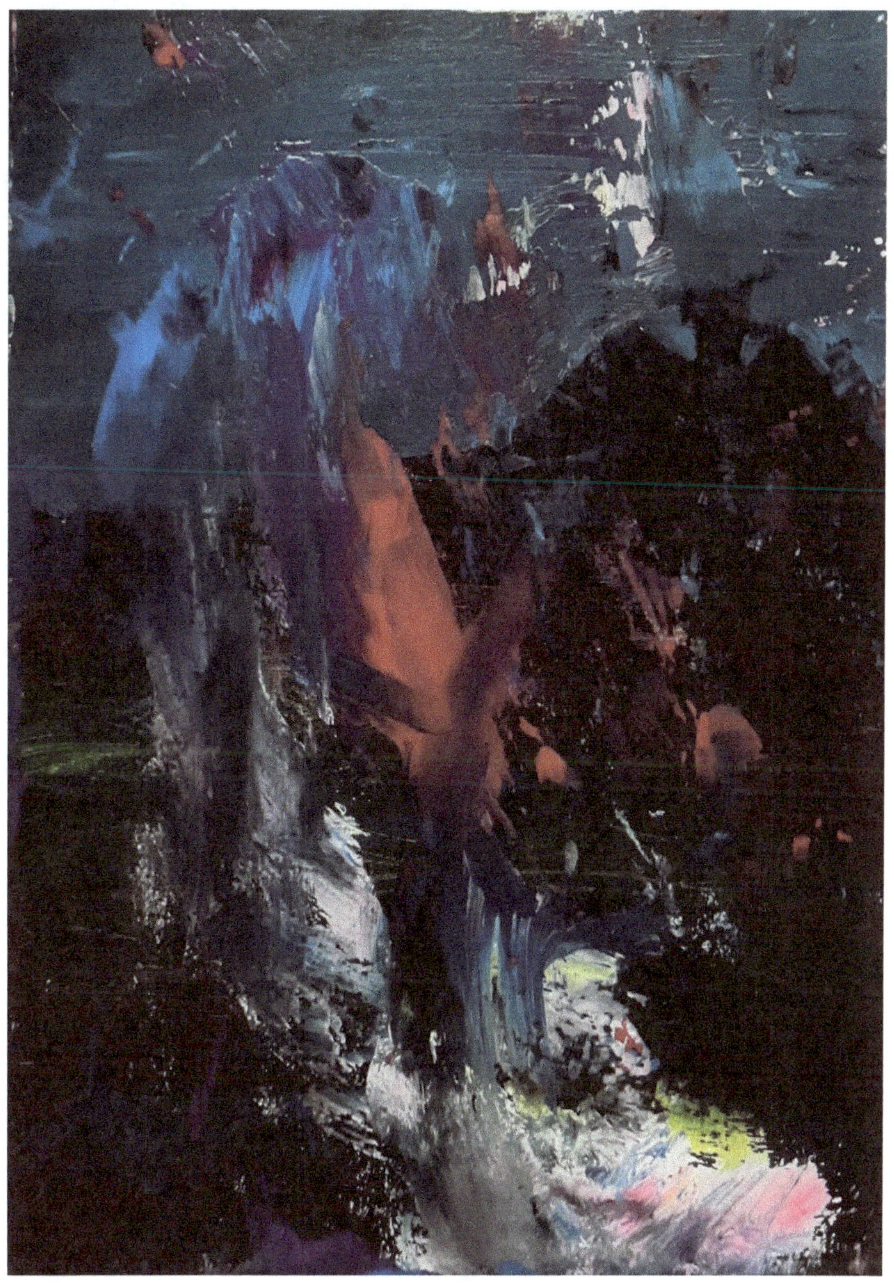

Ballerina Dreams

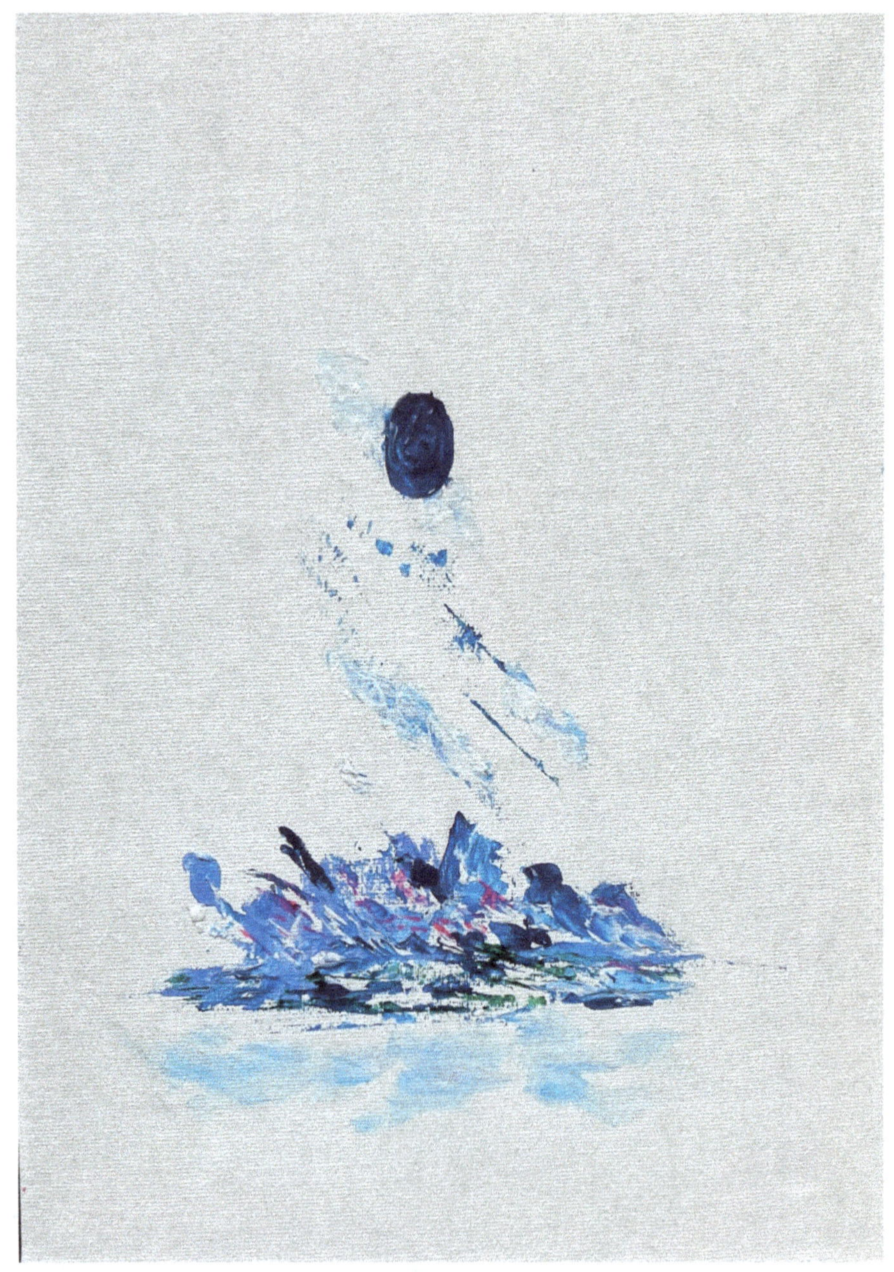

Bird Nest Under Indigo Moon

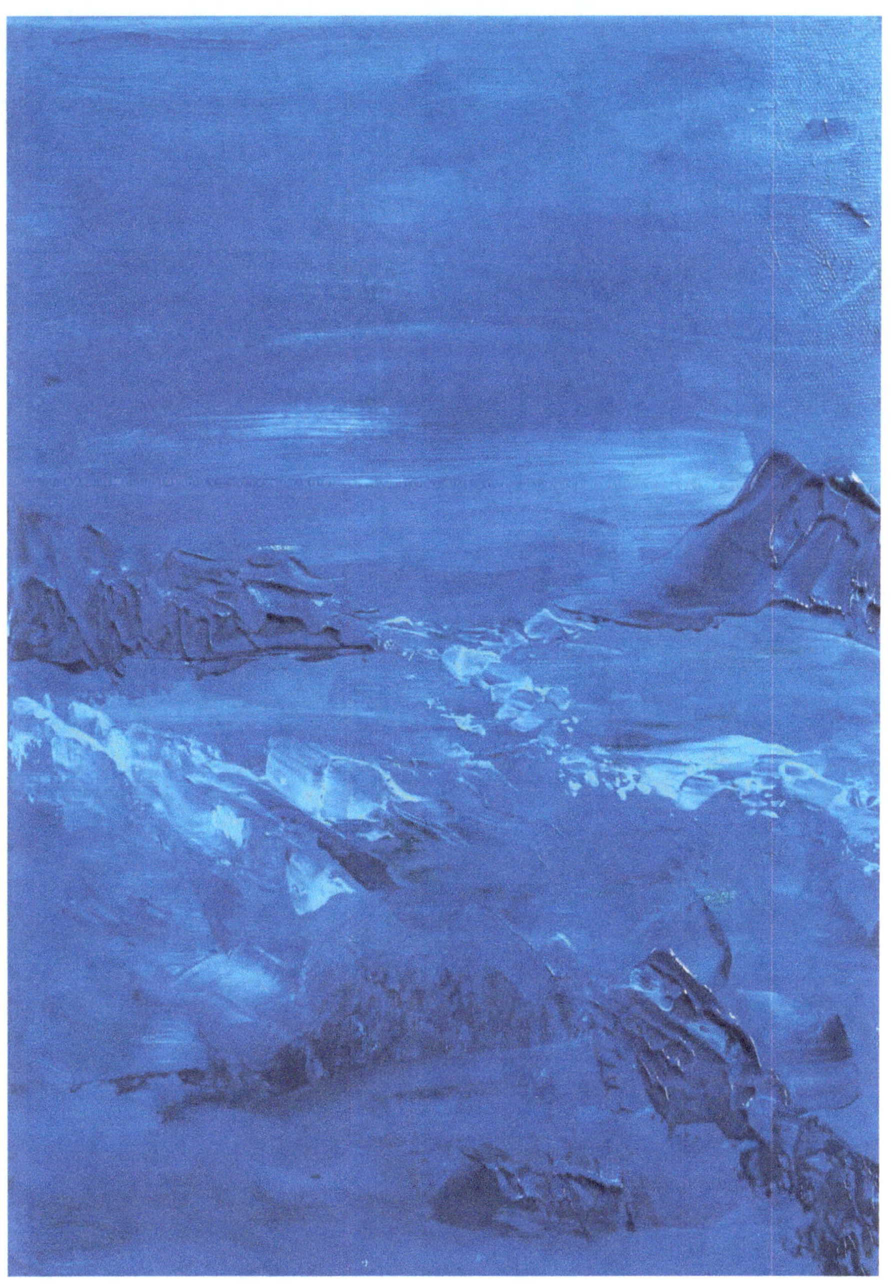

Blue Mountain Waters

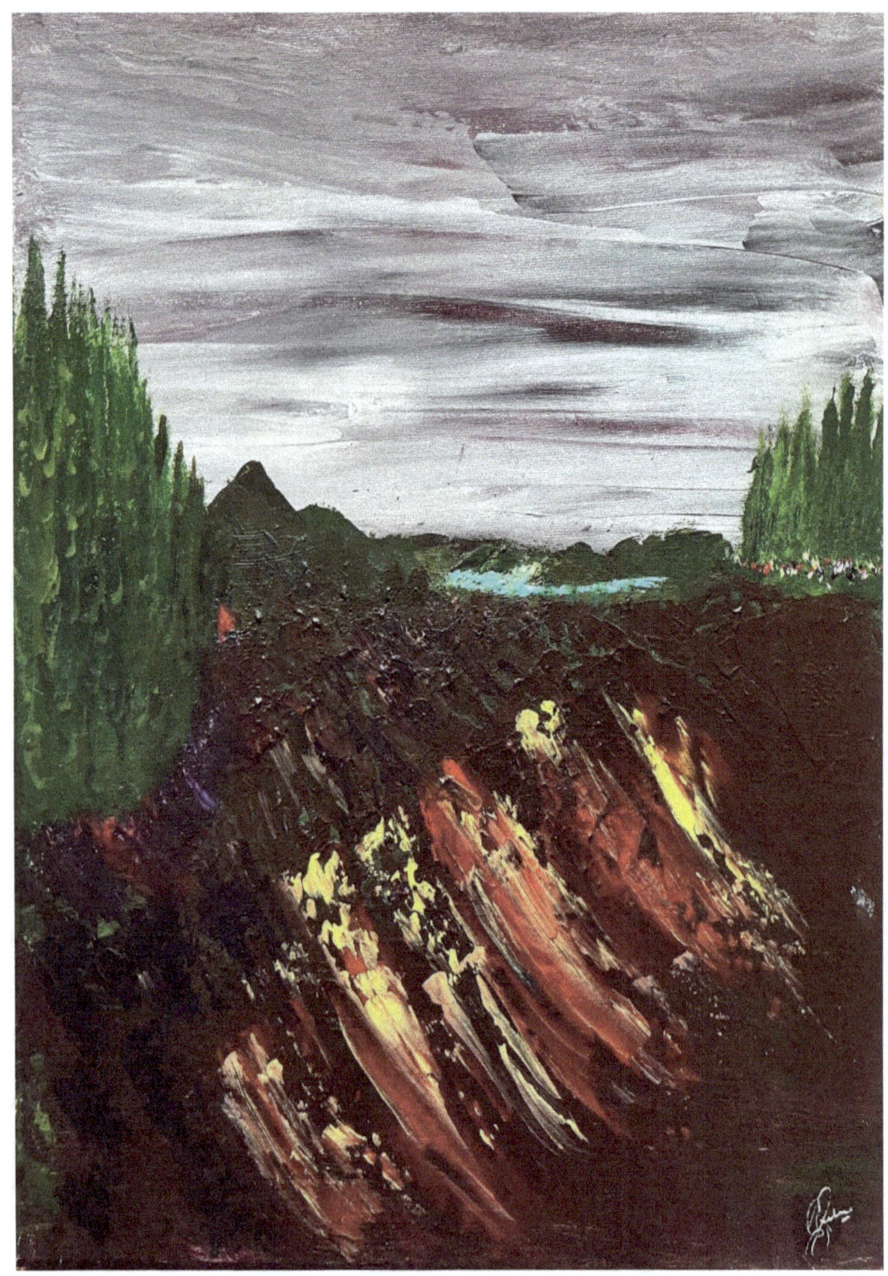

Bloom

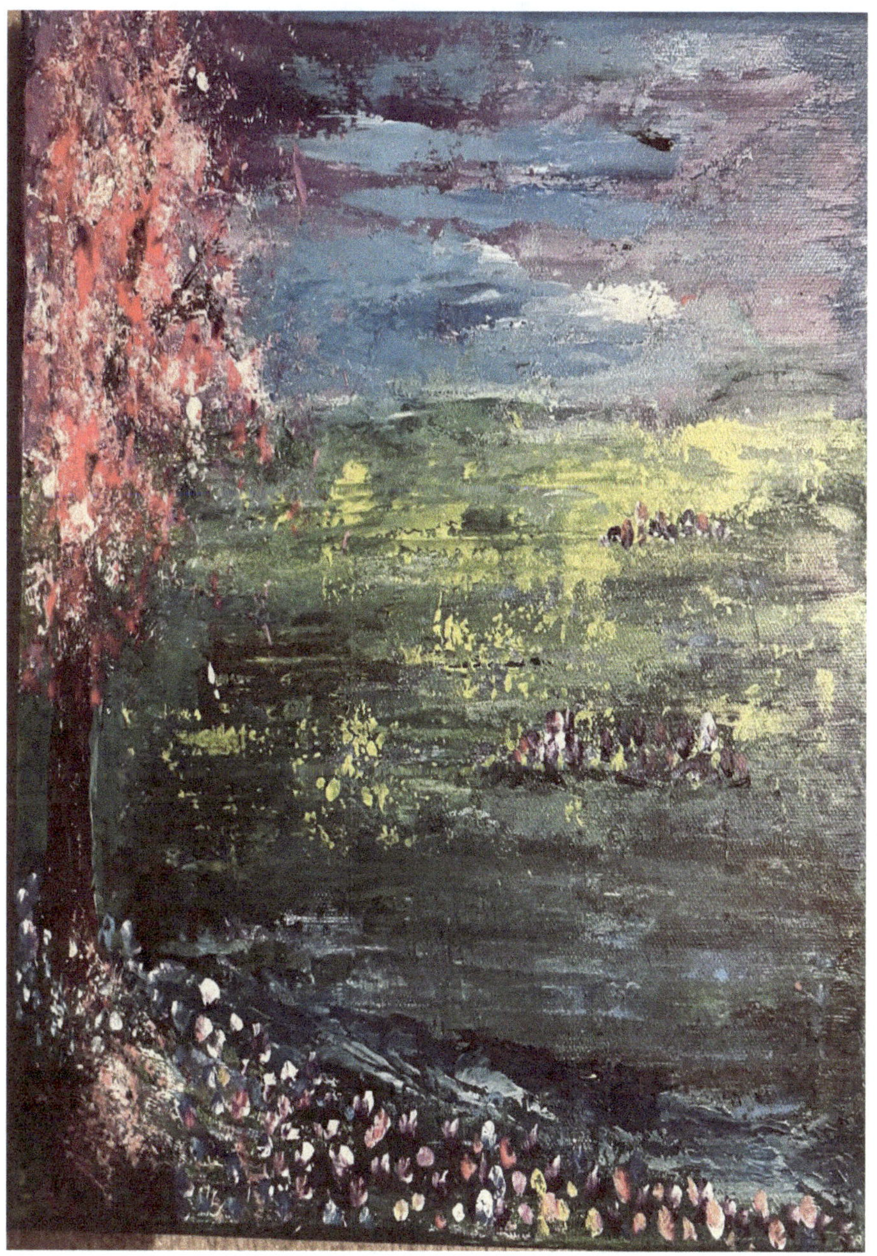

Contrary Mary's Other Garden

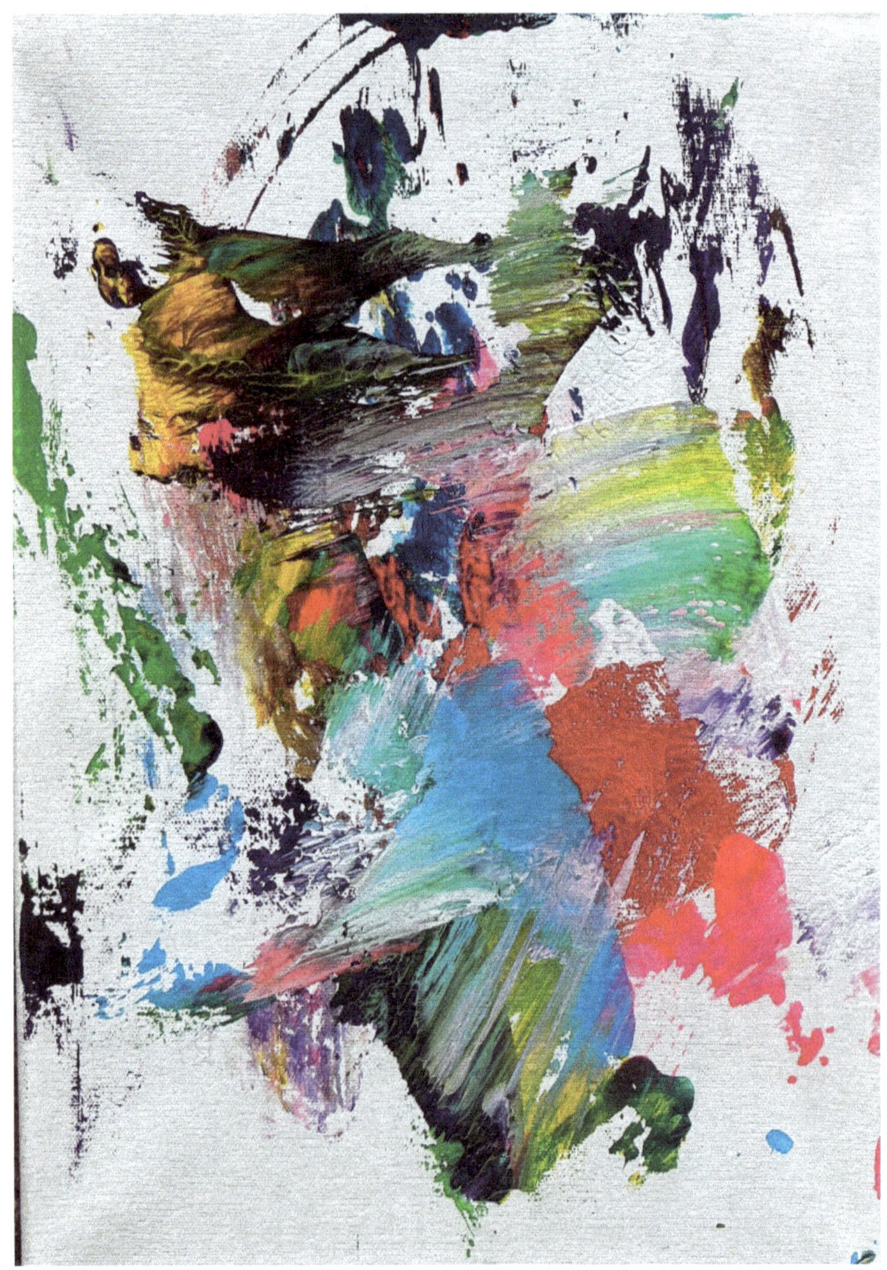

Dance Of The Butterflies

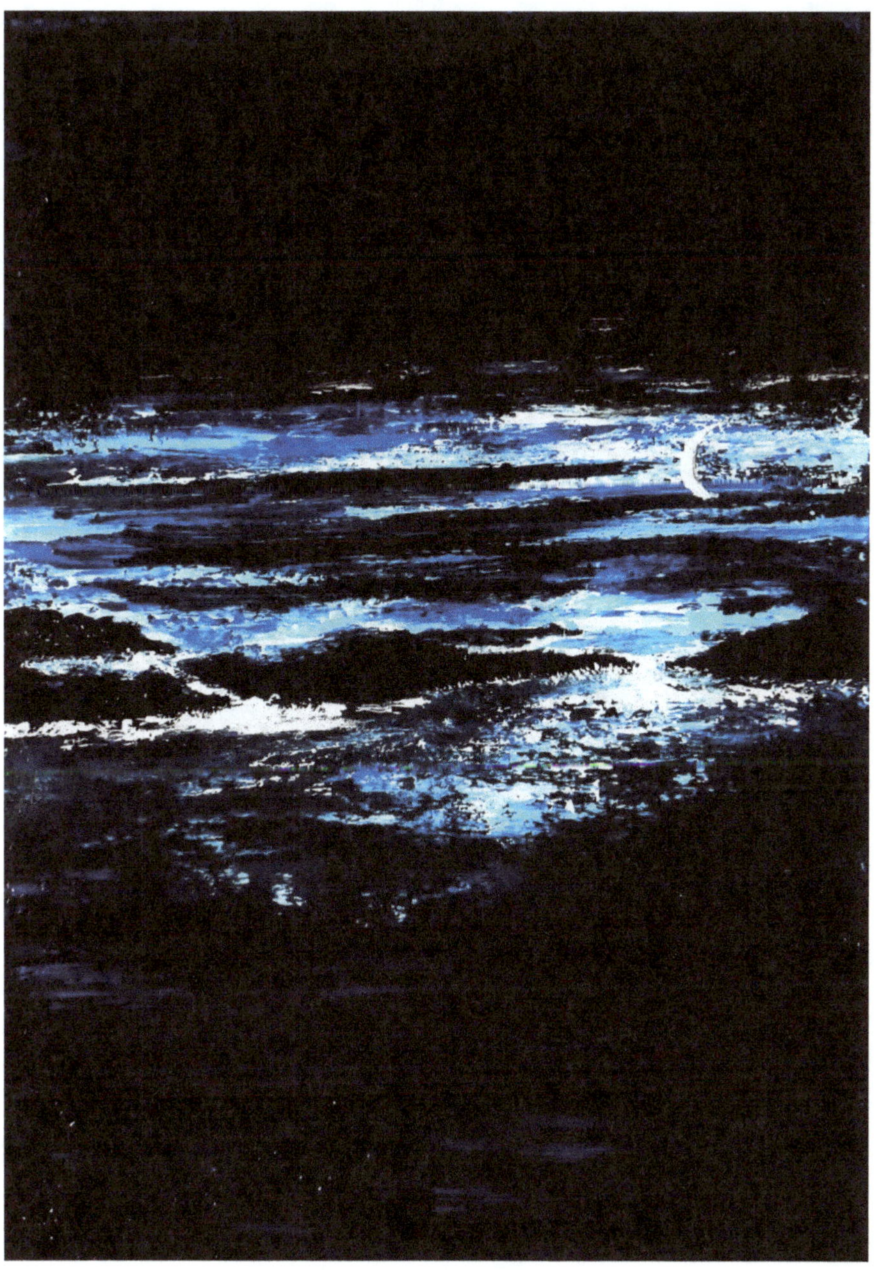

Above Indio Waters

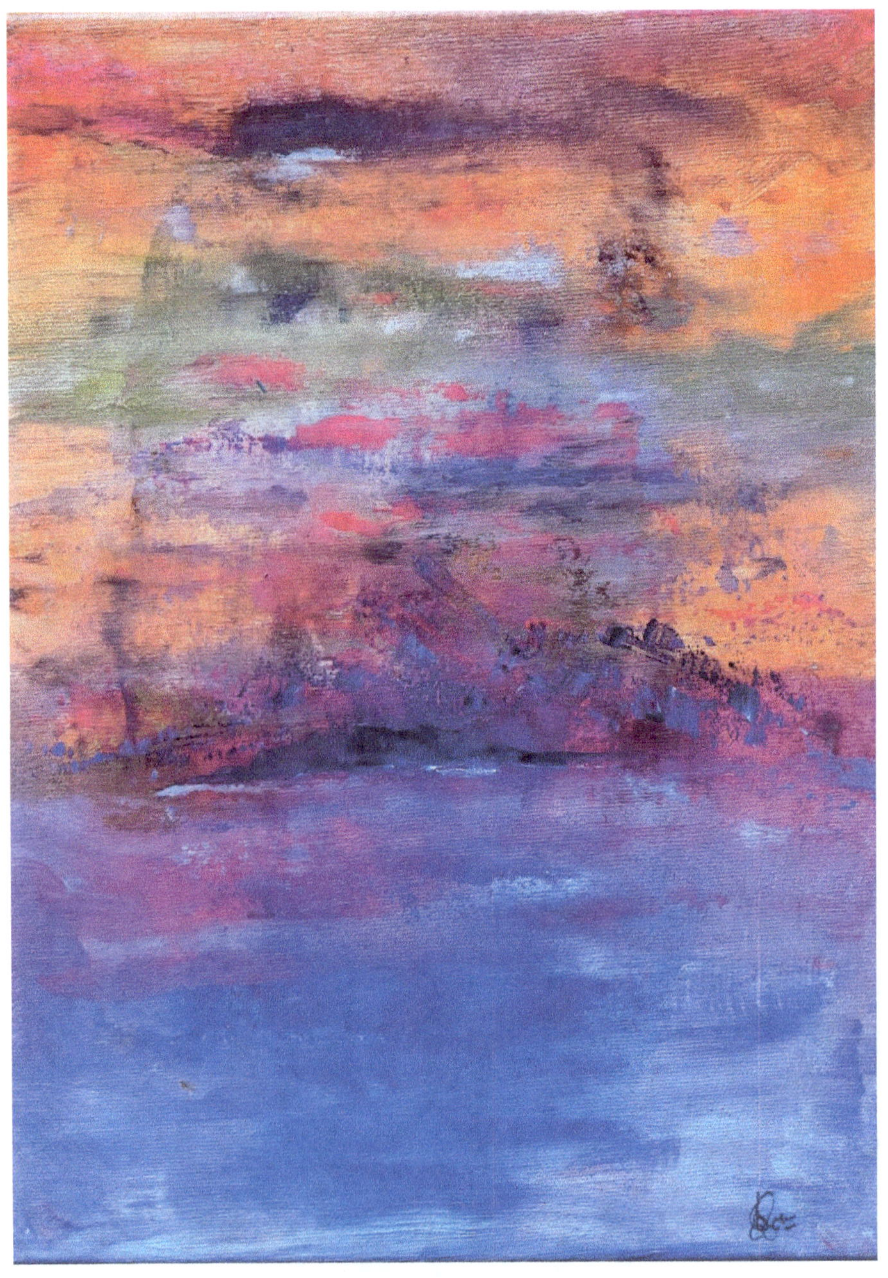

A Special Place In My Mind

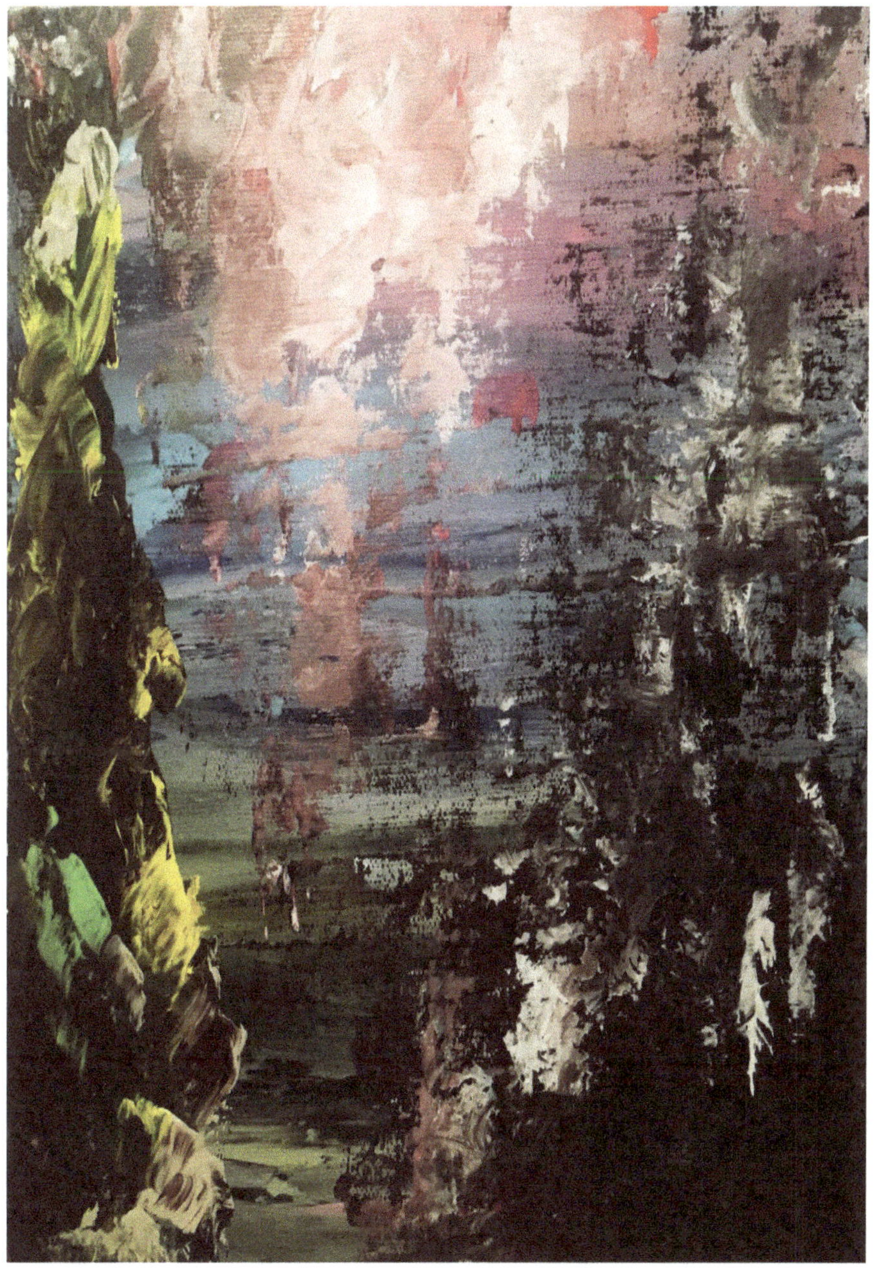

Aladdin In The Land Of The Lamp

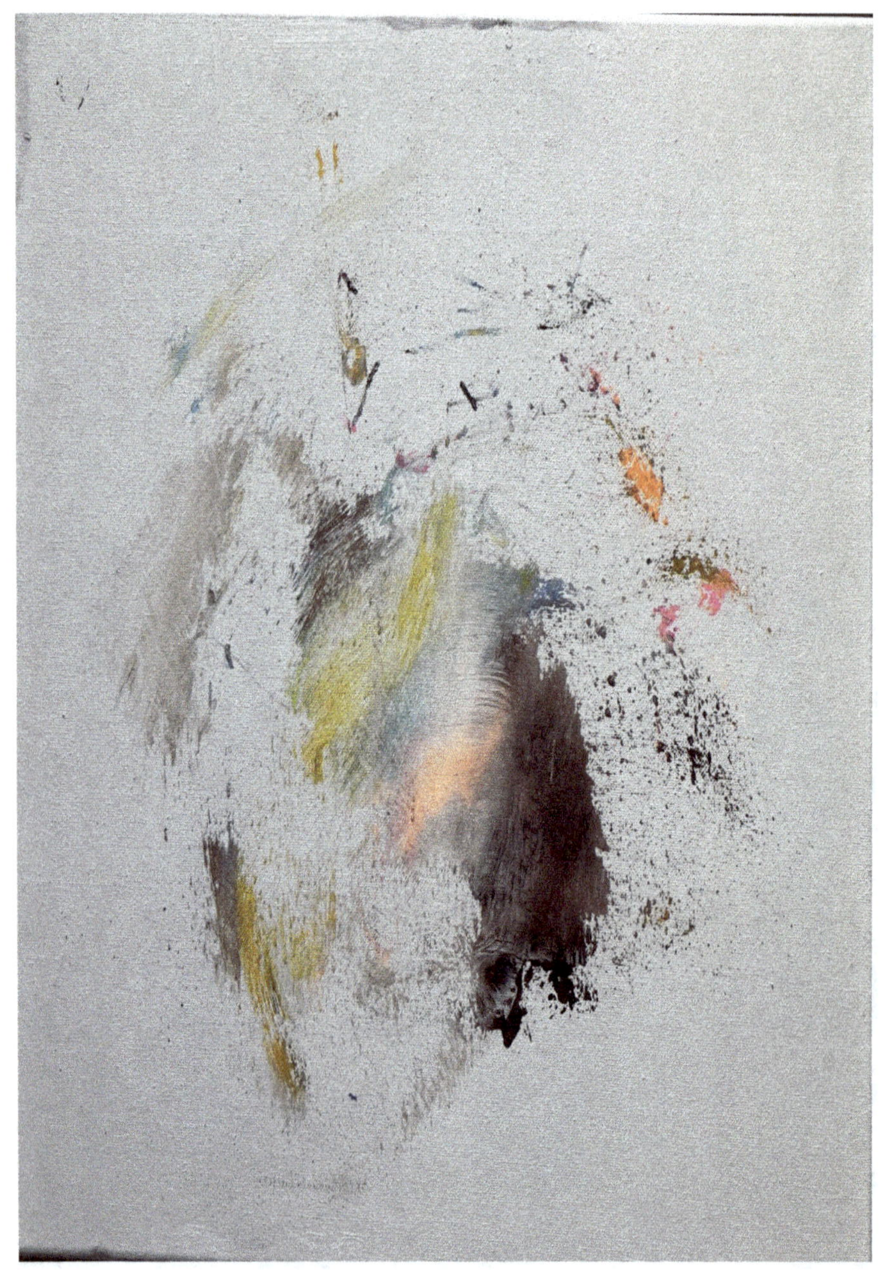

Asleep In The Dream

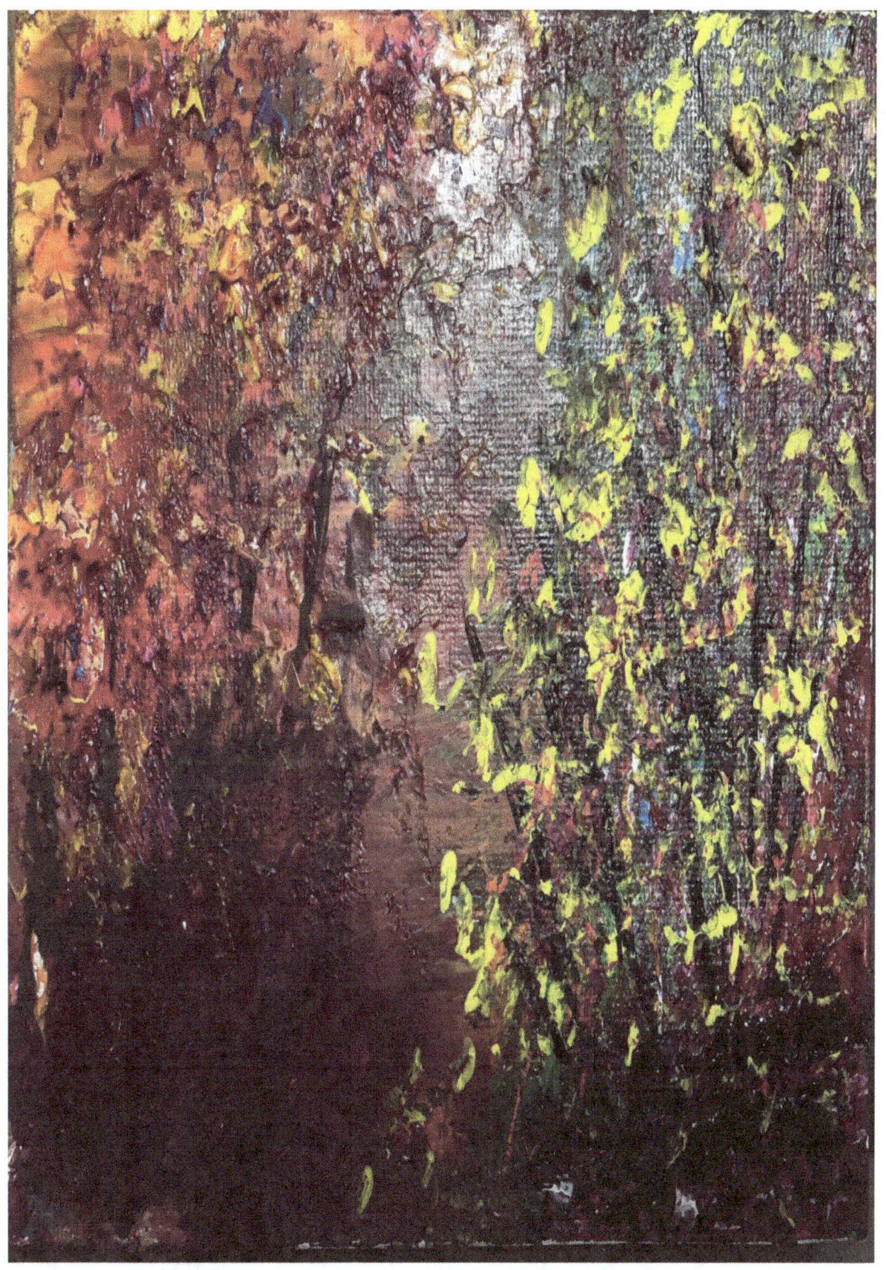

Autumn Forest

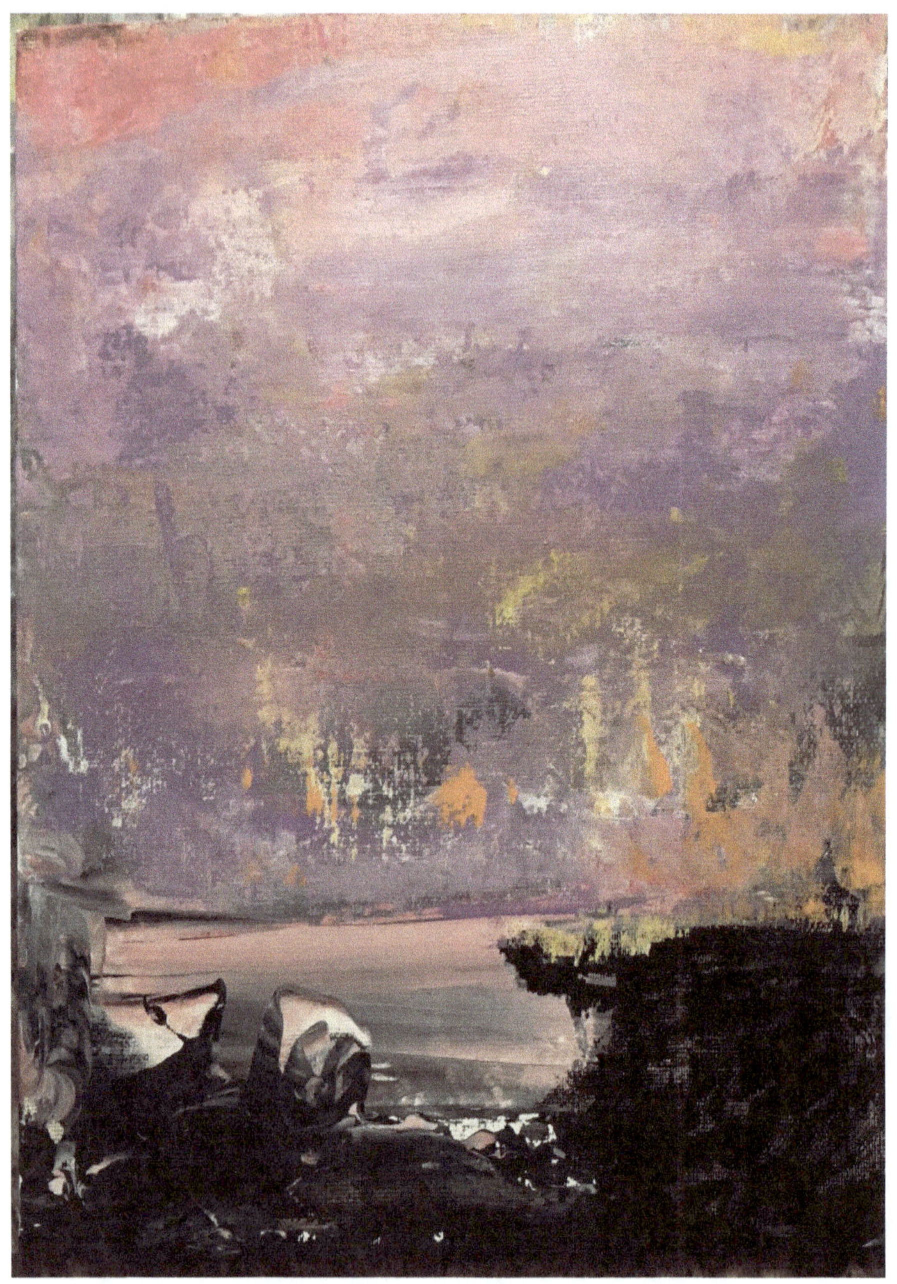

The Boat, The Rock And The Dog

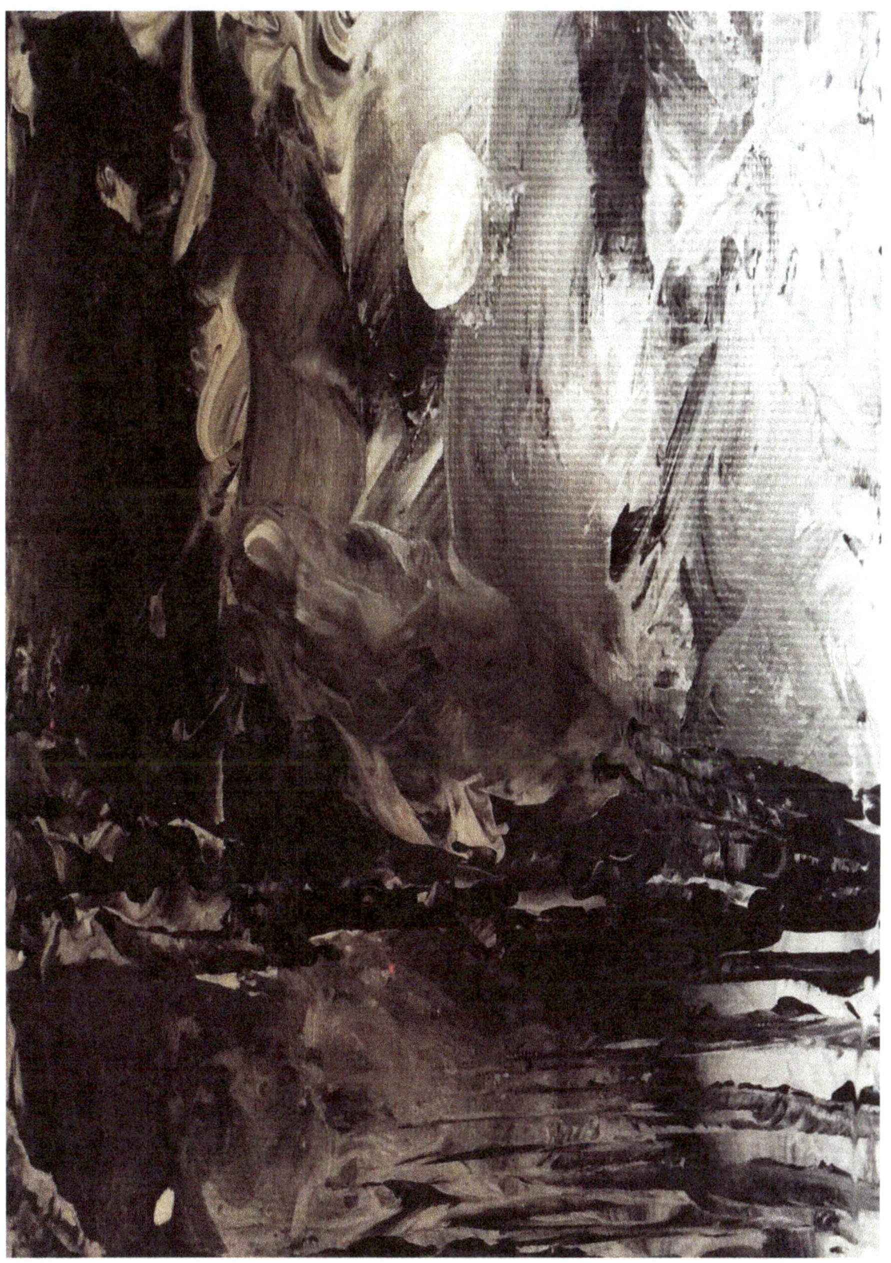

Burnt Almond

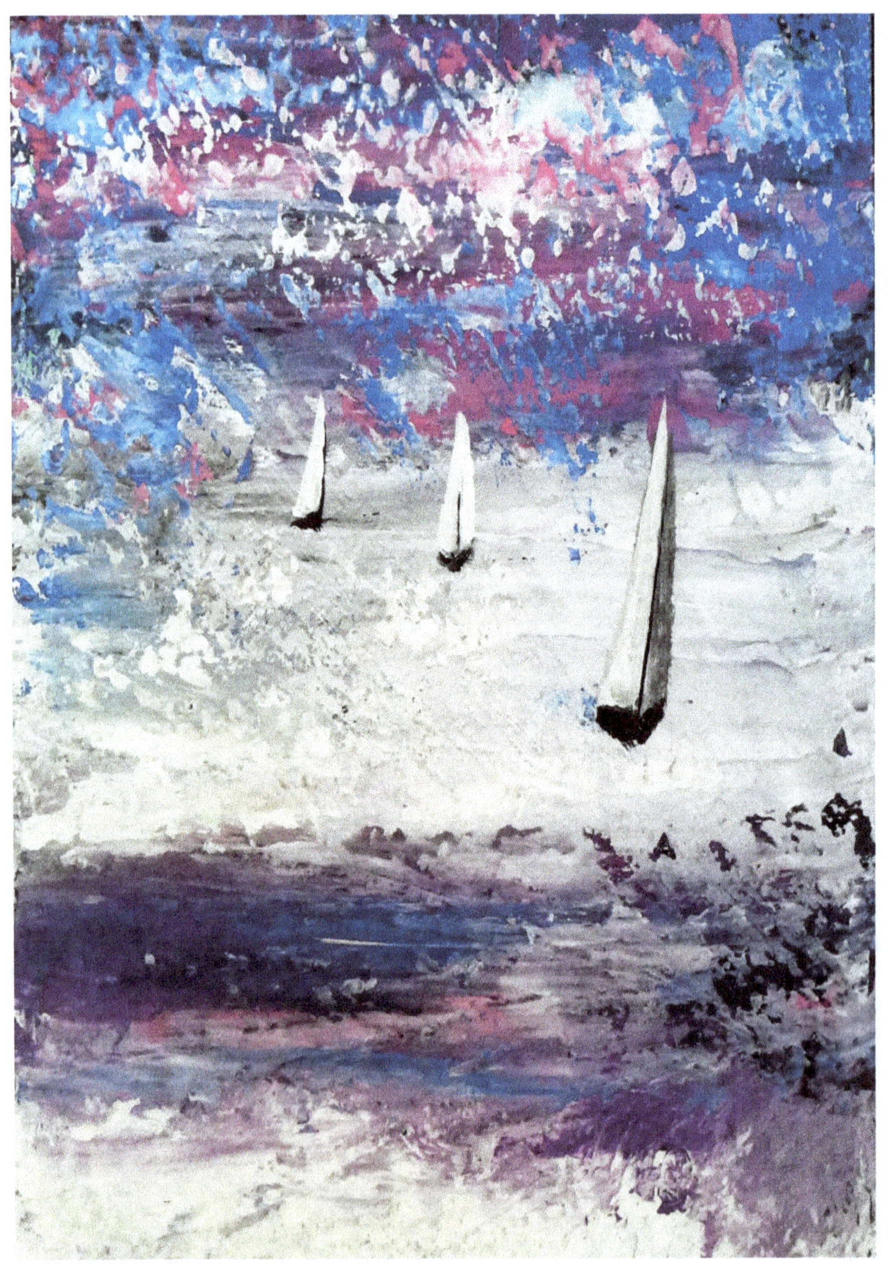

Camels Of The Arctic

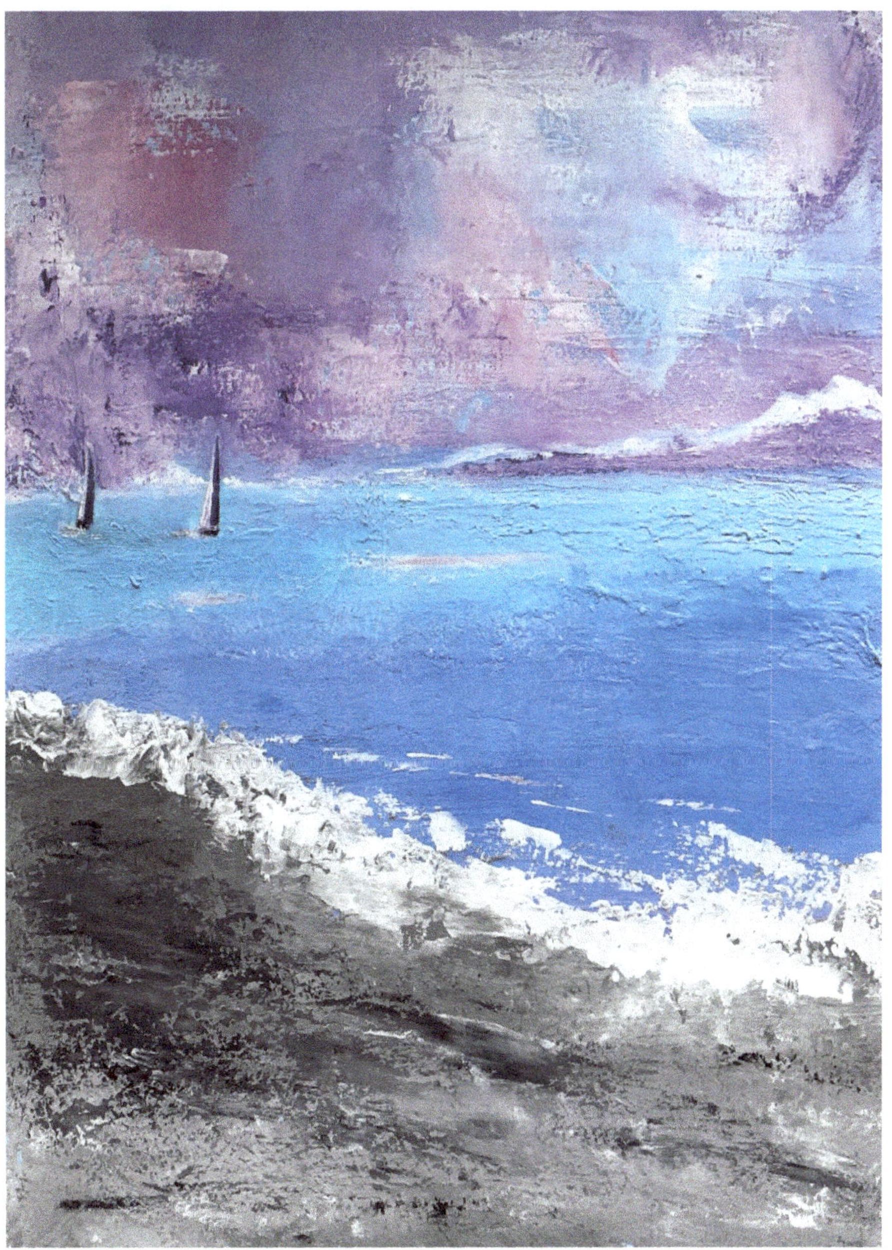

Coming Home

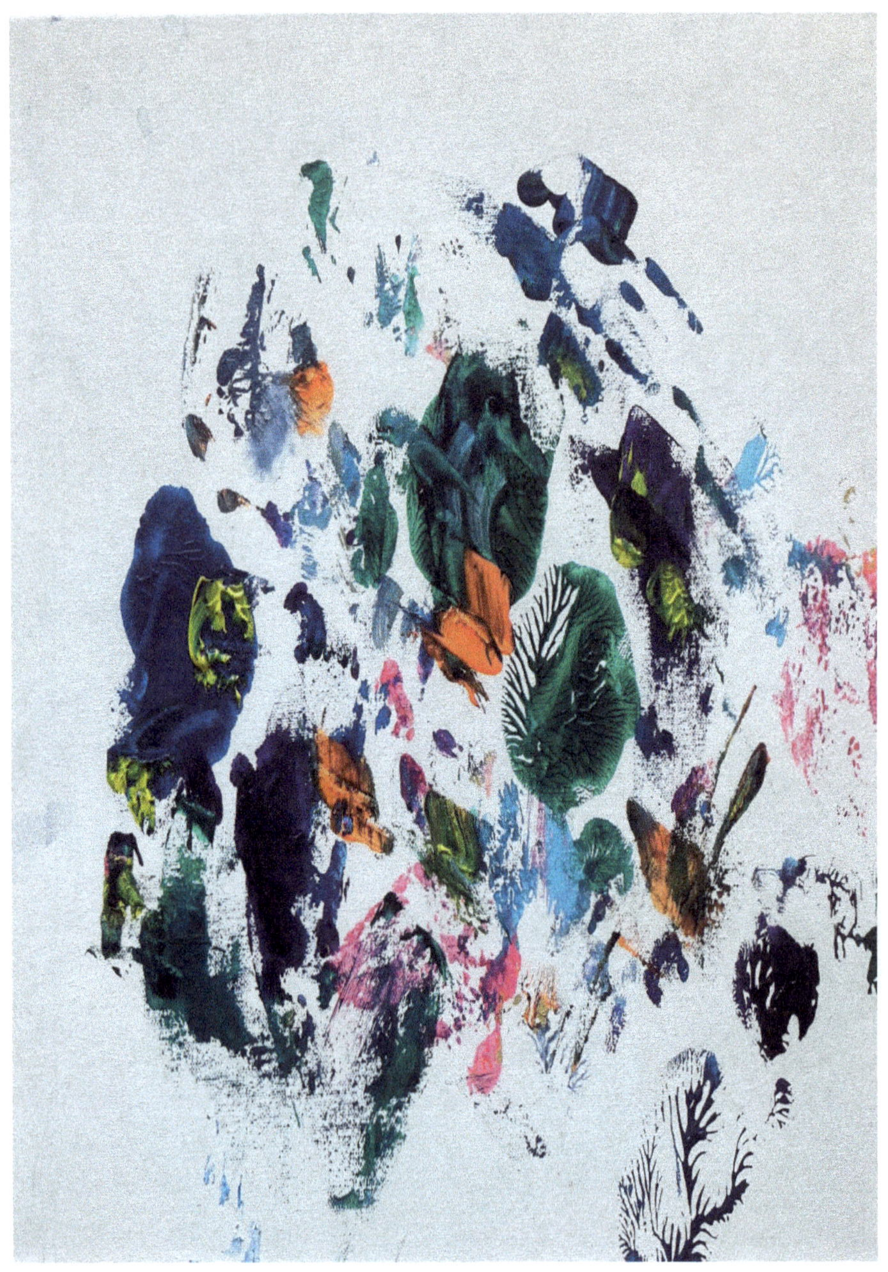

Circle Game Swirl

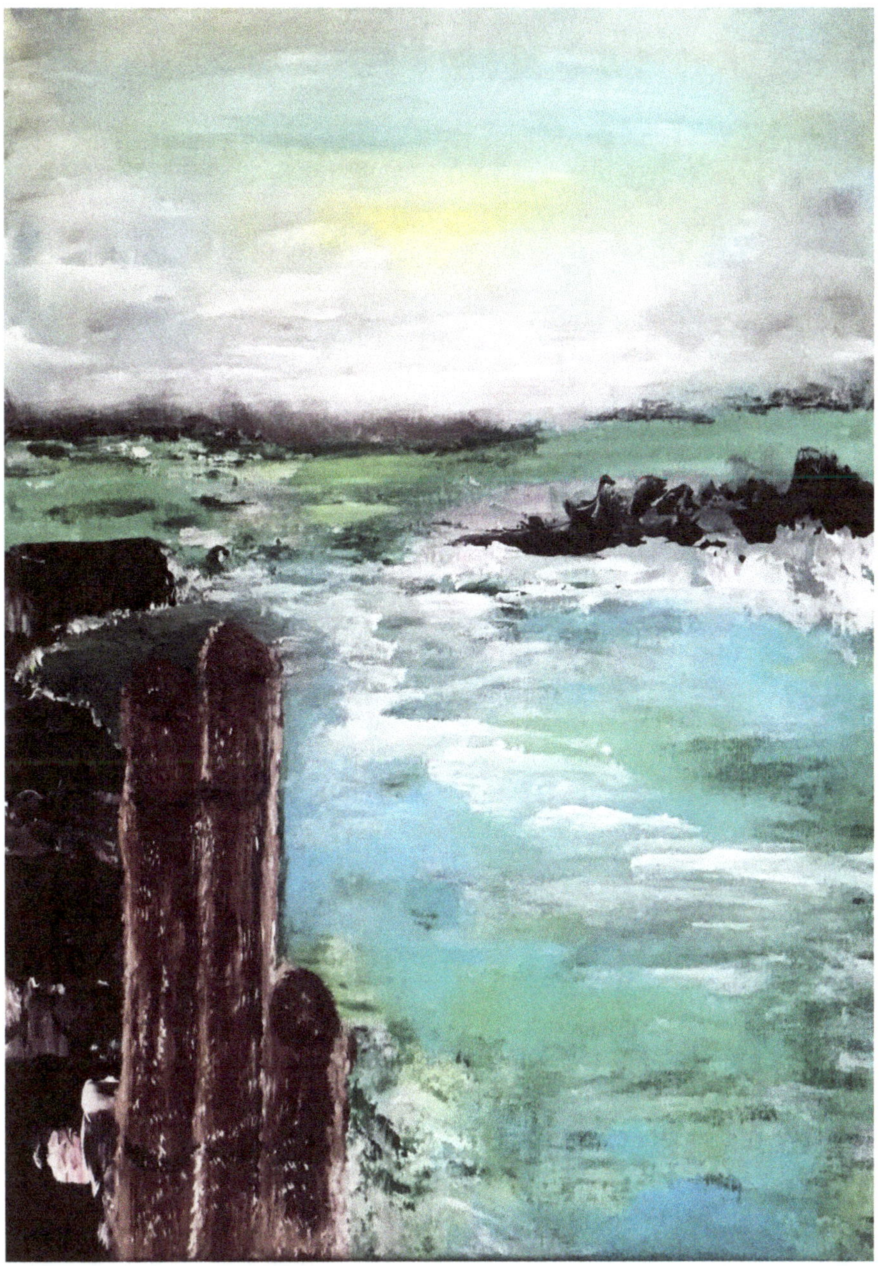

Crescent Beach

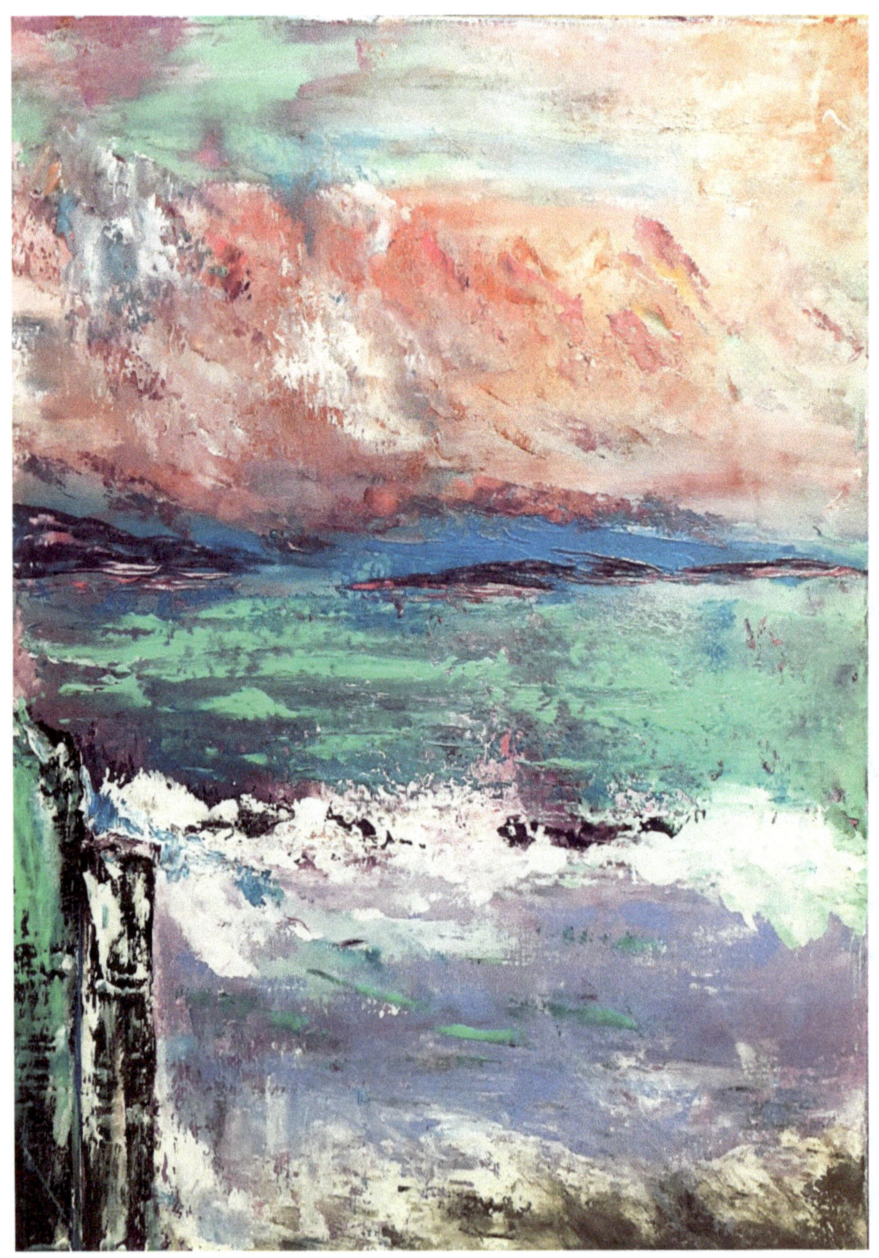

Crossing The Reef

d

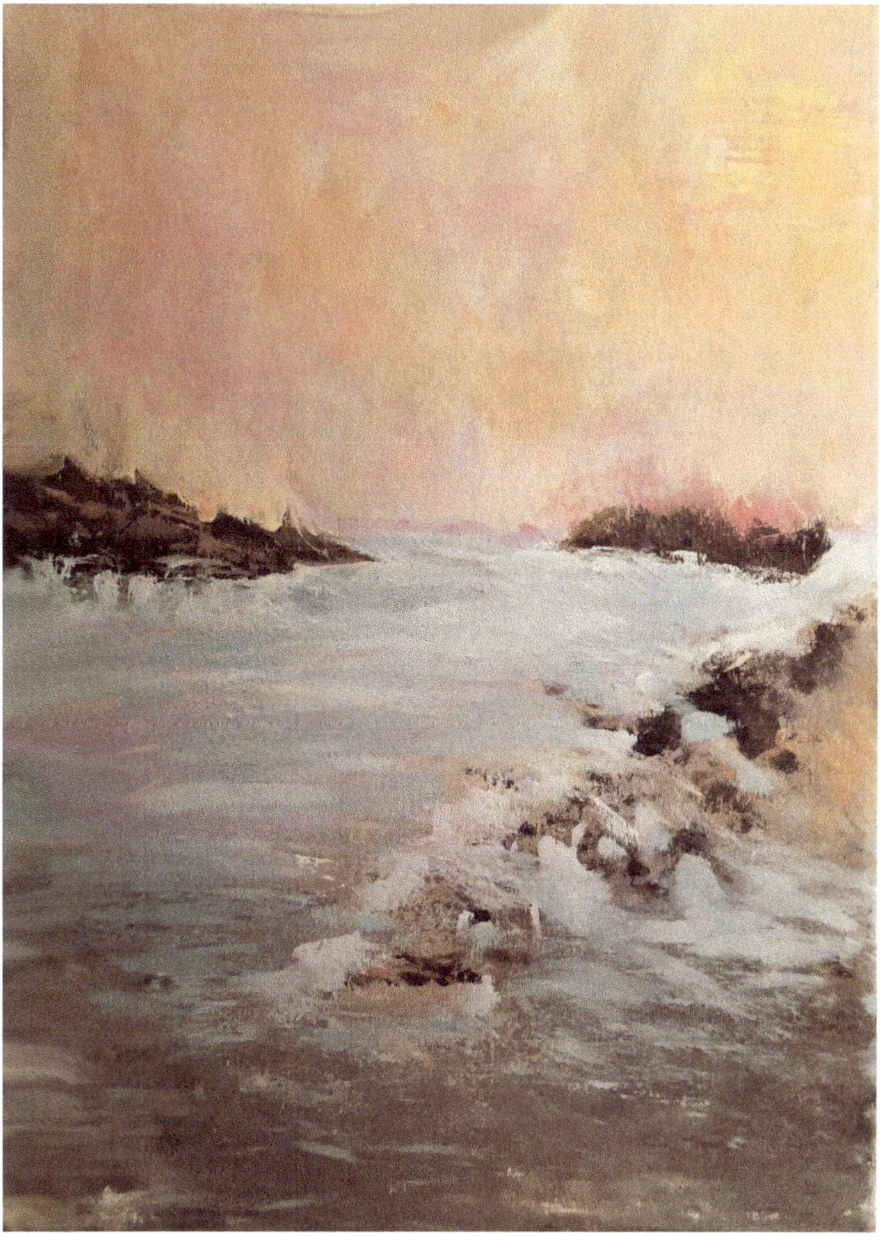

Cove

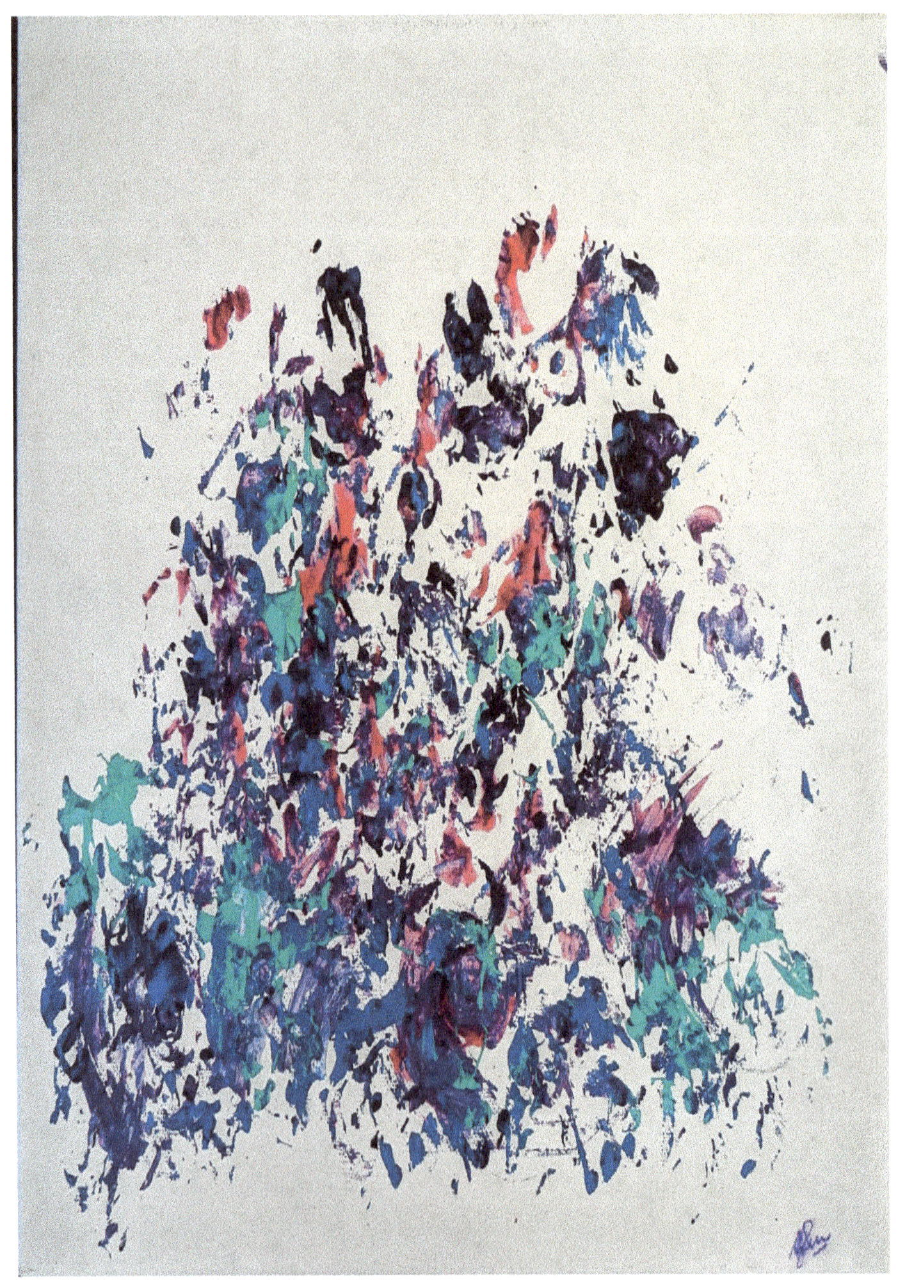

Dance Of The Sugar Plum Faeries

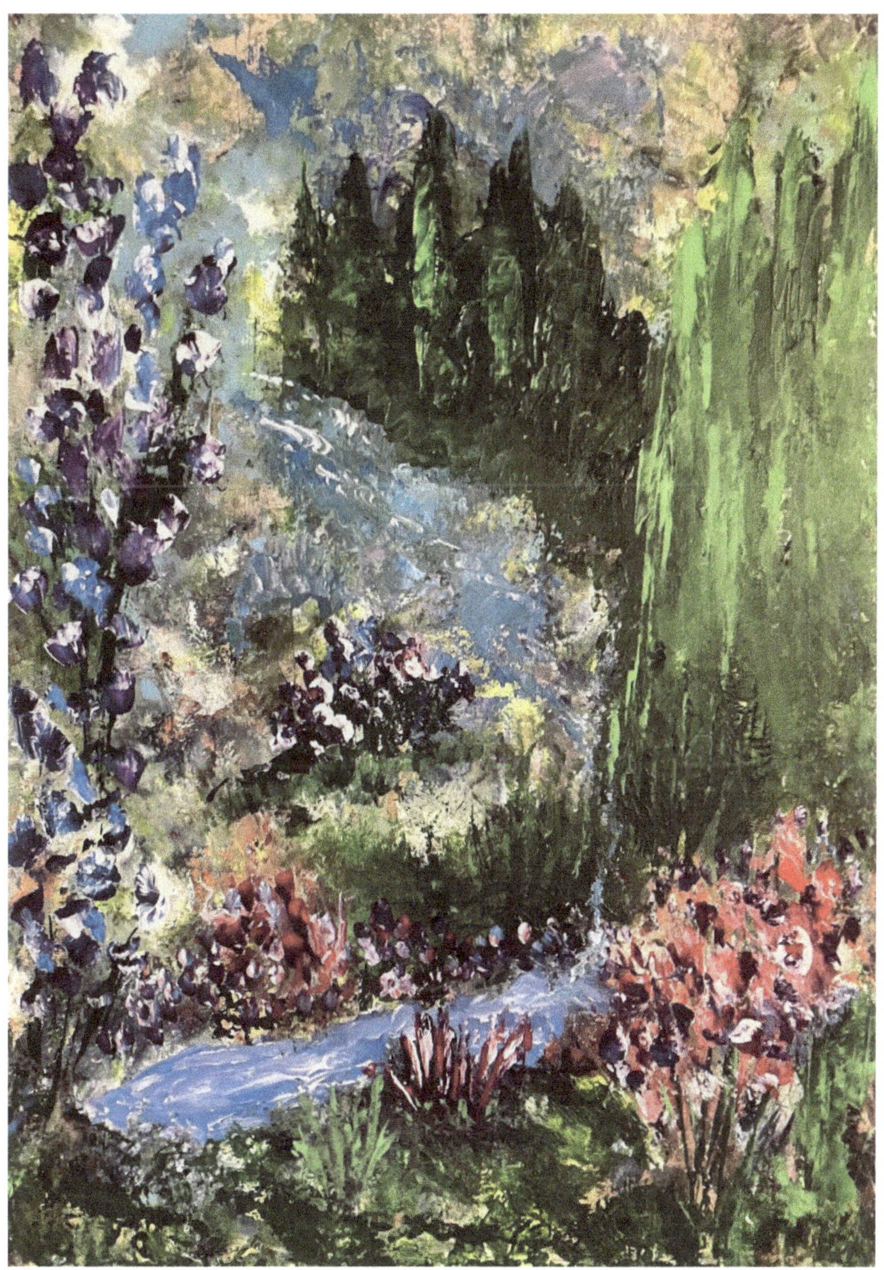

Deep Inside The Magic Forest

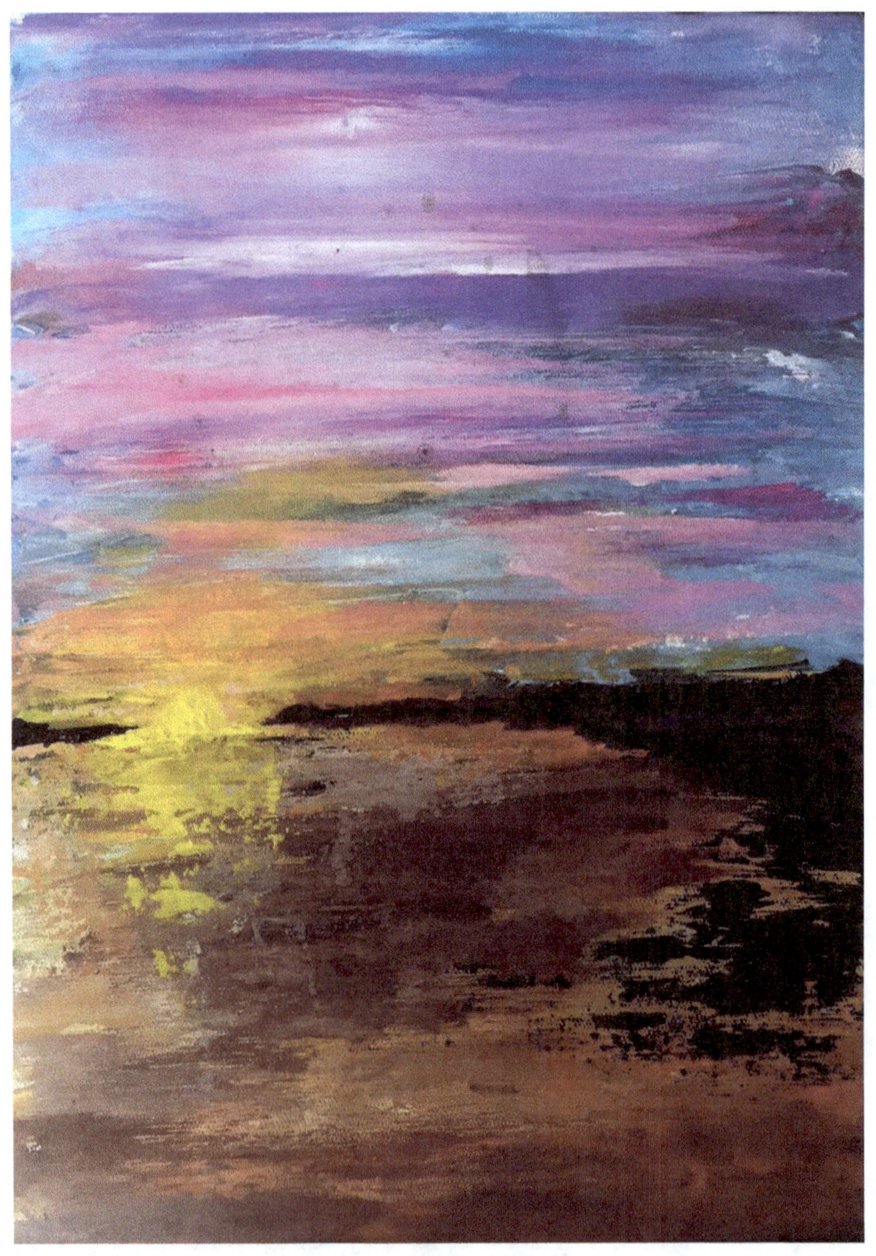

Death Valley Mirage

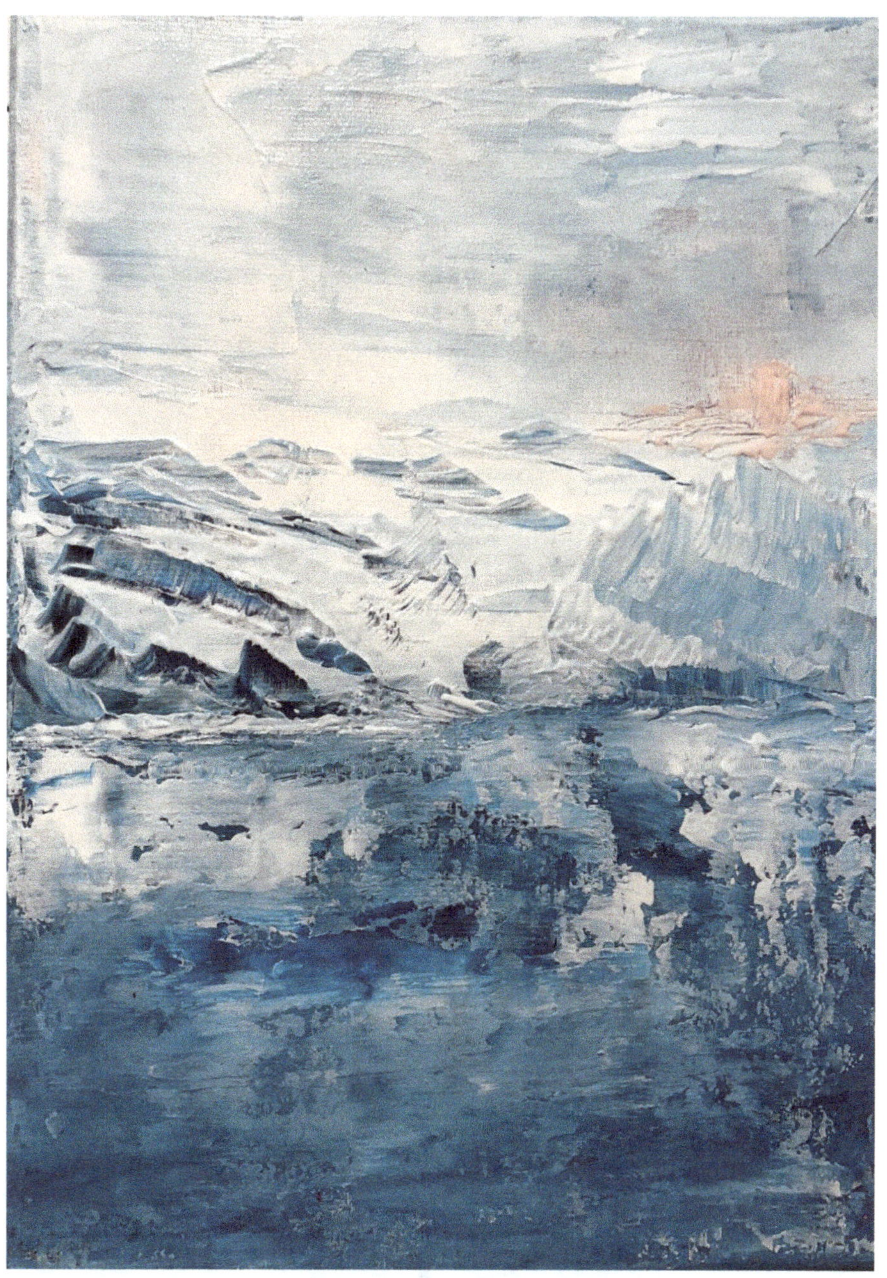

Antarctic Sunrise

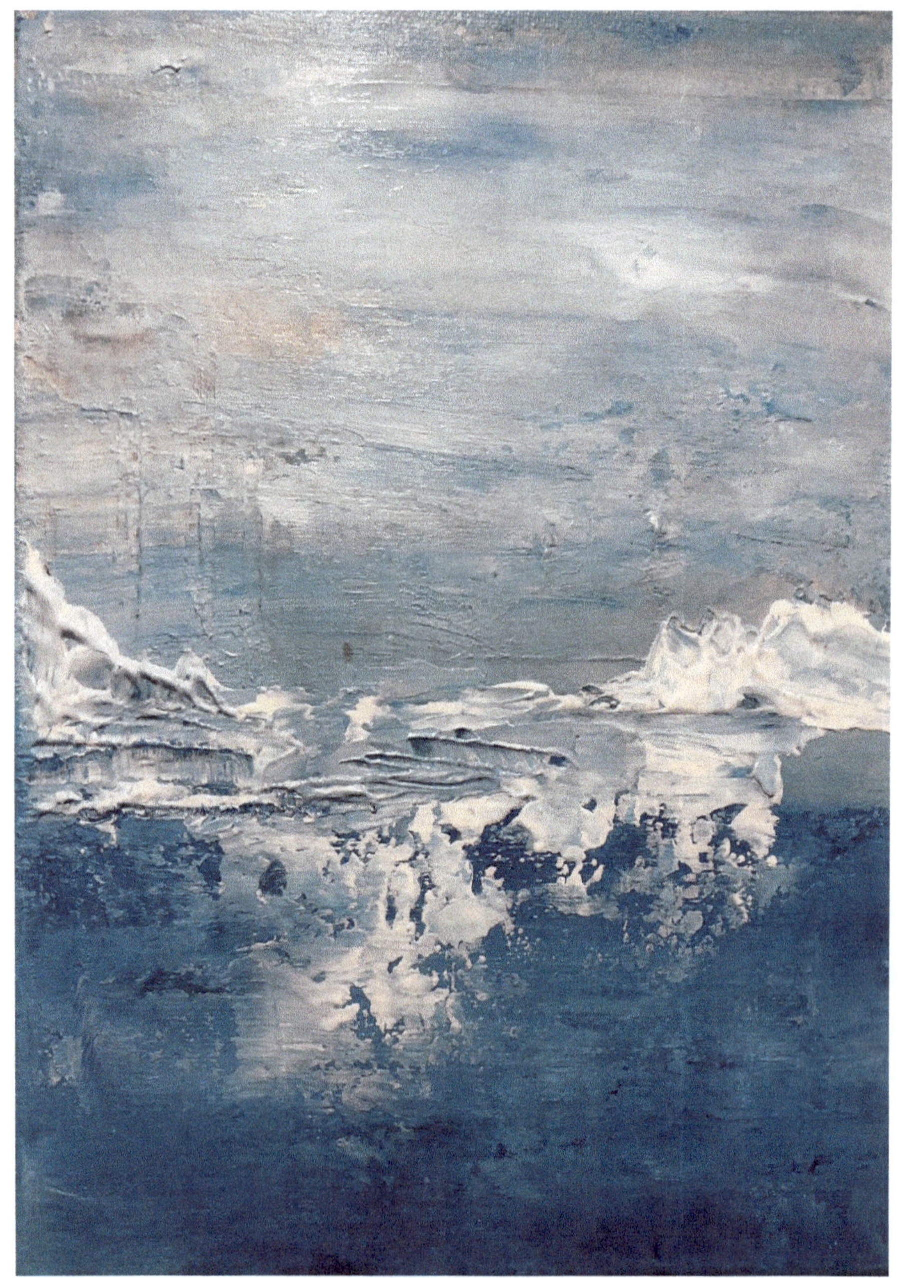

Antarctic Sundown

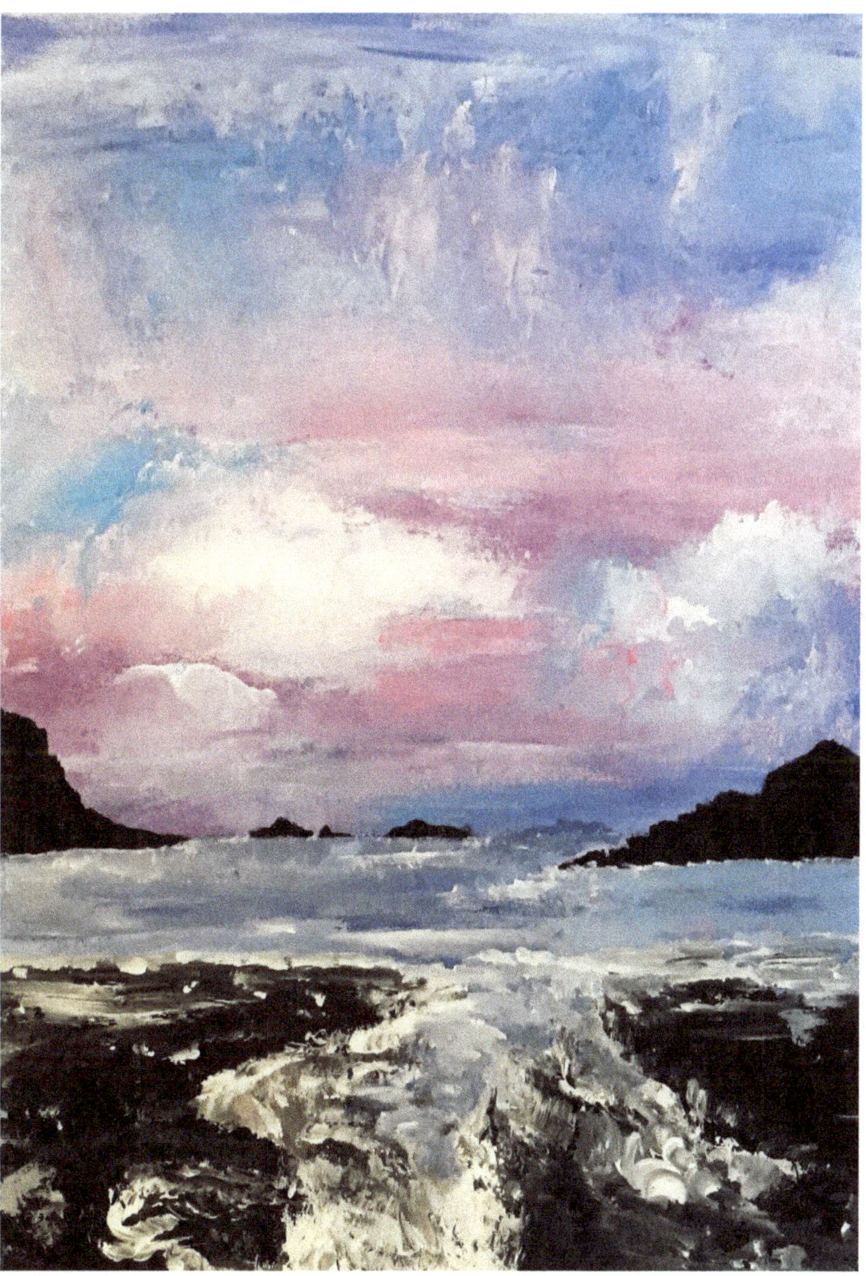

Ebb Tide

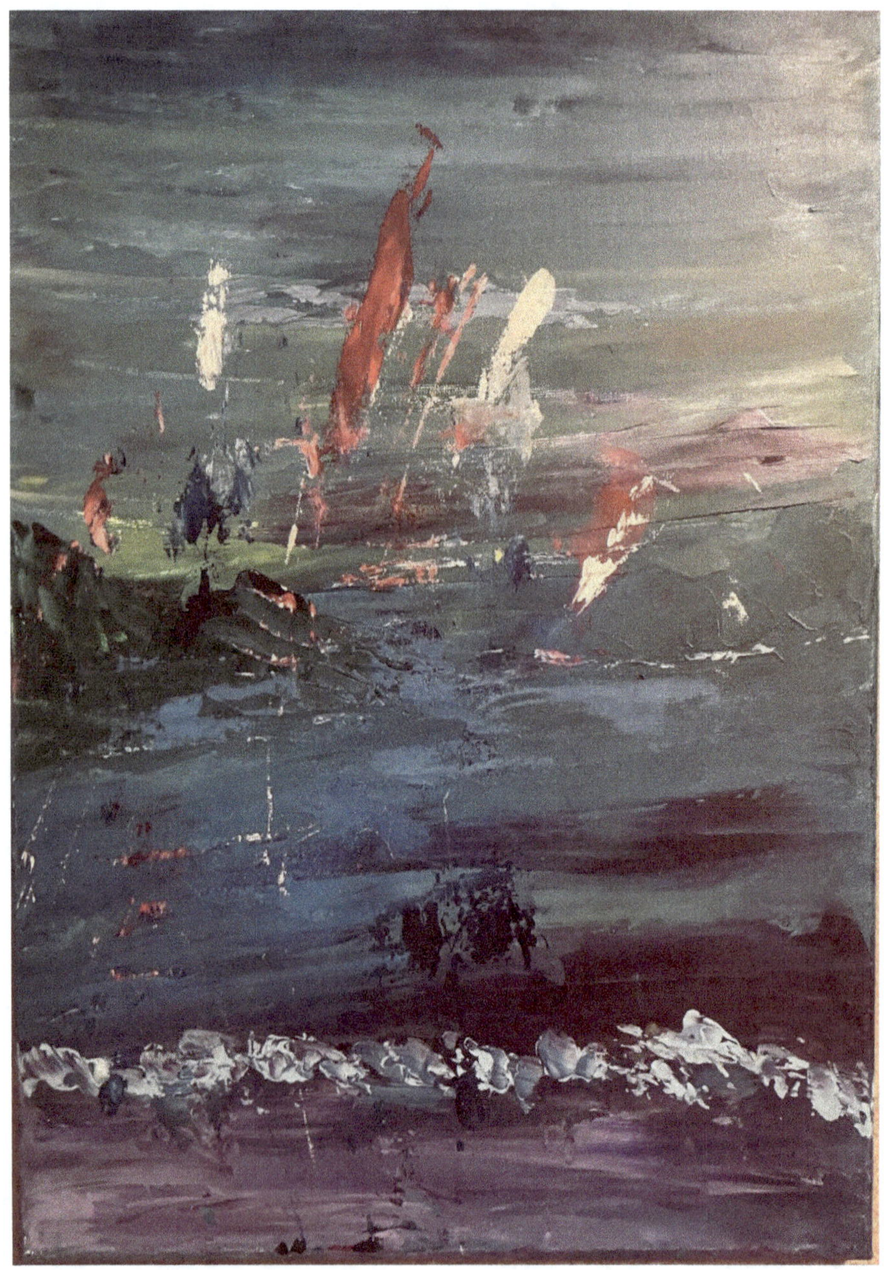

Feathers On The Water

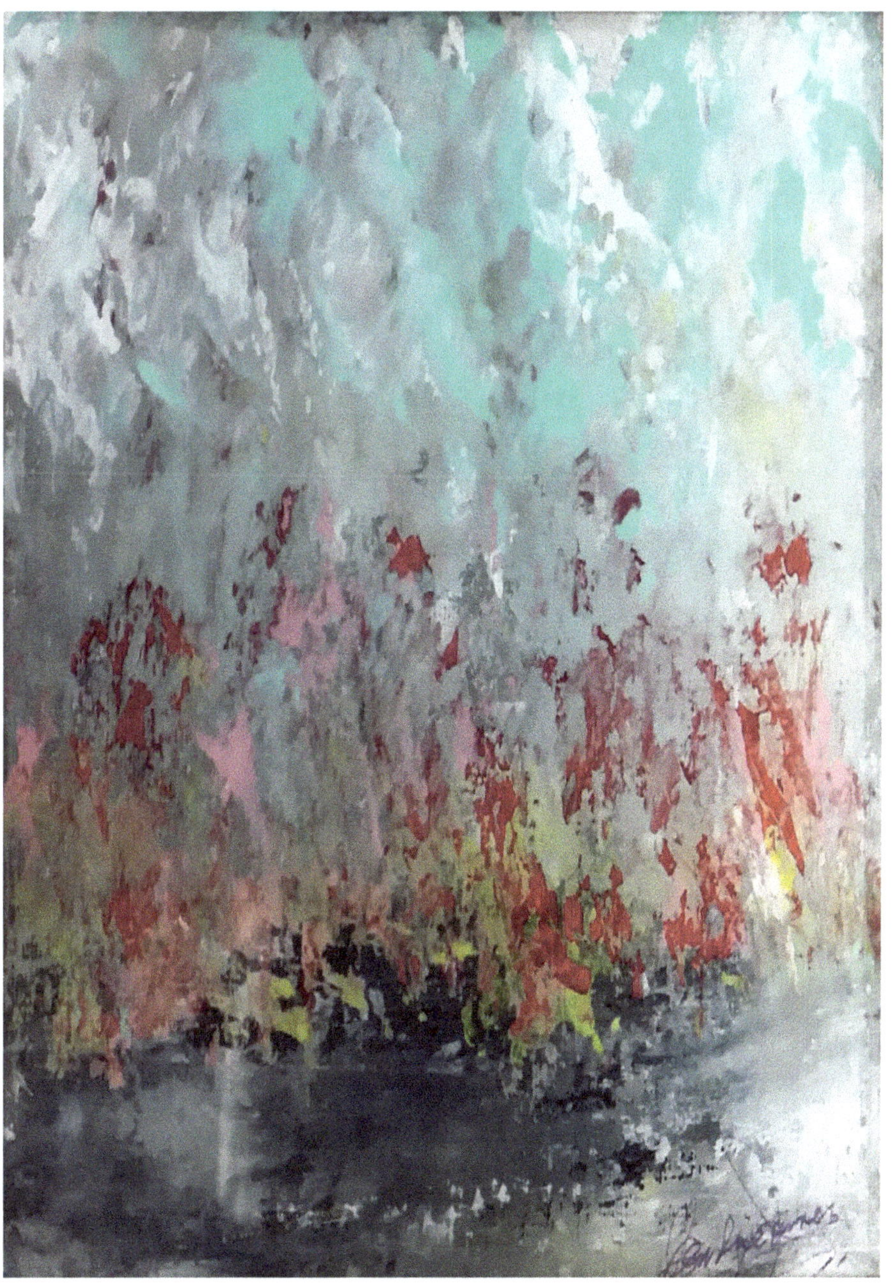

Fire Flowers

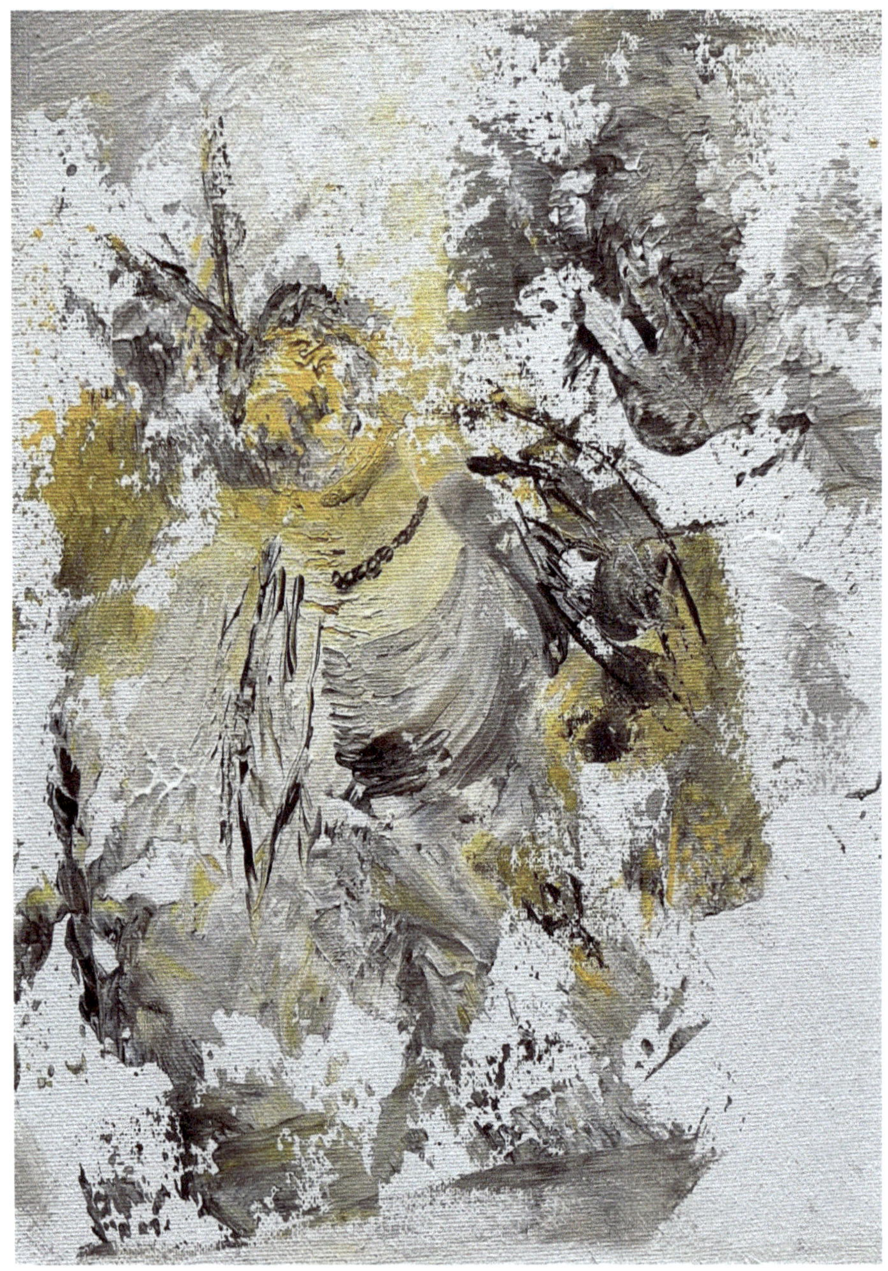

Flight Of The Bumblebee

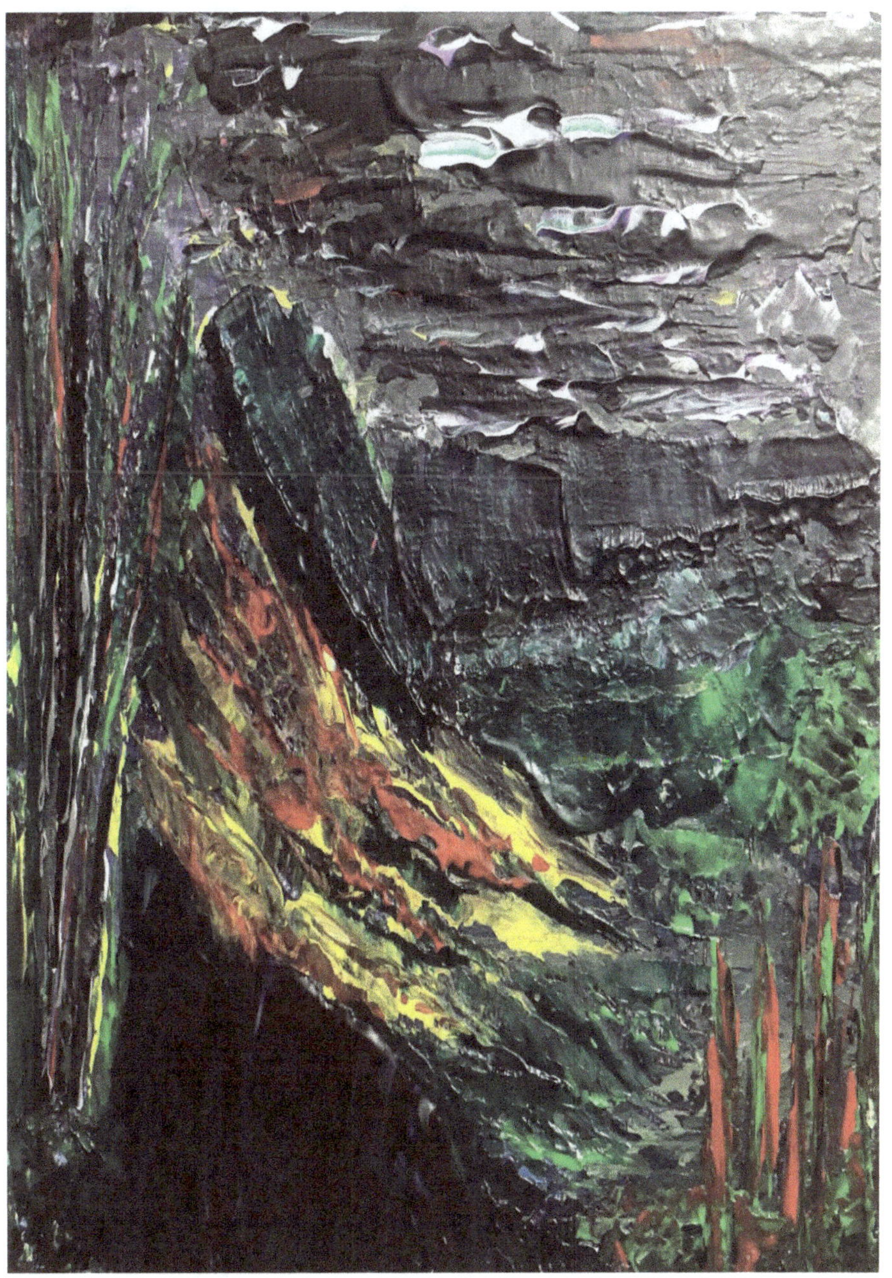

Fire Flow

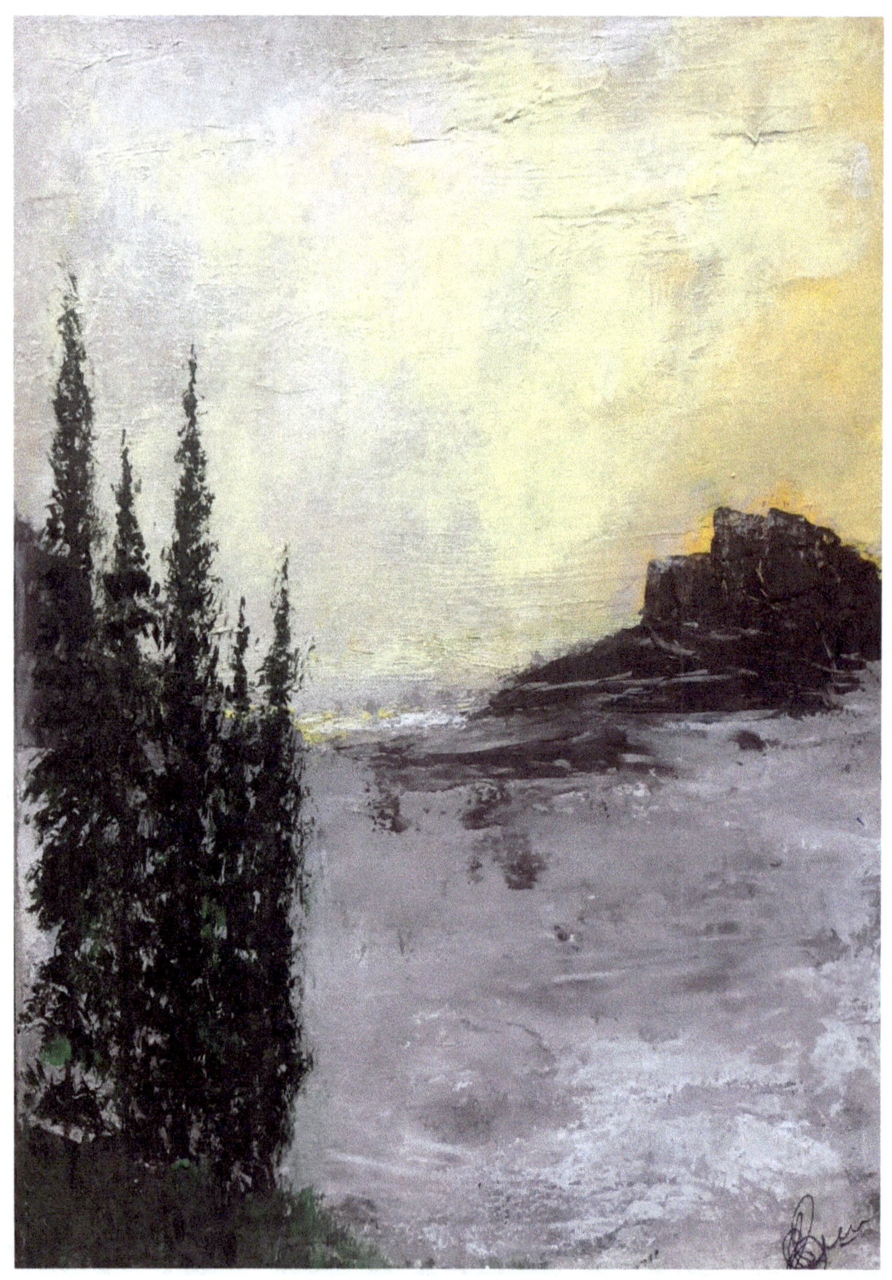

Distant Sunrise

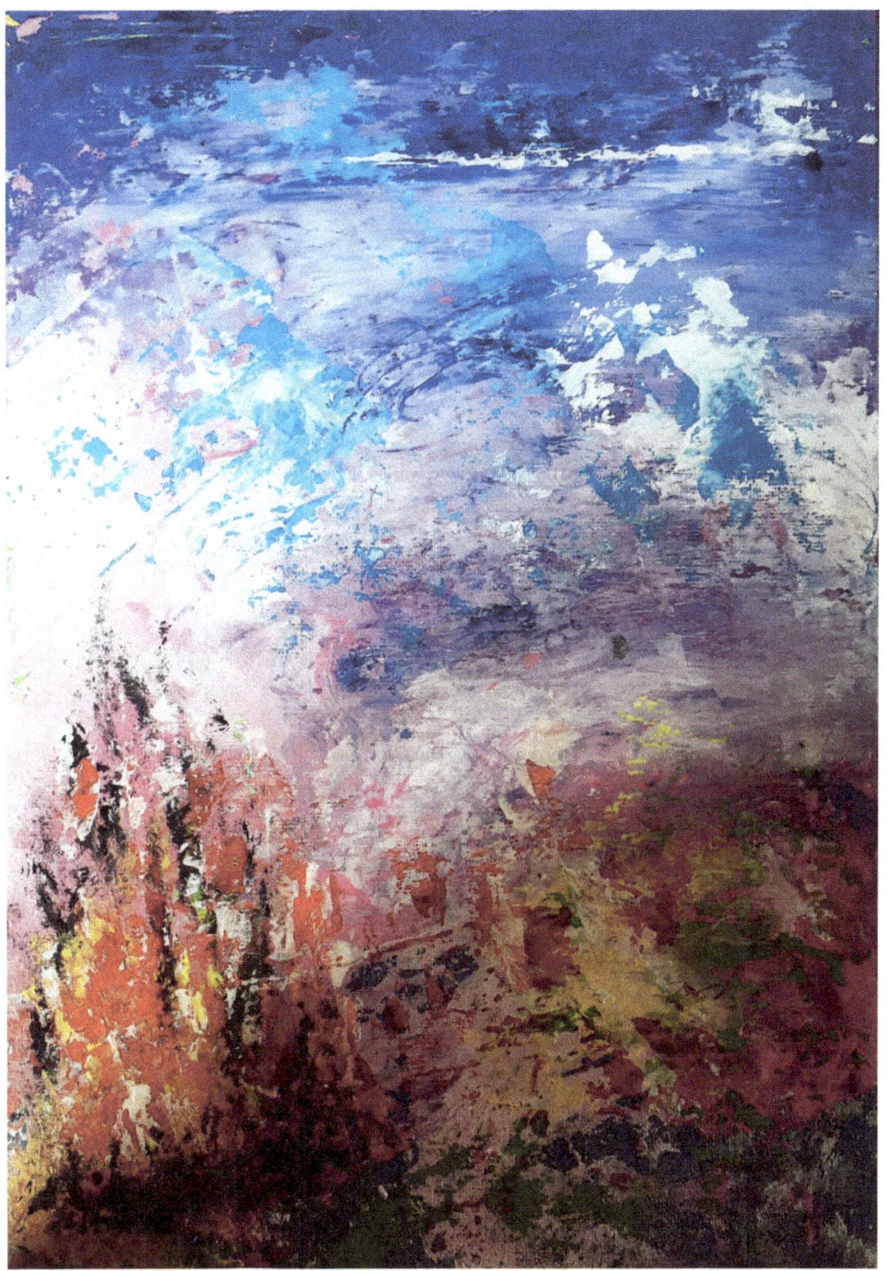

Floral Dawn

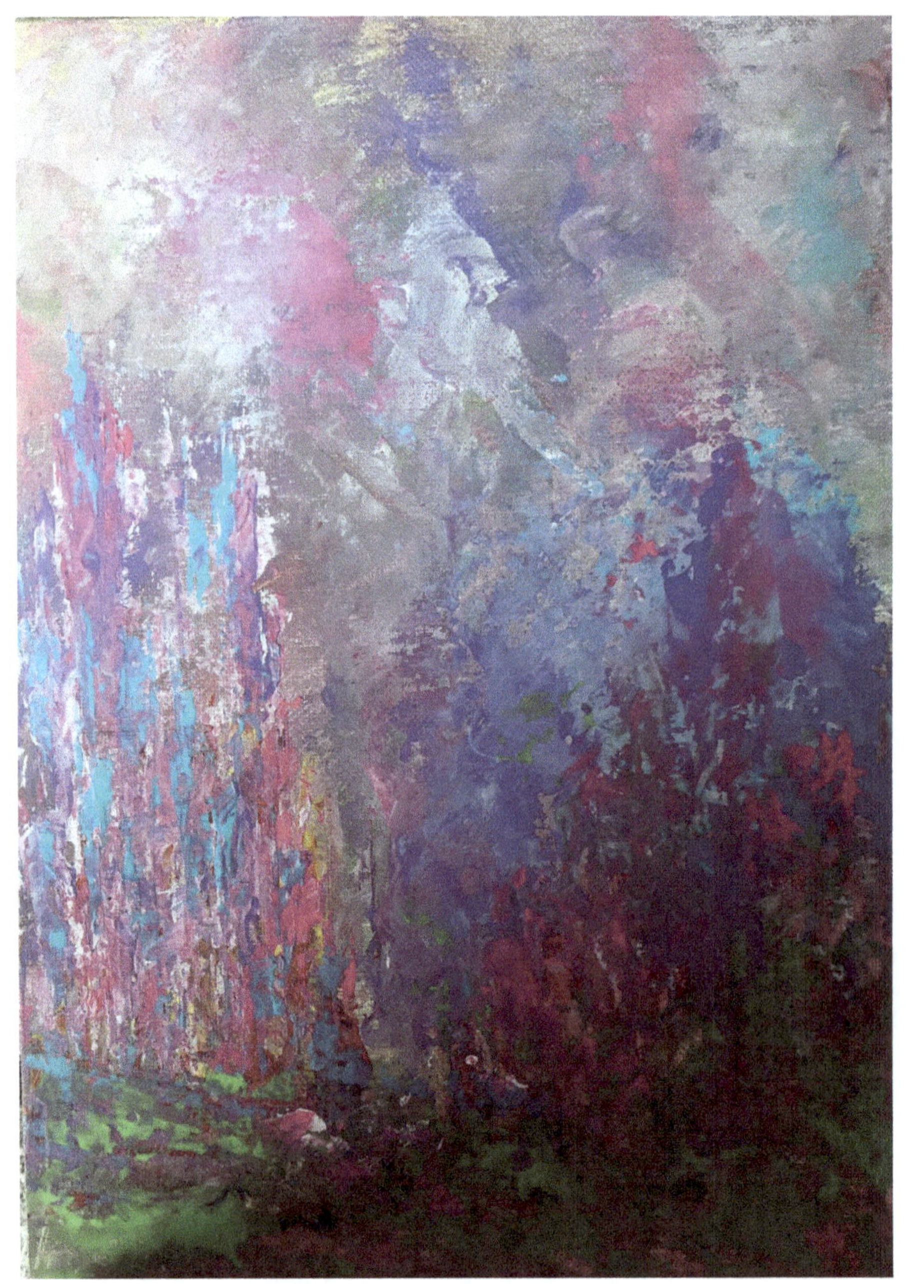

Floral Dusk

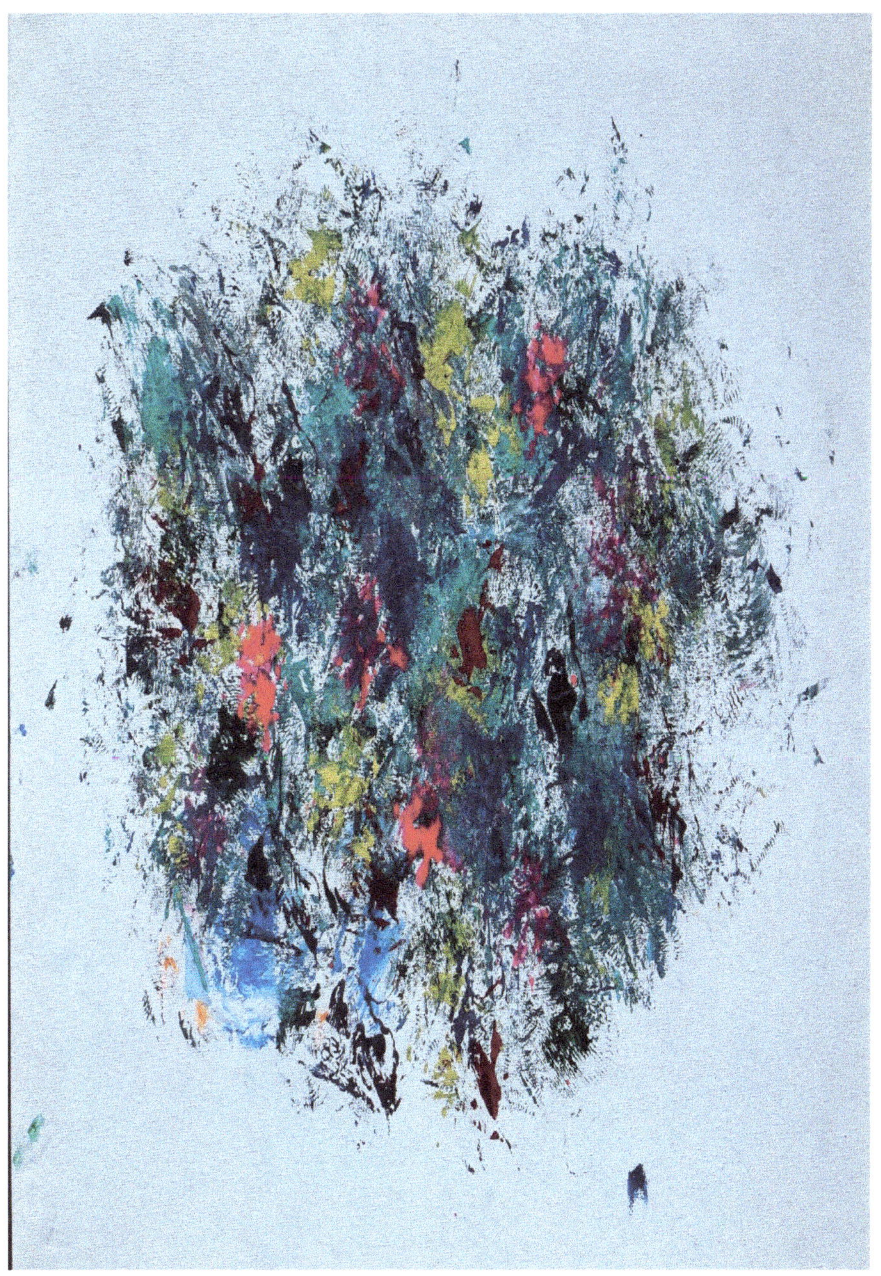

Floral Synaptic

Storm Brewing

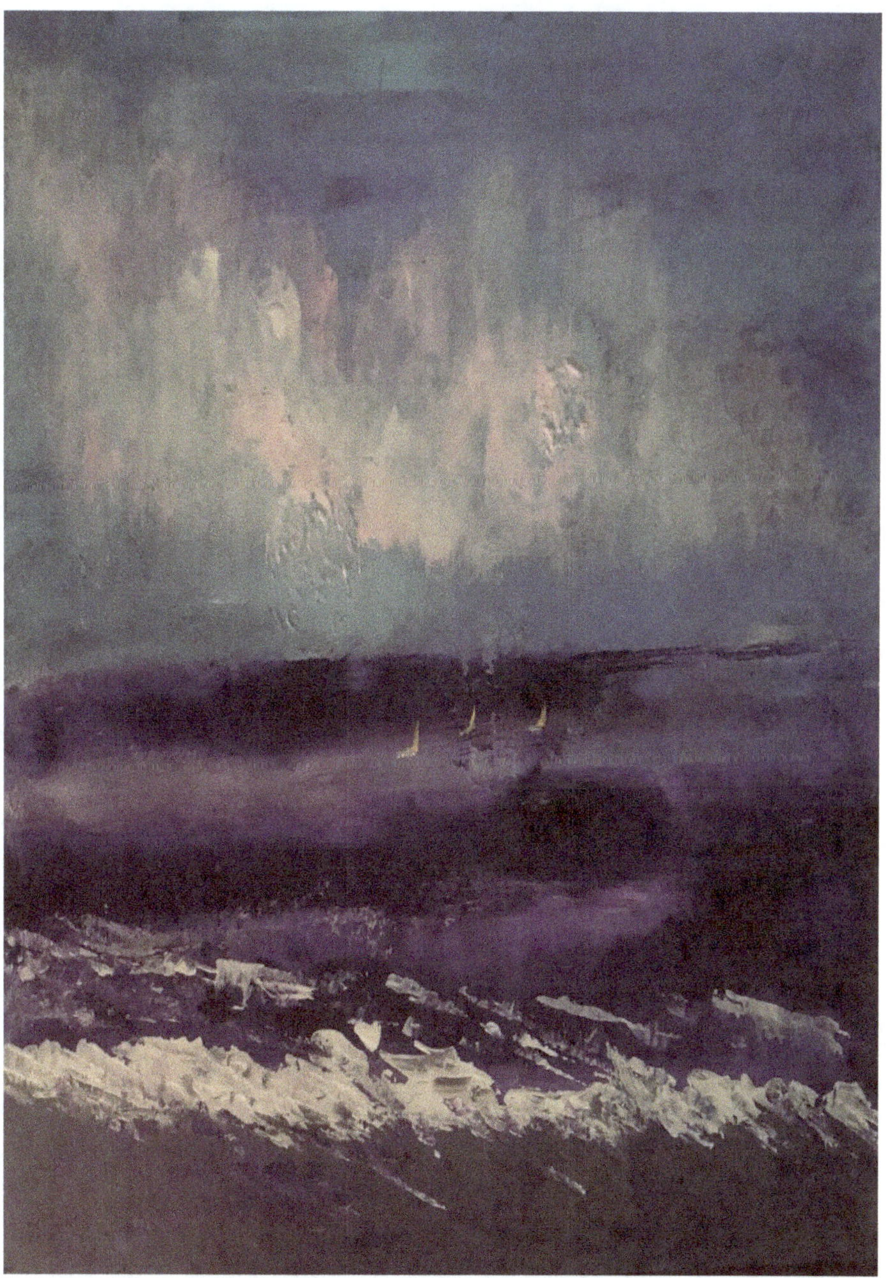

Golden Sailboats

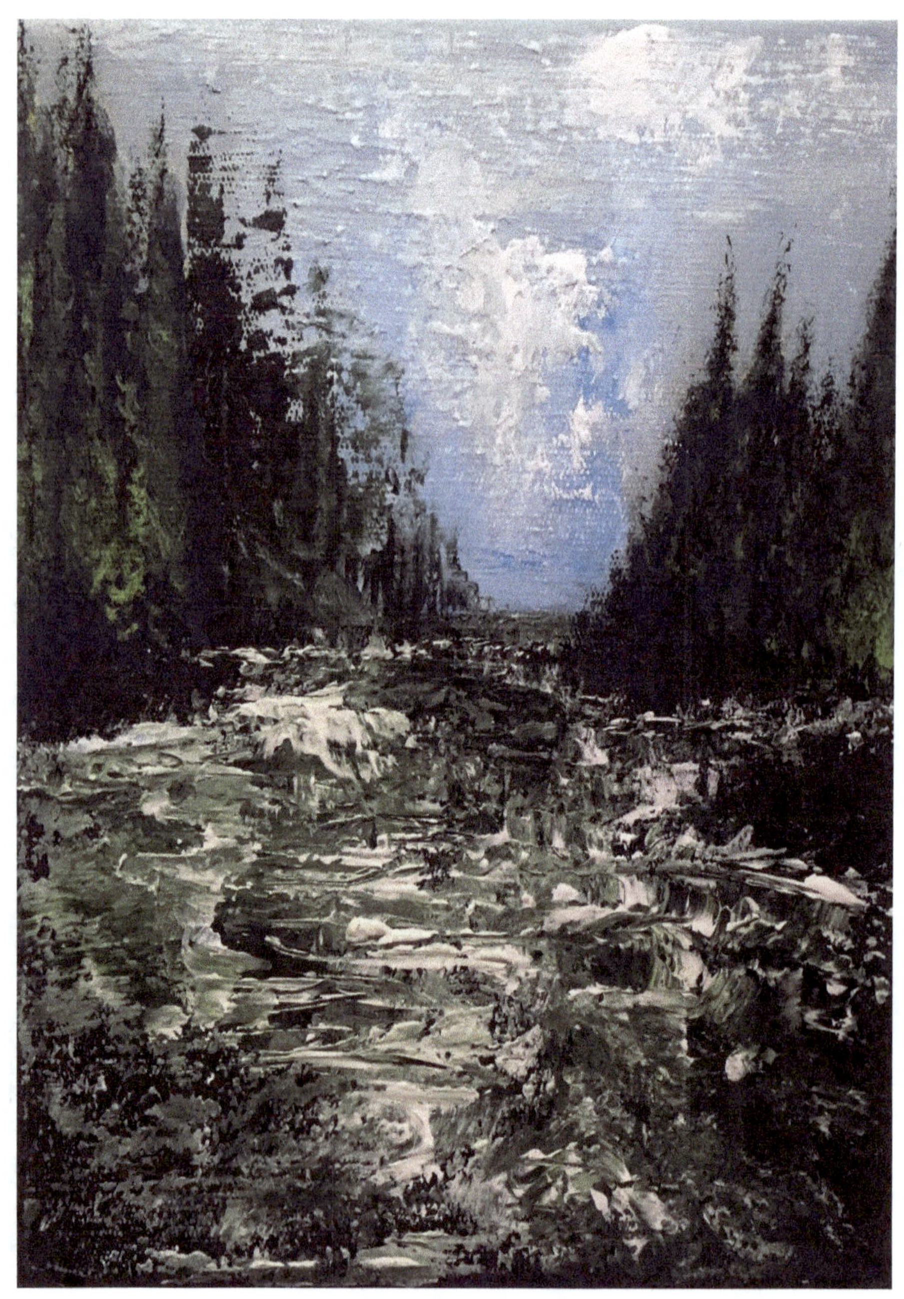

Green River Rapids

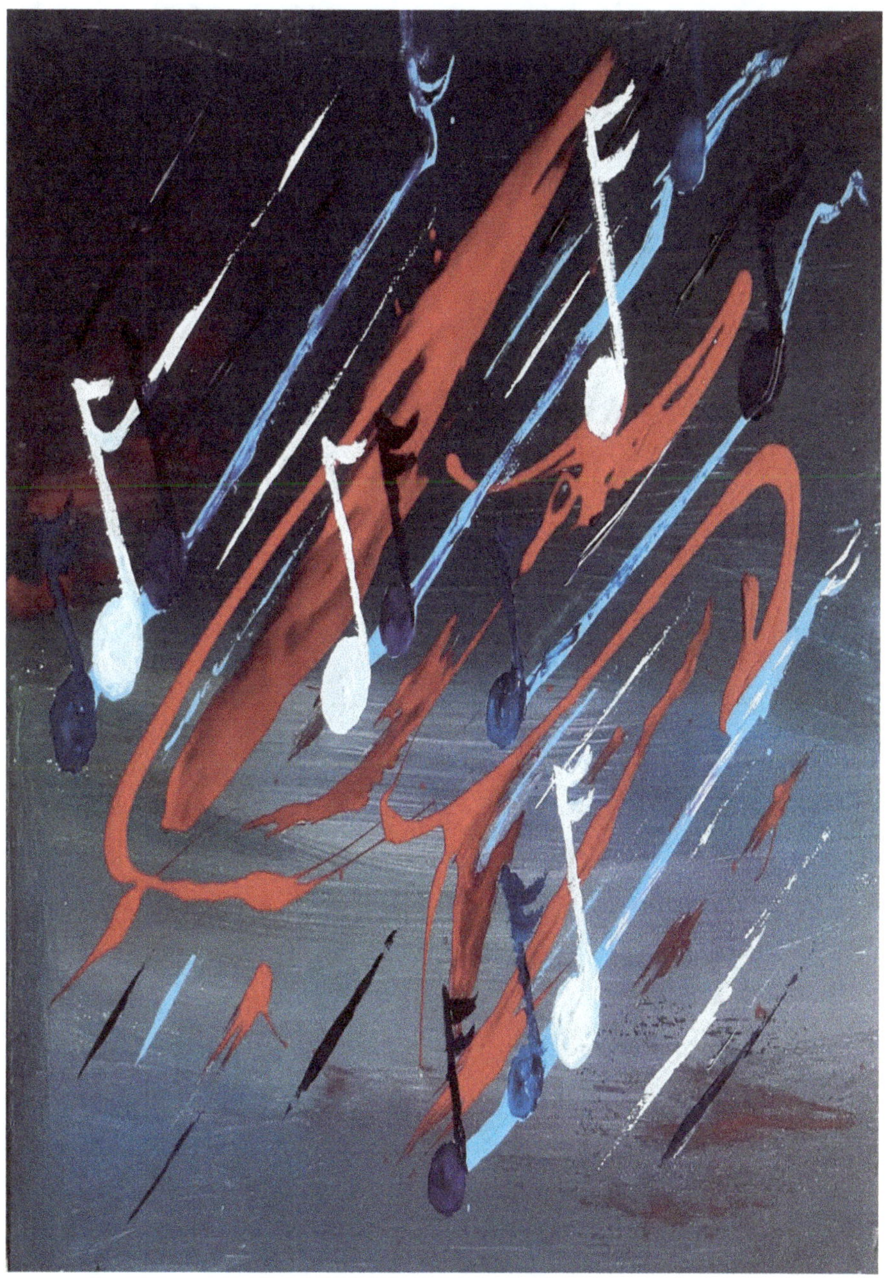

Heartbeat Of The Music

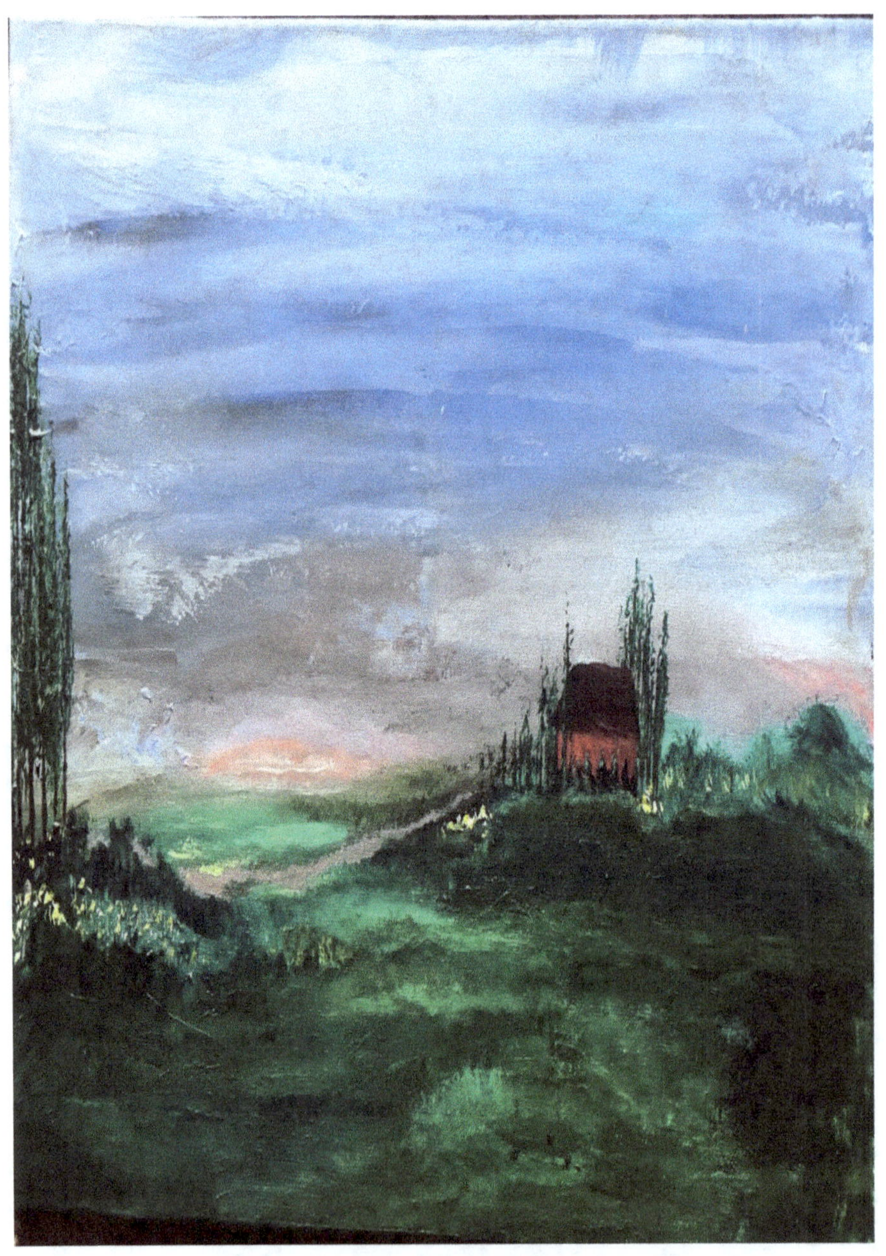

Homestead Indian Mountain
(Moncton New Brunswick CANADA circa 1898)

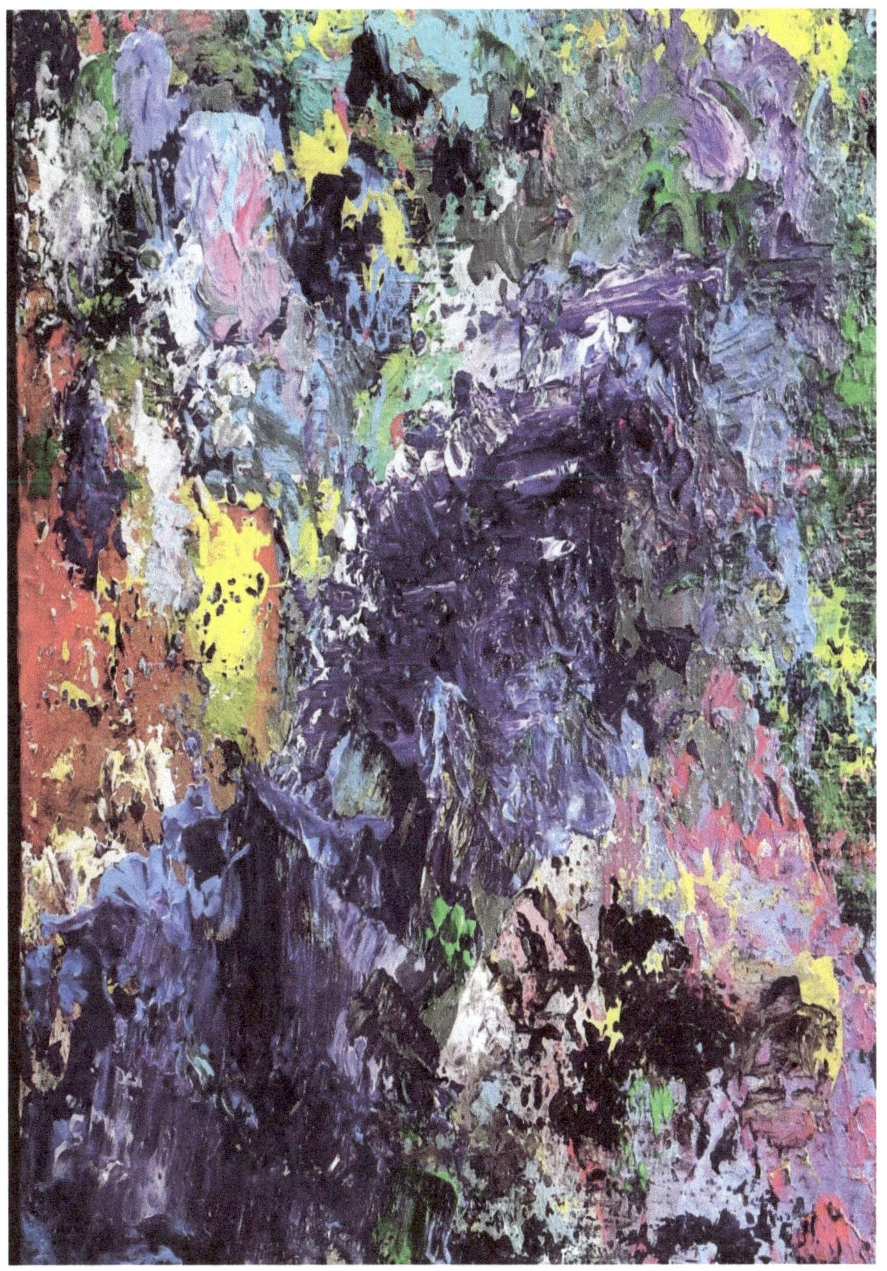

Horse Of The Rising Sun

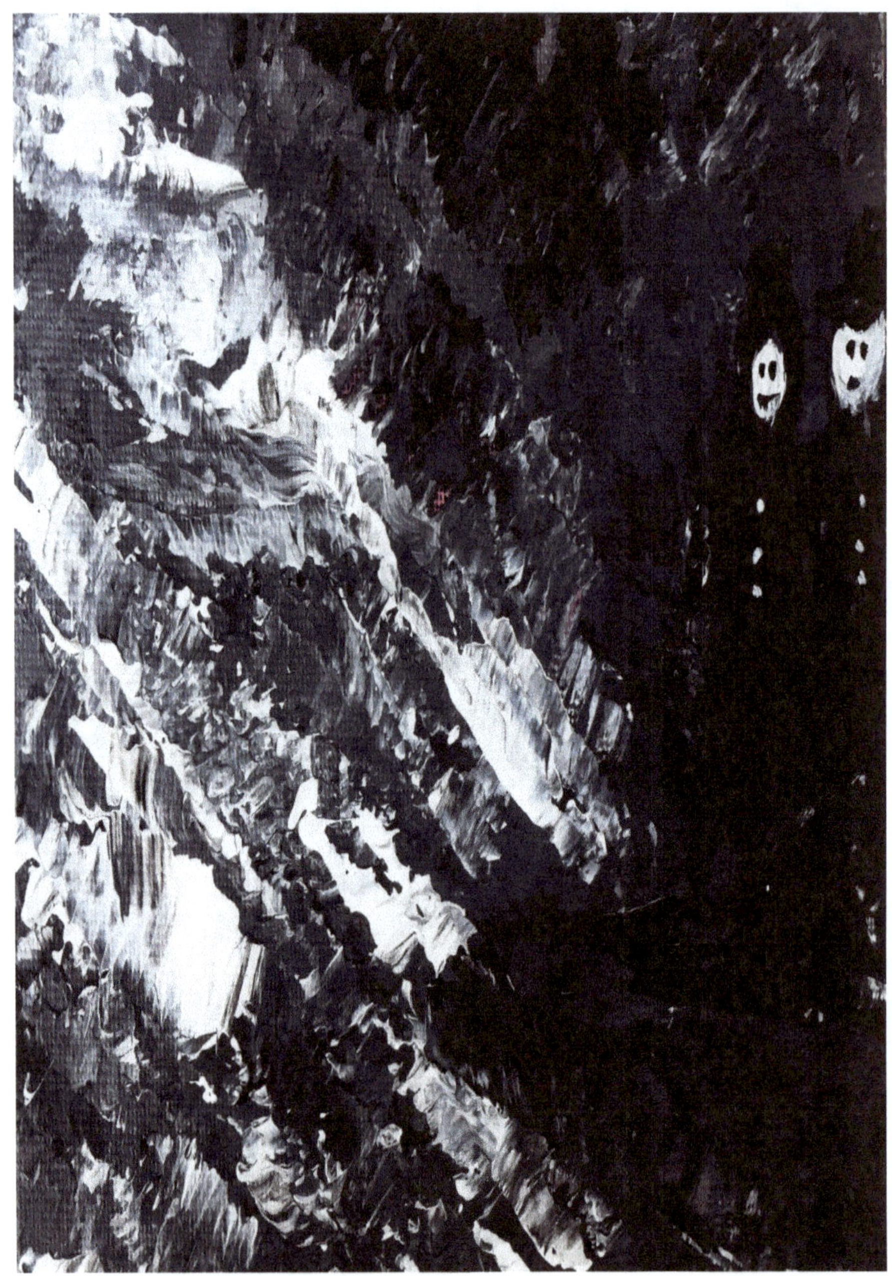

Frosty And Wife In Disguise At The Final Deluge

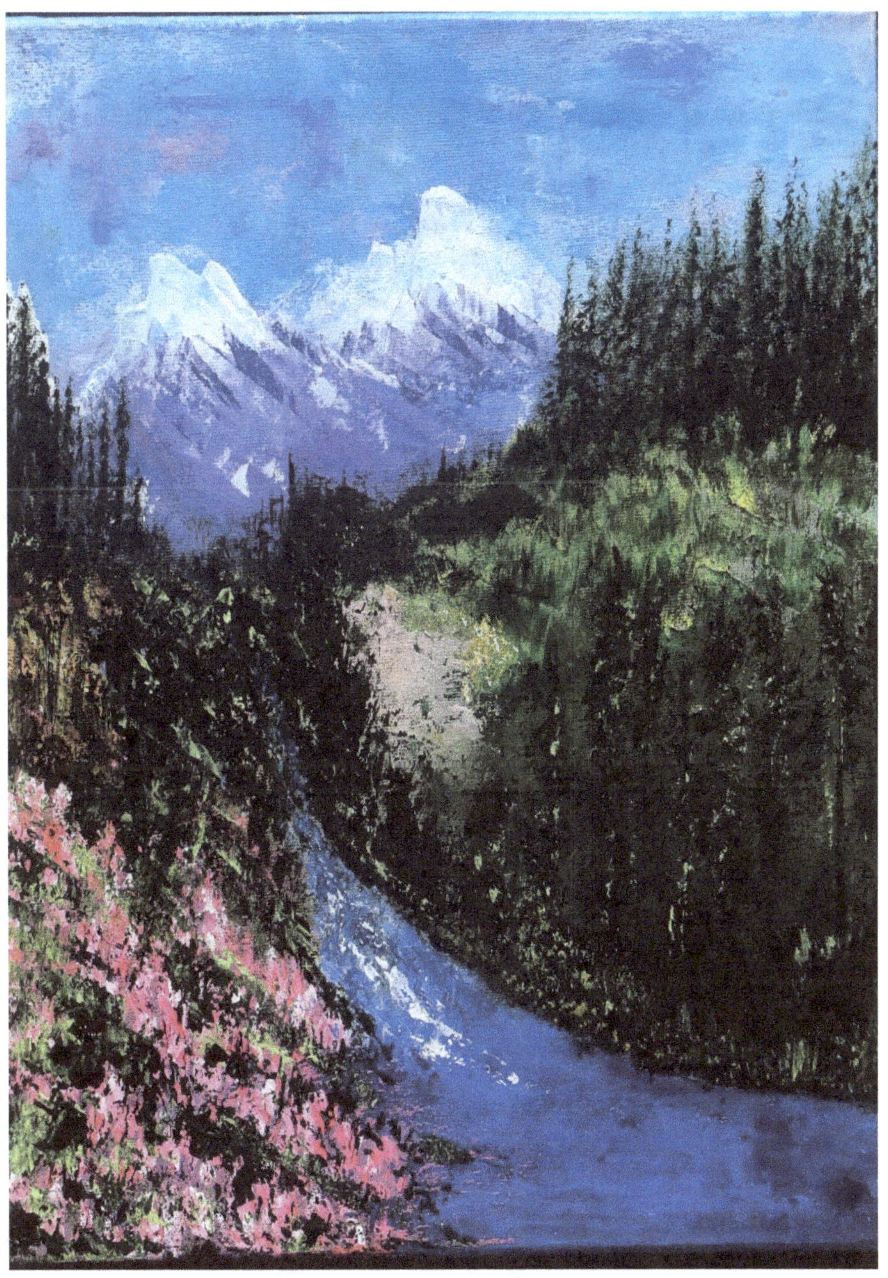

Indian River

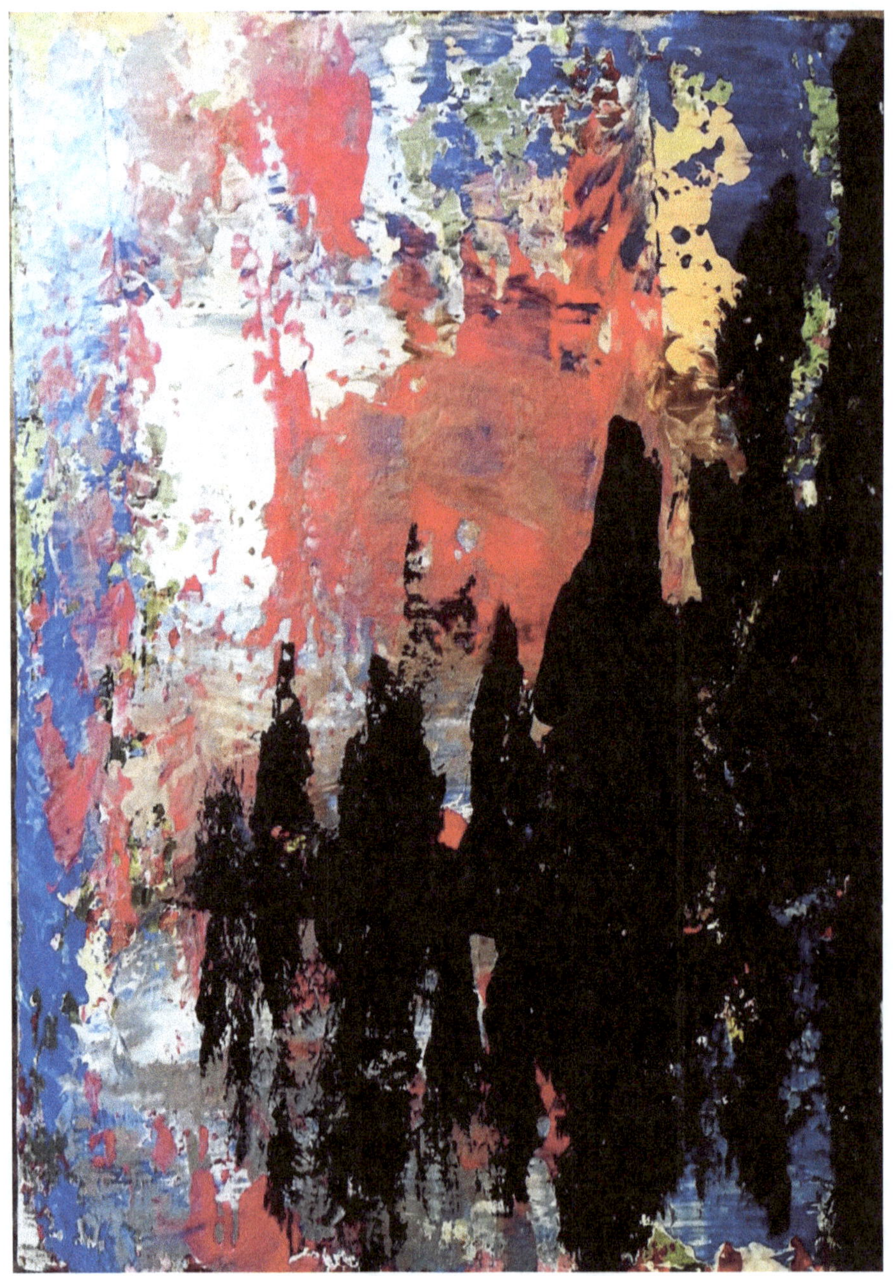

In The Land Of Nebuchadnezzar

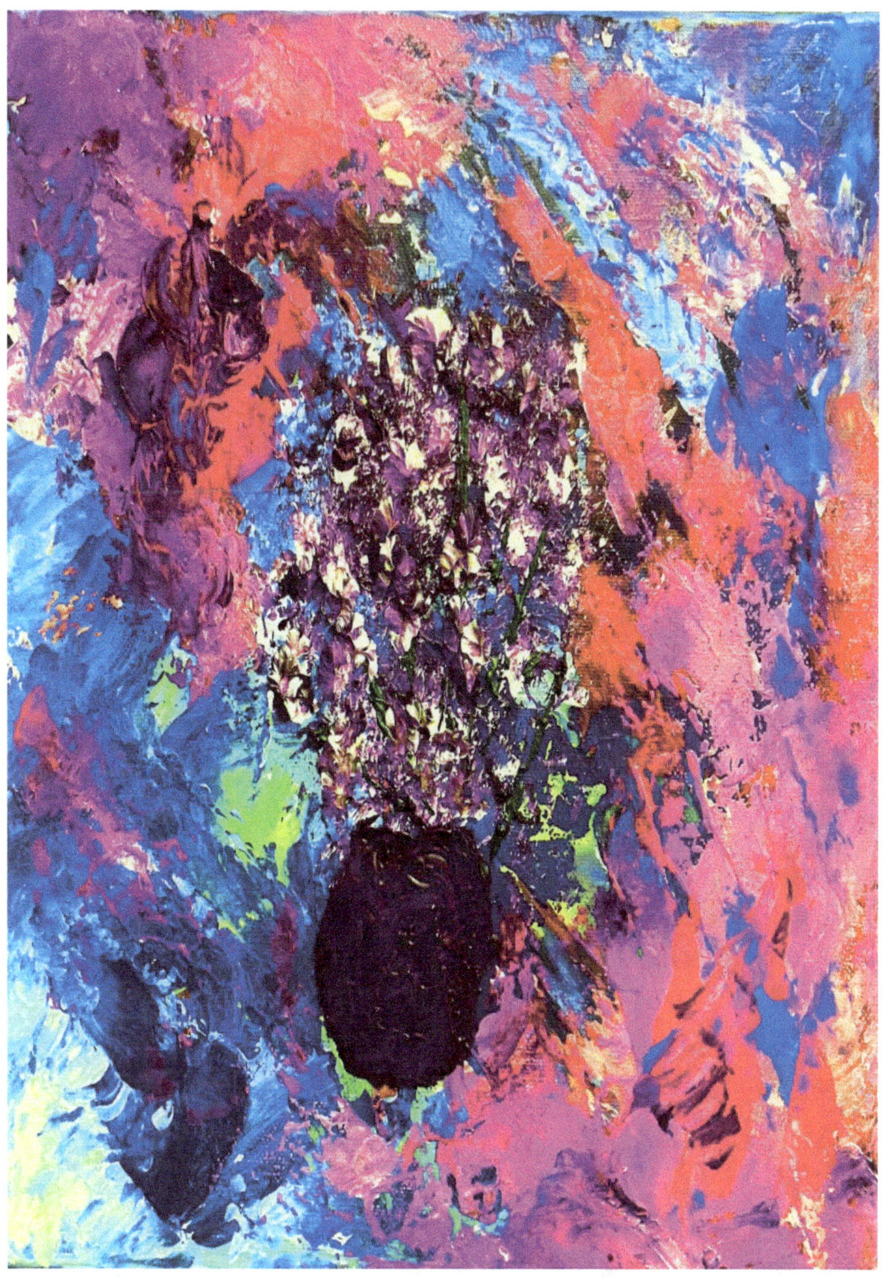

Irises In The Ether

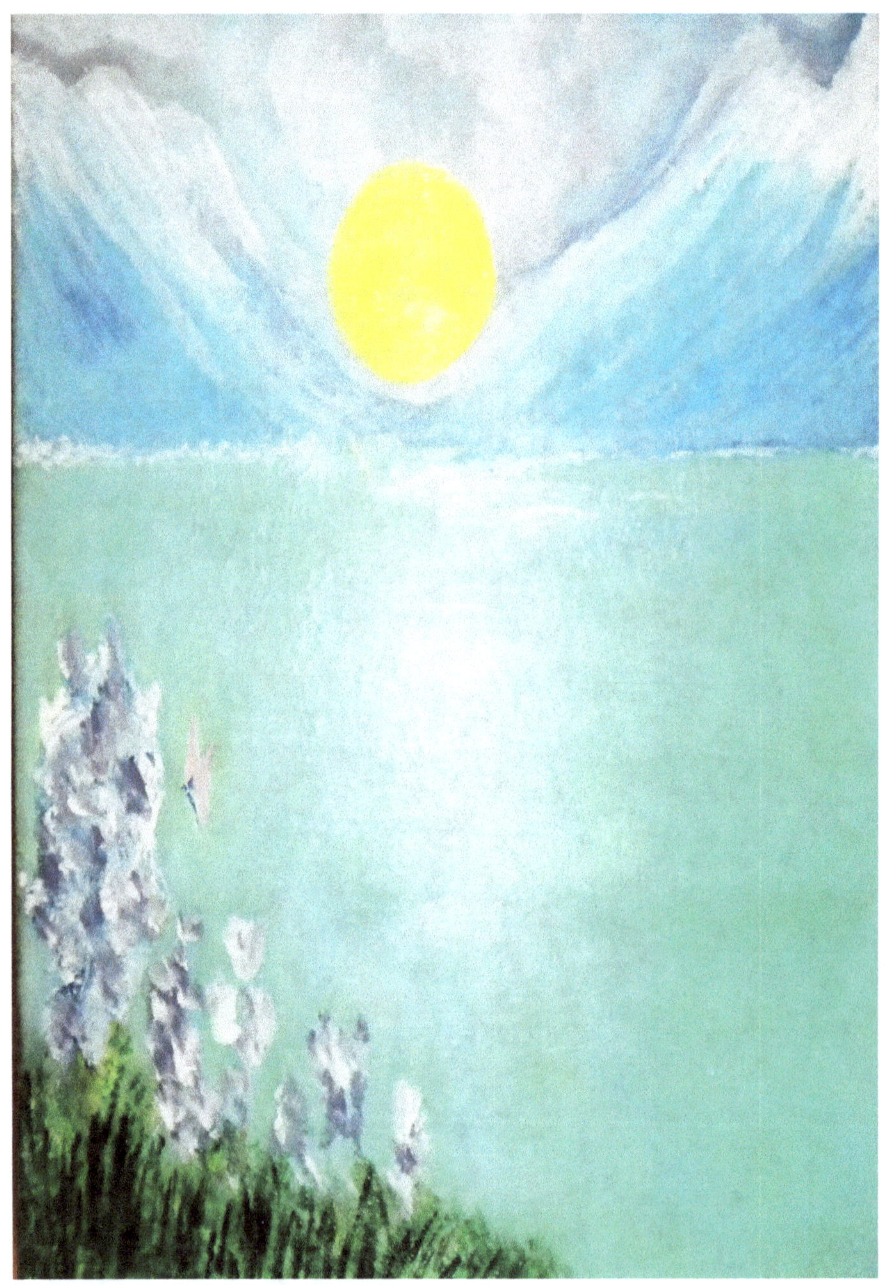

Lake Louise Sundown

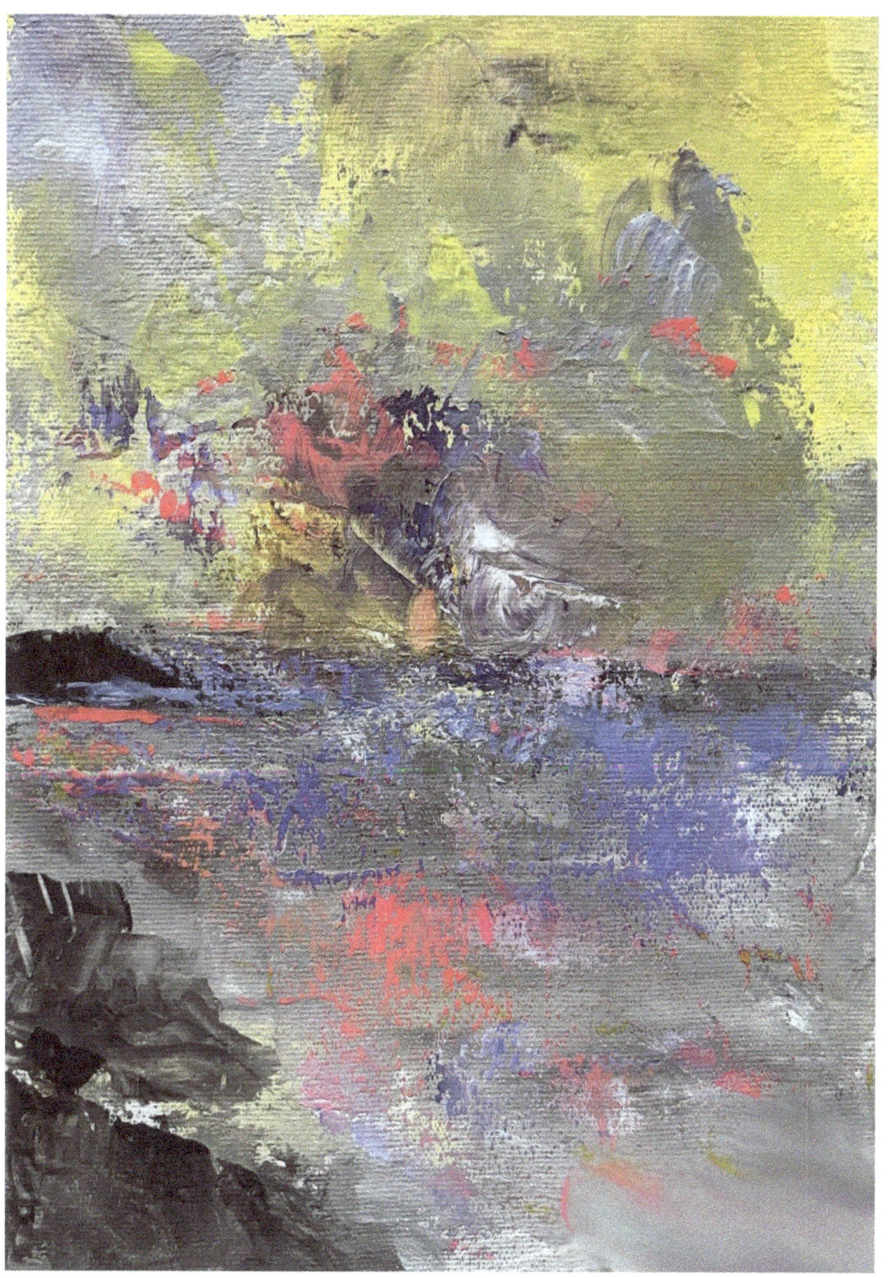

Lavender Waterfalls

Lawnmower Man

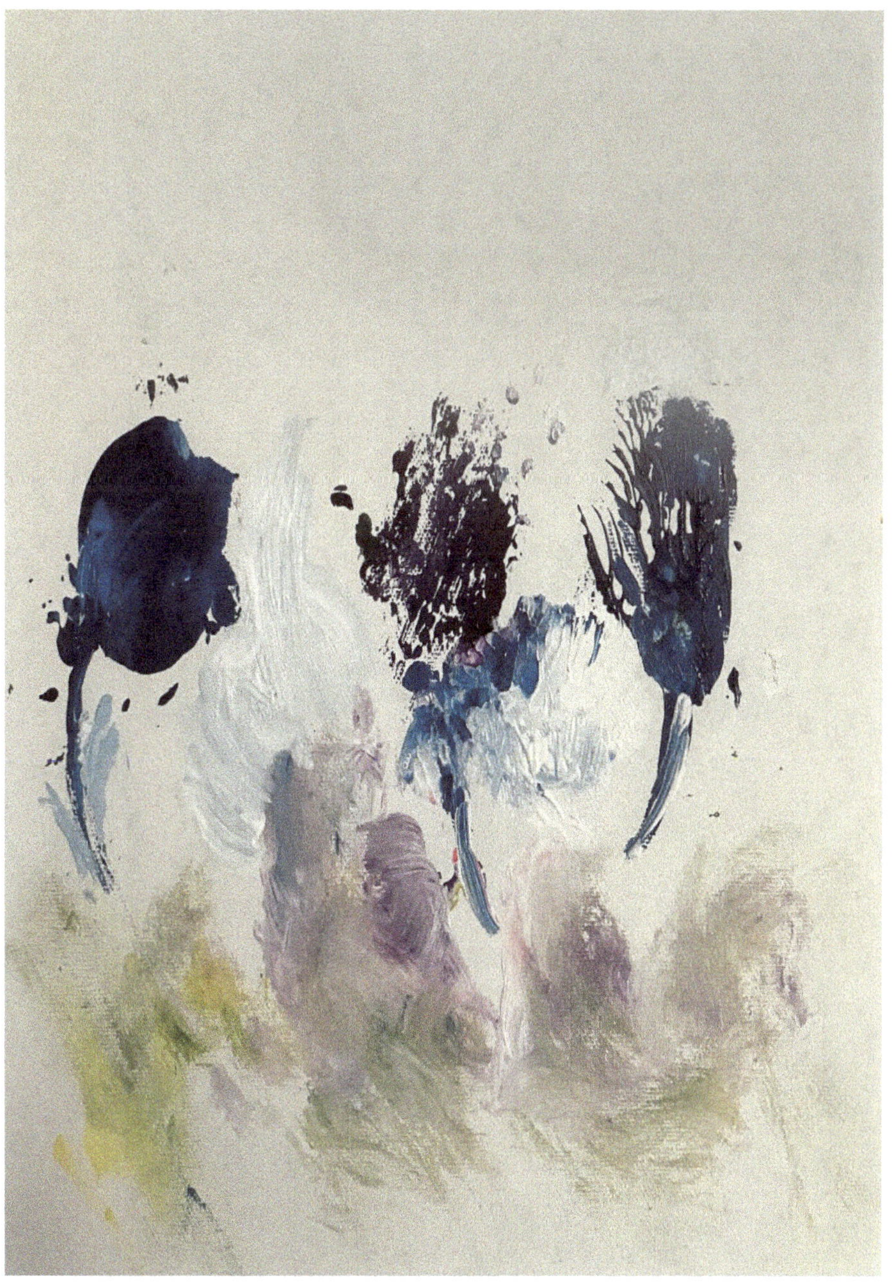

Blue Tulips

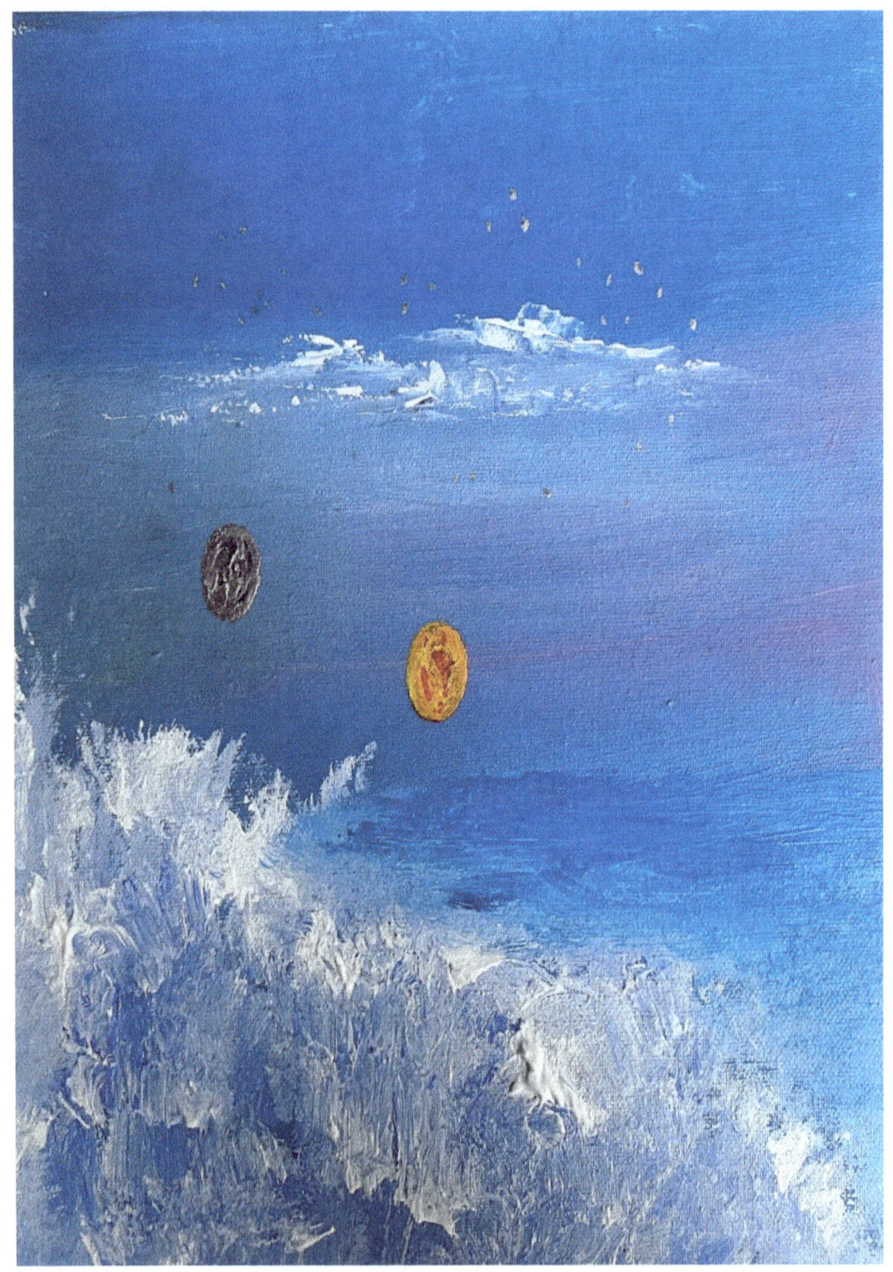

Luke 21:25 King James Bible

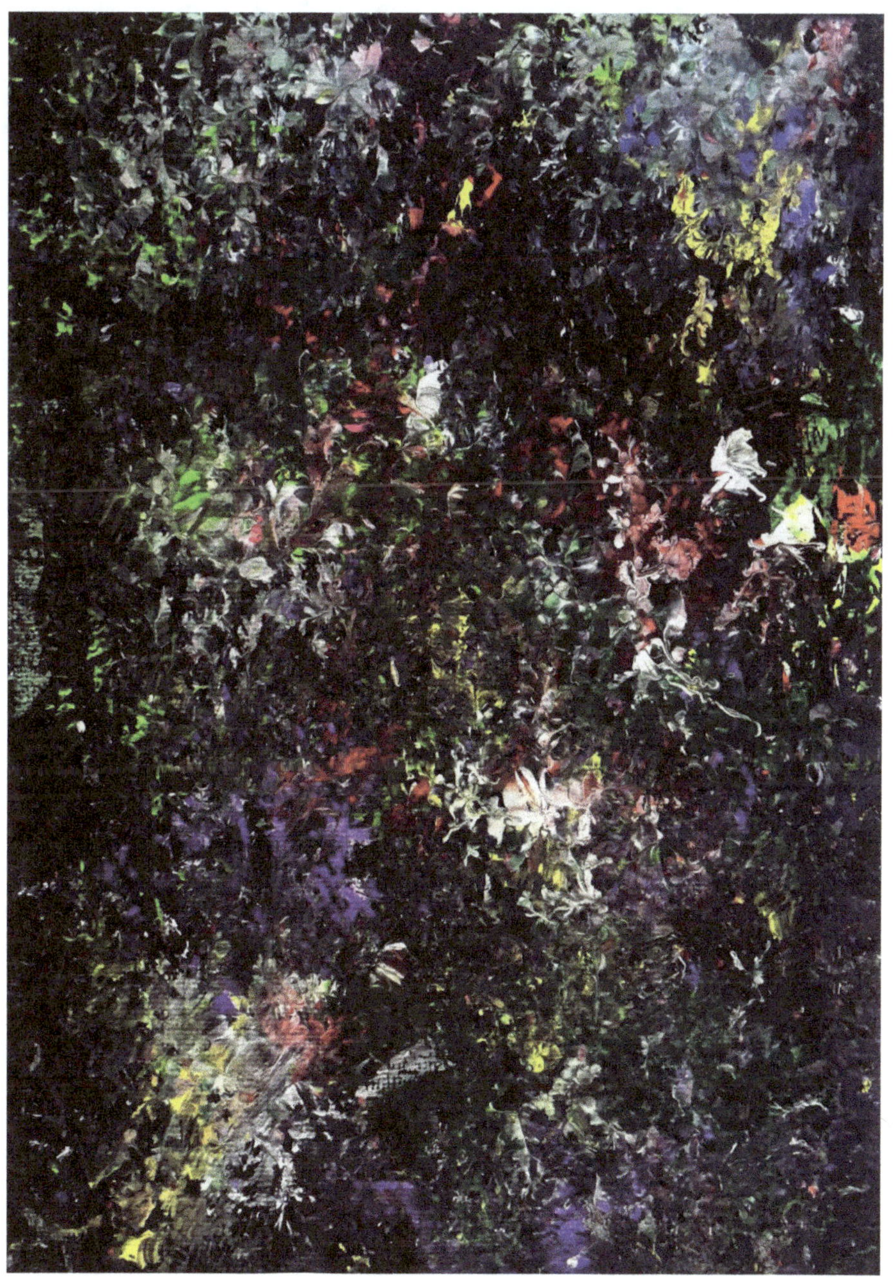

Magic Forest

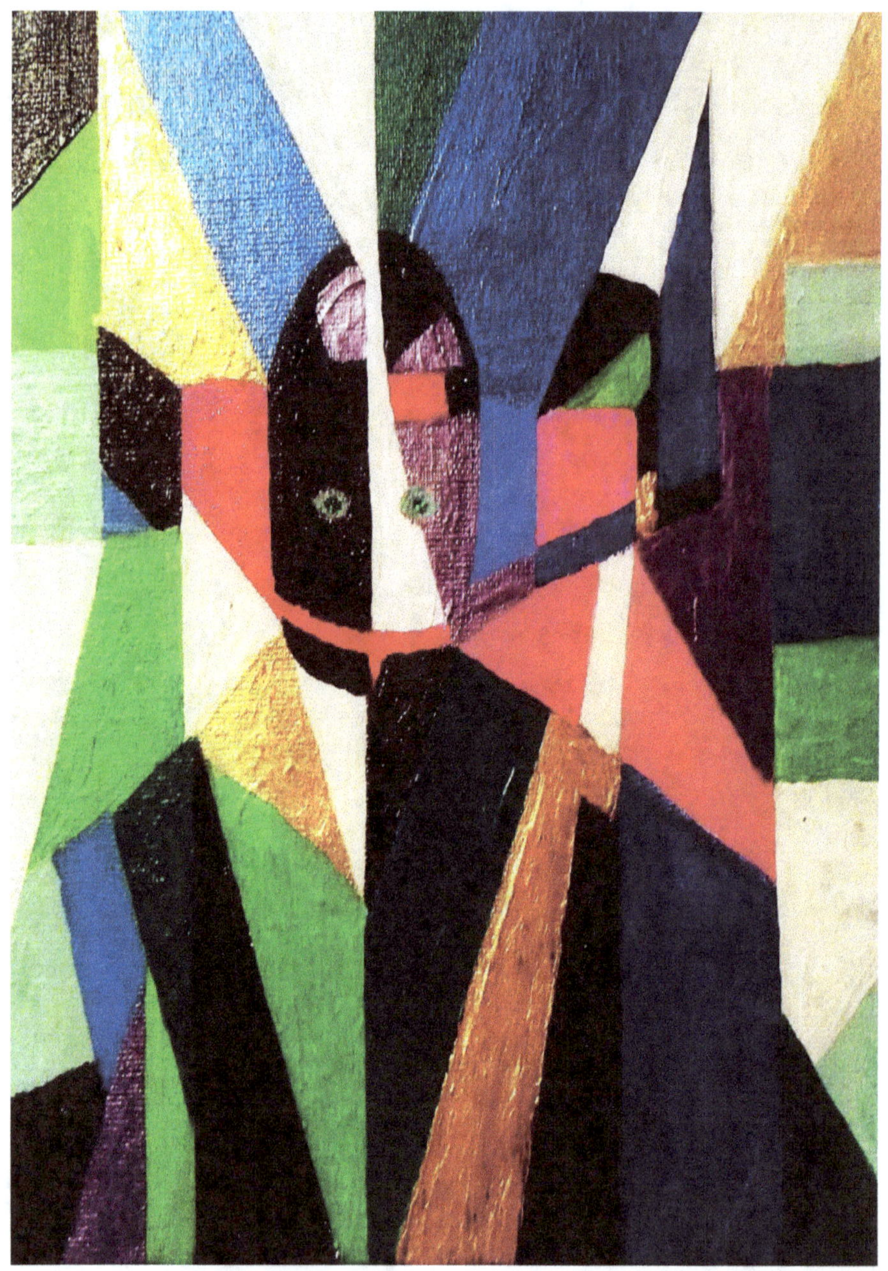

Masked Enigma

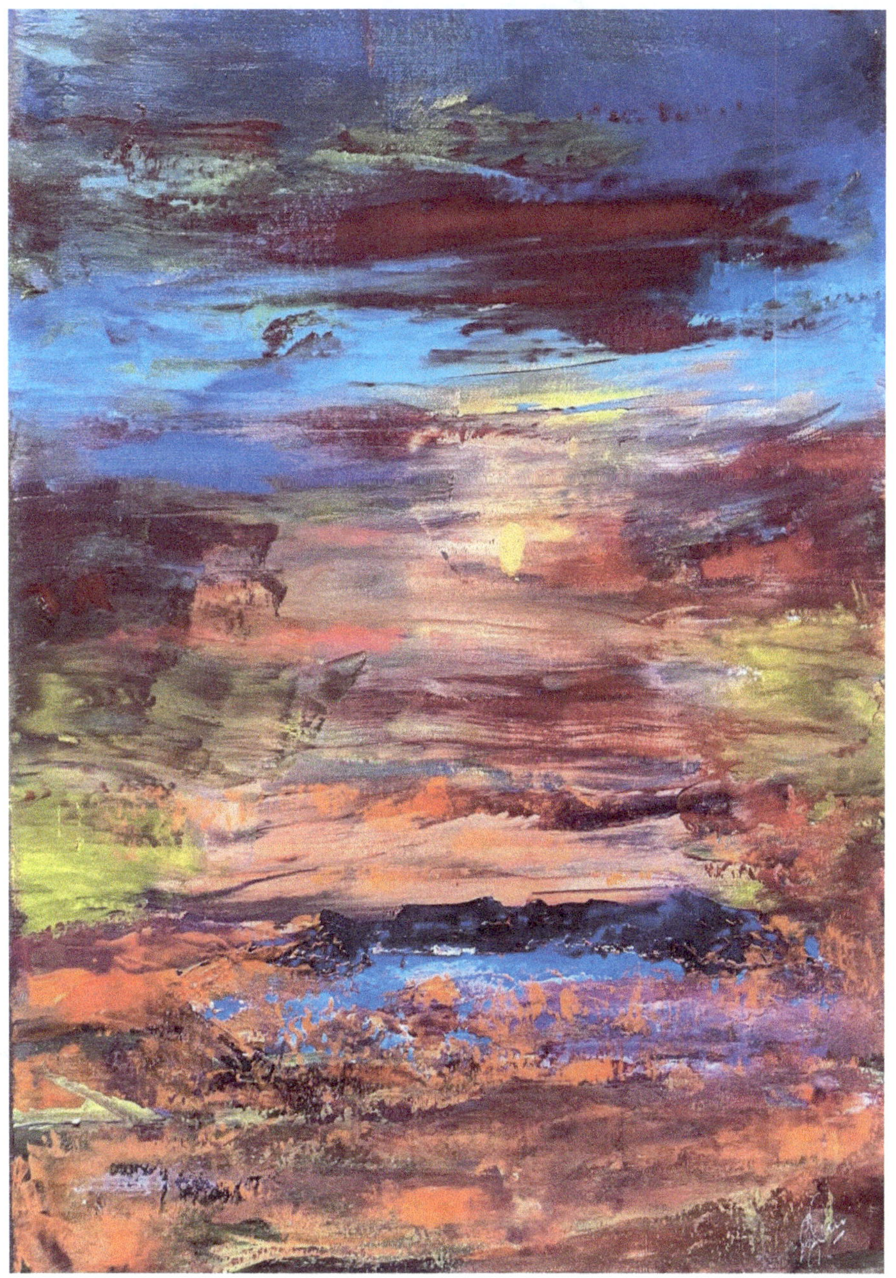

Mirage

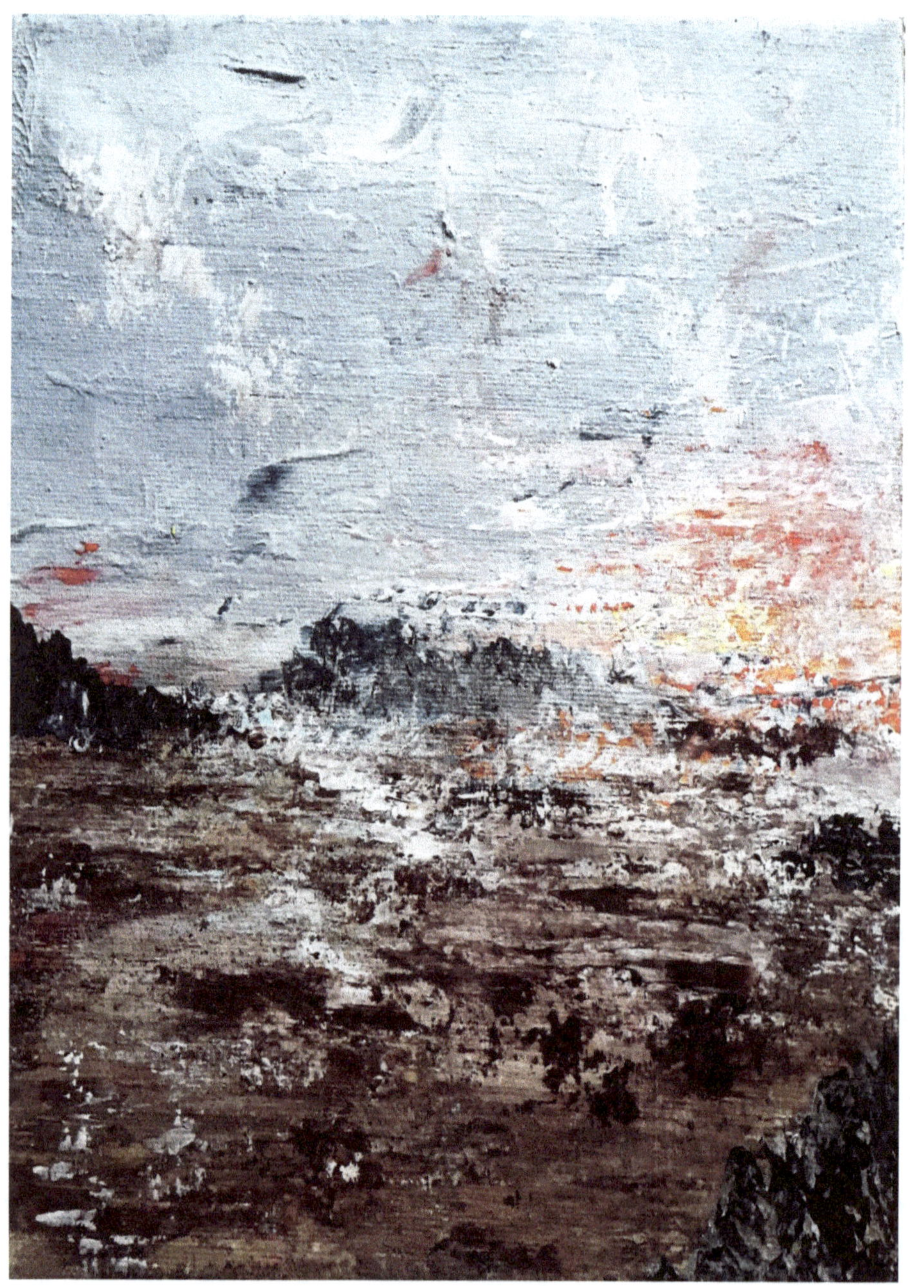

Long Beach Sundown

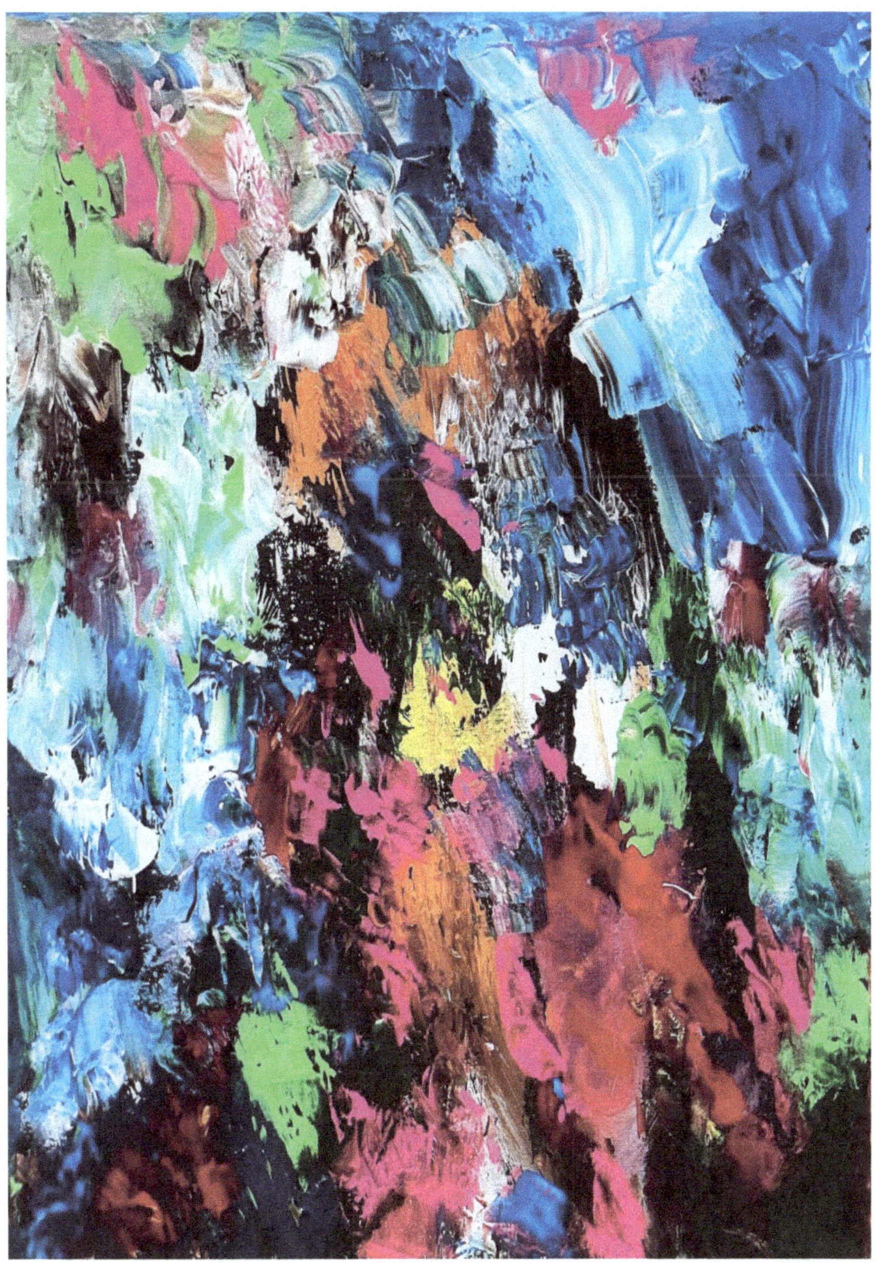

Monet's Hidden Garden

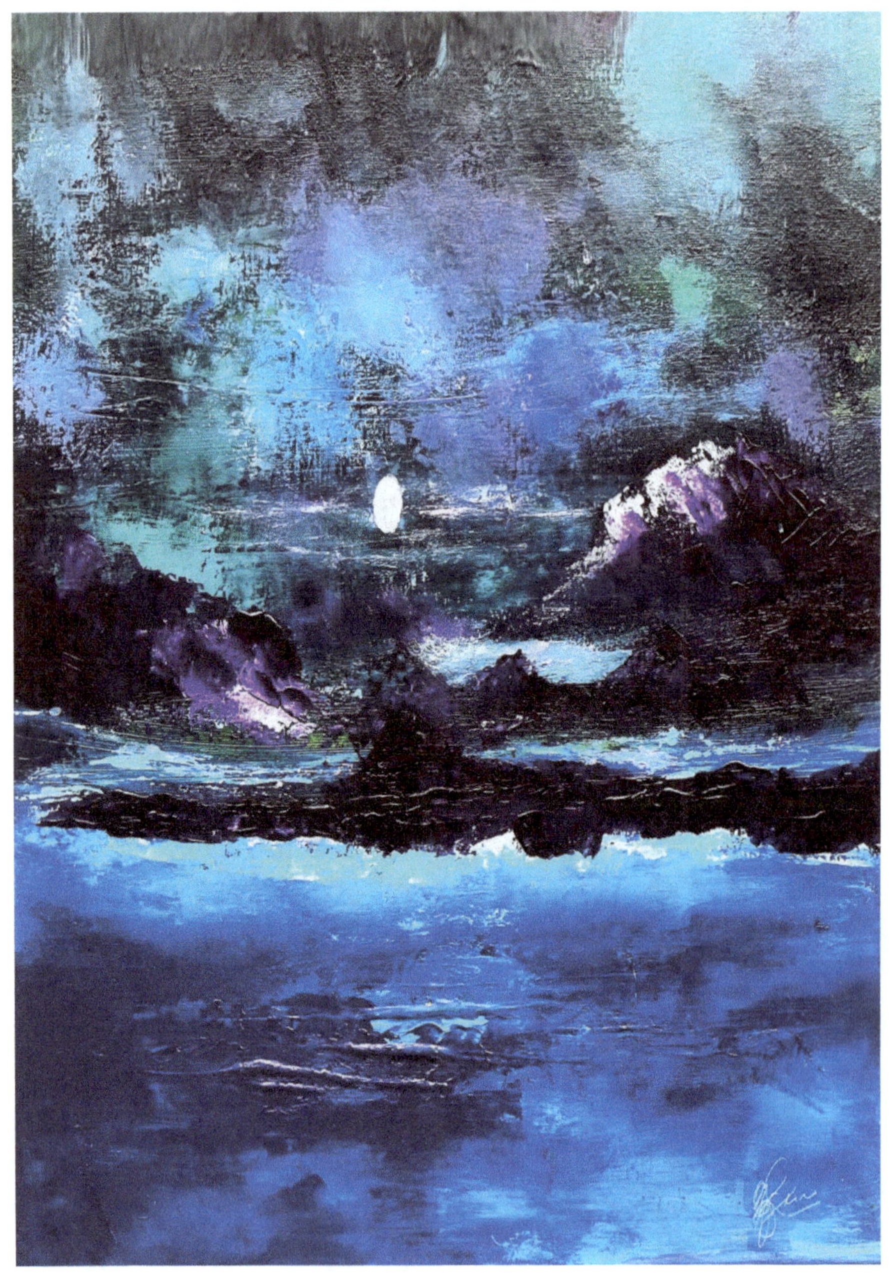

Moody Night Sky

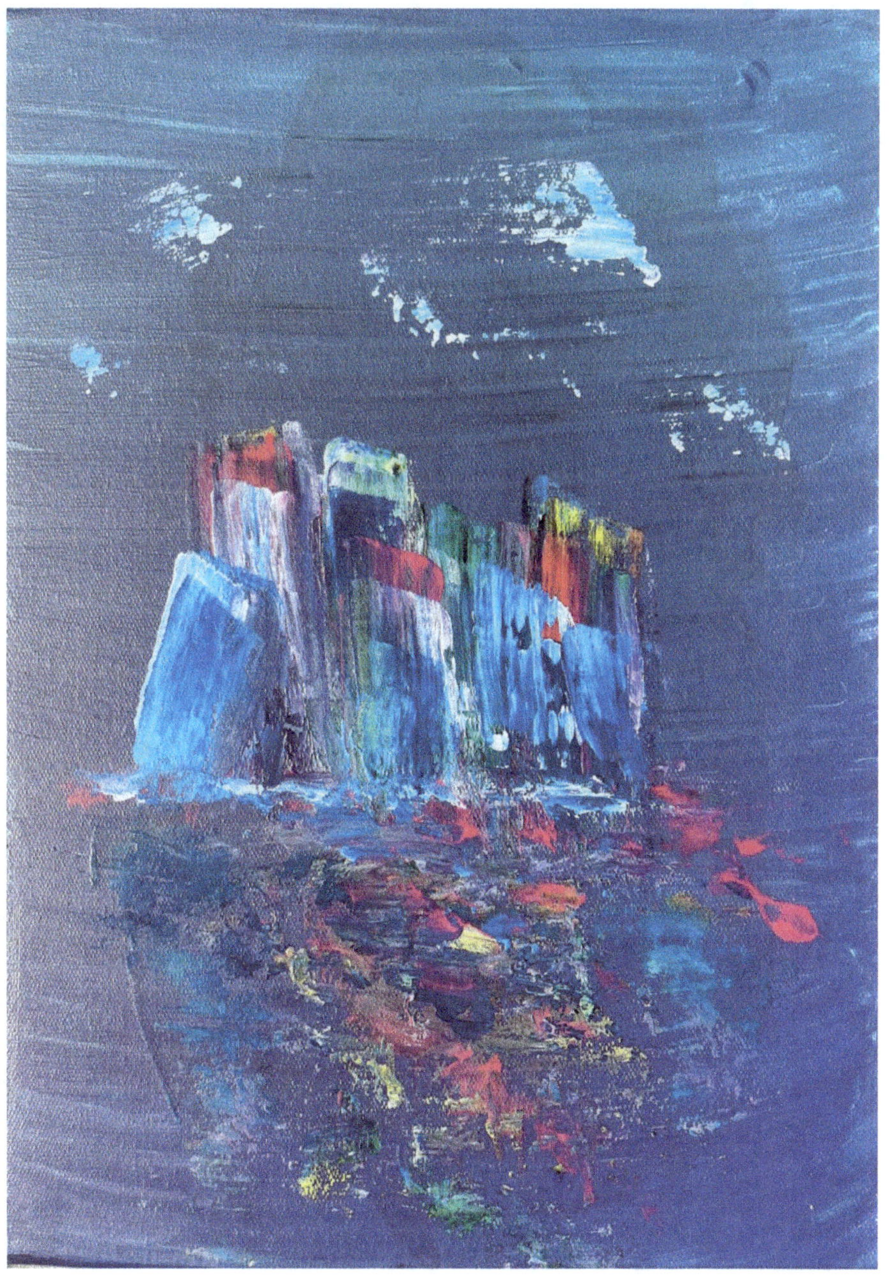

On A Painted Ocean

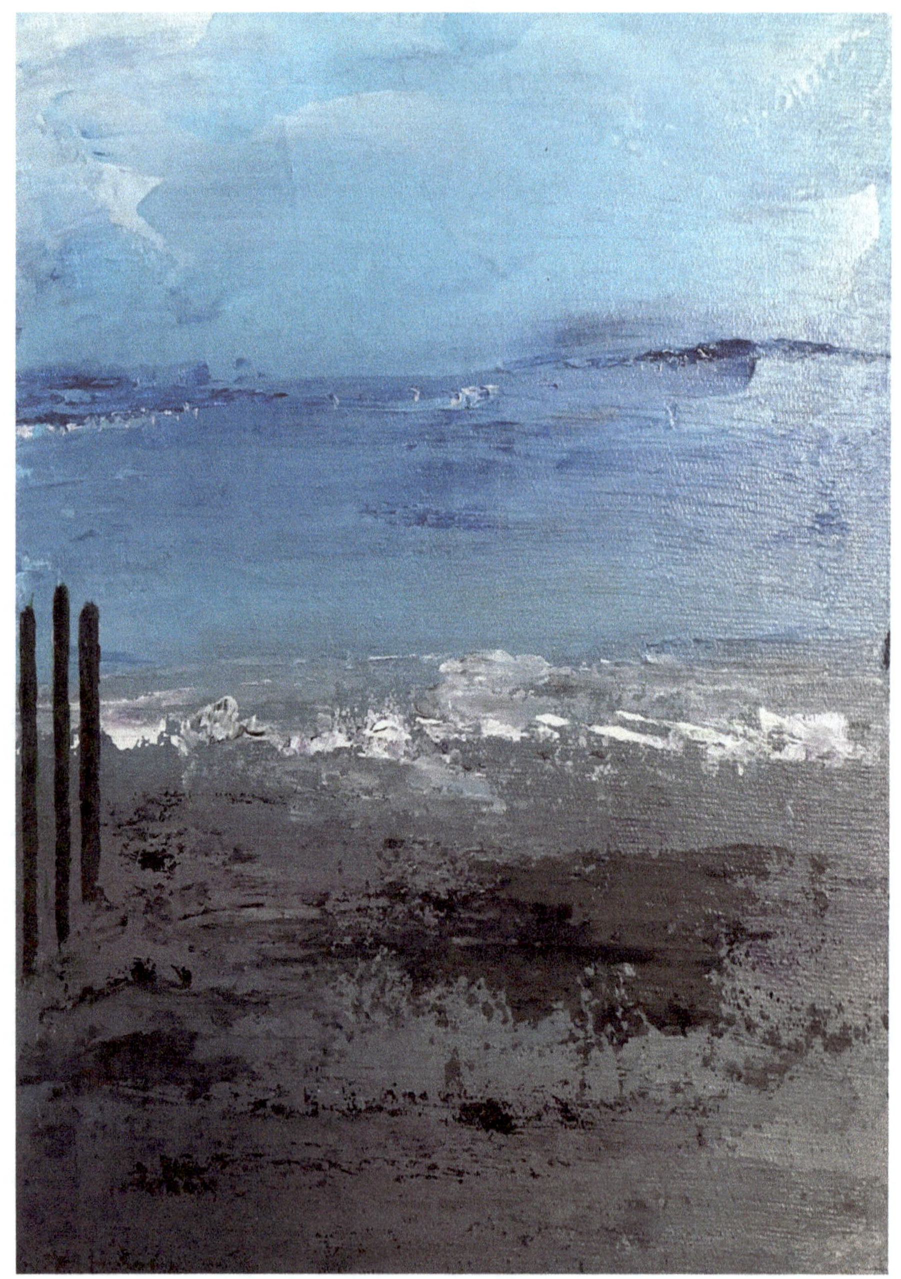

November Beach

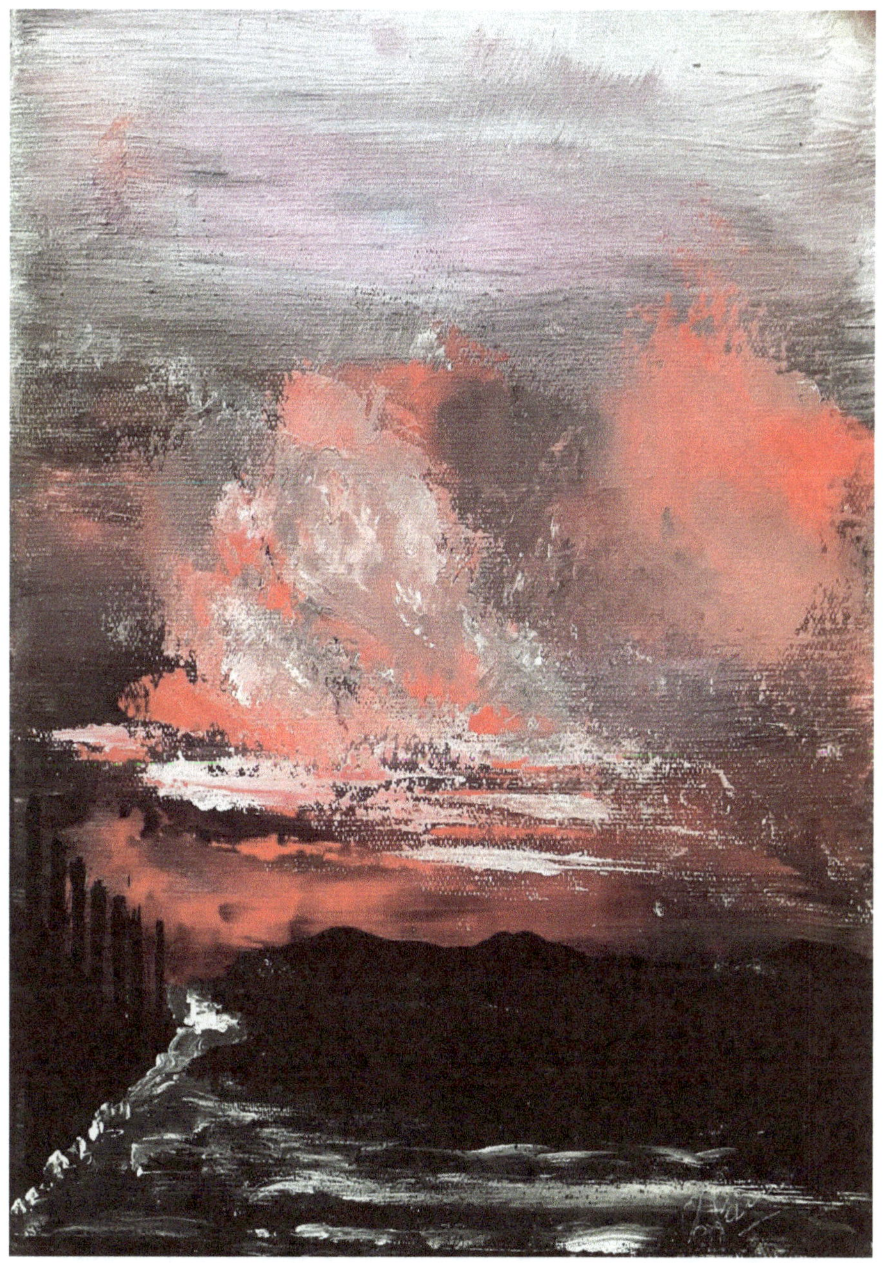

Orchestral Sky

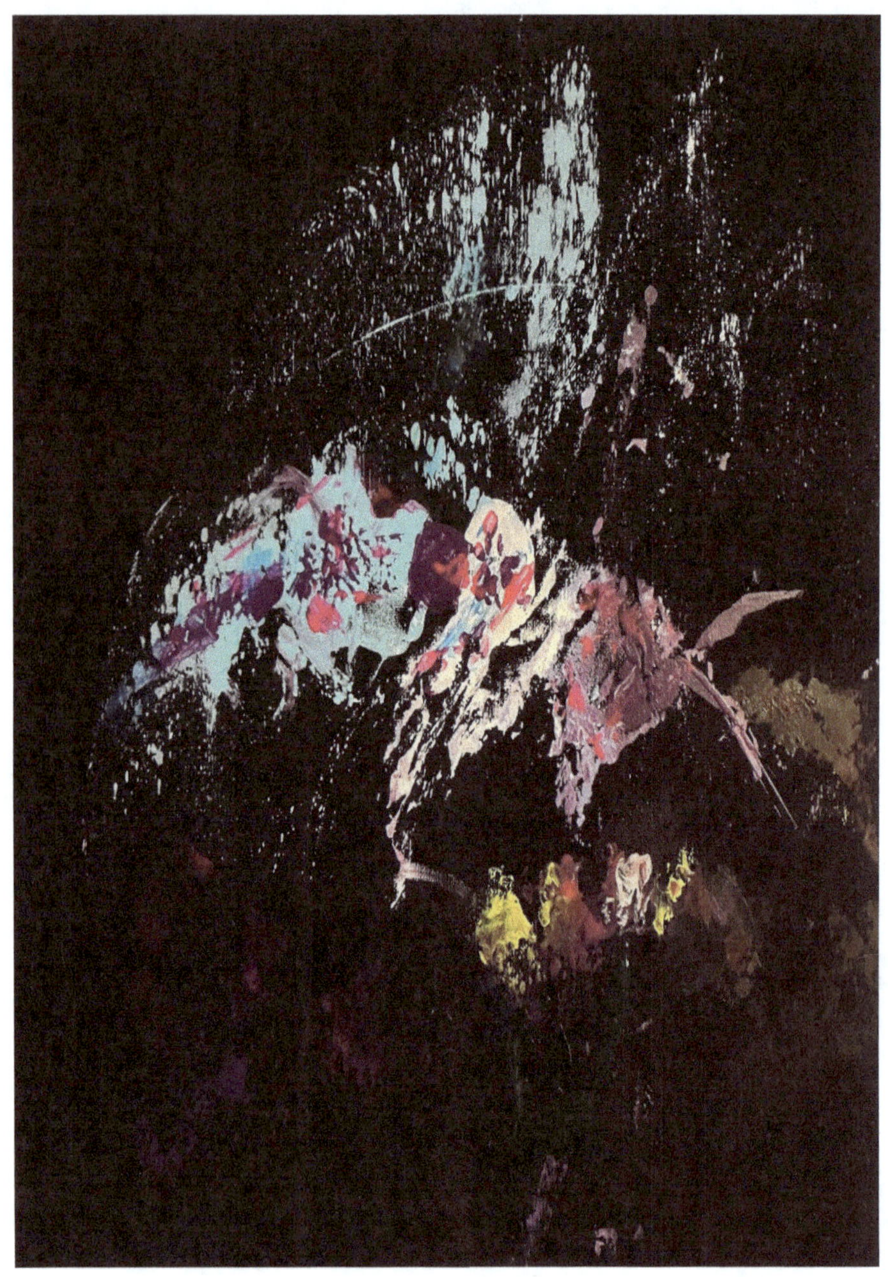

Pollination

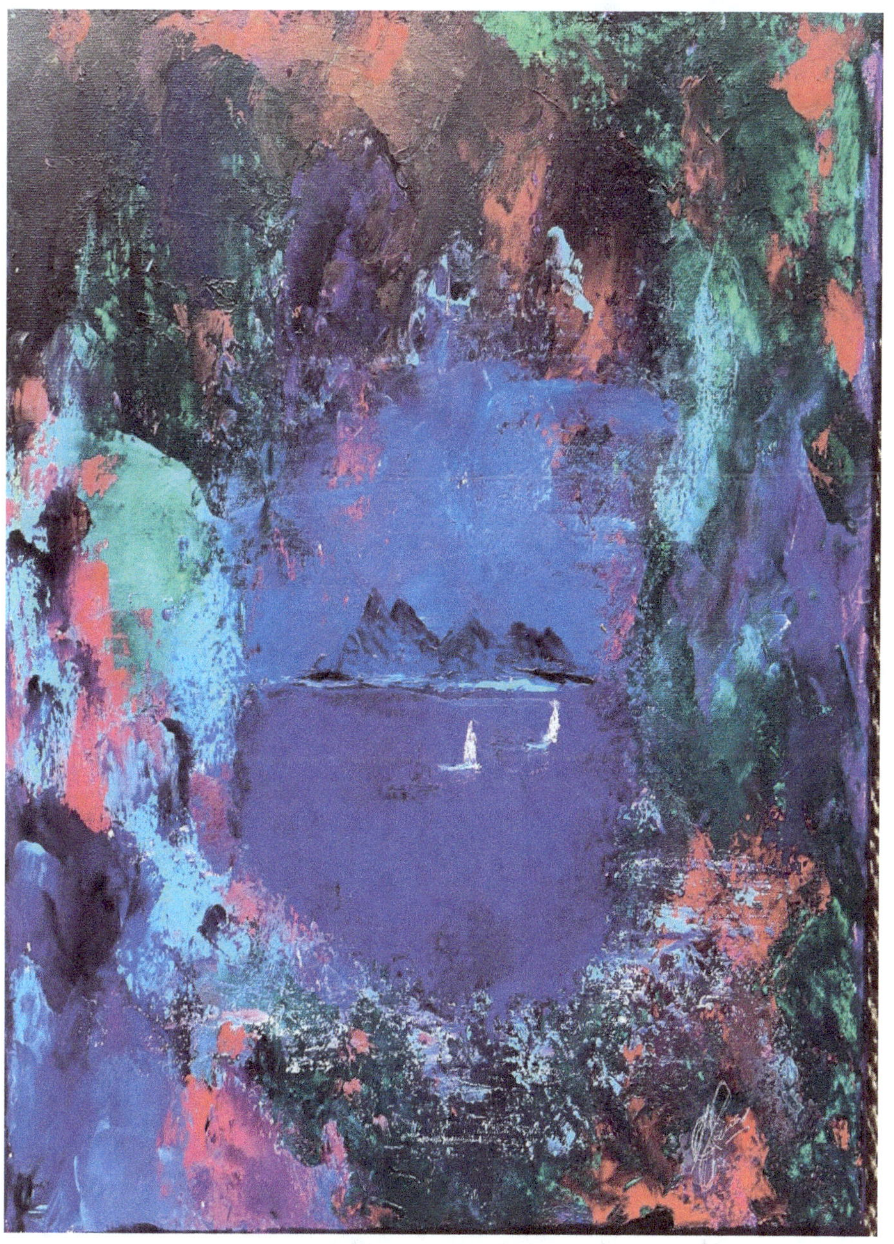

Once Upon A Dream

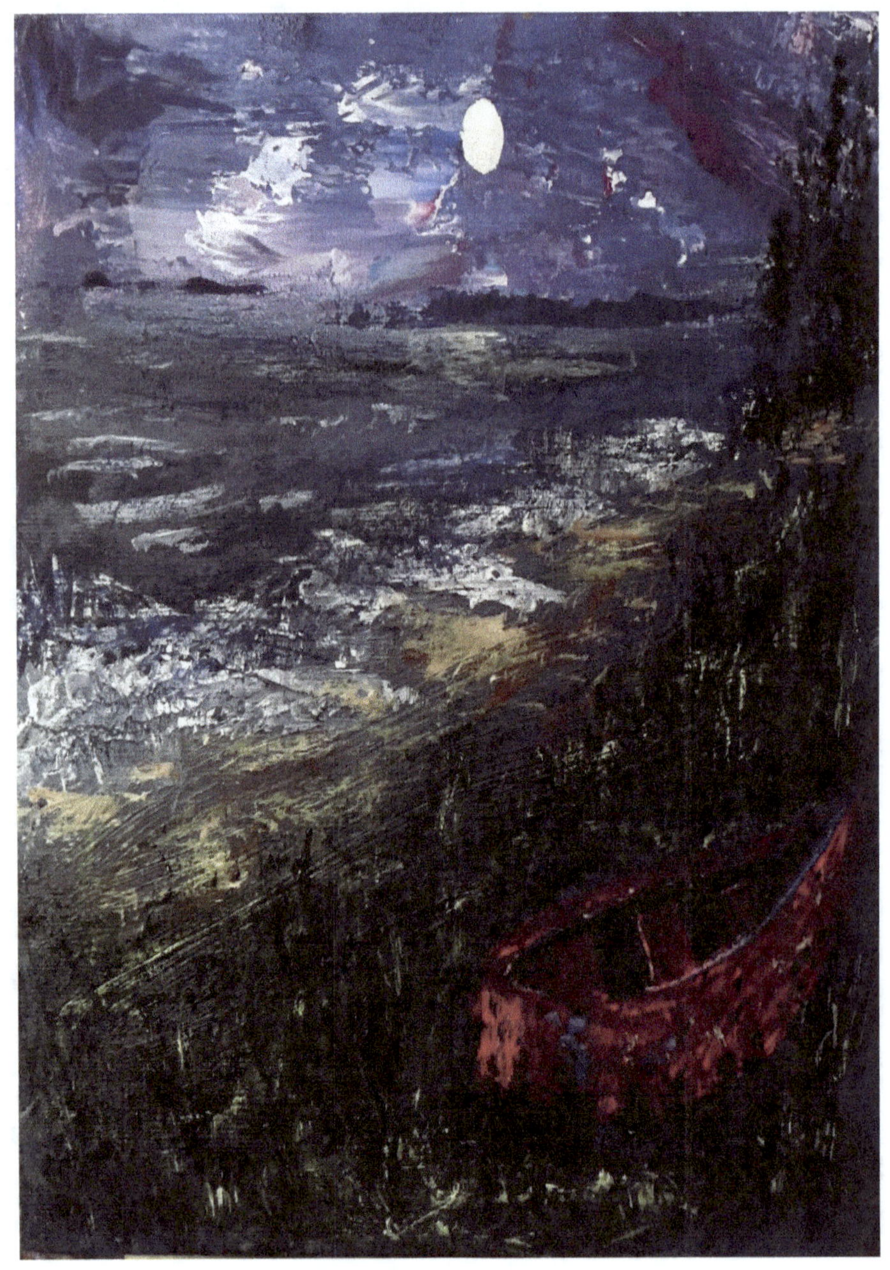

Red Rowboat

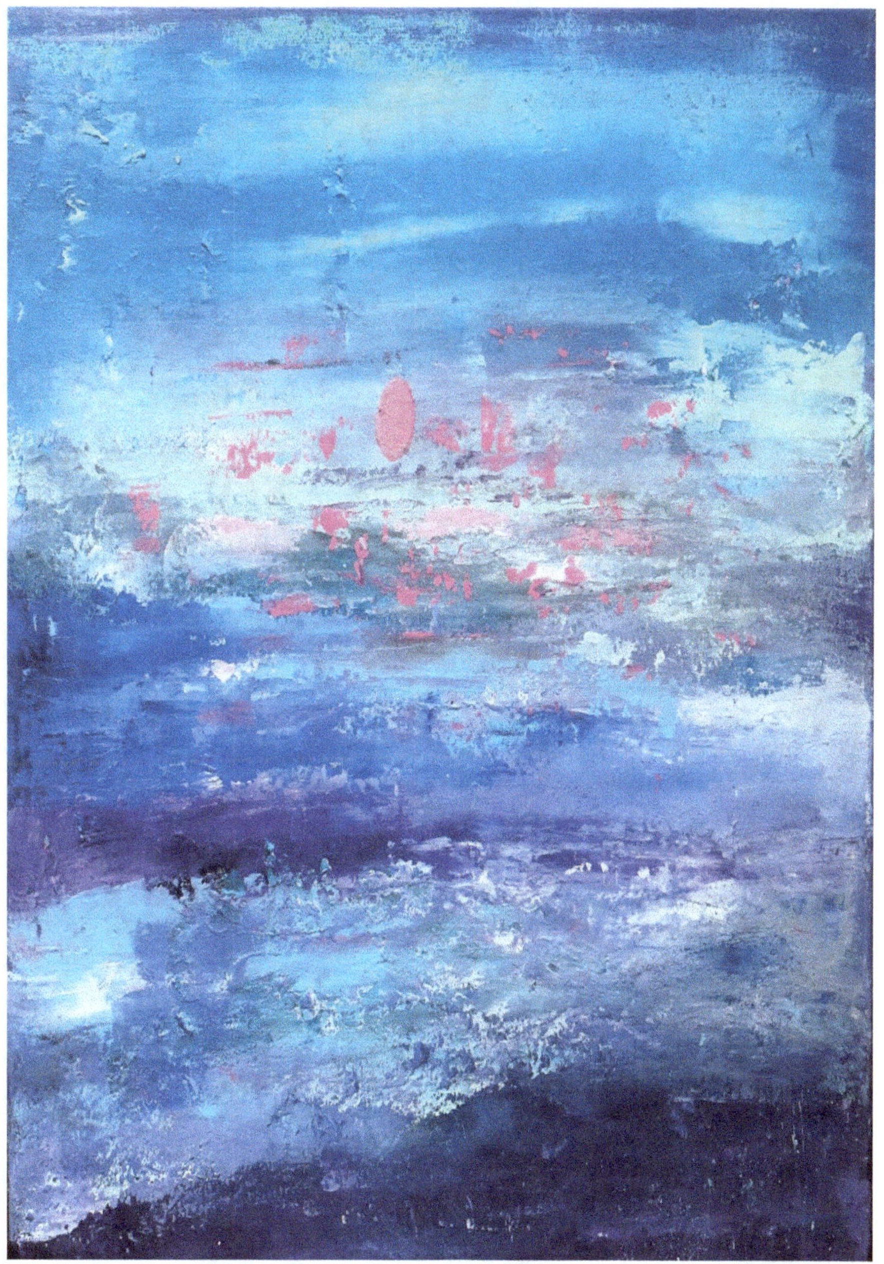

Daylight Stars Of Evidaris

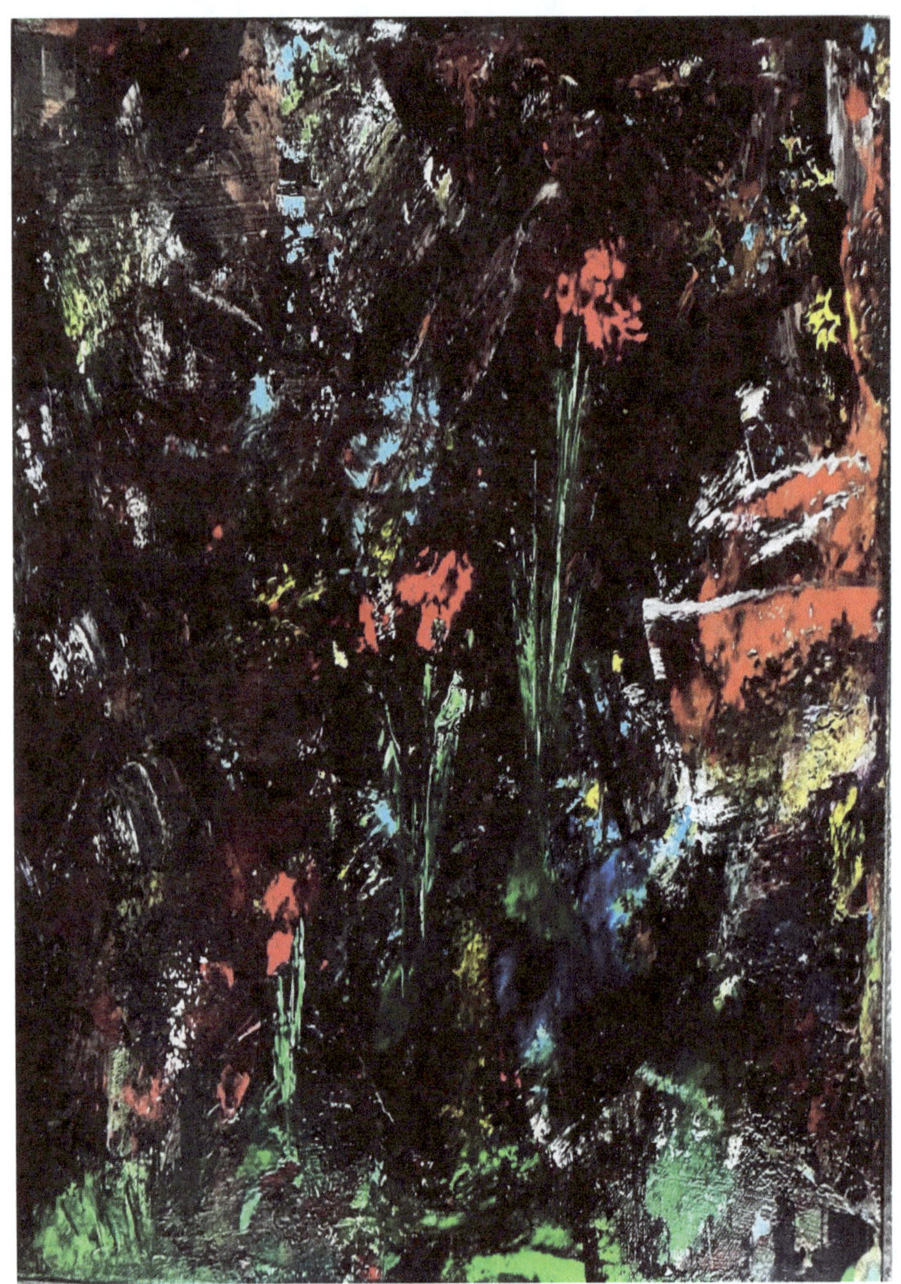

Shipyard Flowers

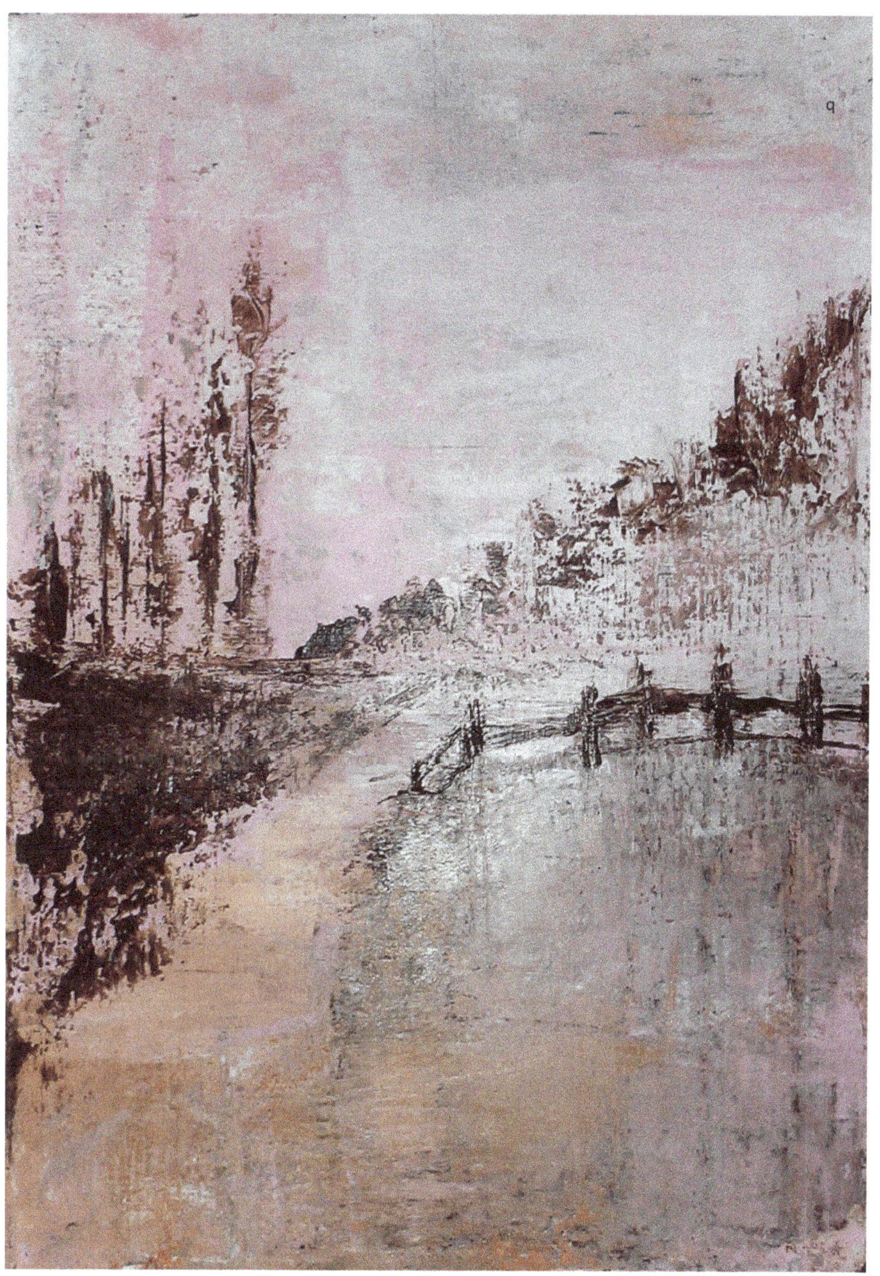

A Silence Of Echoes

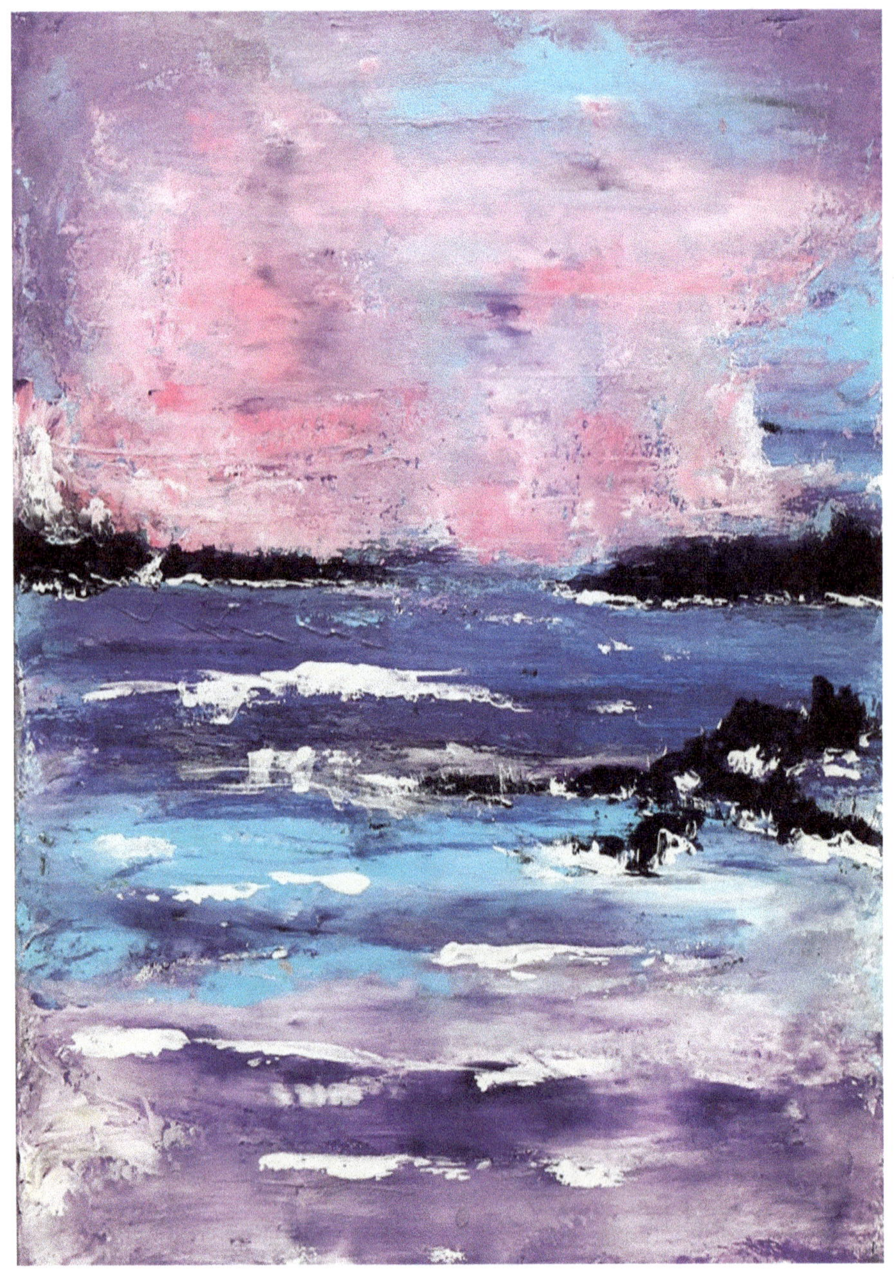

Sky Pastels

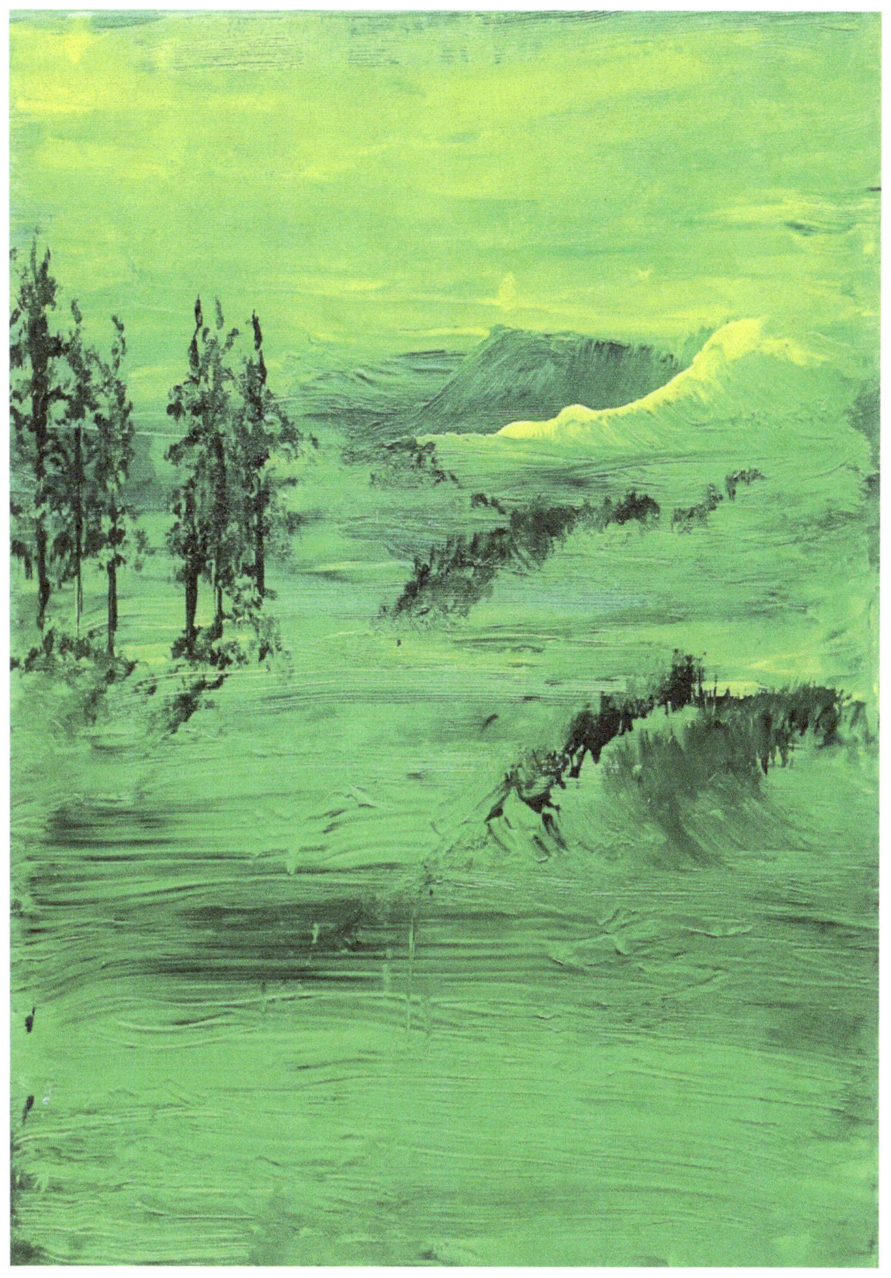

So Green My Valley

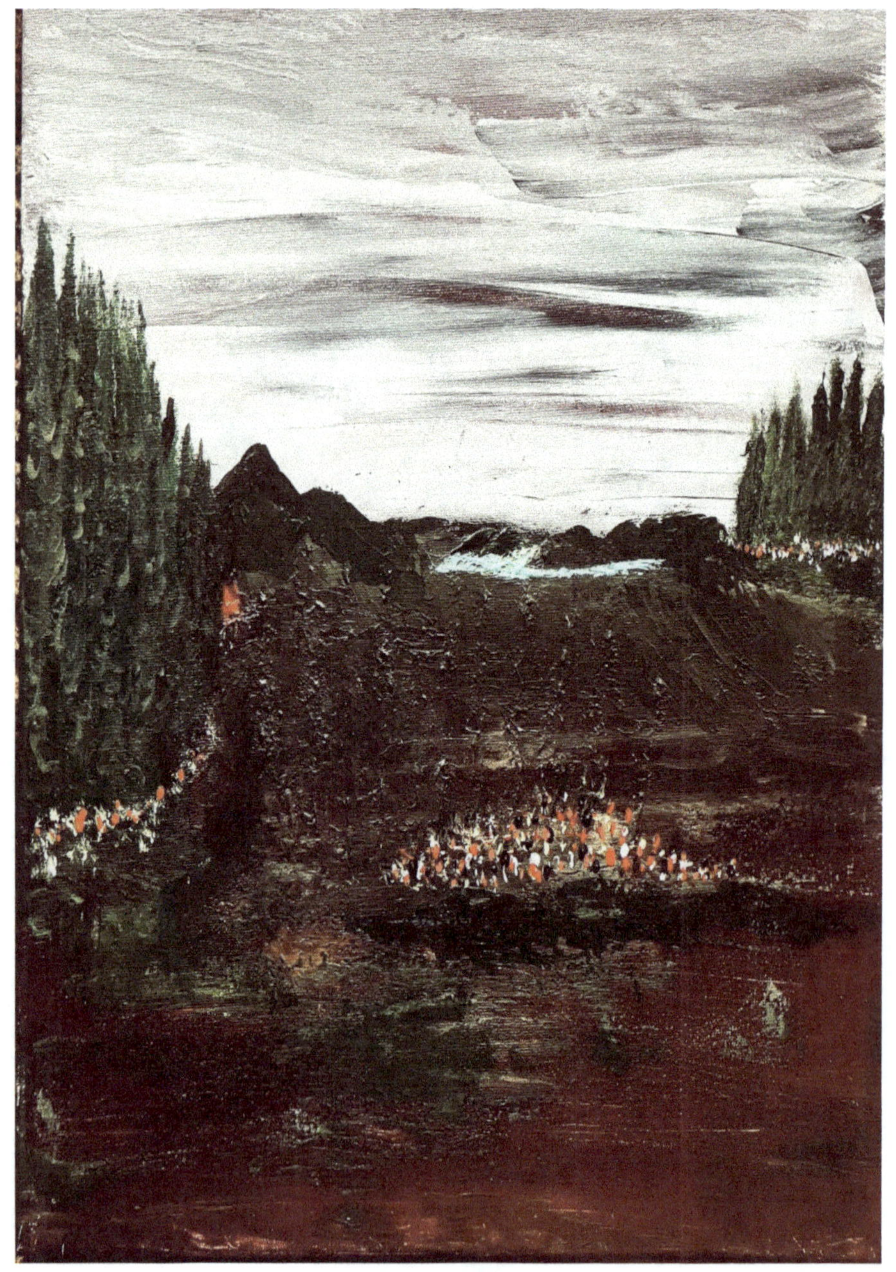

Spring On The Hill

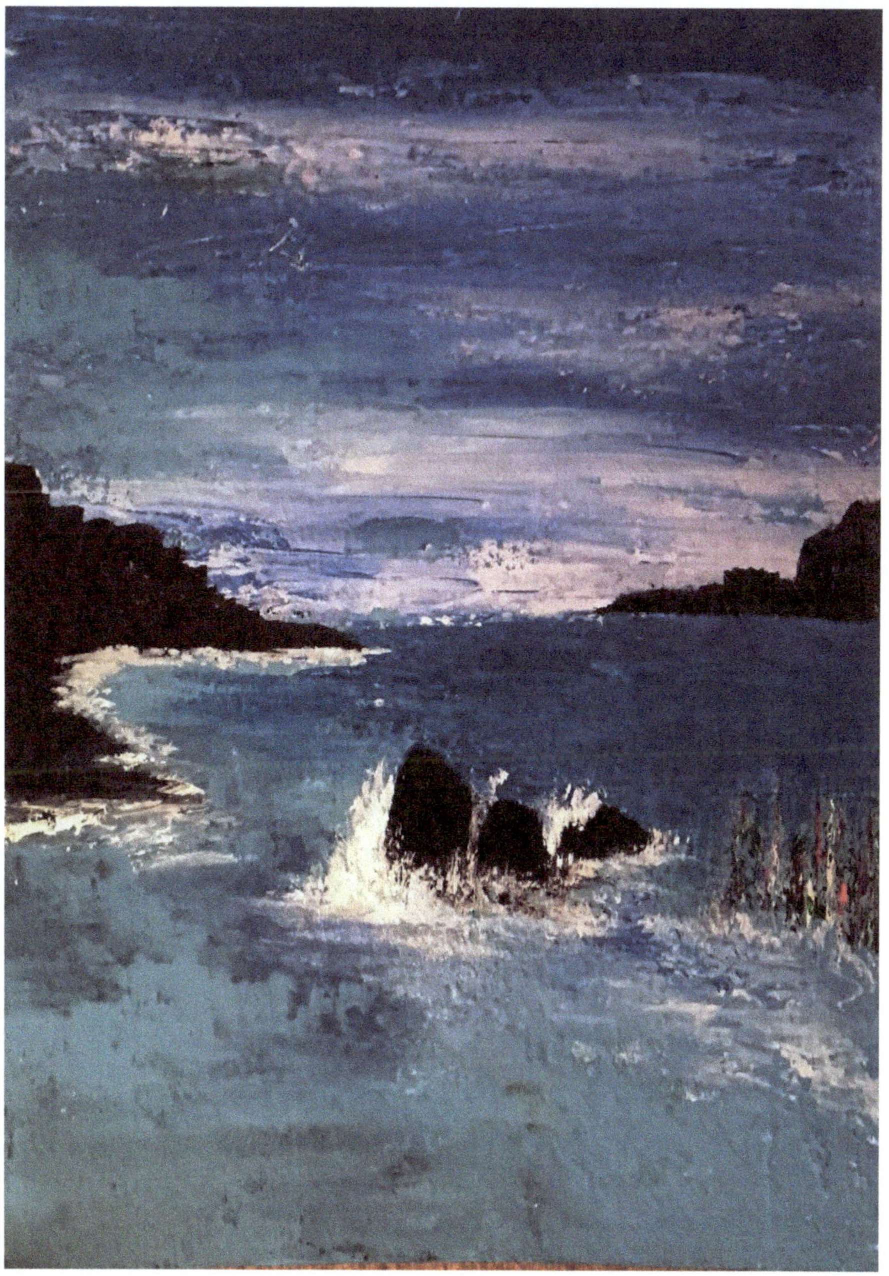

Rock Crescent

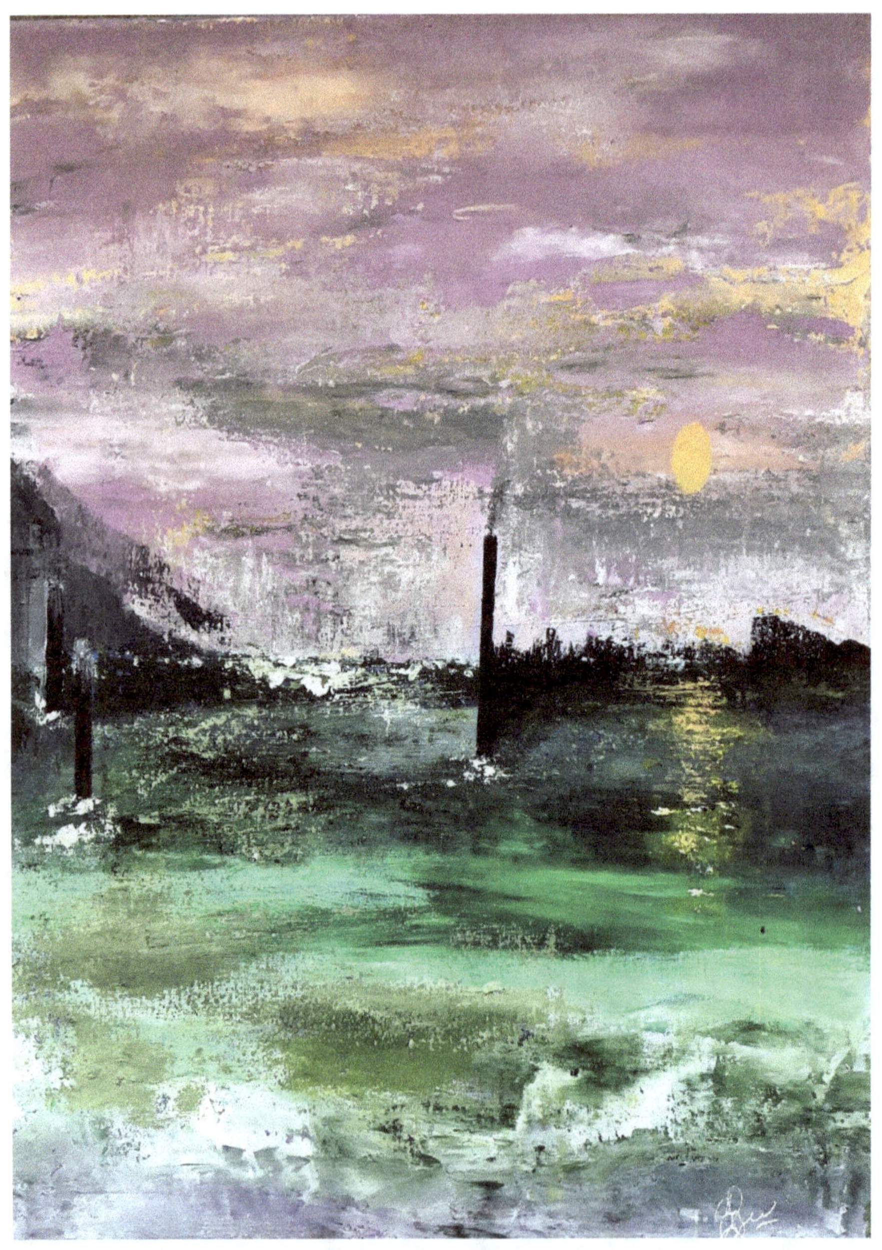

Industrial Revolution
Liverpool circa 1898

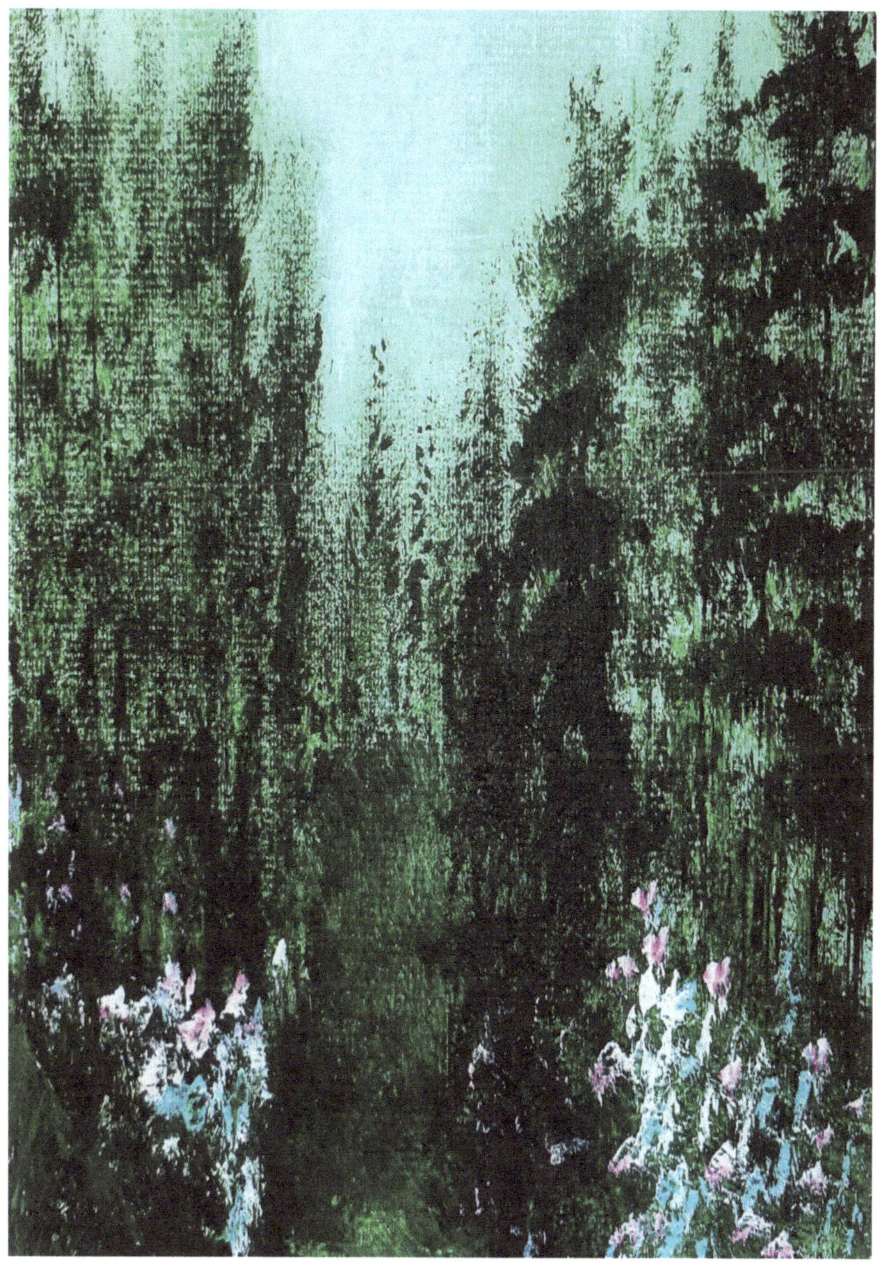

Summer Evening Stroll

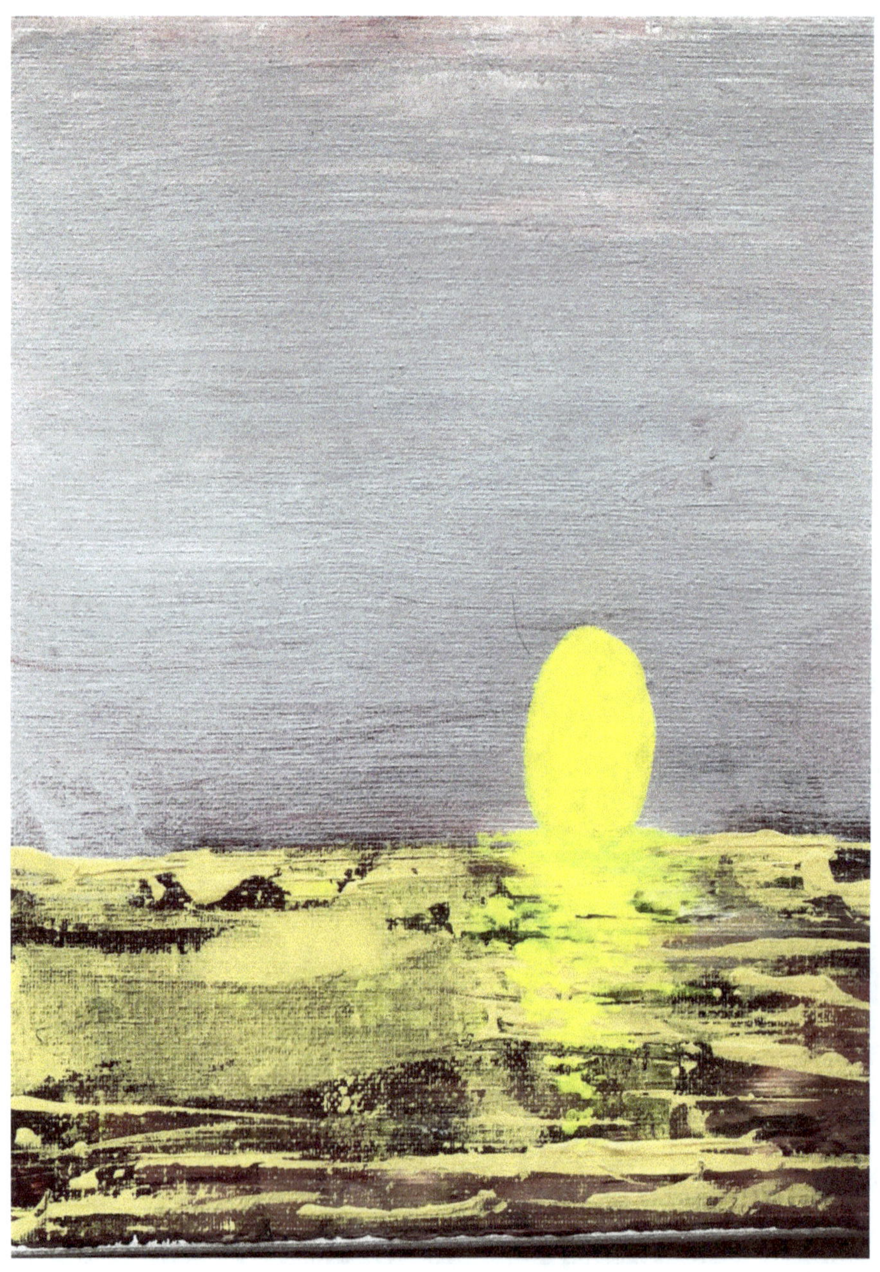

Sun Down

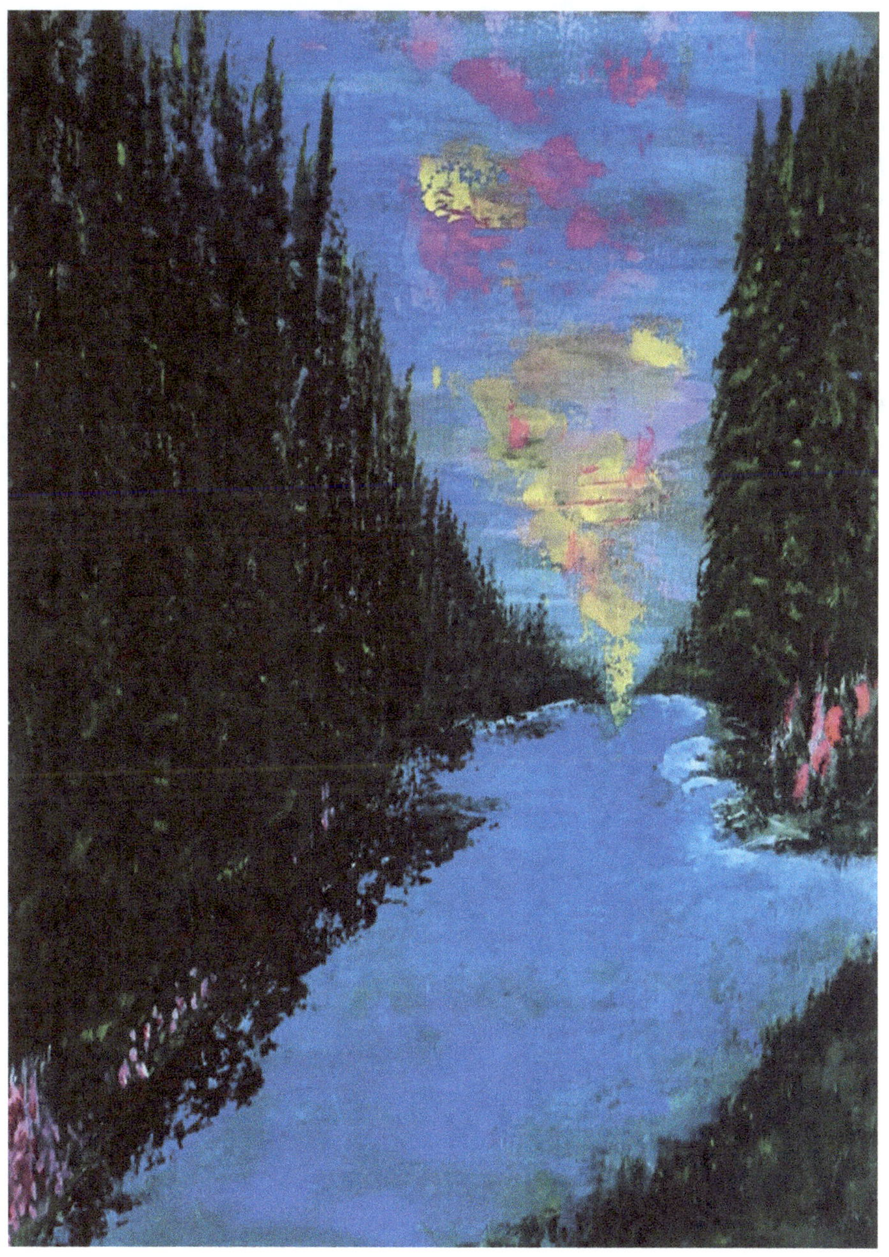

Sun Drill Down

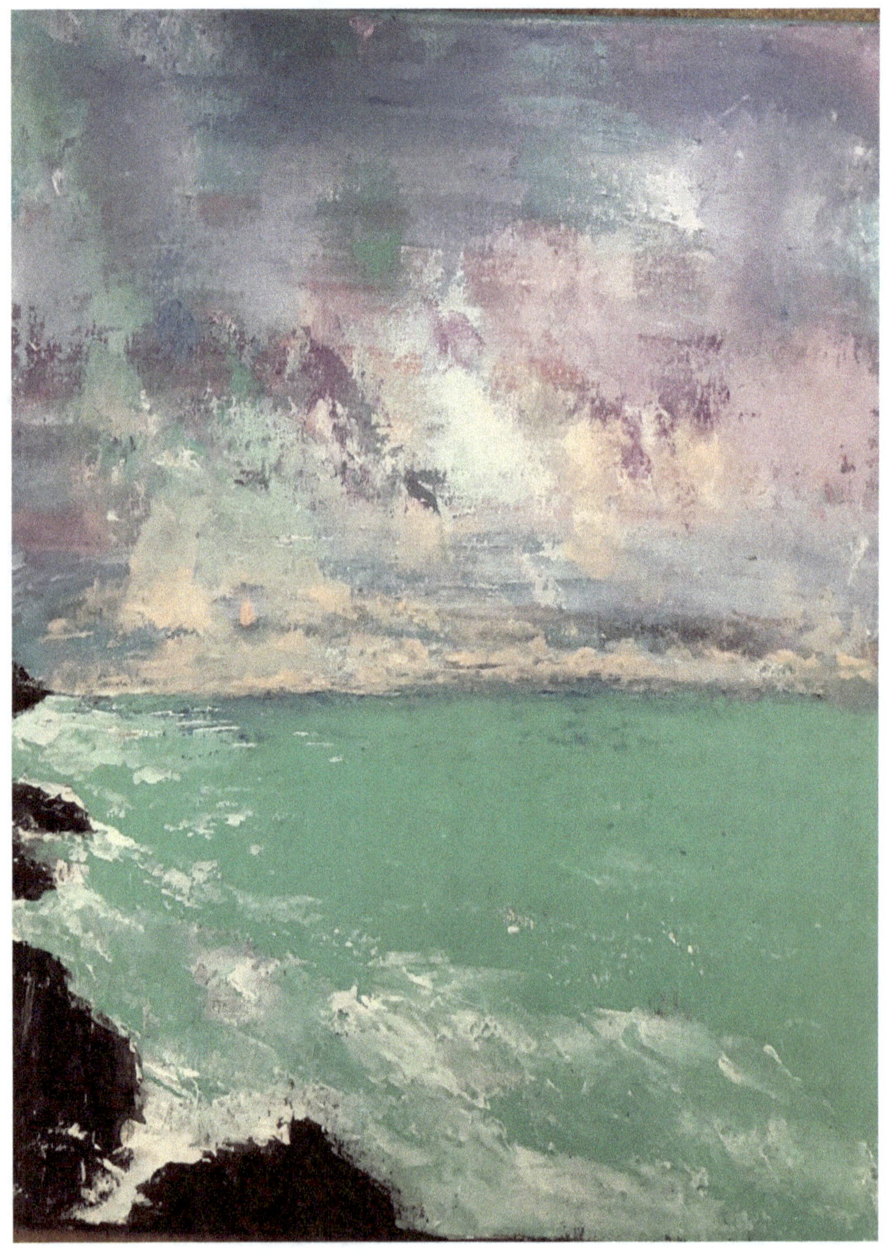

Sun Fog

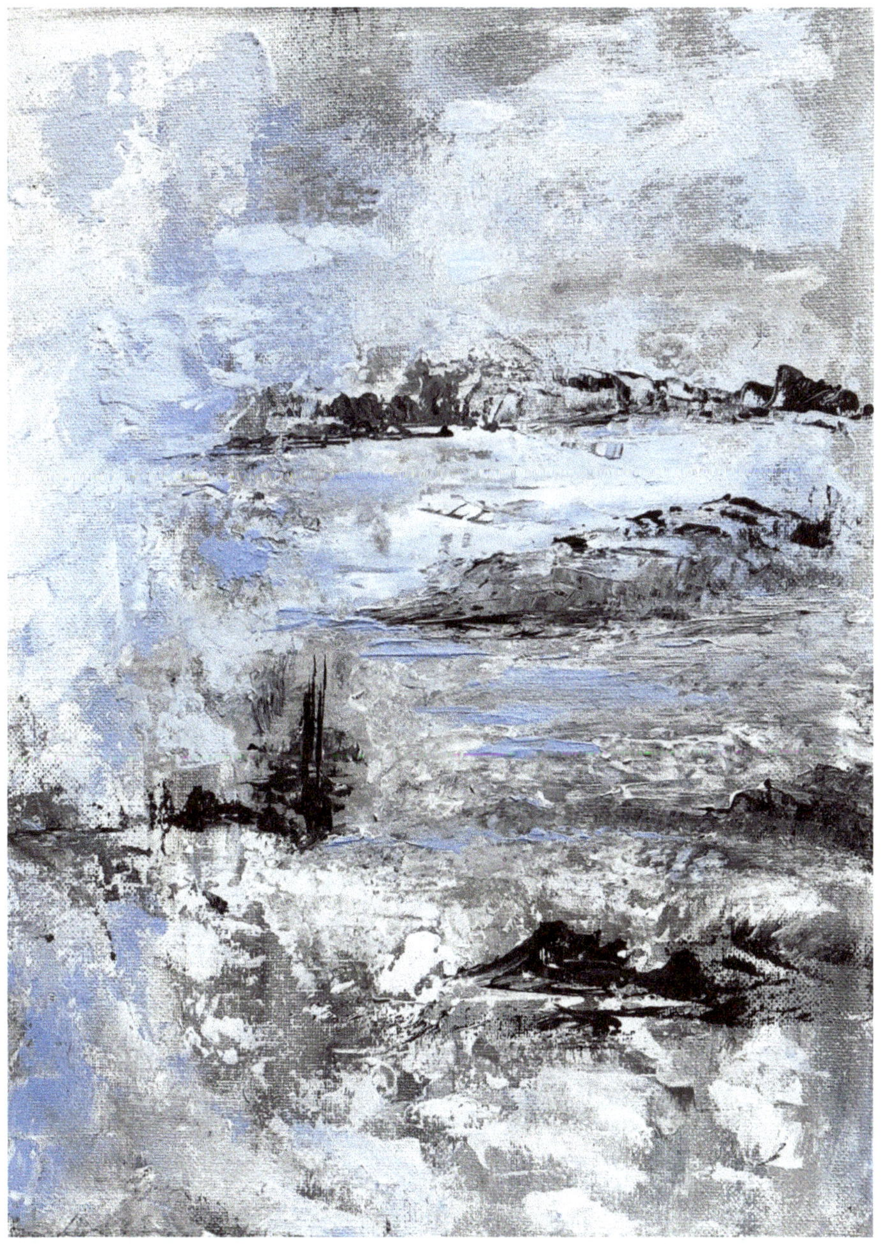

Navigating 'The Harbor

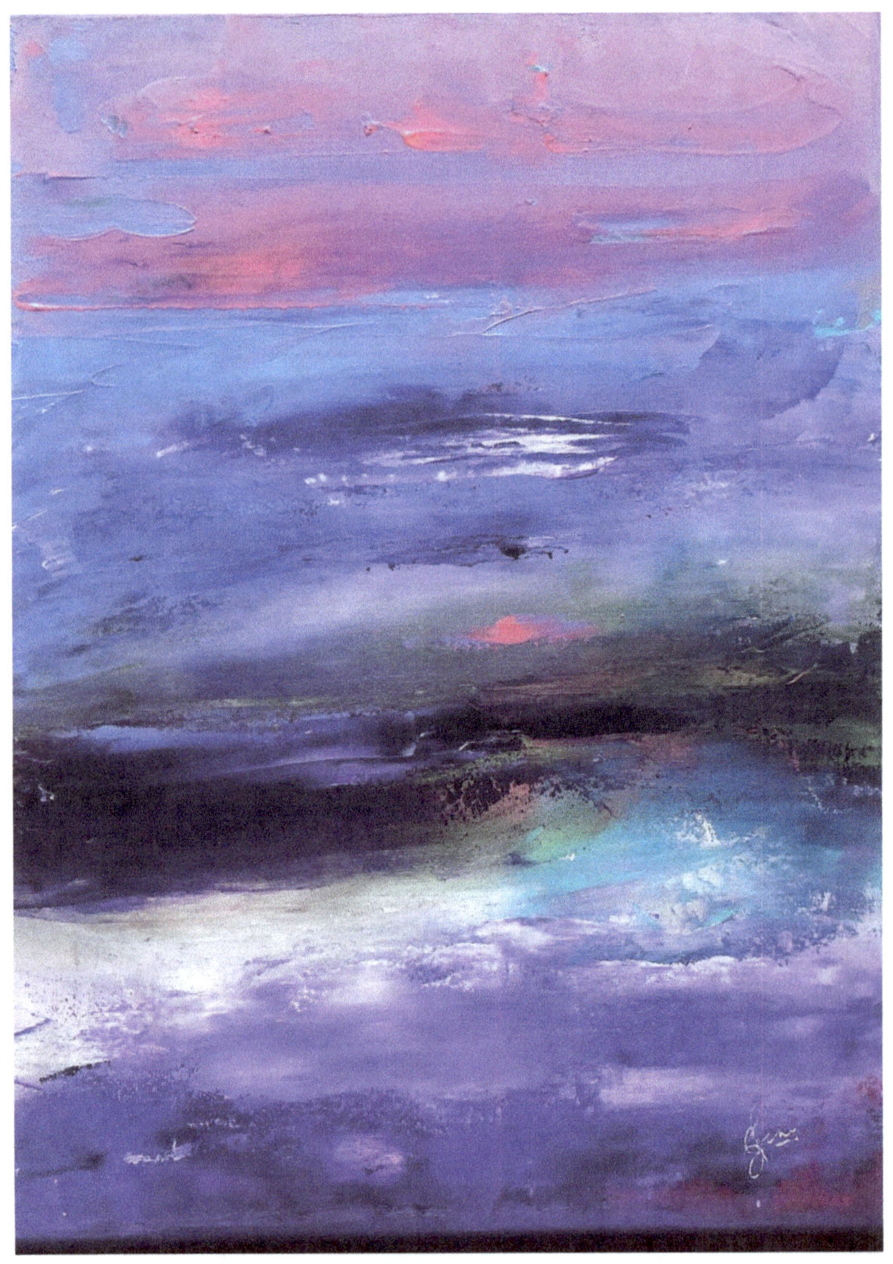

High Plains Oasis

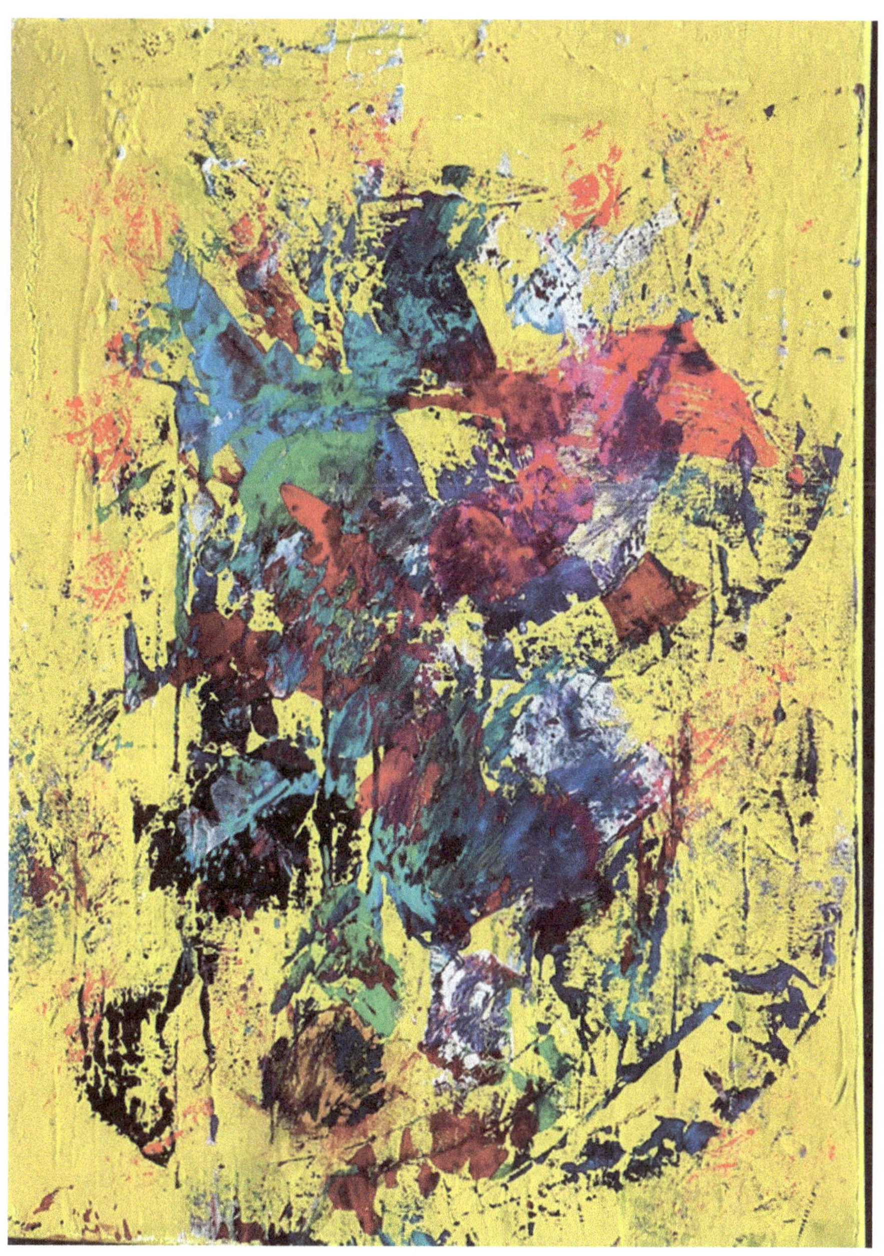

Rocking Horse Dreams

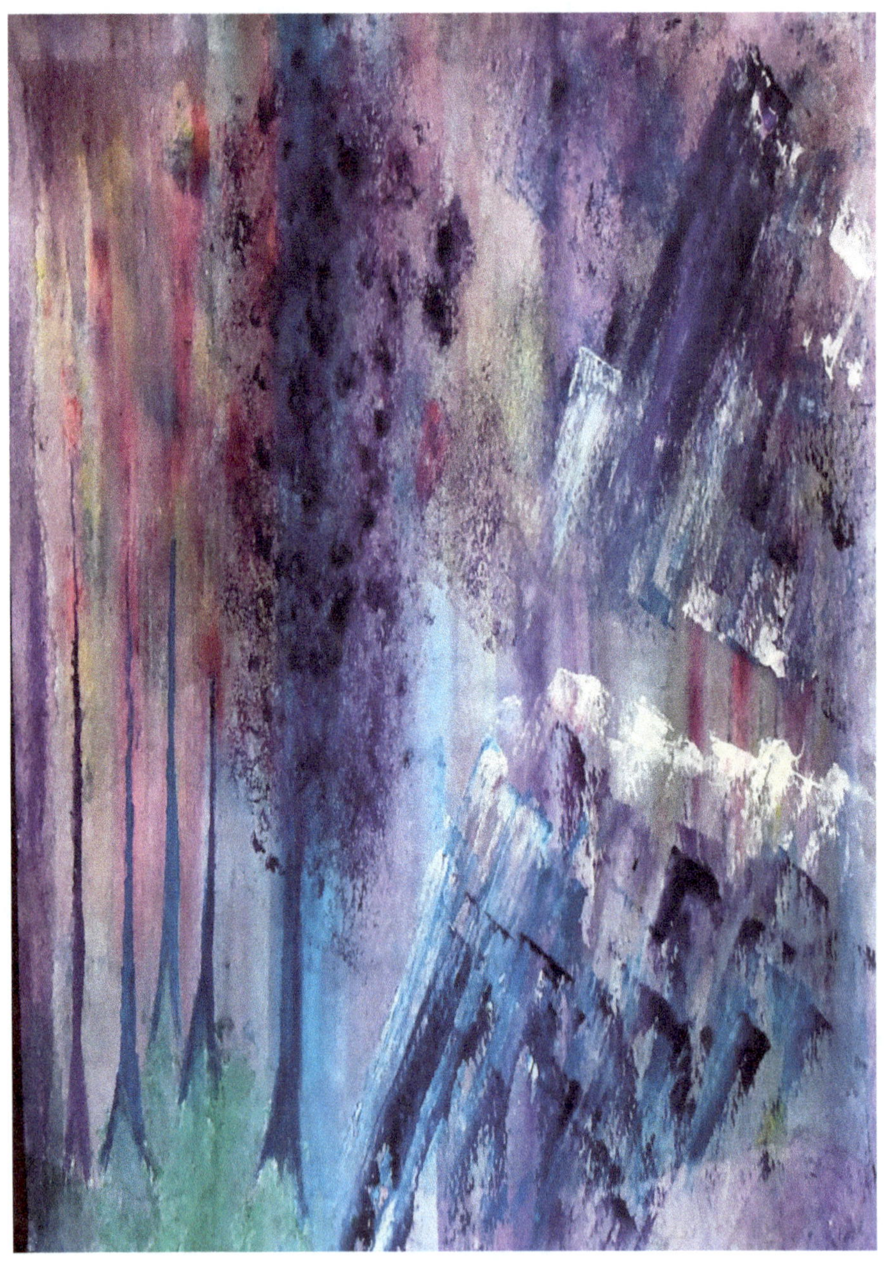

The Parrot and the Mulberry Tree

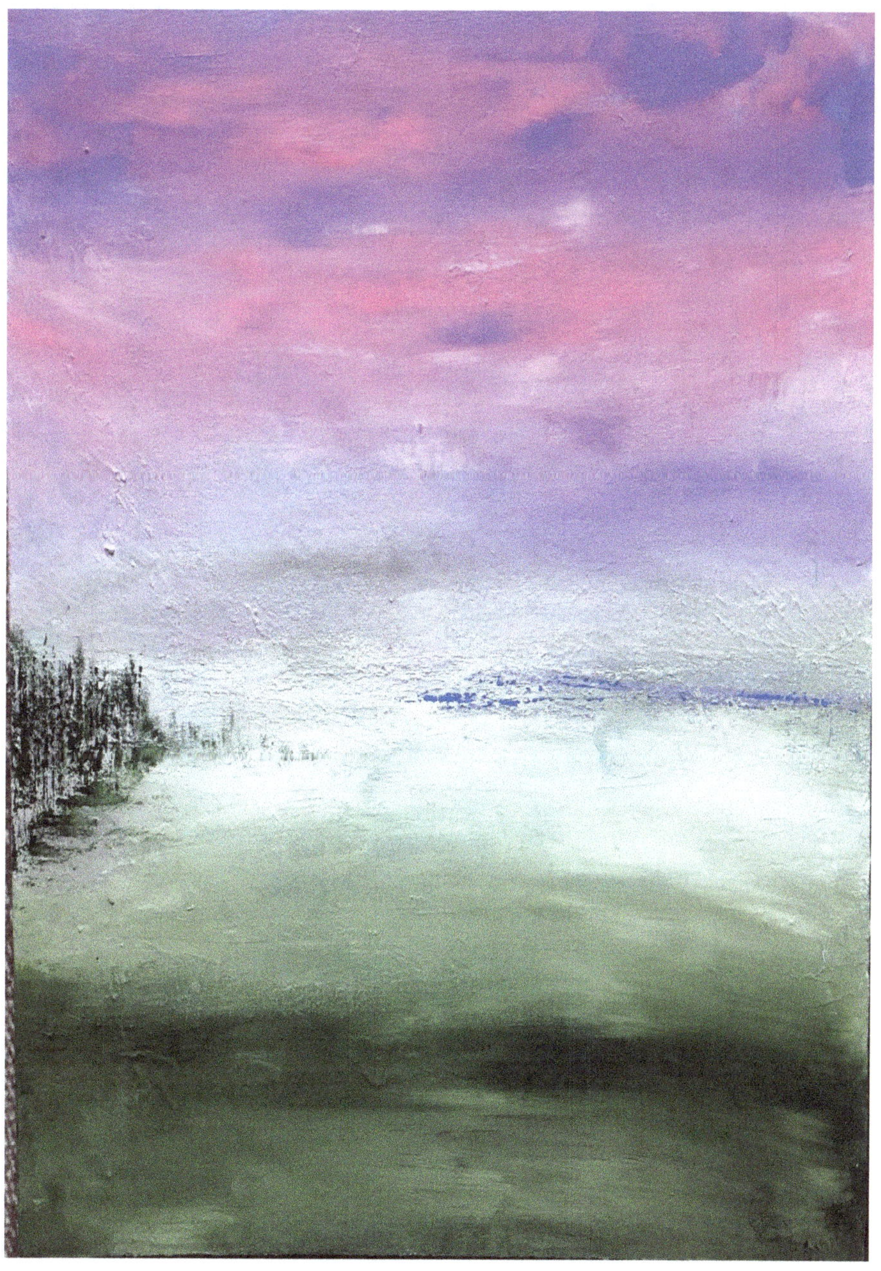

Morning Mist

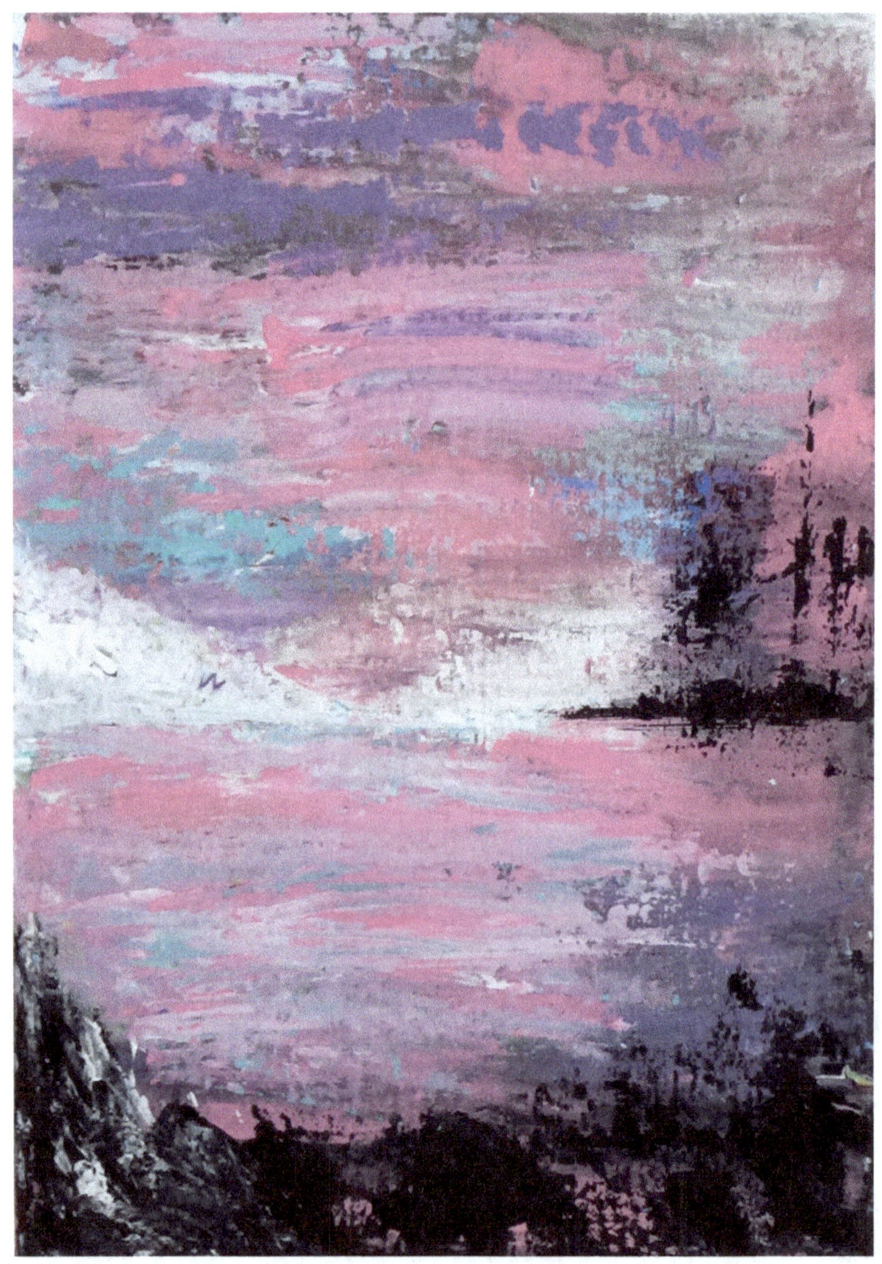

Aglow

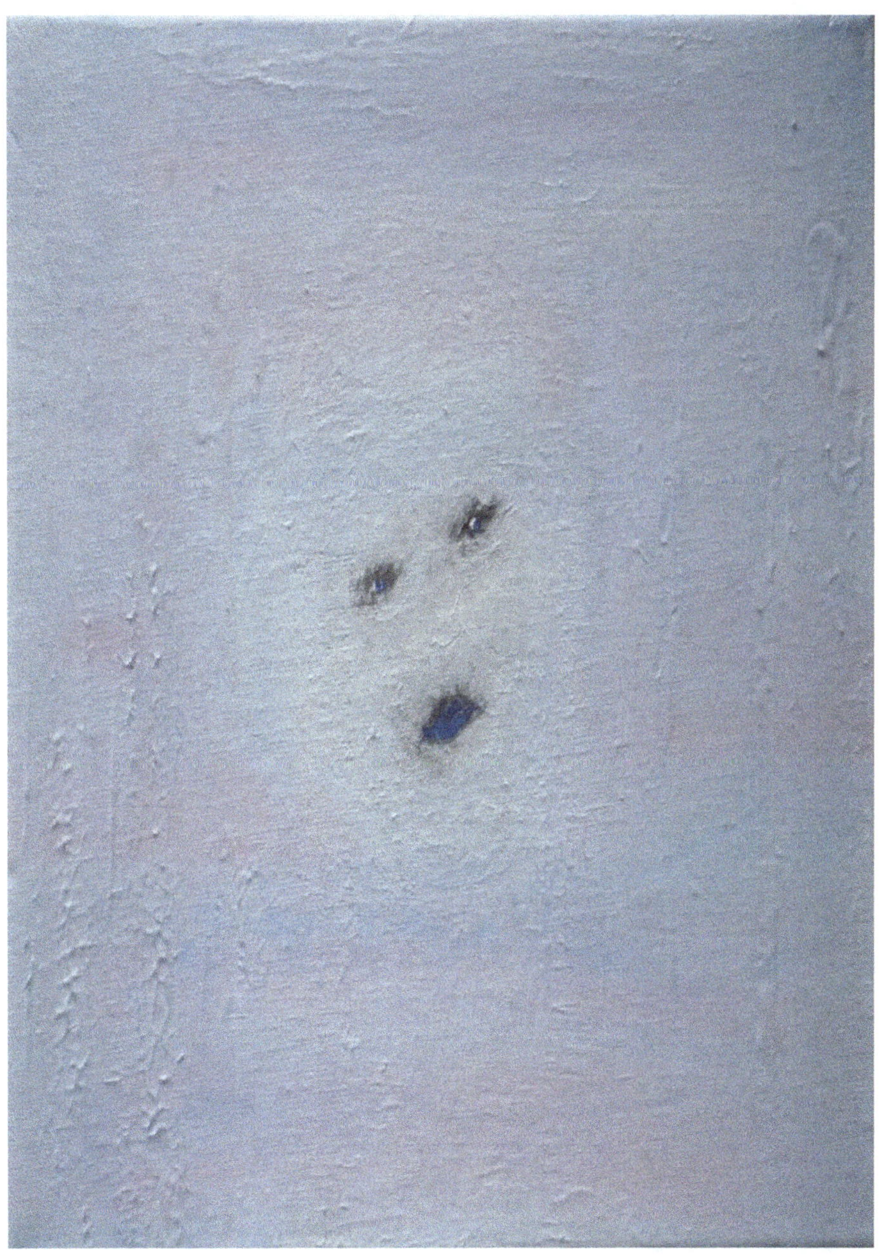

Seeing Through

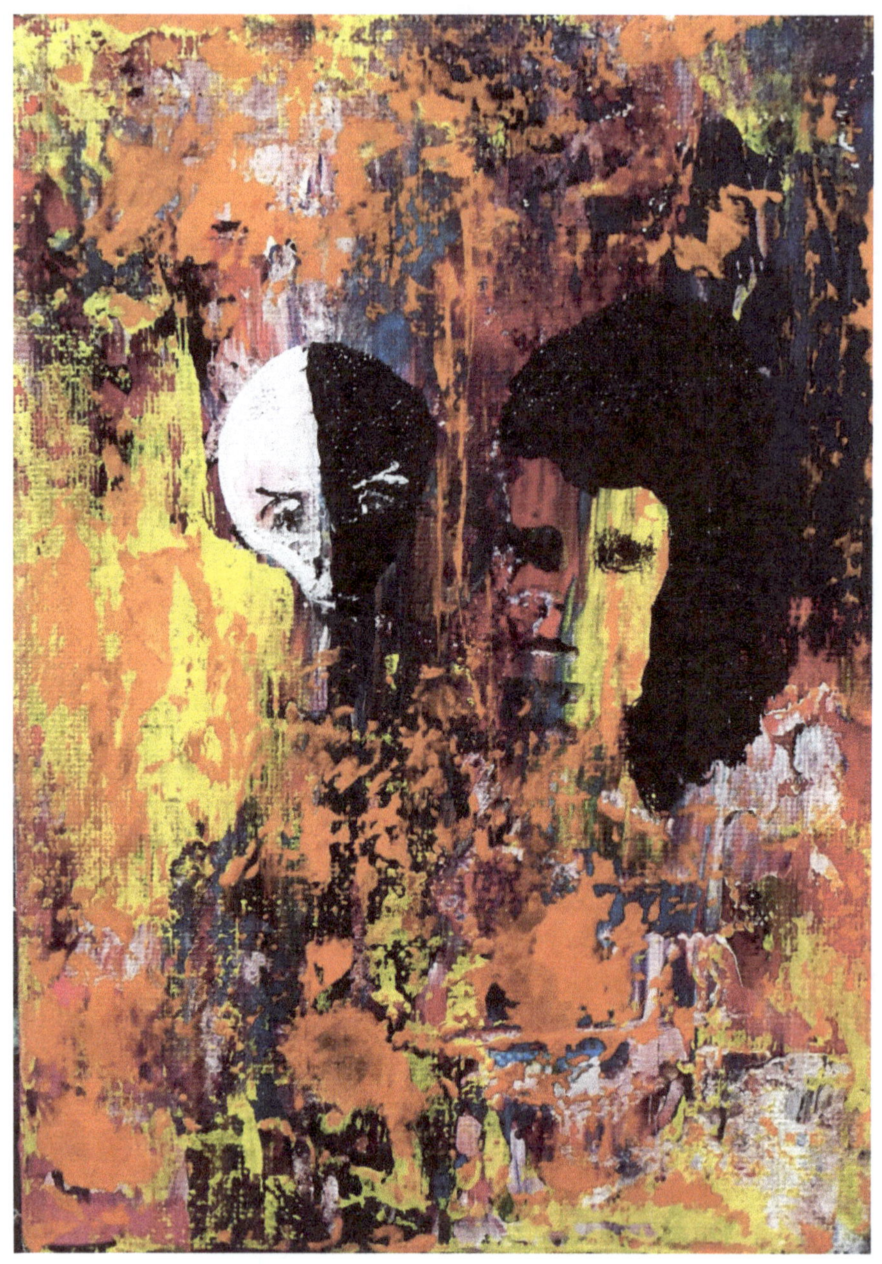

Unmasked

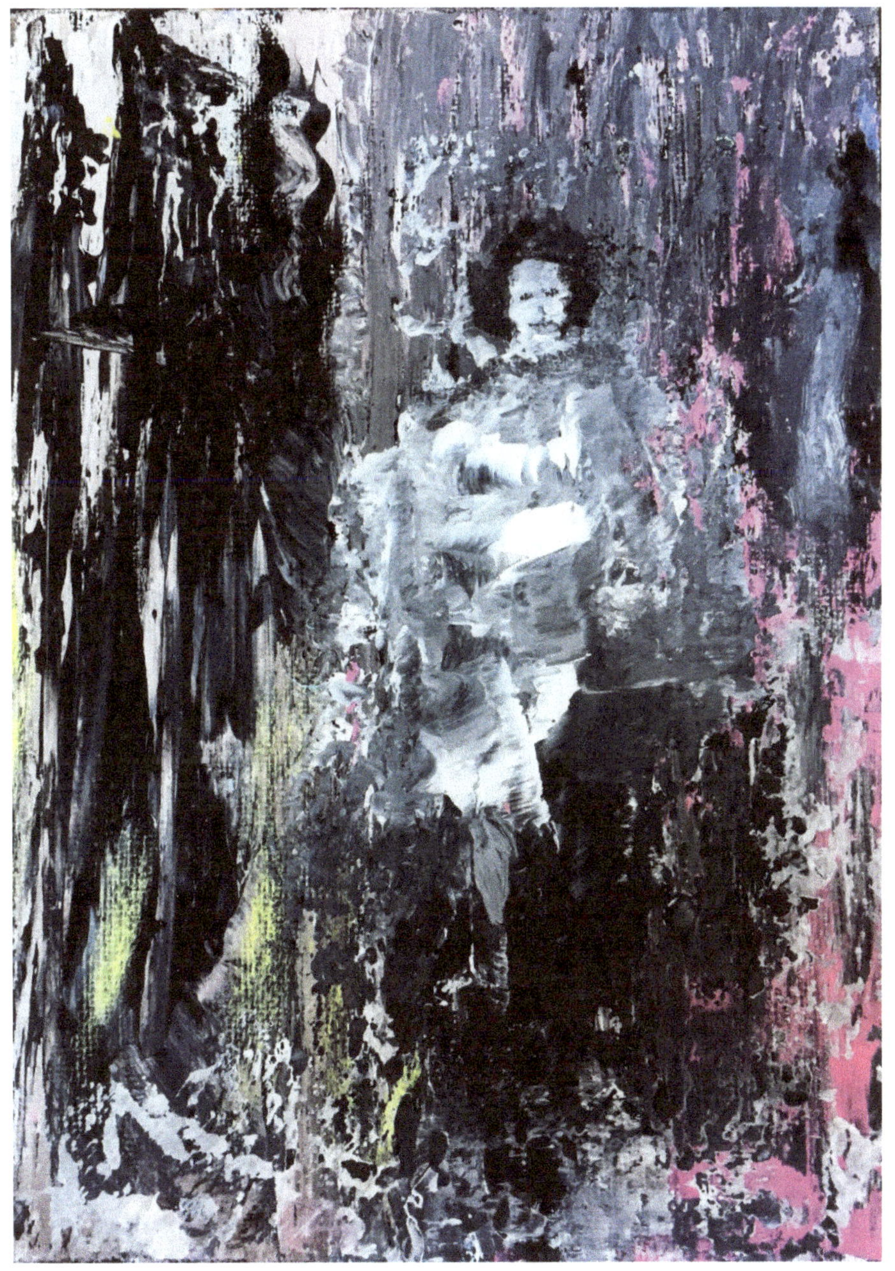

The Dancer And The Watchers

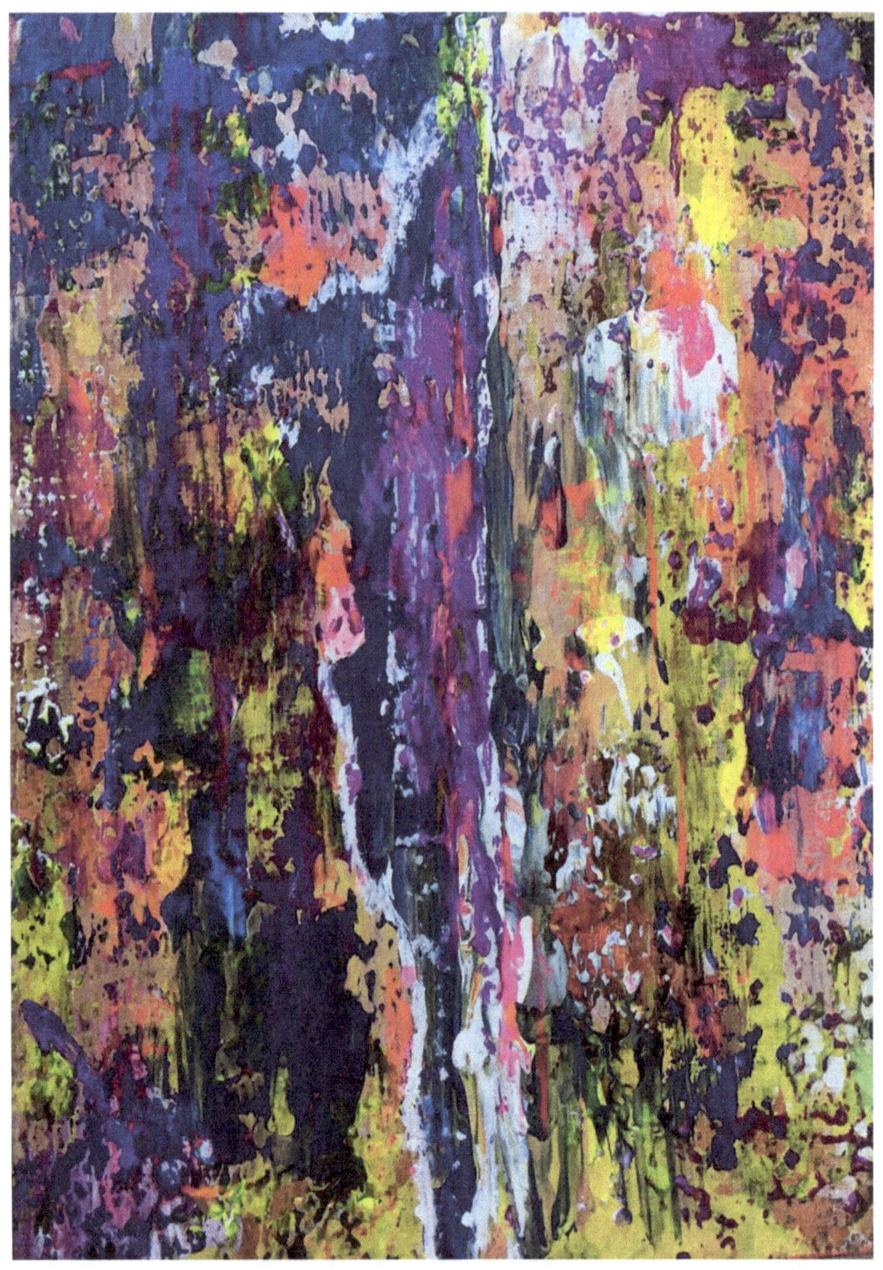

Leaving The Past Behind

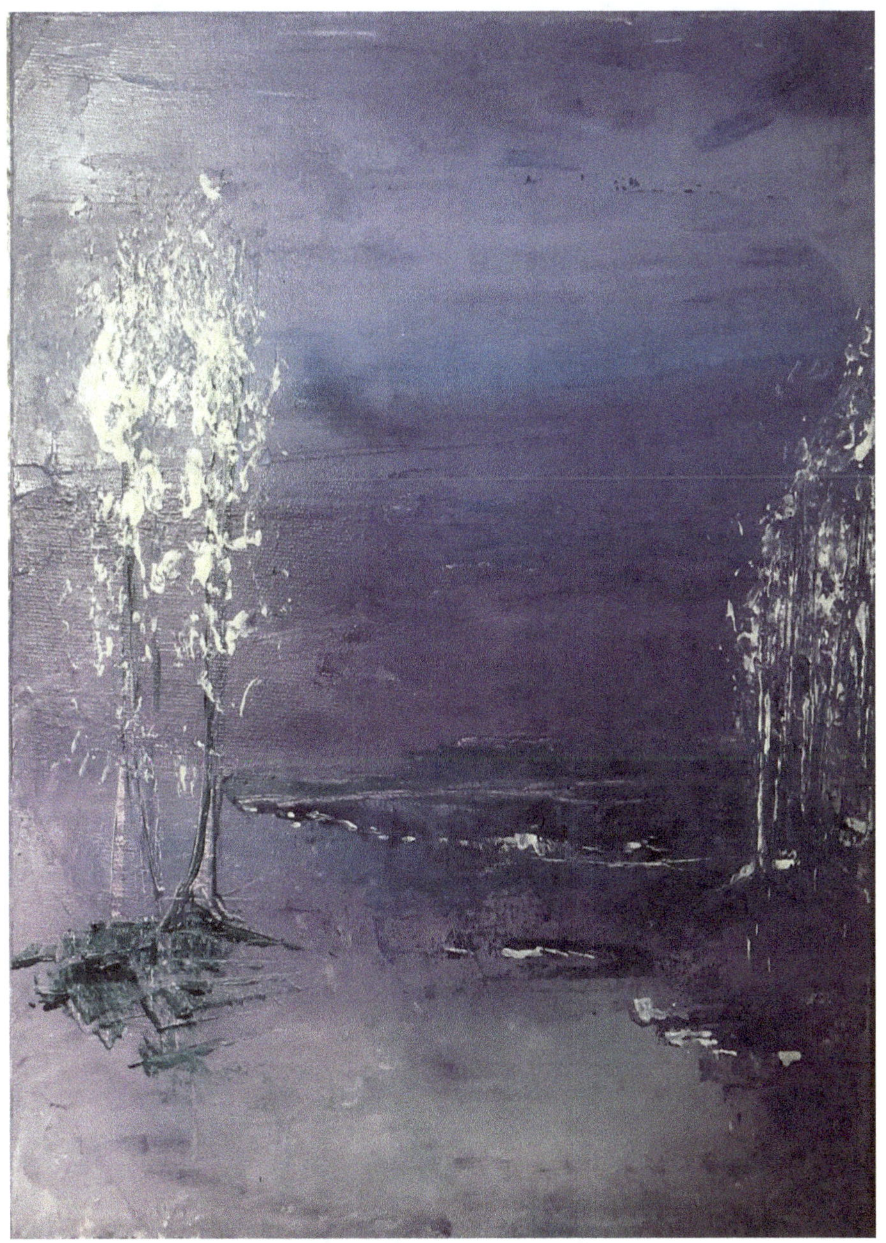

Deep Inside The Dream

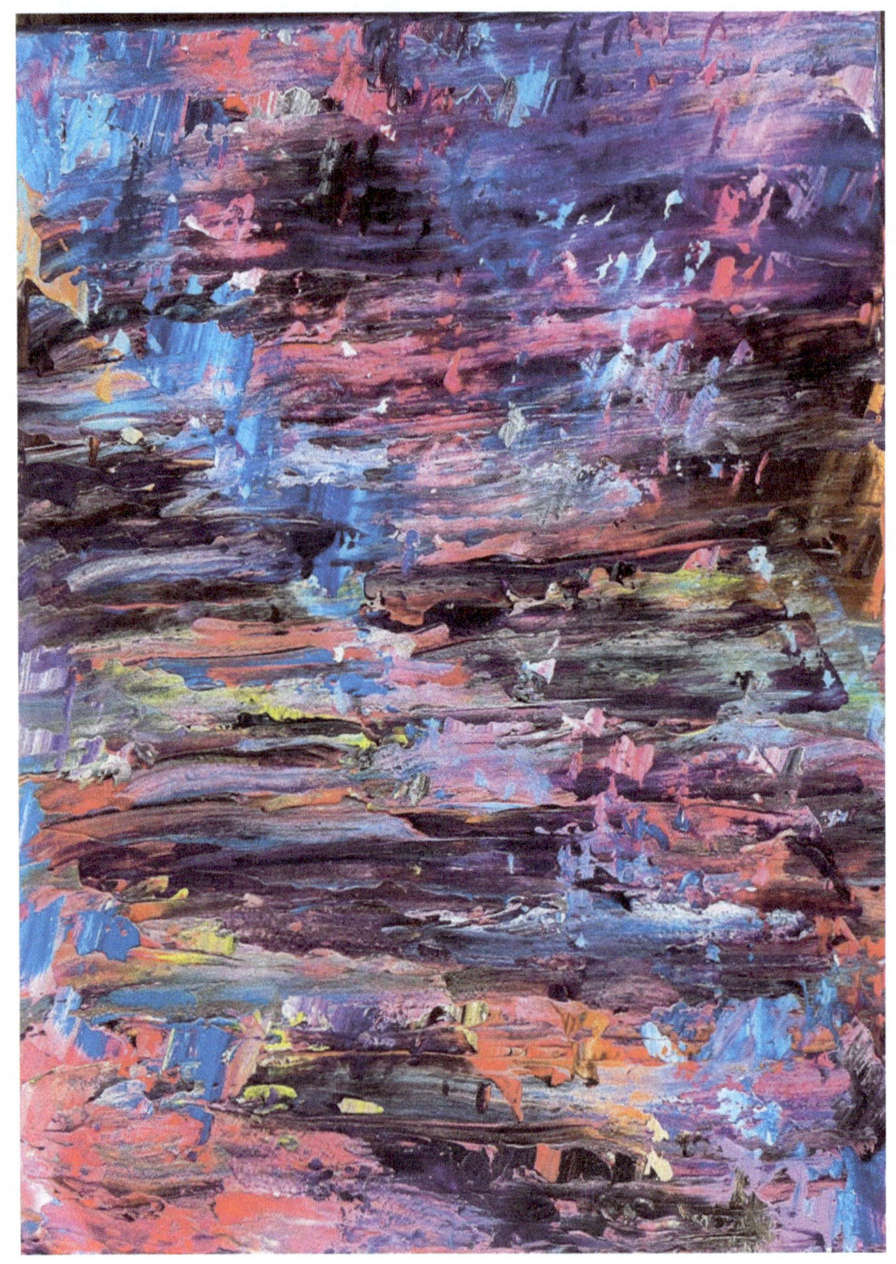

B Minor 7th b5

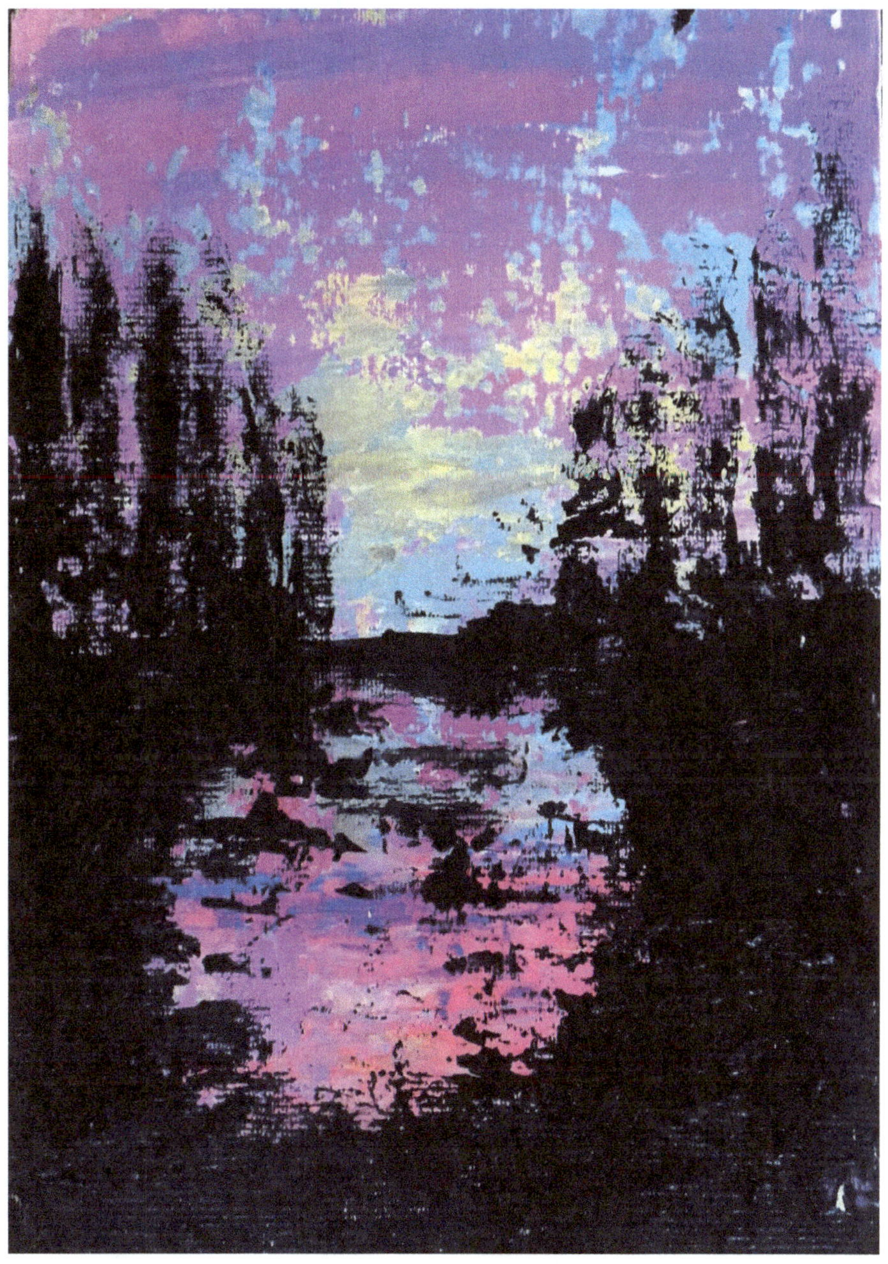

Bridge Over Twilight Waters

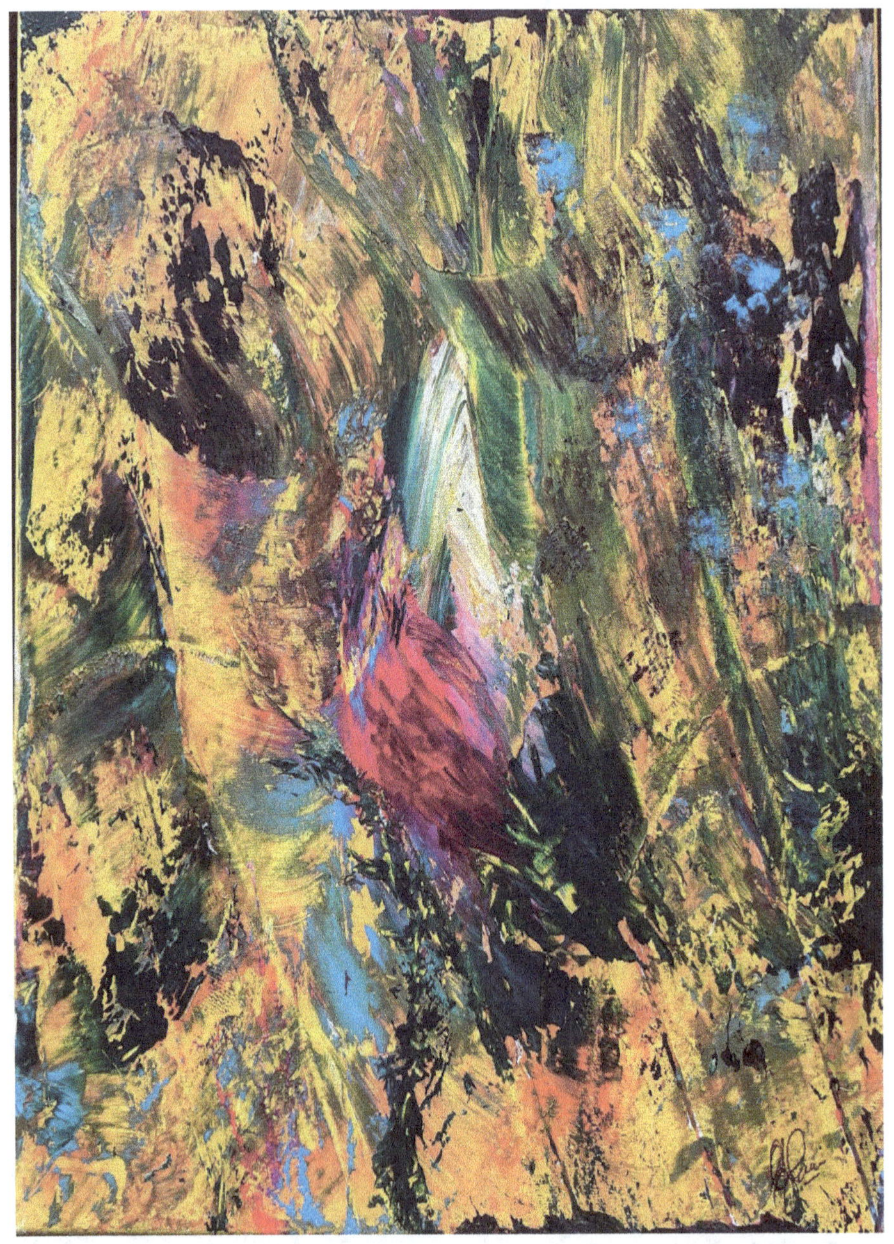

Brad Pitt And The Bird Of Paradise

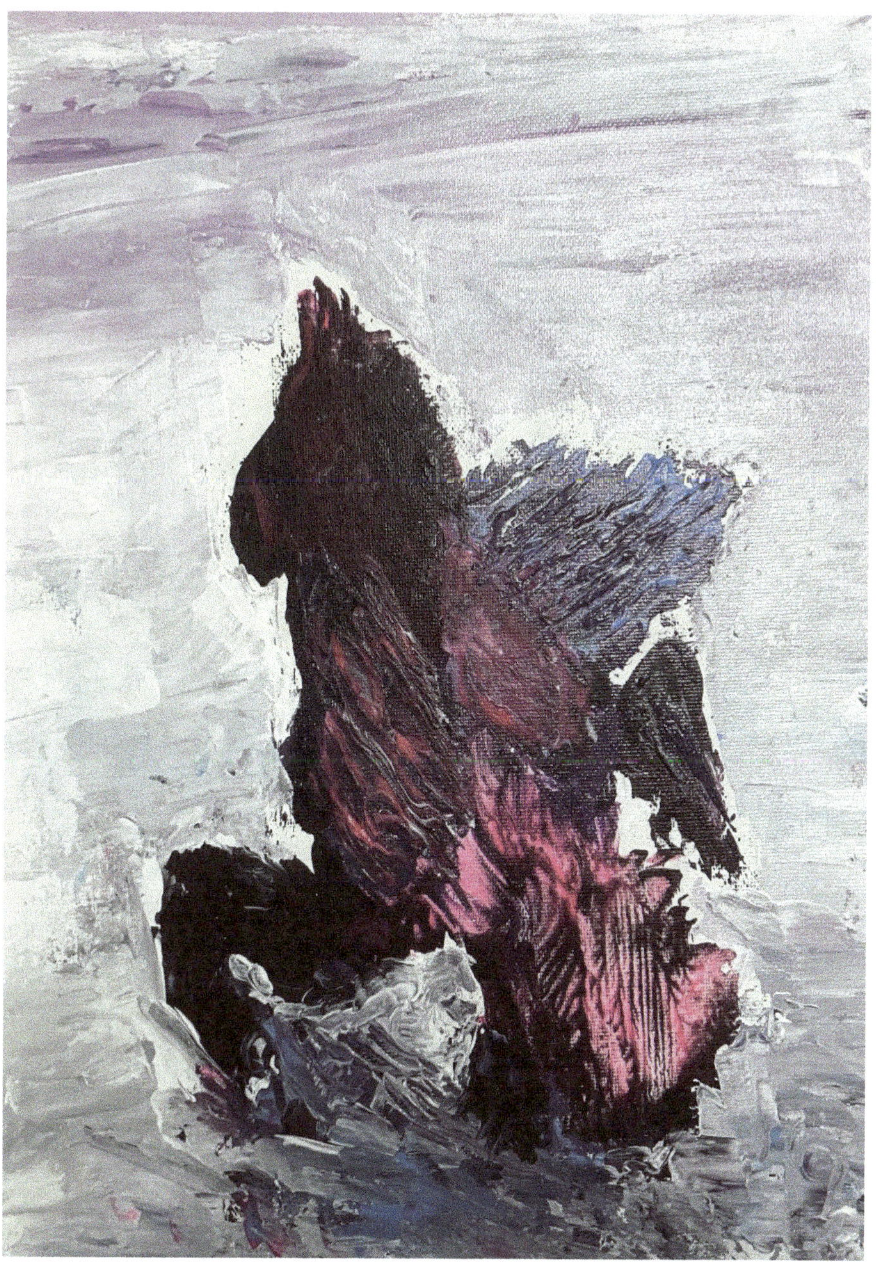

Escape

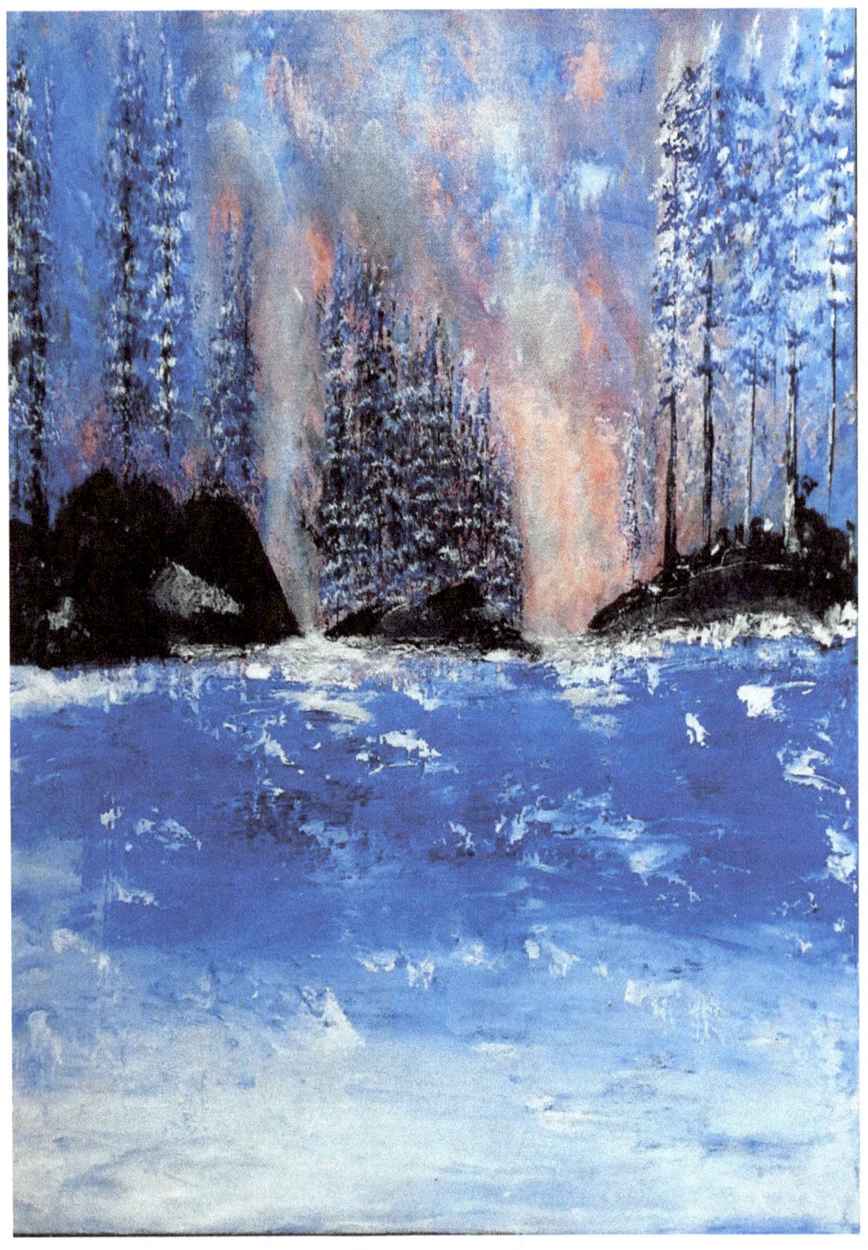

Early Morning Haunting

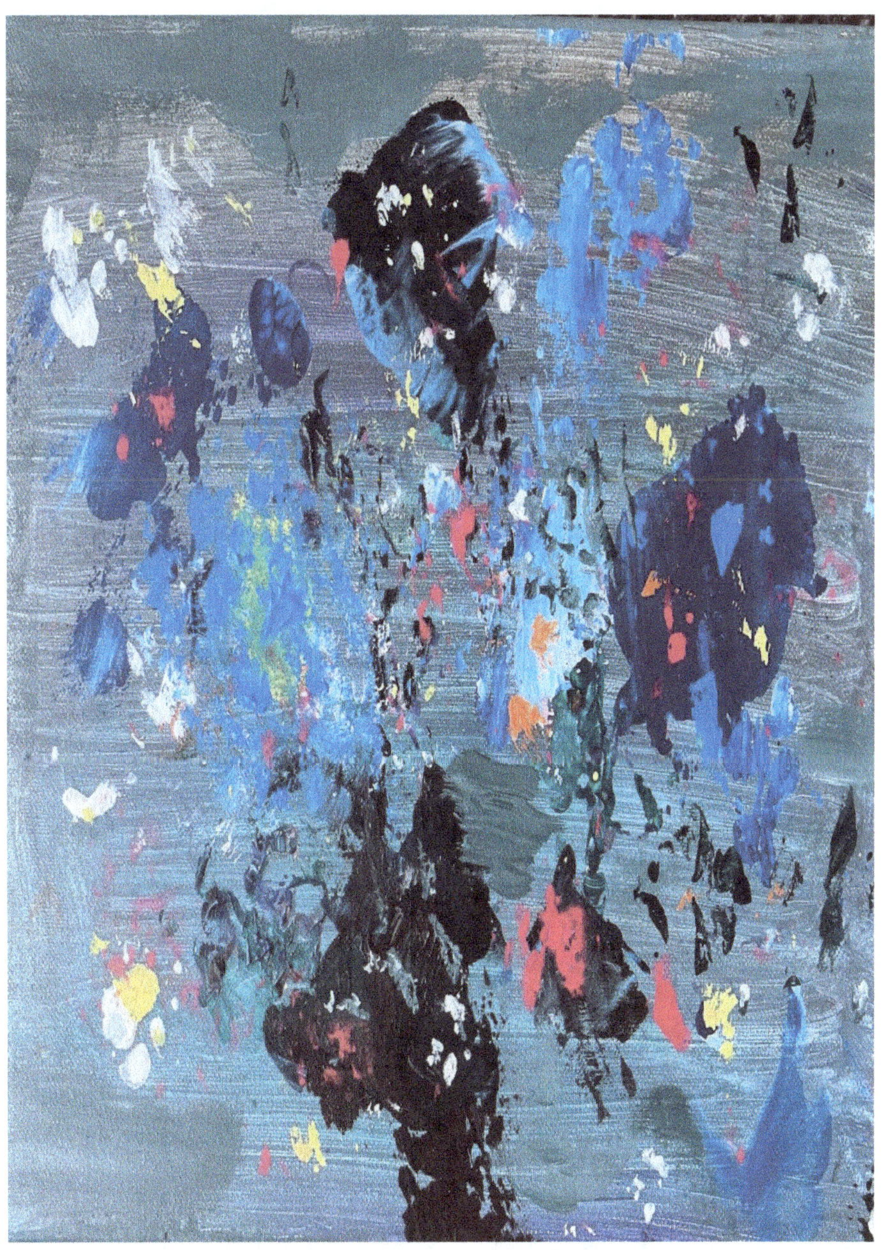

Dog Dreams

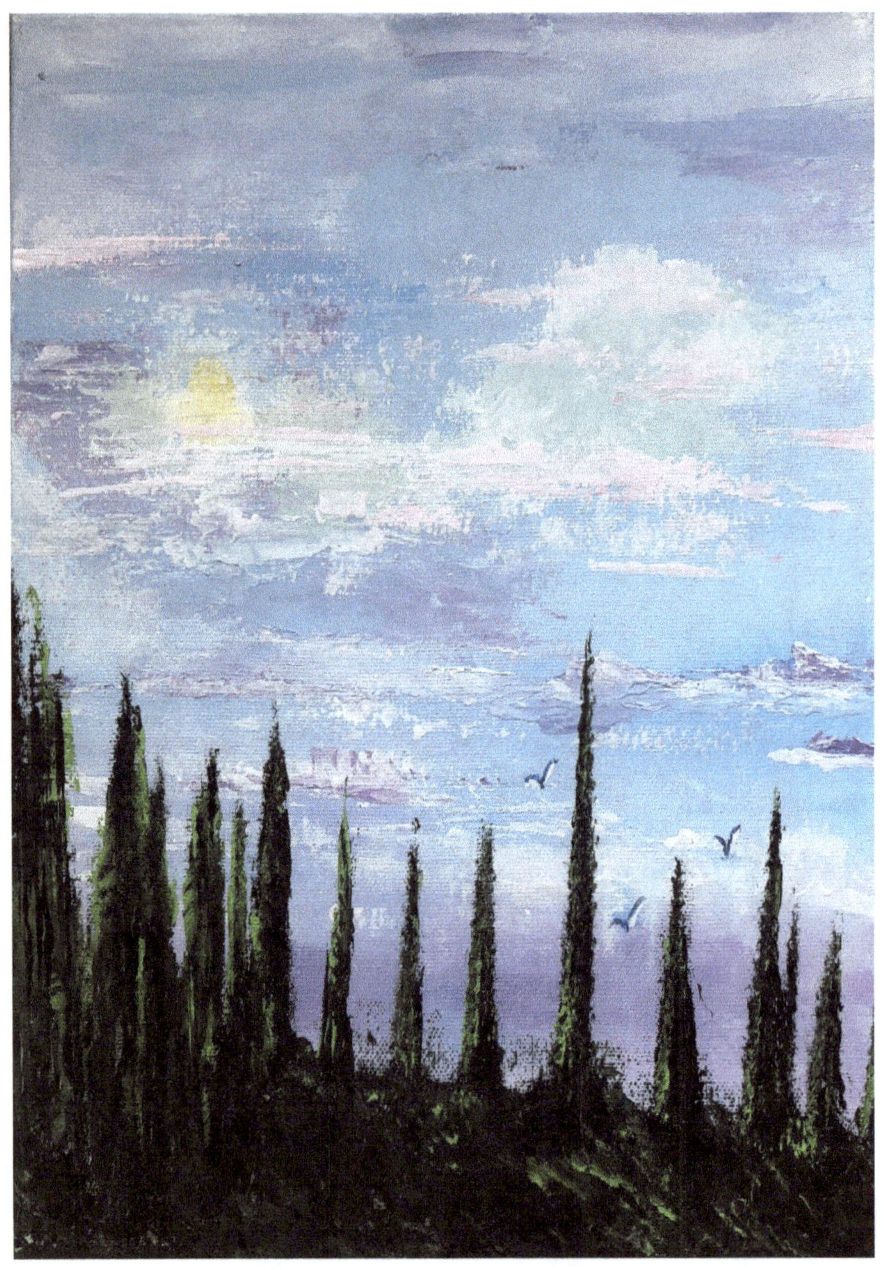

The Faithful At Prayer

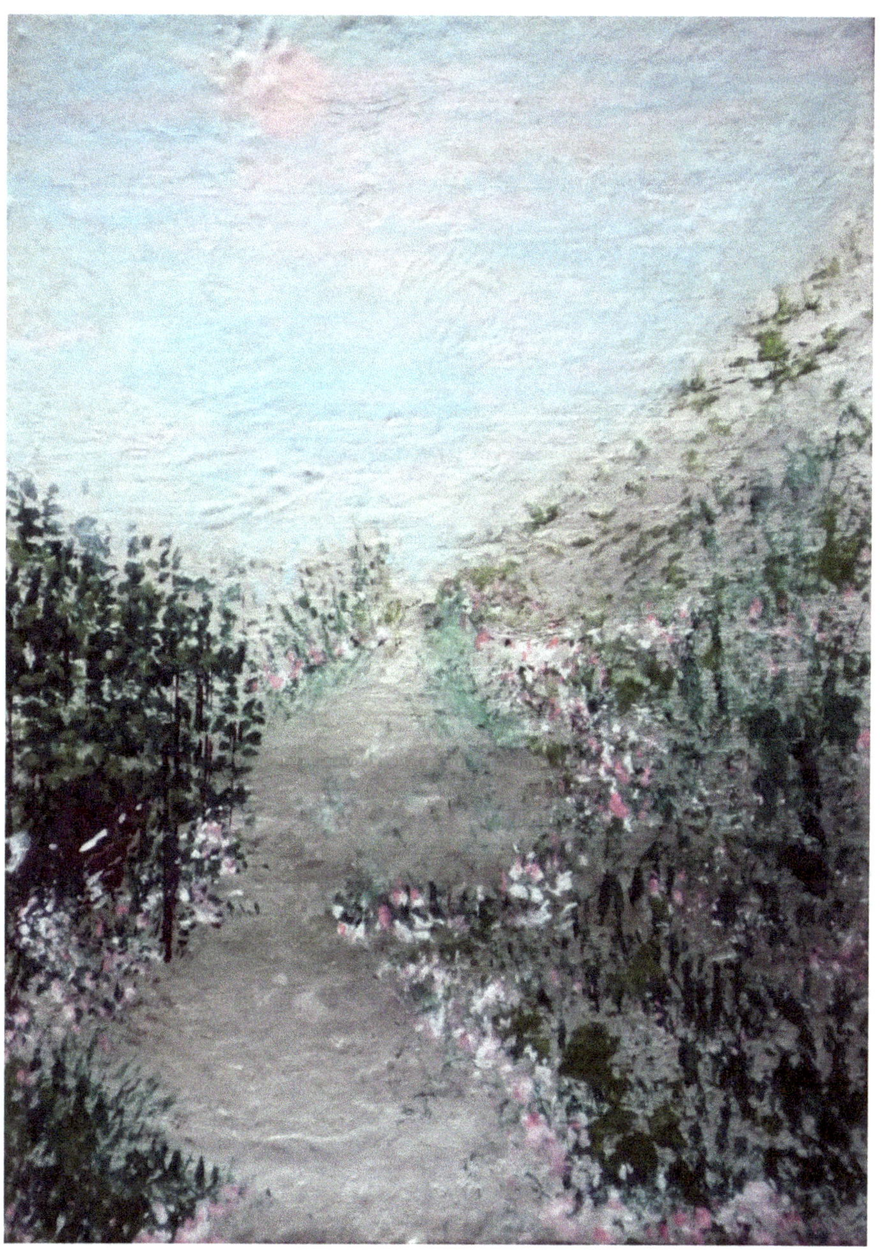

Backwoods In The Spring

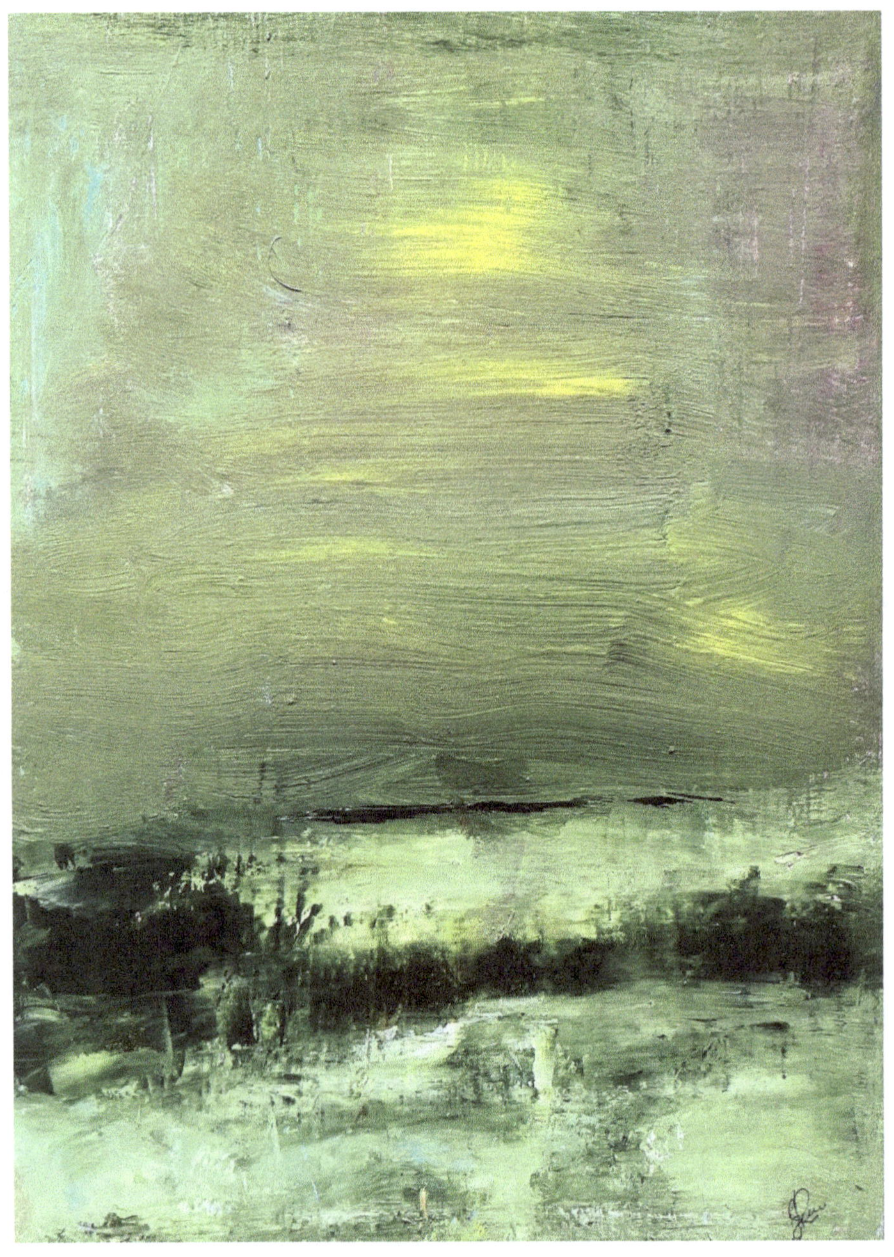

An Hour Before The Hurricane

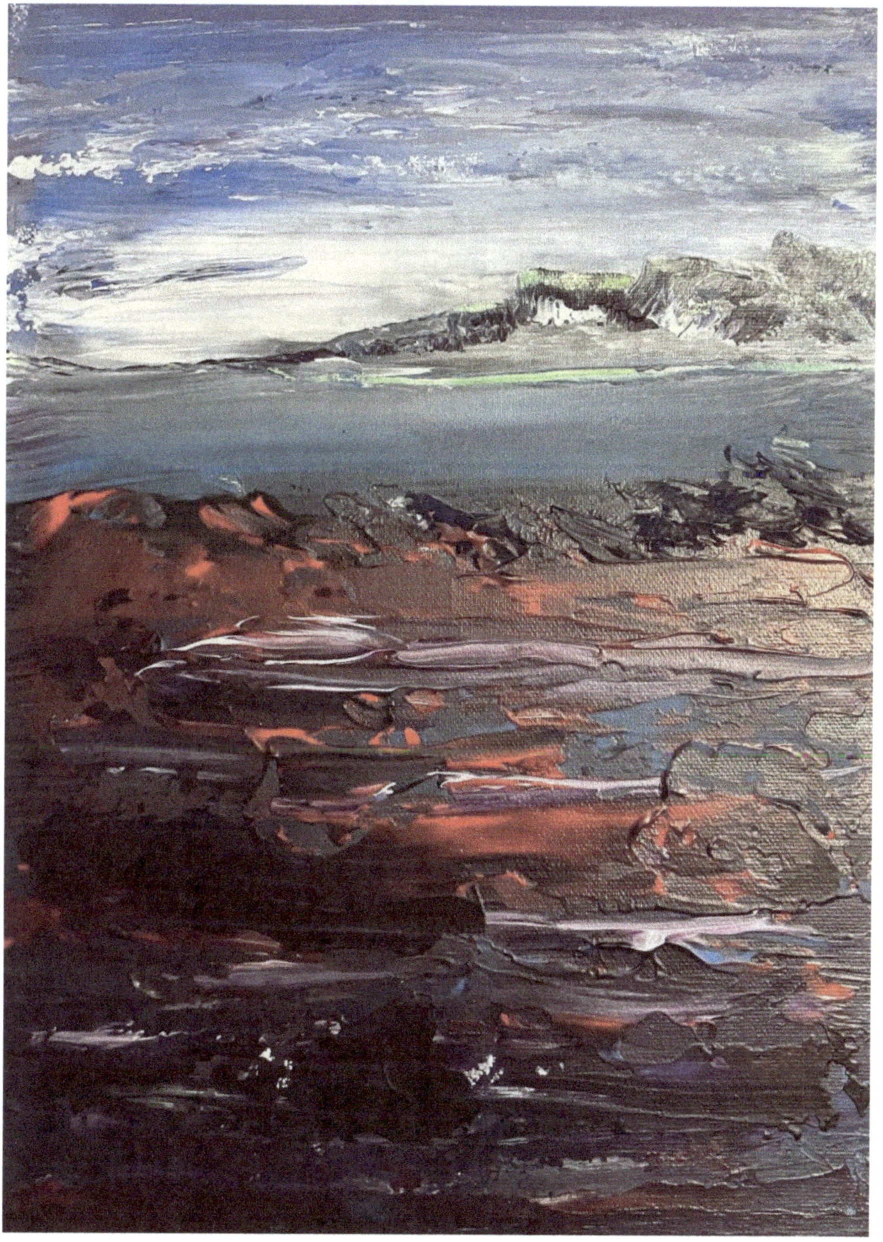

Before The Eruption

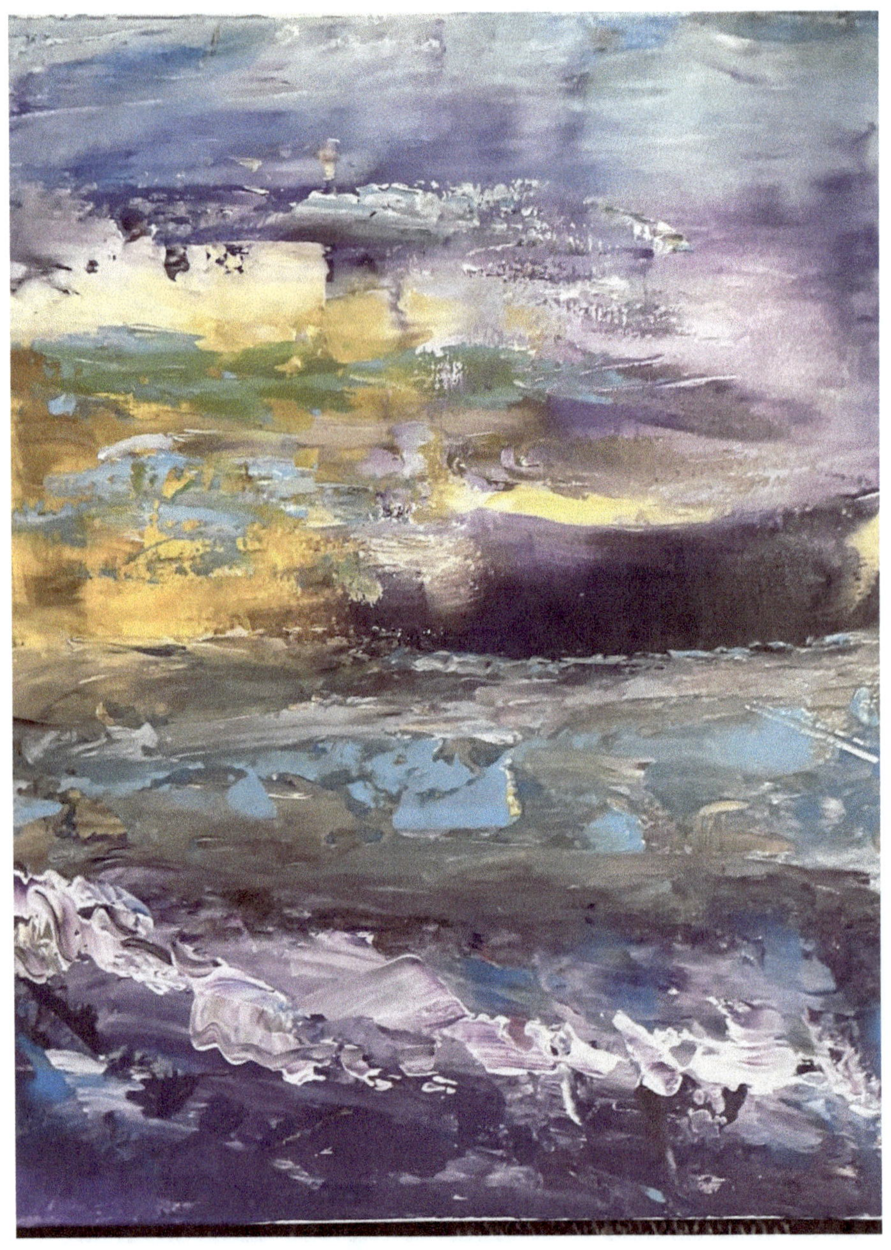

At End Of Day

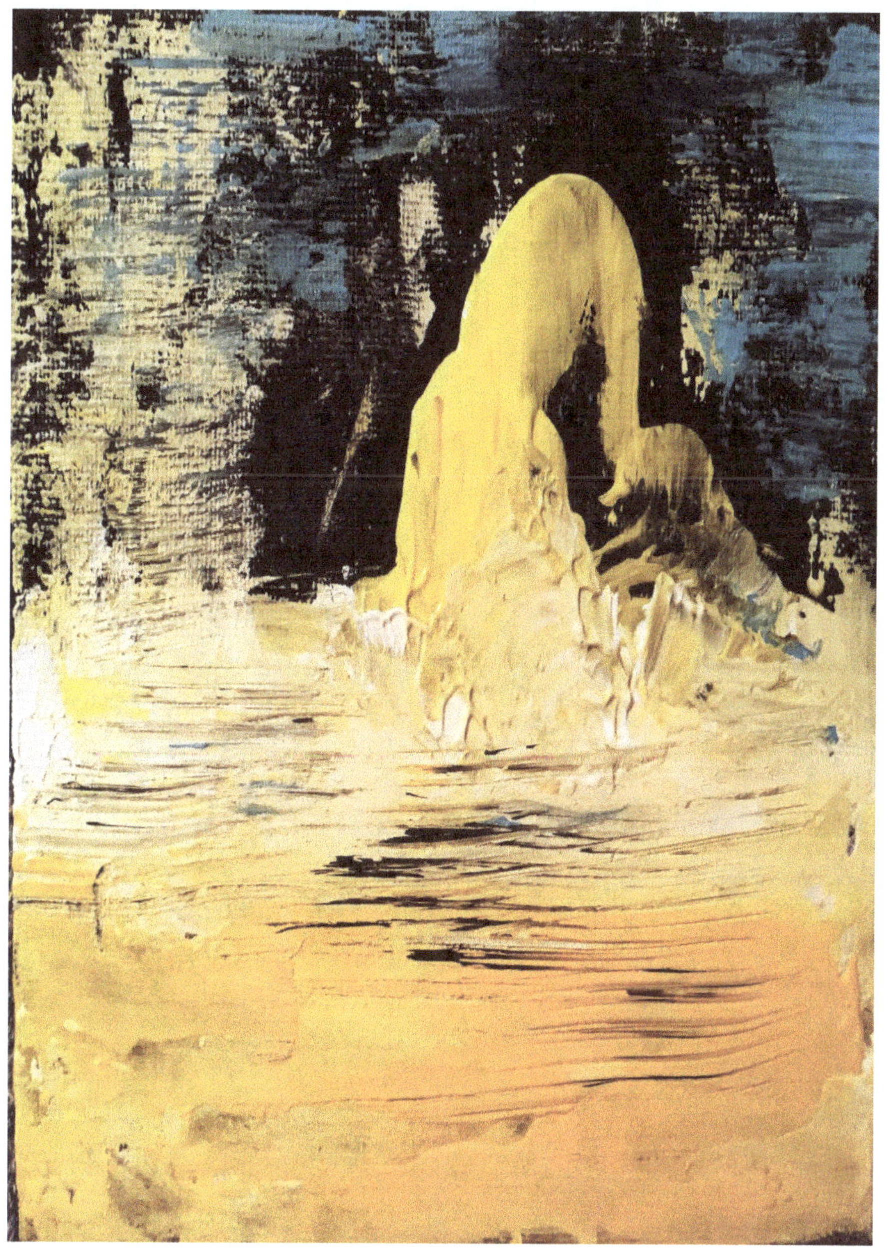

Cosmic Kiss

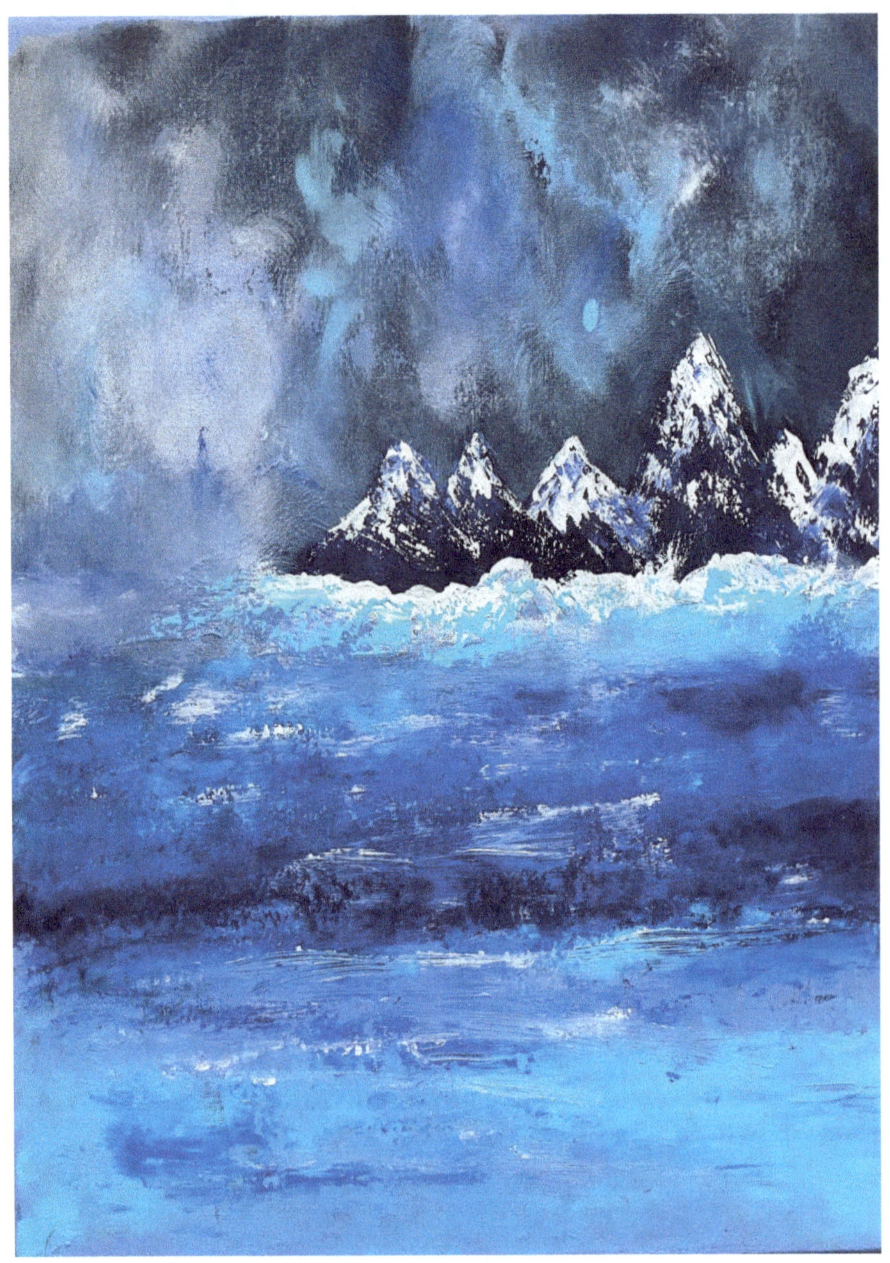

Diamonds Of The Arctic

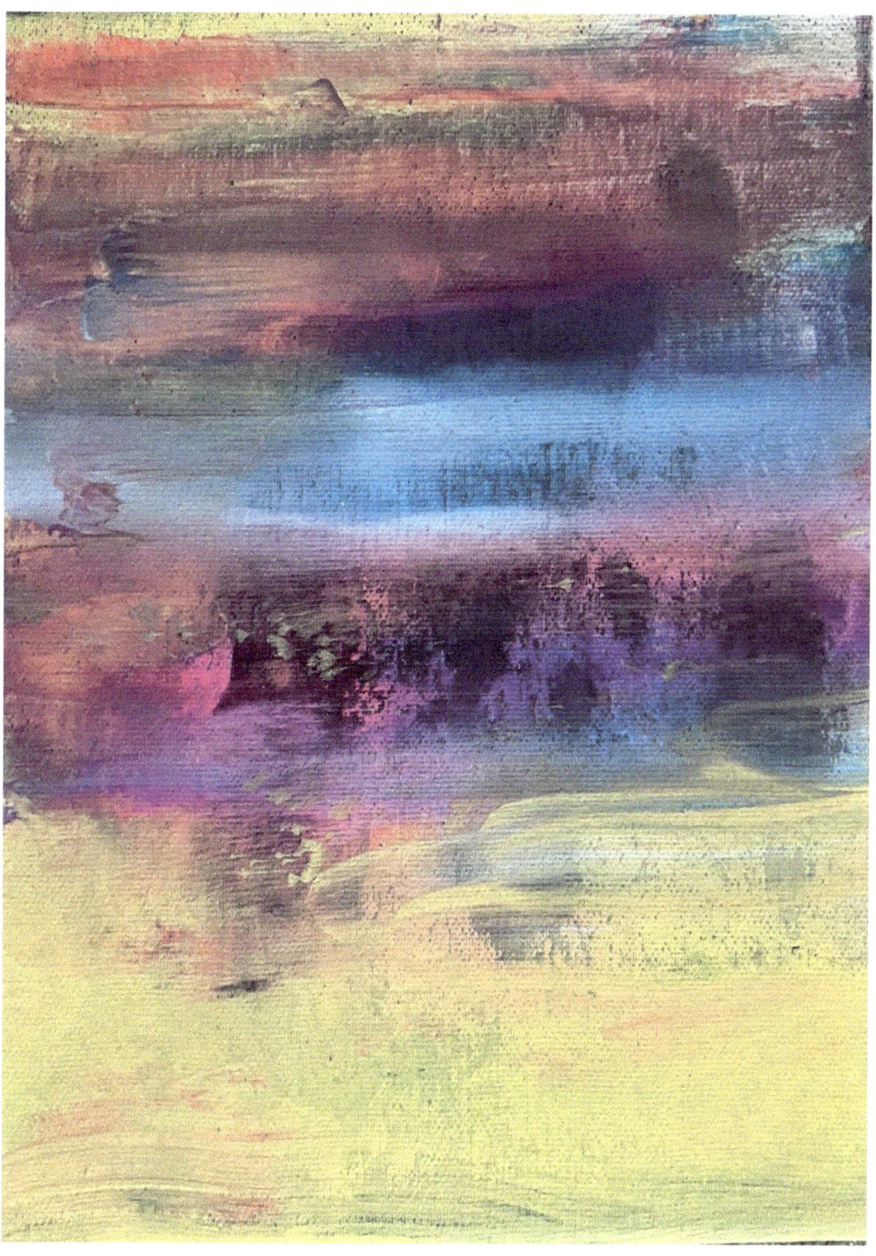

Distant Pink Plateau

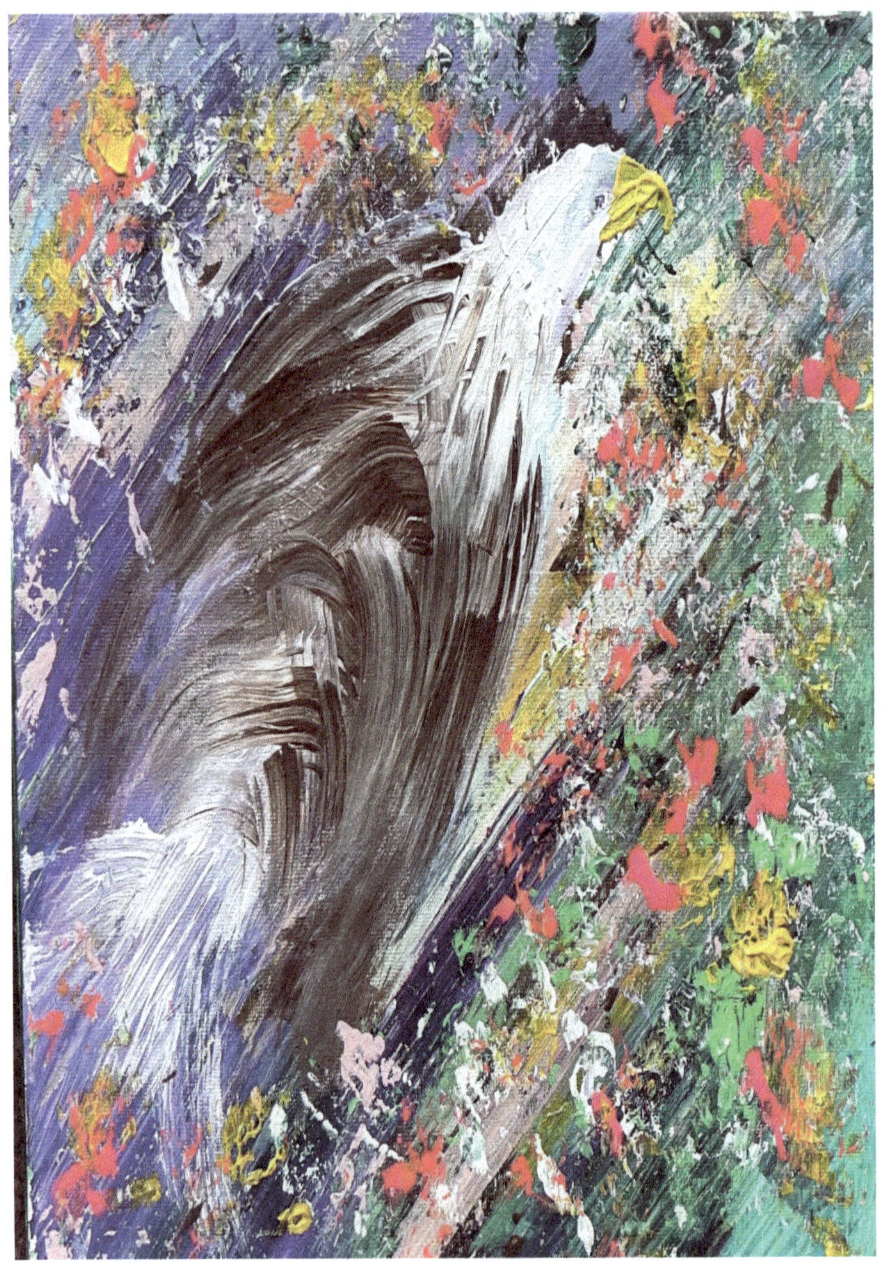

Eagle Dreams

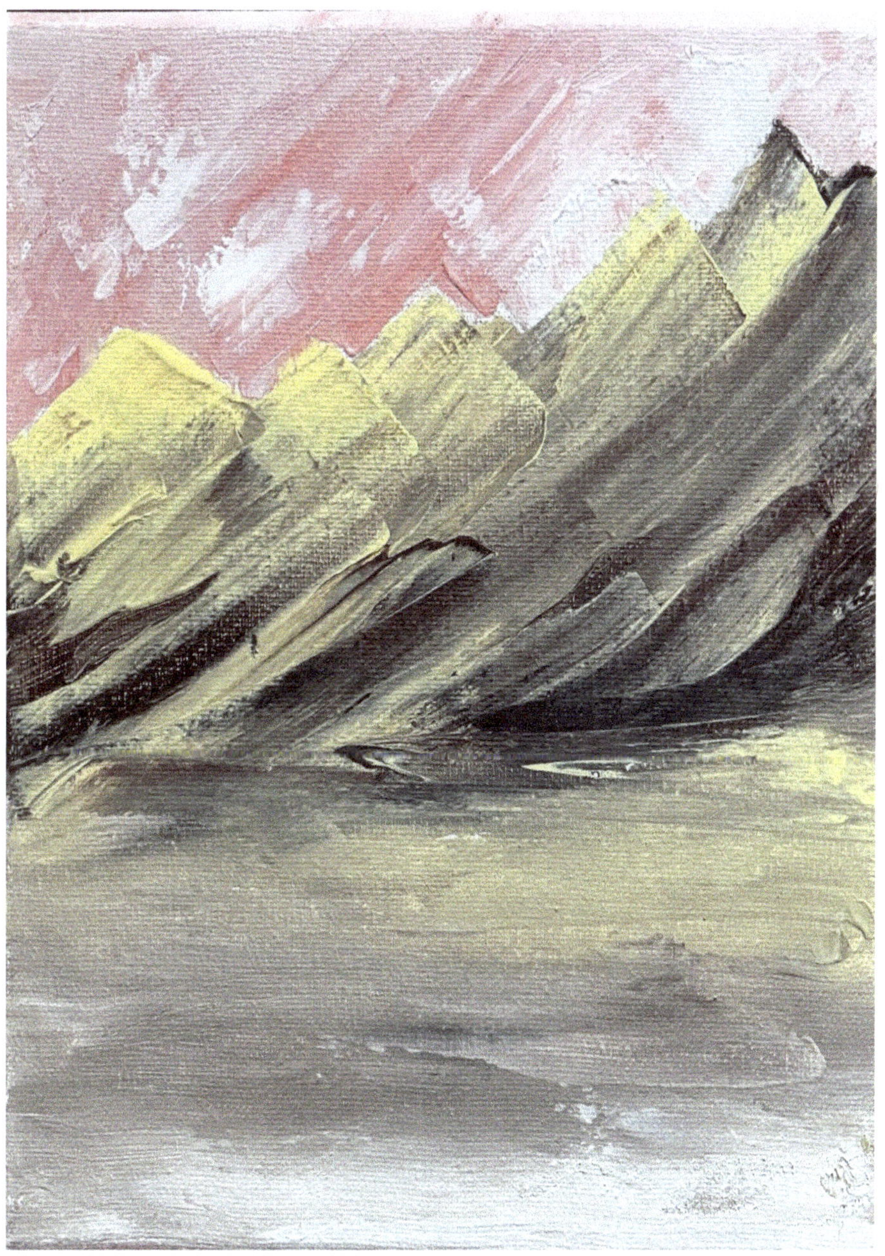

Bieszczady Mountains, Carpathians, Poland

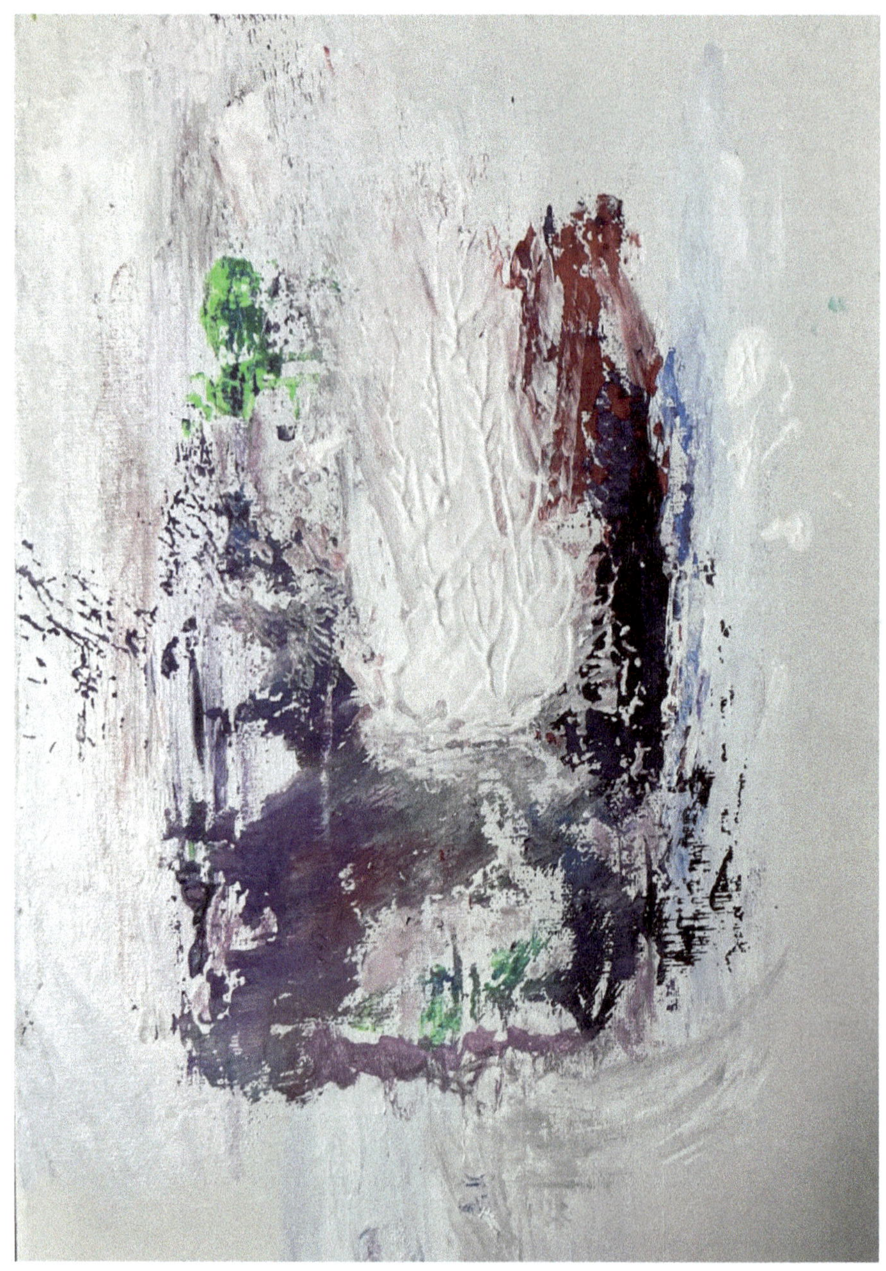

Heaven's Swing

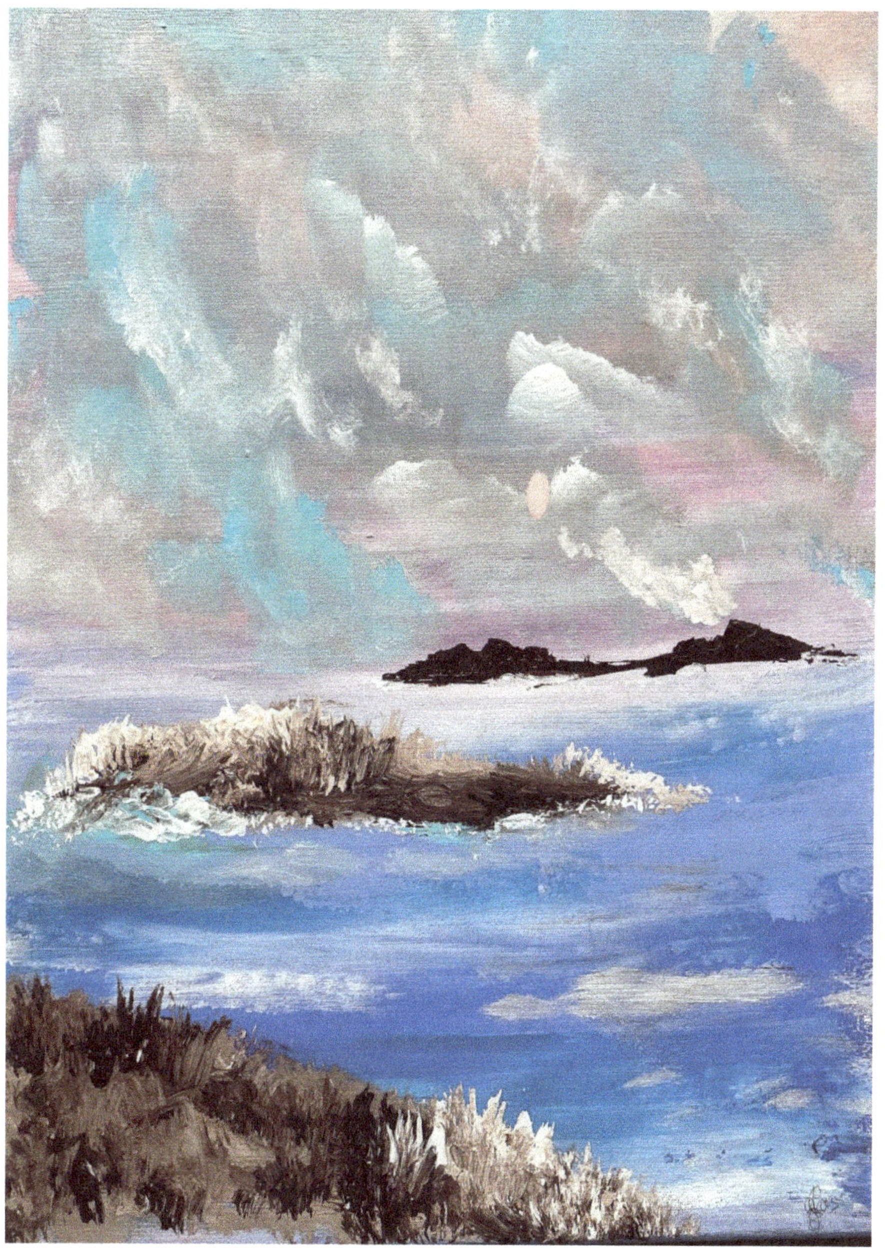

South Seas Afternoon

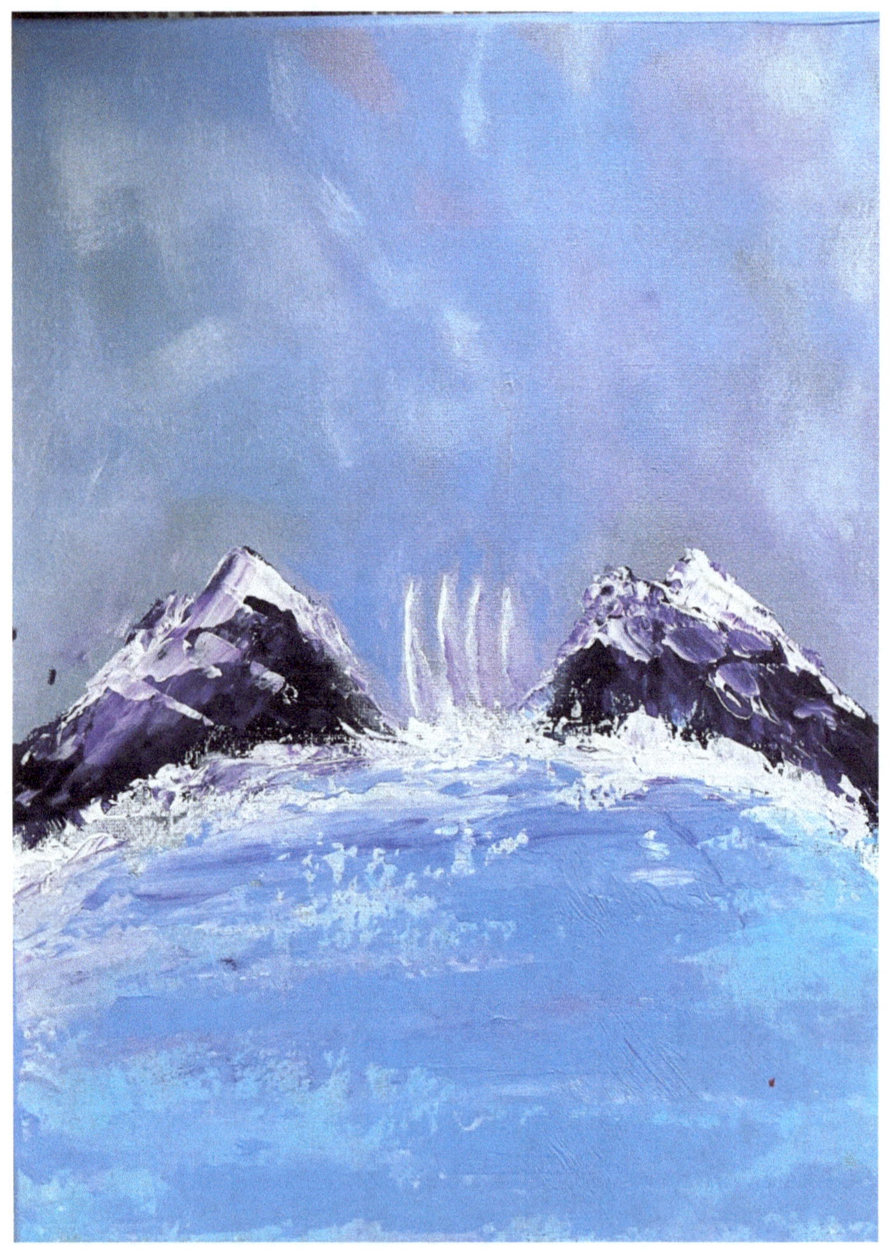

A Quartet Of Sailboats In The Pass

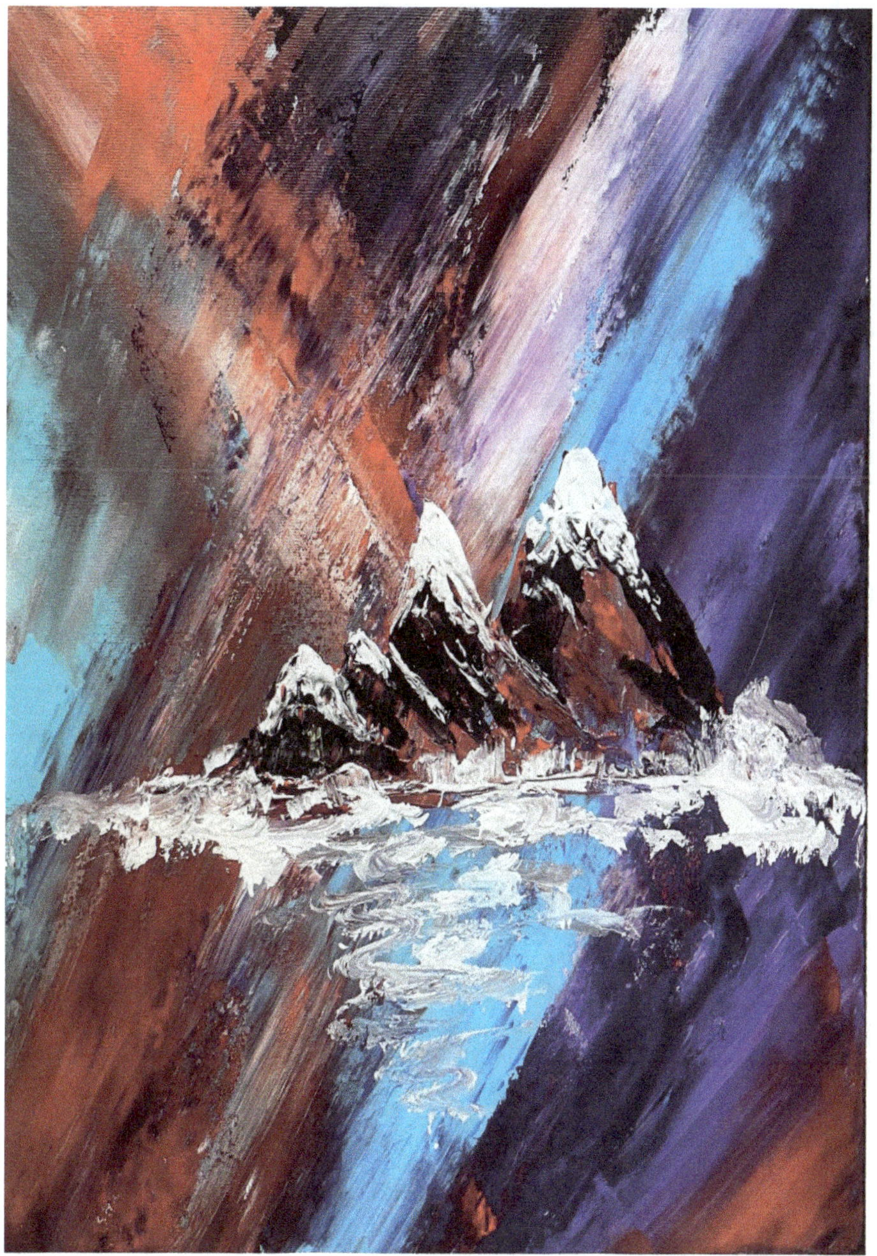

Mountains Of The Plaid

Warm Summer Night, Athabasca, Alberta

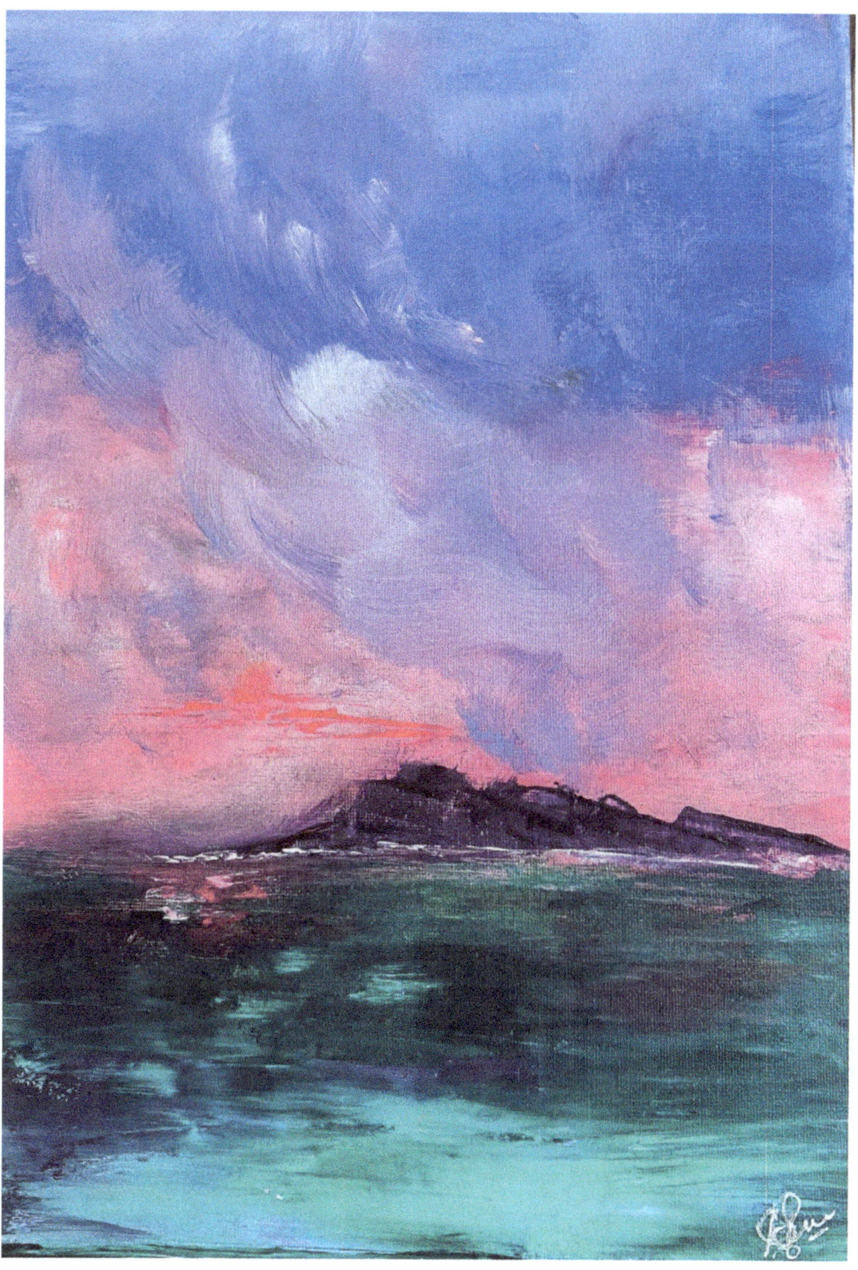

Tropical Sunglow

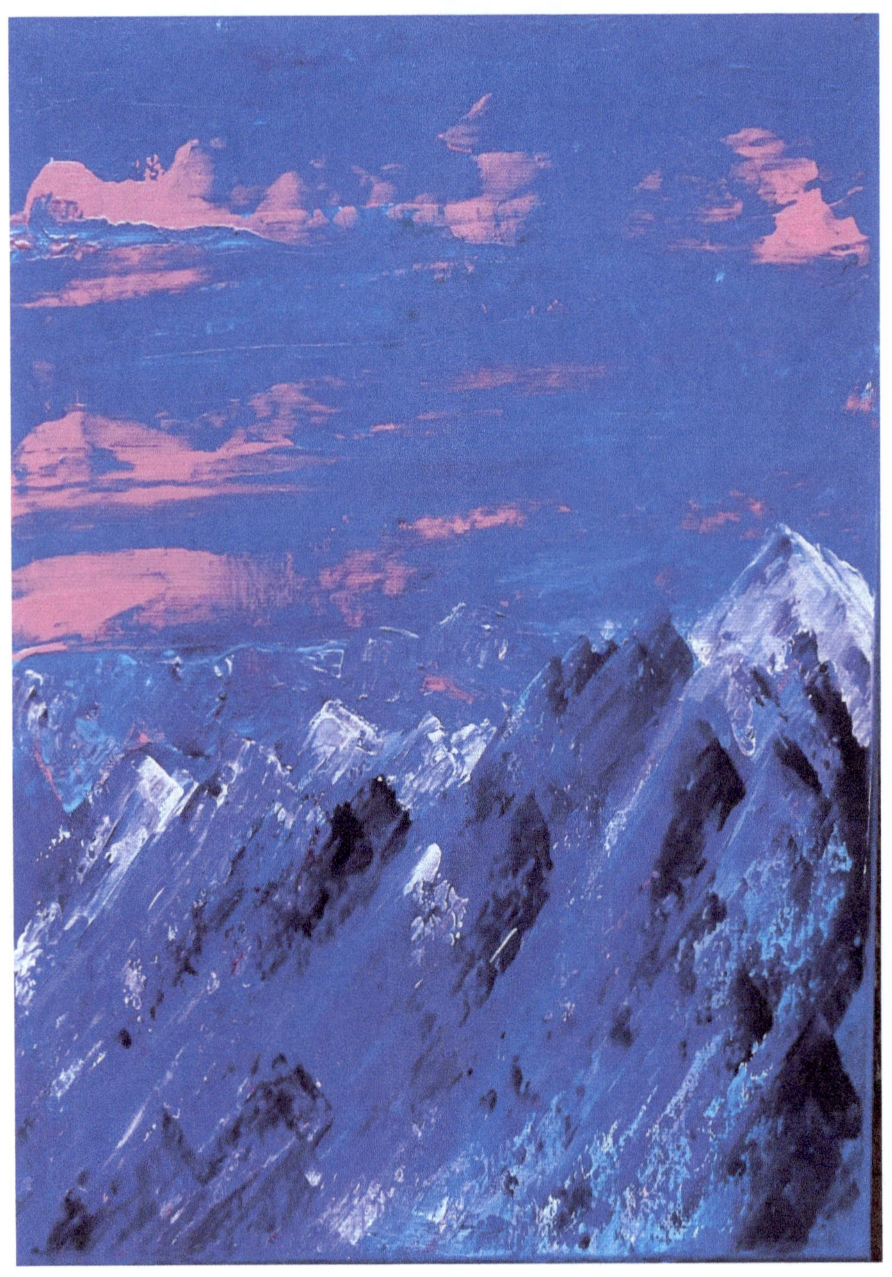

Land Of The Midnight Sun

The Fraser Mills

Series

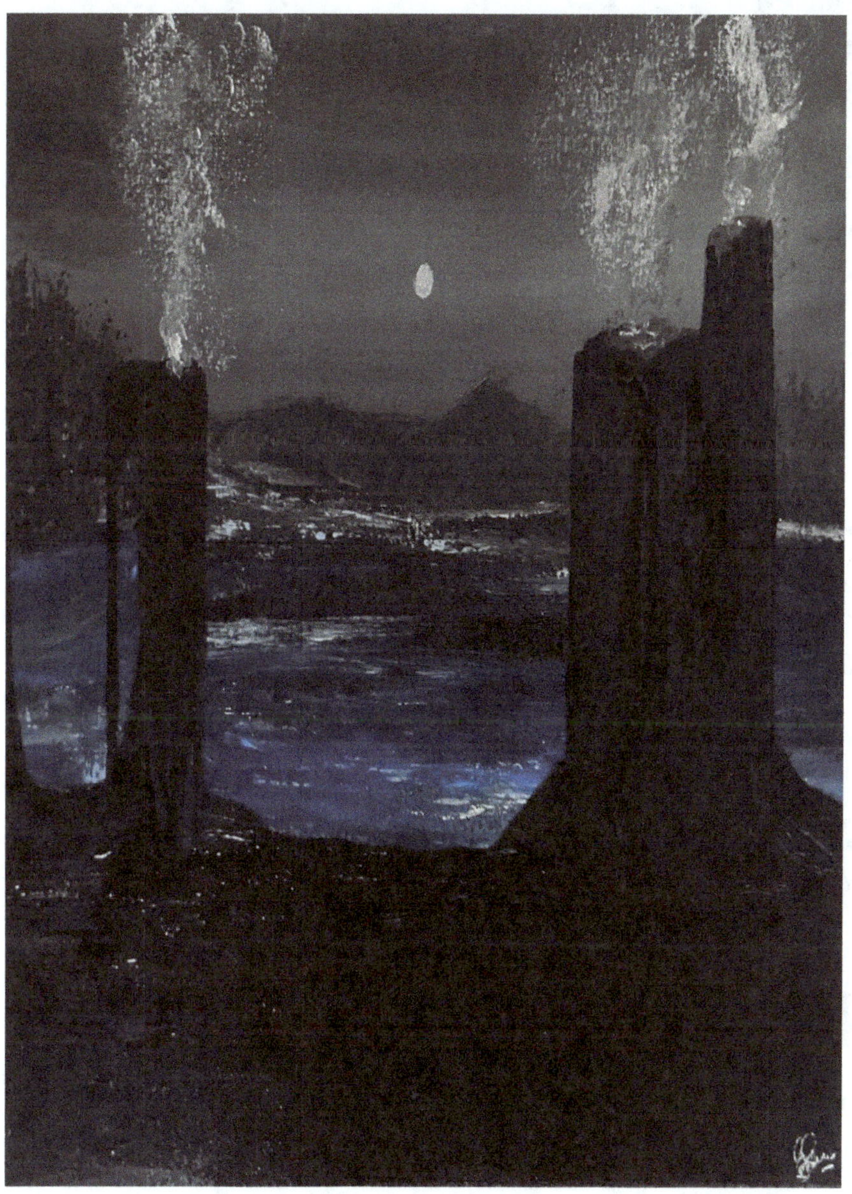

Fraser Mills circa 1890

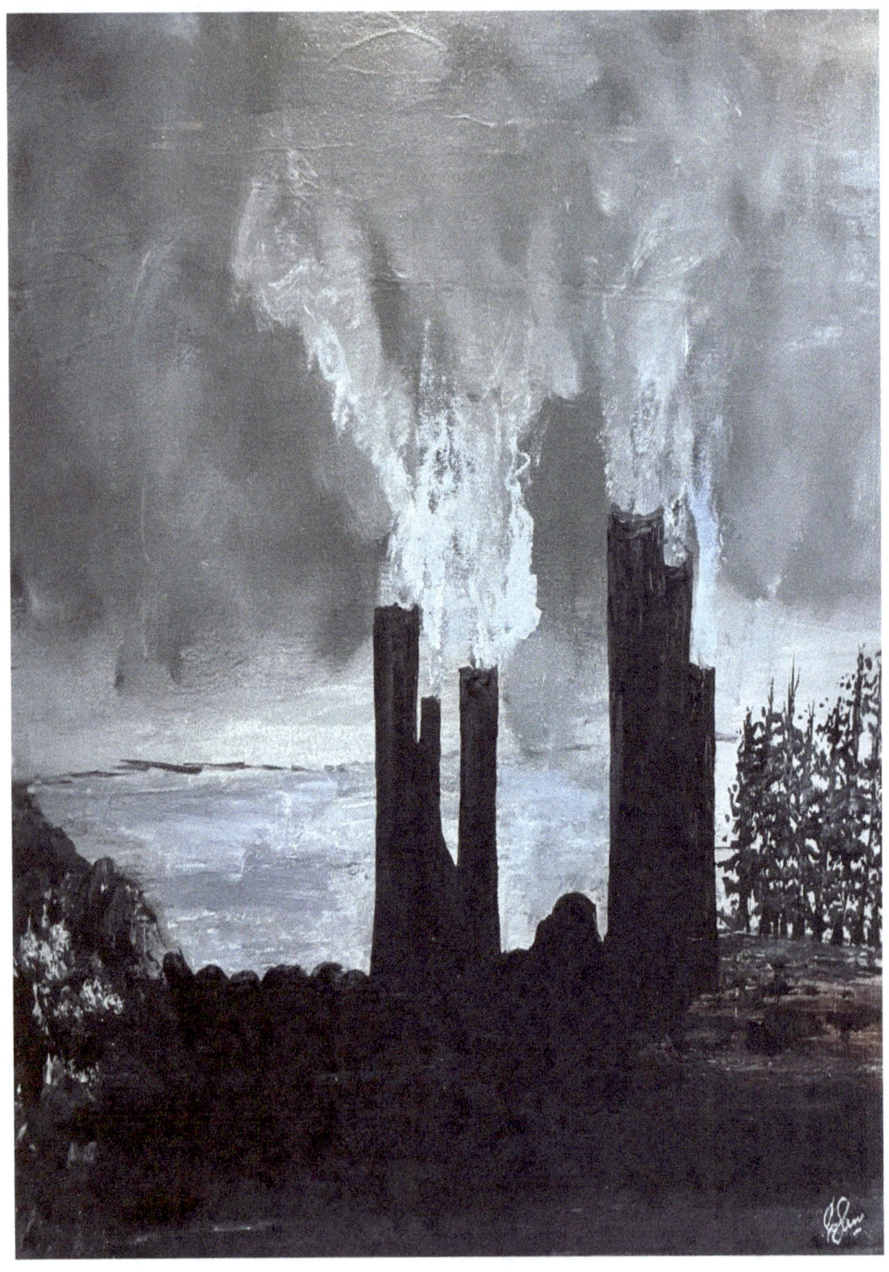

Fraser Mills circa 1891

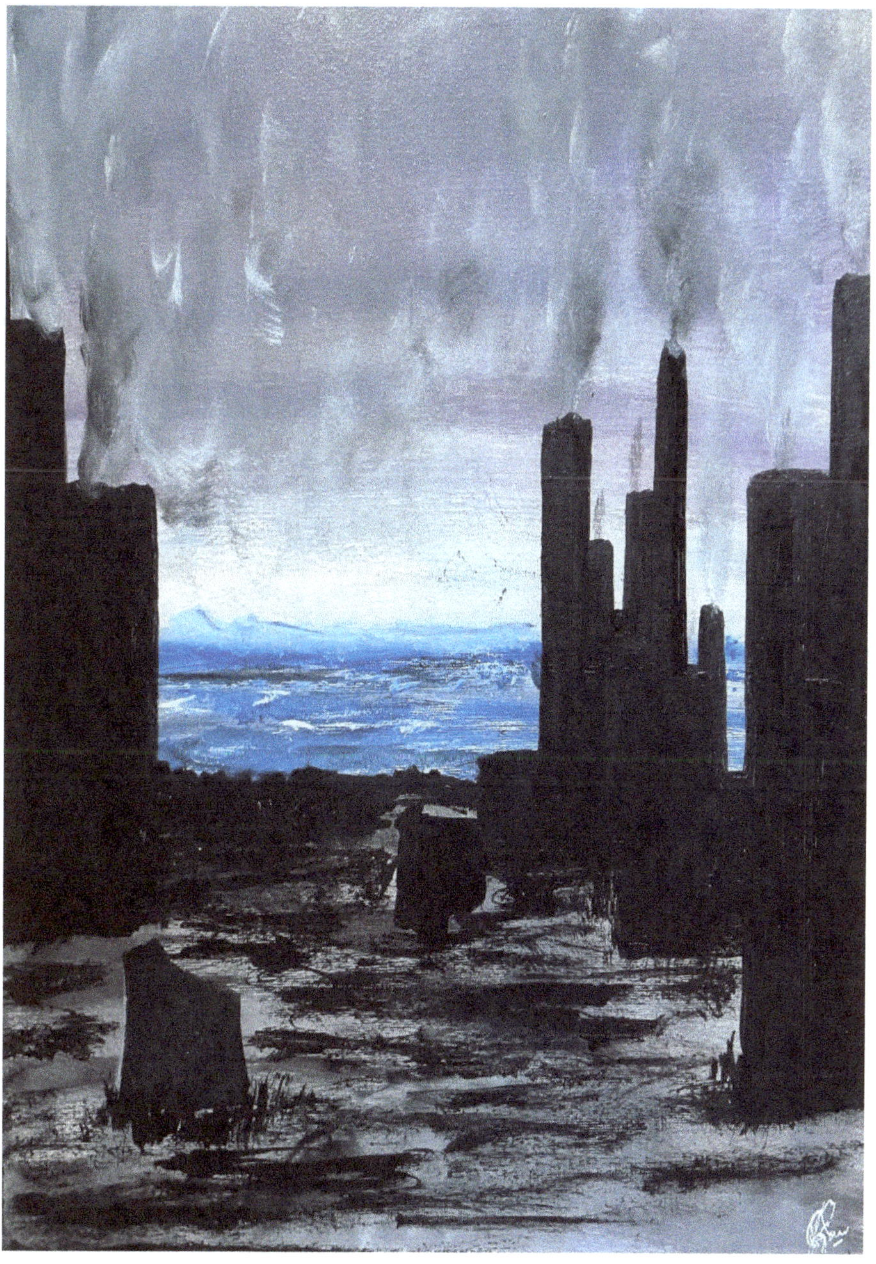

Fraser Mills circa 1892

The Arctic Ice Flow

Series

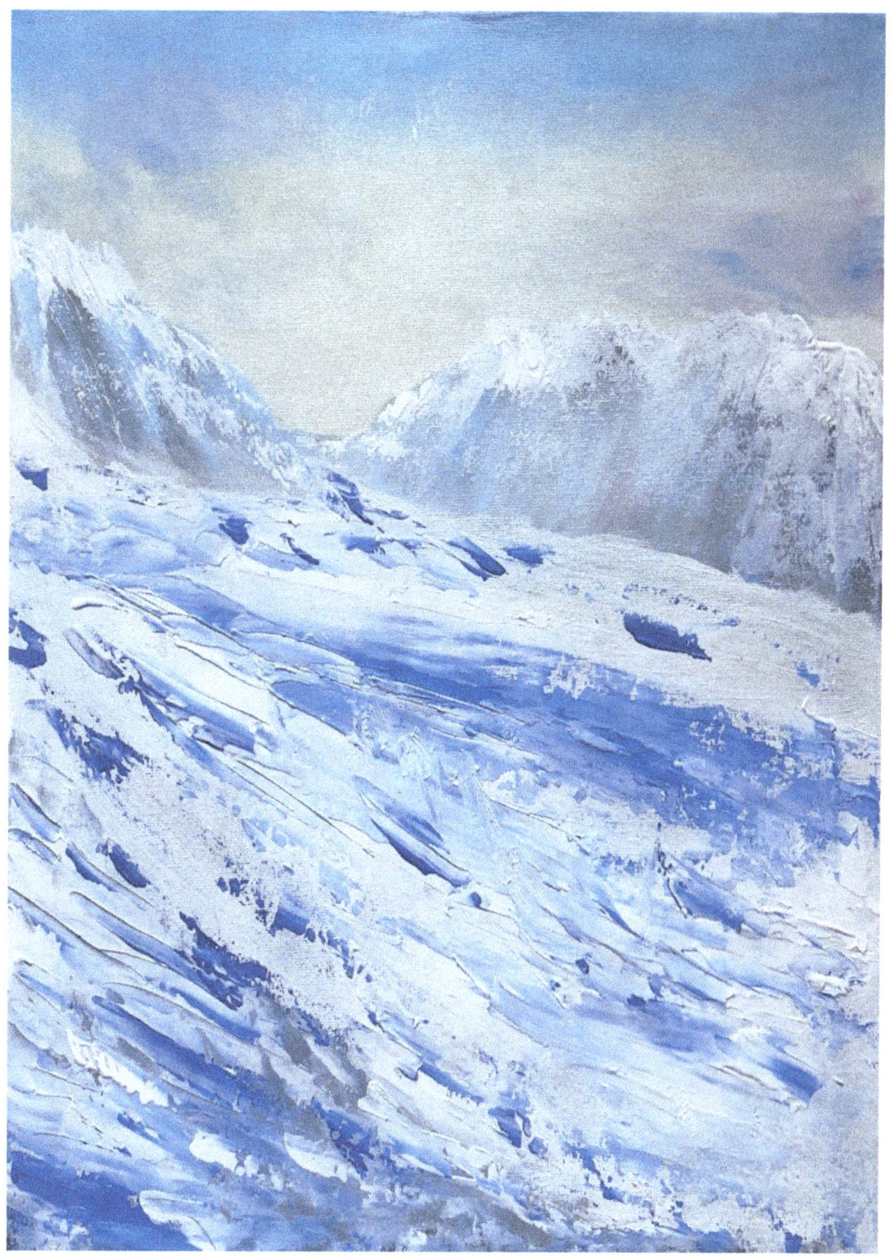

Arctic Ice Flow 1

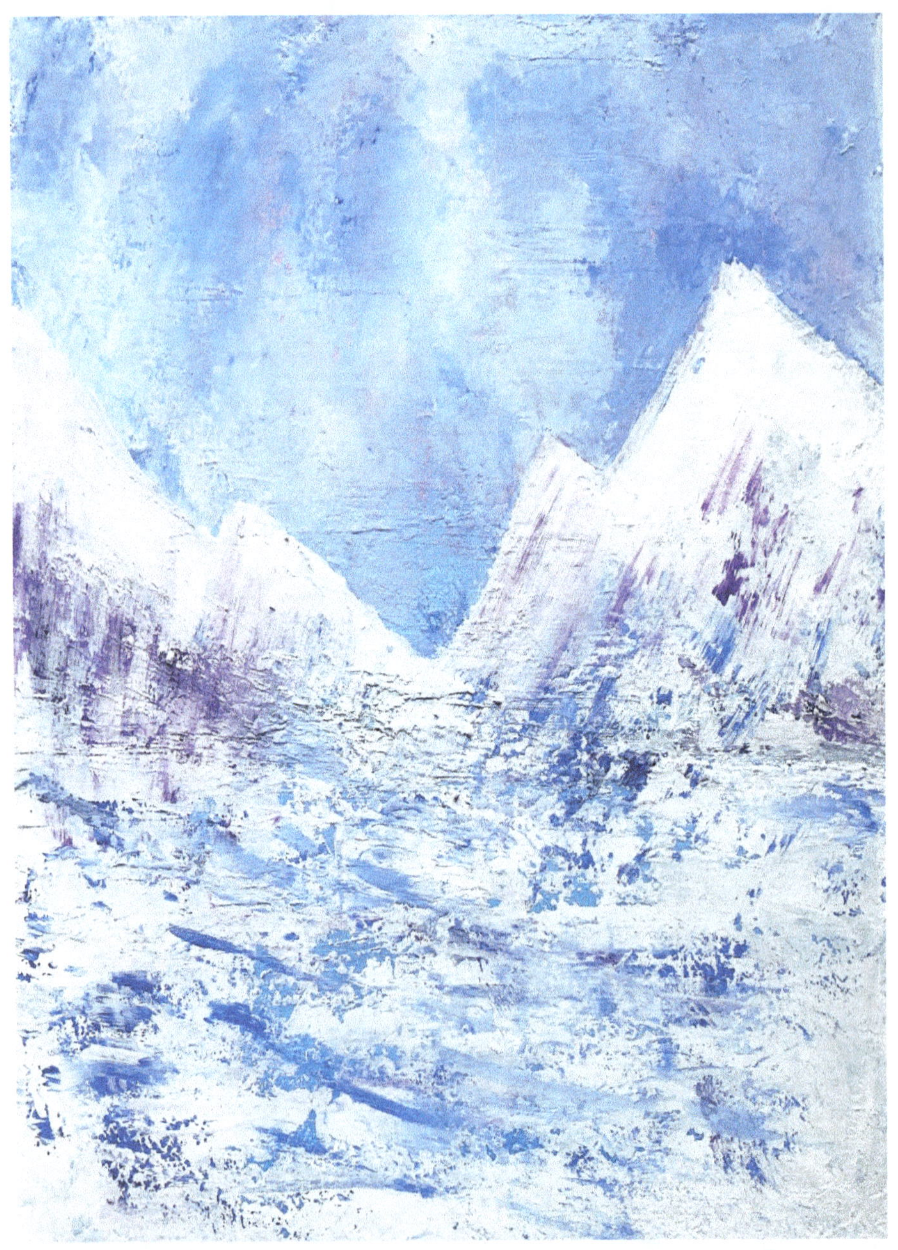

Arctic Ice Flow 2

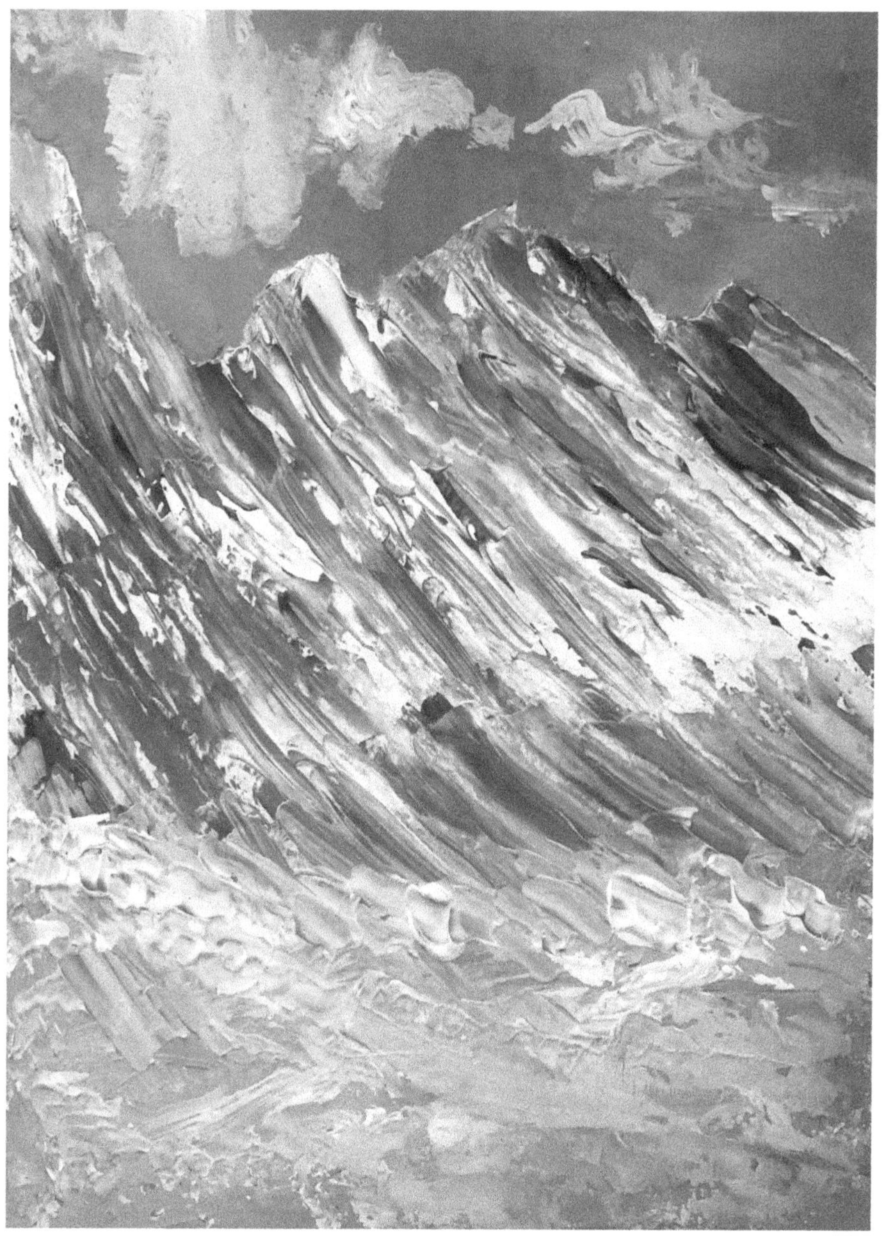

Arctic Ice Flow 3

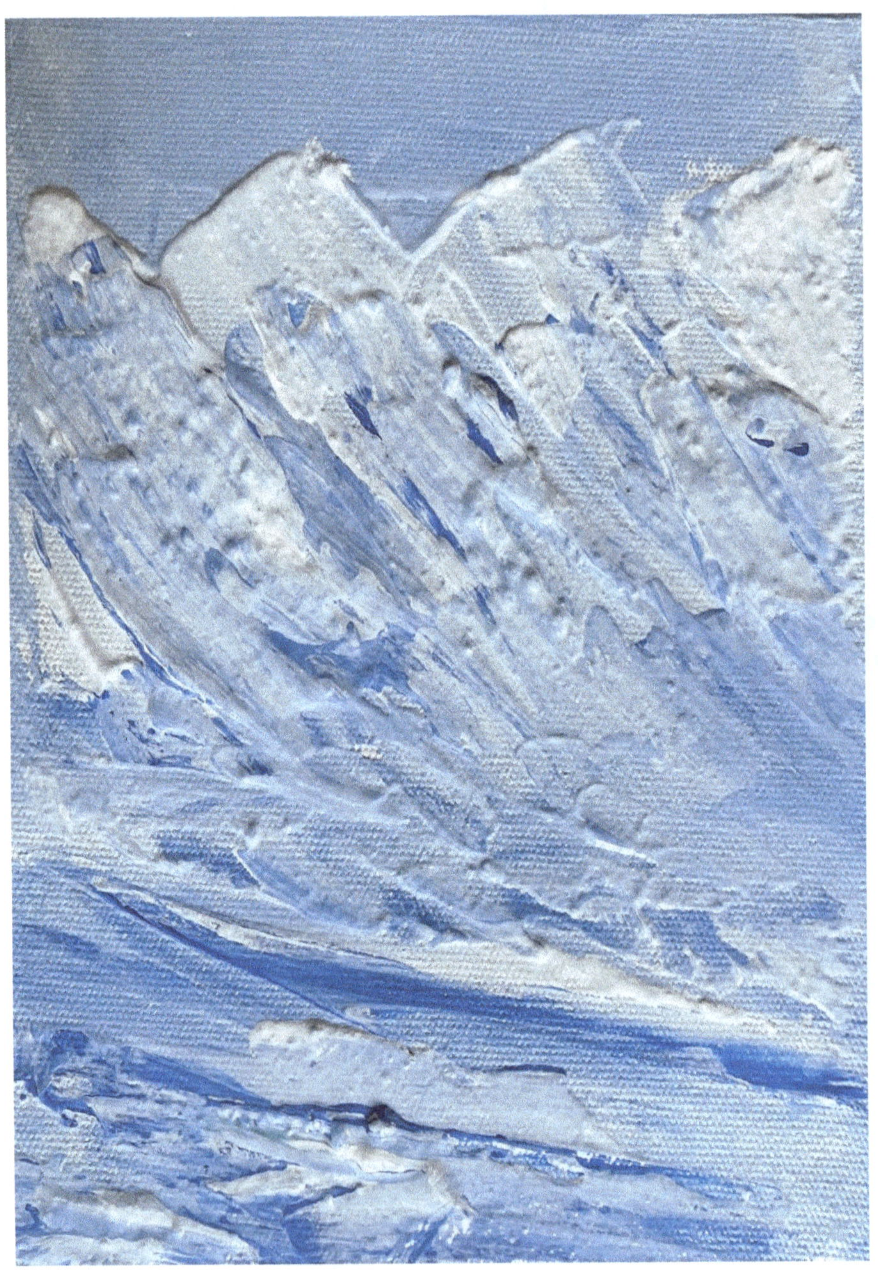

Arctic Ice Flow 4

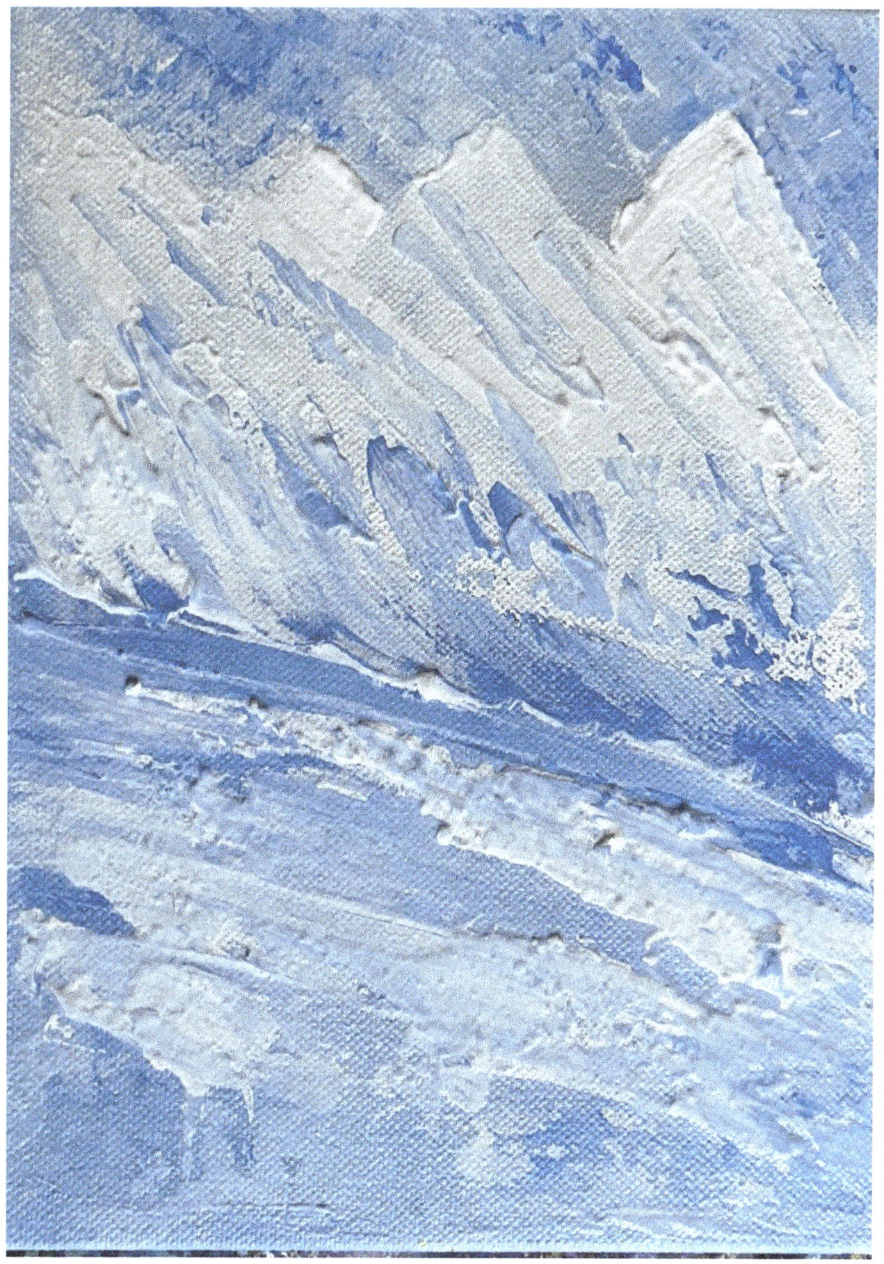

Arctic Ice Flow 5

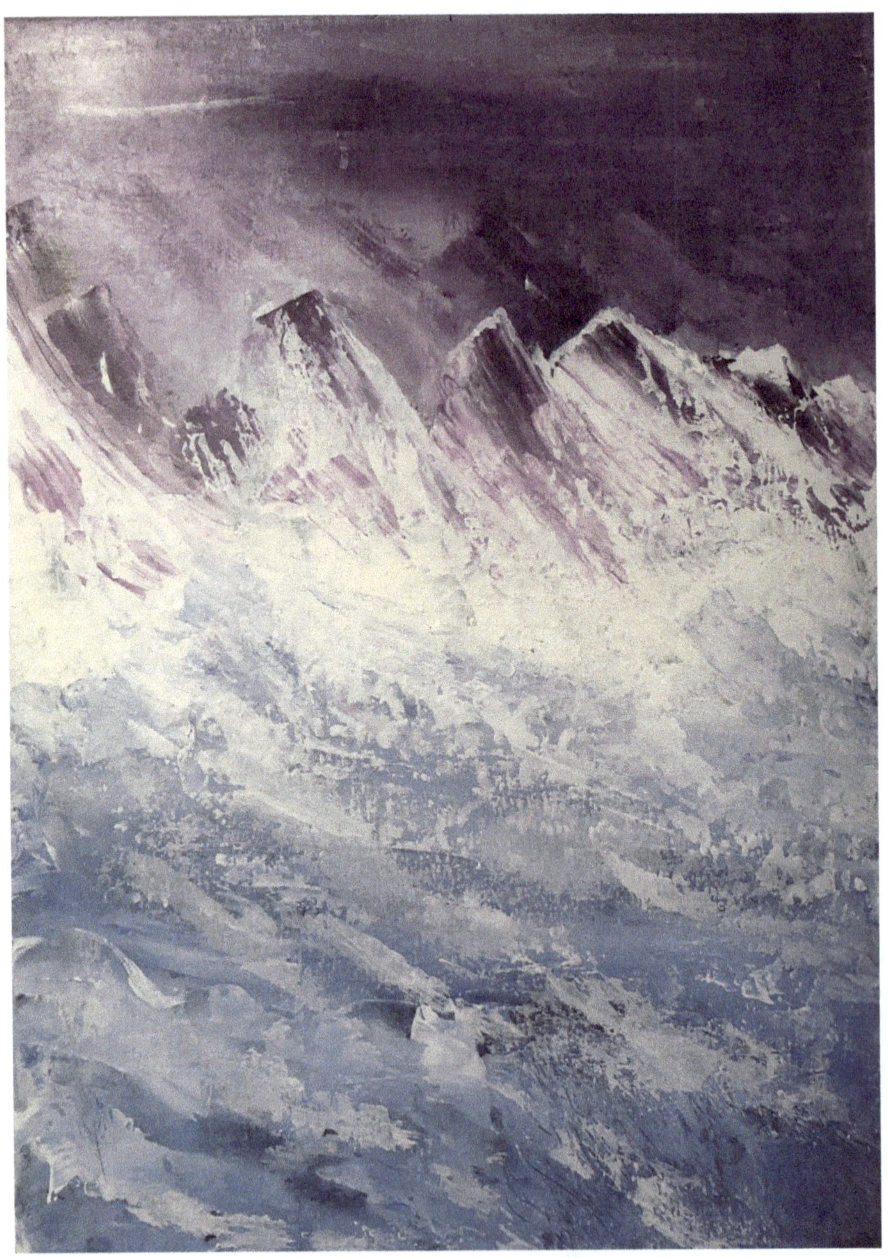

Arctic Ice Flow Twilight

The Earth

Series

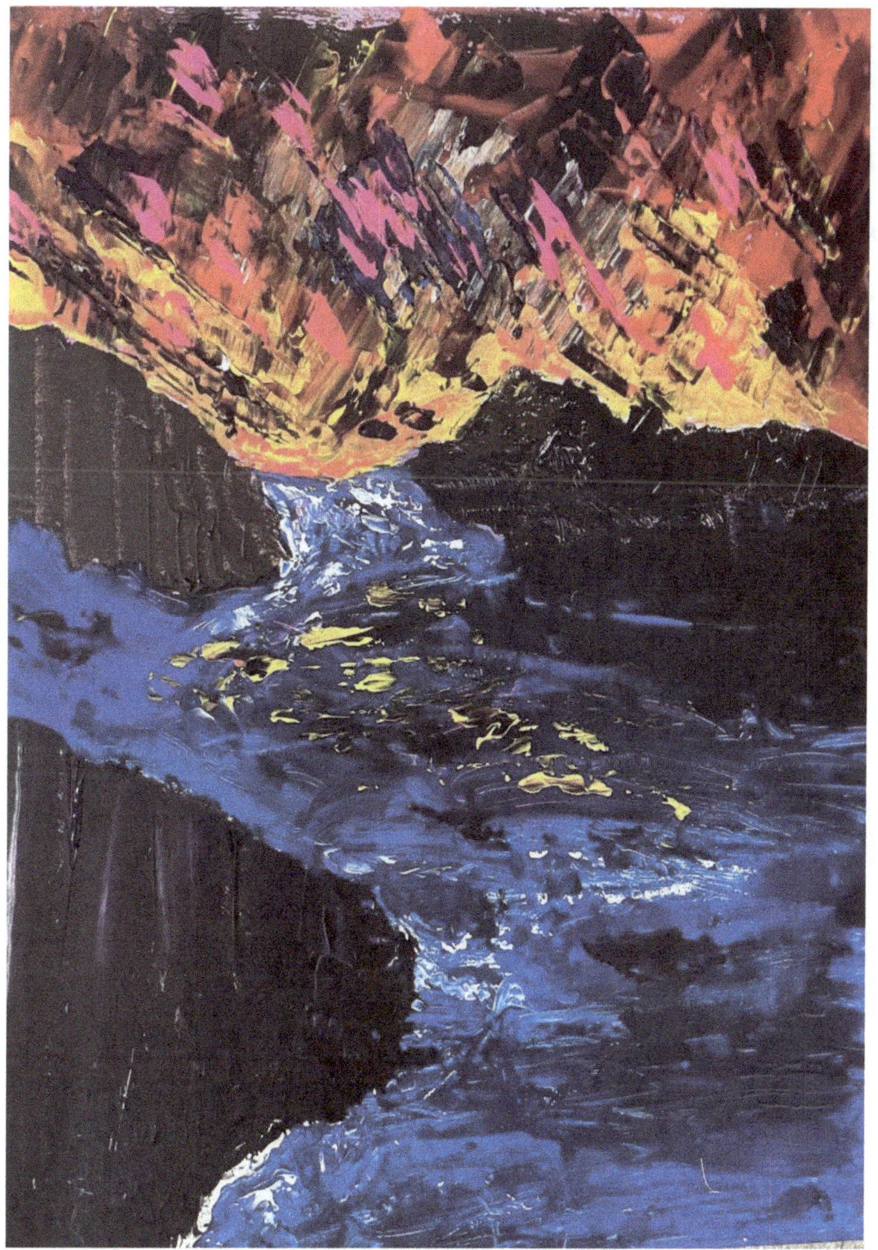

Earth – In The Beginning

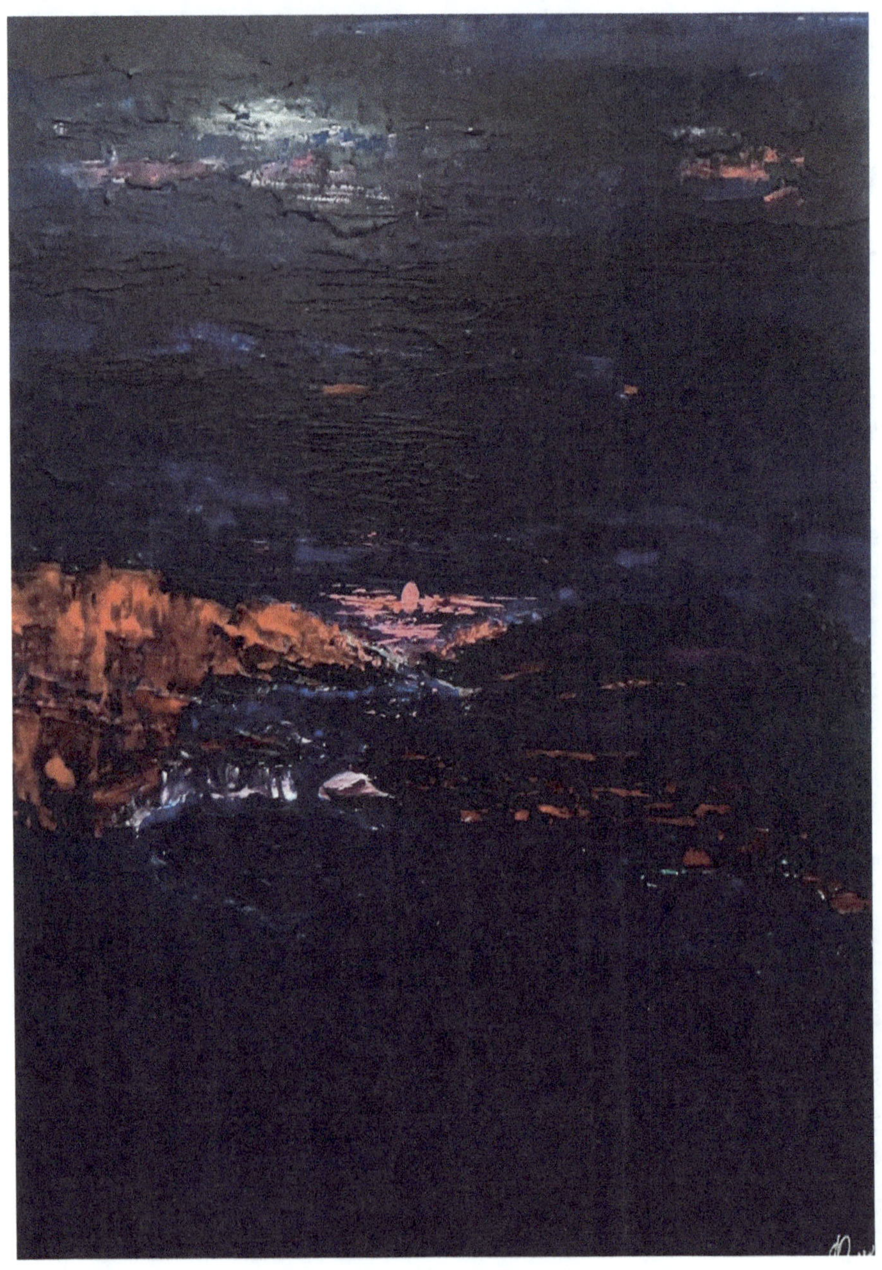

Earth – Day 1

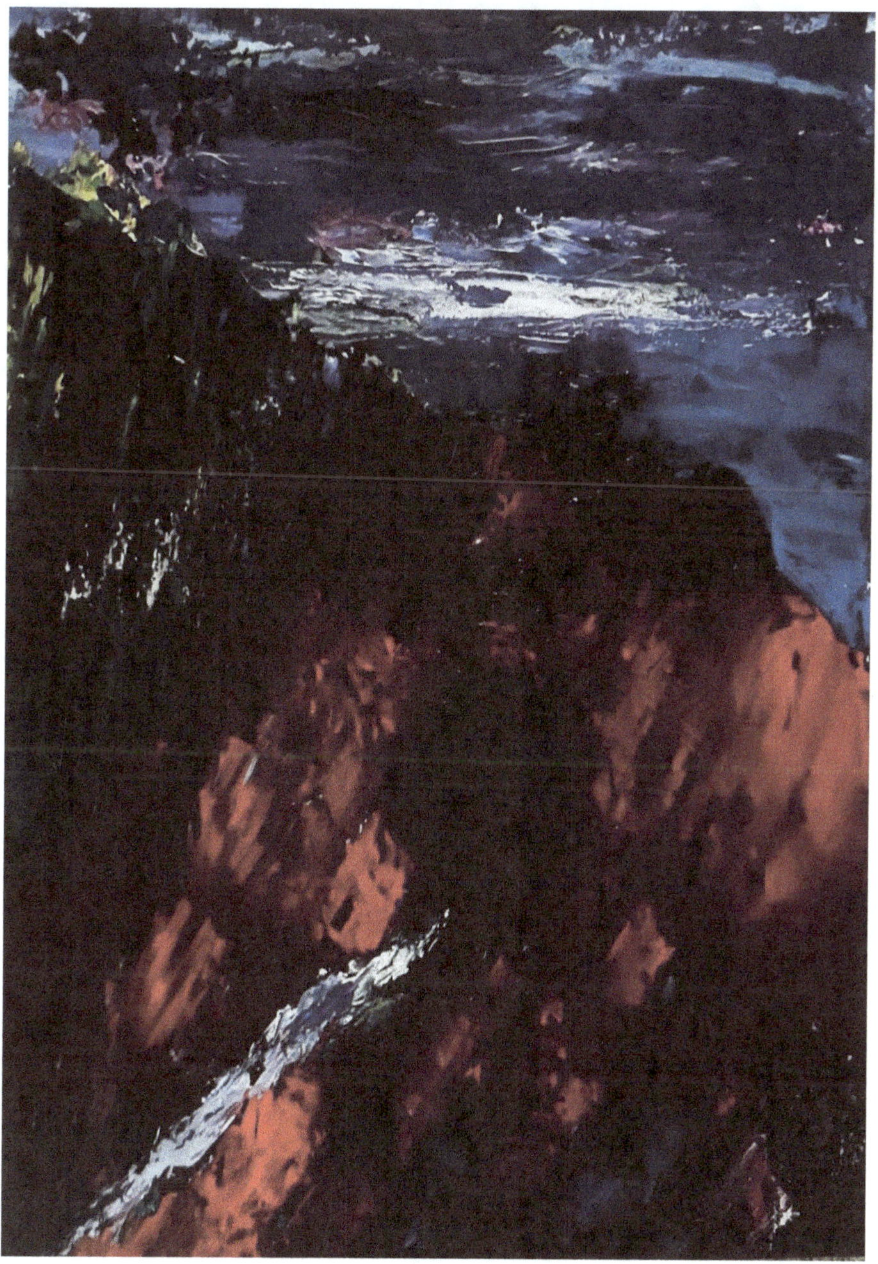

Earth – Day 2

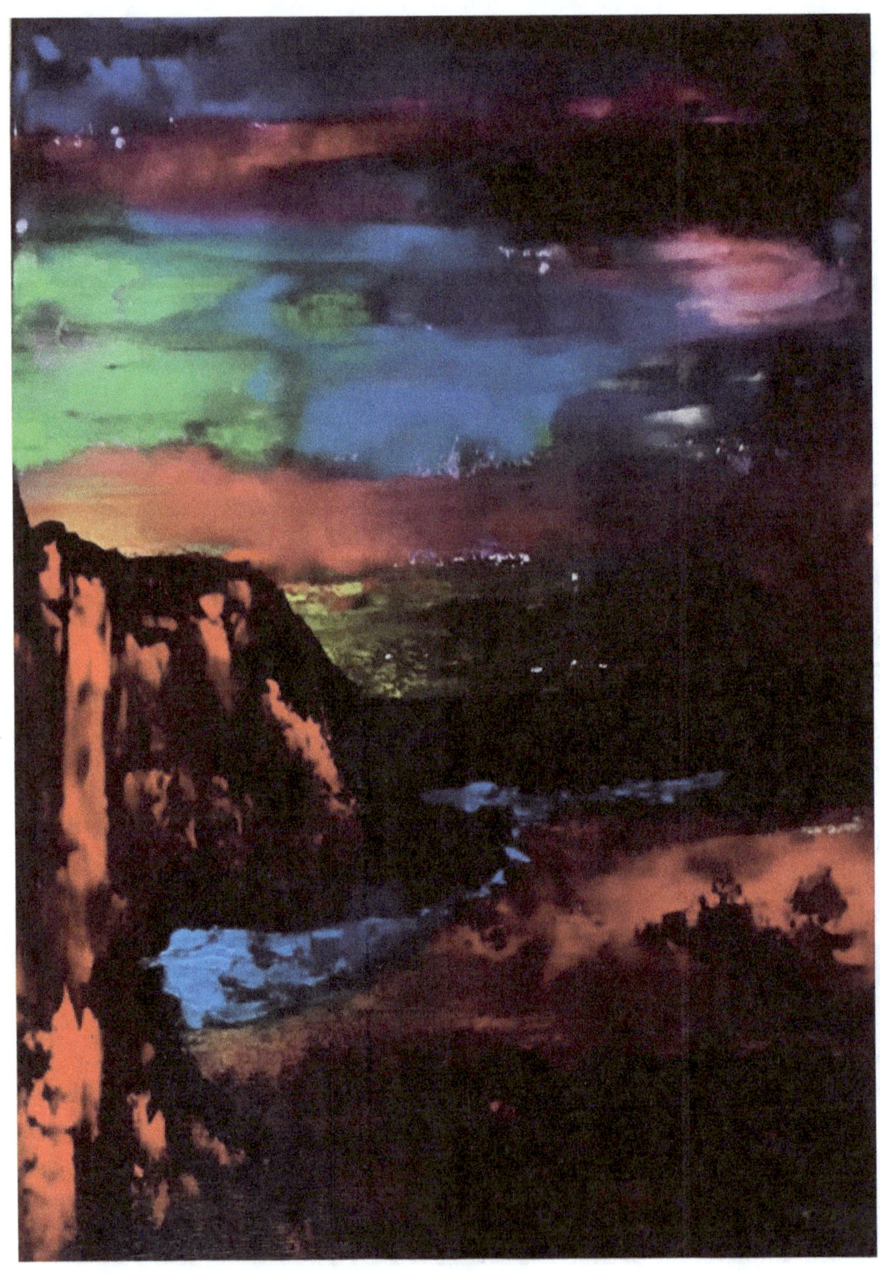

Earth – Day 3

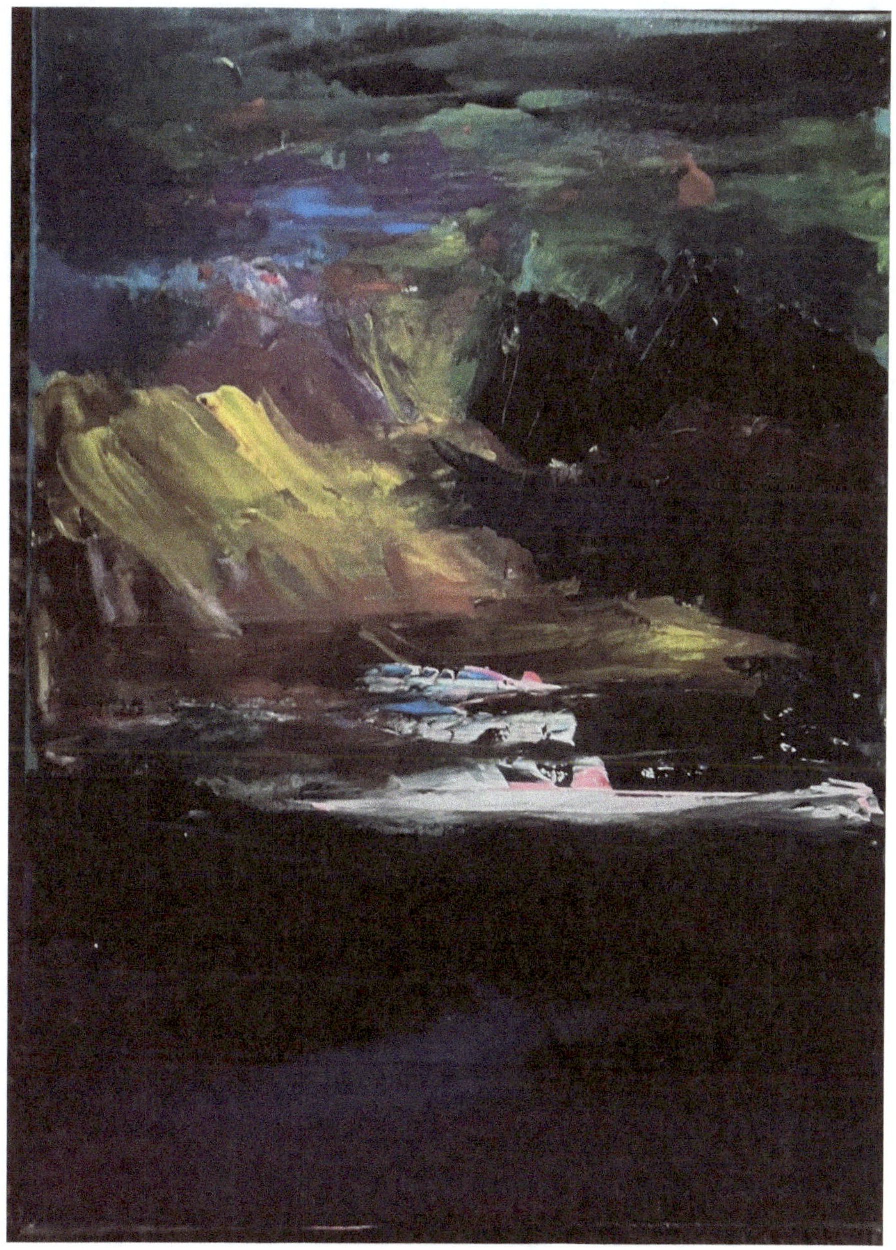

Earth – Day 4

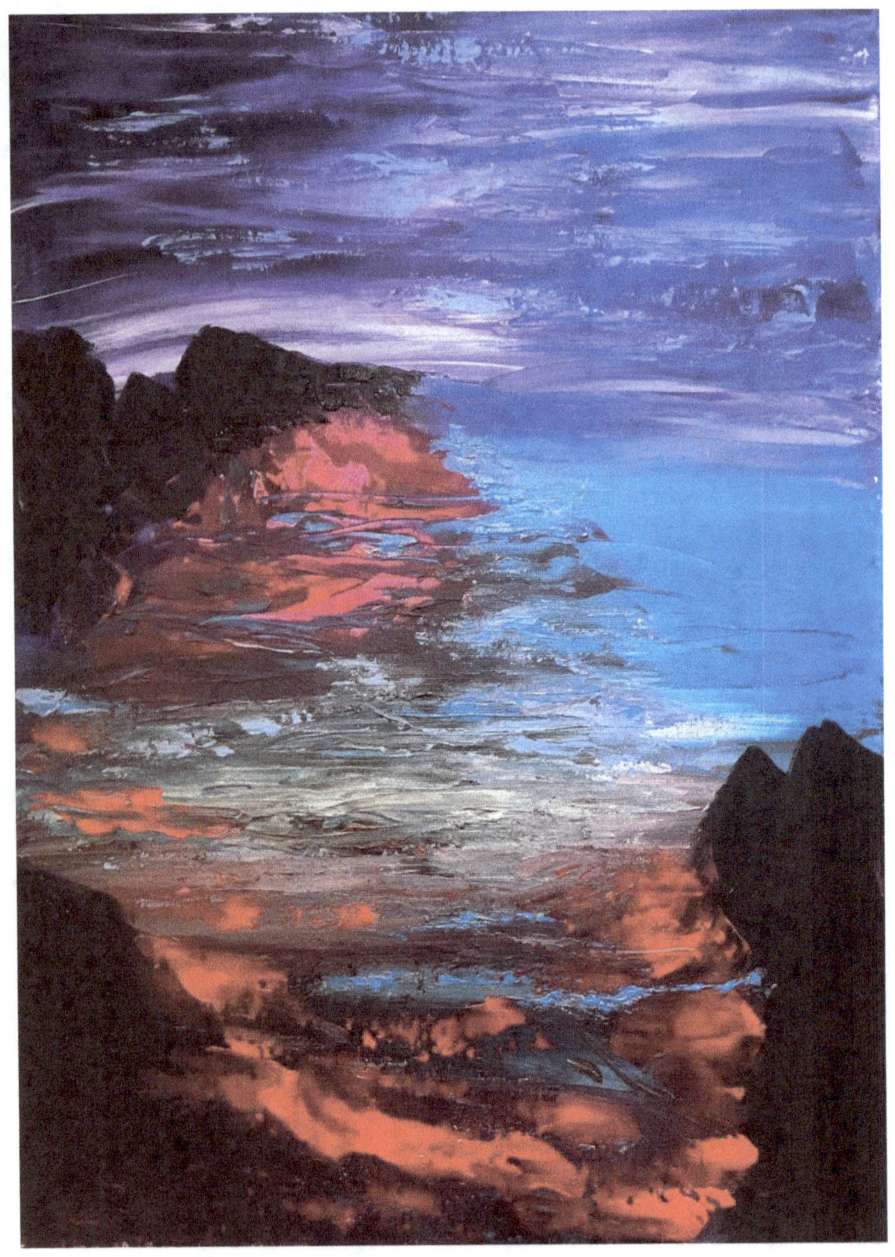

Earth – Day 5

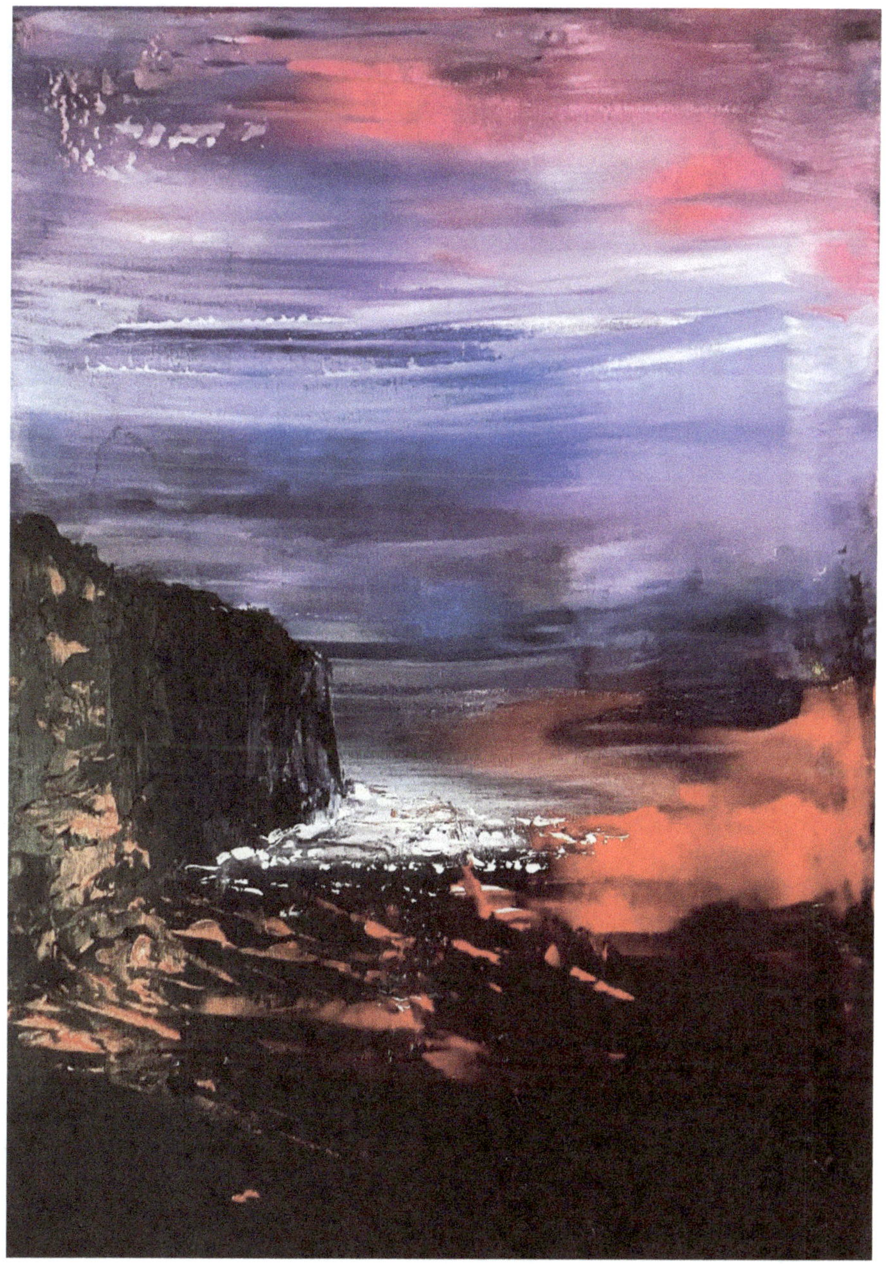

Earth – Day 6

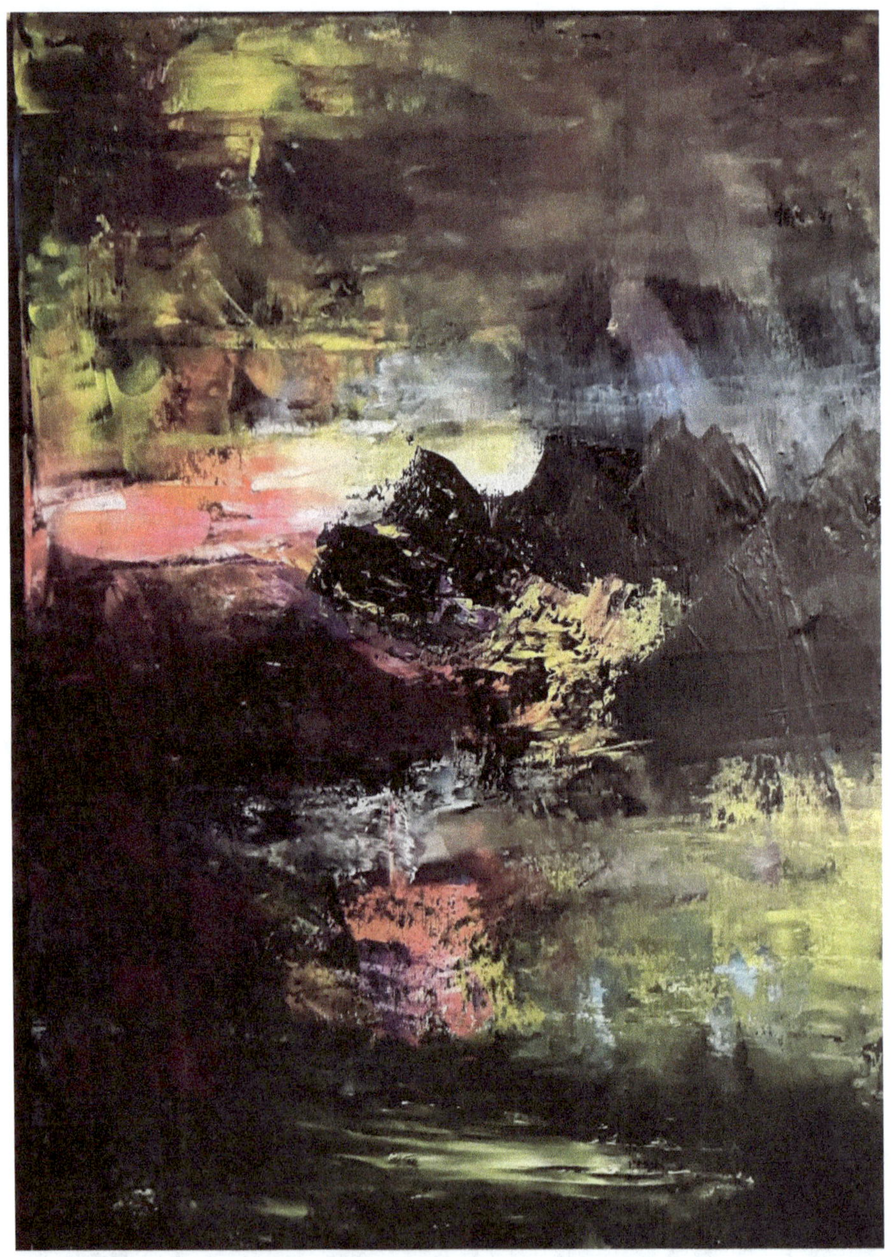

Earth – Day 7

CANDICE JAMES
Poet Laureate (2010 – 2016)
City of New Westminster, BC CANADA
appointed Poet Laureate Emerita
by City Council Nov 2016

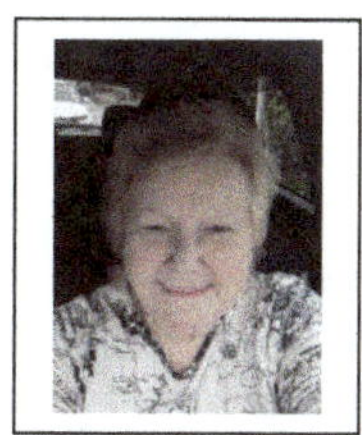

Candice James is a poet, visual artist and musician. She is founder of Royal City Literary Arts Society; founder of The Fred Cogswell Award For Excellence In Poetry and she is a full member of The League of Canadian Poets, Past President of the Federation of British Columbia Writers, creator of series "Poetic Justice;" "Poetry in the Park" and "Slam Central.

Her art has been featured in many art shows in the British Columbia Lower mainland and Greater Vancouver area. She has sold will over 100 paintings over the years internationally. She is a prolific painter and paints 5 or 6 paintings a month. Her main medium is acrylic, but she does some watercolors. She leans toward the surreal and abstract in her stylings.

She is the Author of 26 poetry books, The first one: "A SPLIT IN THE WATER" - Fiddlehead Poetry Books 1979; The latest one "DEEP BLUE SILENCE" Silver Bow Publishing 2024

She is recipient of the following awards "Chamber of Commerce Bernie Legge Artist of year"; Pandora's Collective "Citizen of Year" Writers International Network "Distinguished Poet"; "Woman of Prestige" Pentasi B Poetry Conference, Manila, Philippines and she has judged The League of Canadian Poets "Jessamy Stursberg Canadian Youth Poet Award" and "Pat Lowther Memorial Award "and also judged the "Fred Cogswell Award for Excellence in Poetry"; Candice has featured on "Wax Poetic," "World Poetry Café", and "Story Time". She has led workshops and been keynote speaker, at "Word on the Street;" Black Dot Cultural Collective";" Write on The Beach" and "Lit Fest New West." She has been featured at Crossroads Hospice Donors' Dinners and New Westminster Hospice Society "Dialogues on Death and Dying" reading from her book "Behind the One-Way Mirror" 2023. Her poetry has appeared in a variety of local and international magazines, e-zines and newspapers. She has led online forums, reviewed books and written prefaces and testimonials for authors and poets internationally and hosted National Poetry month for the League of Canadian Poets 6 times.

For Further information visit www.candicejames.com

The Herbalist's Compendium: Nature's Healing Power

From Ancient Remedies to Modern Applications: A Thorough Exploration of Herbal Medicines and Their Benefits

Lysander Bennett